MAHARANAS

A Thousand Year War For *Dharma*

MAHARANAS
A Thousand Year War For *Dharma*

Omendra Ratnu

Published by
PRABHAT PRAKASHAN PVT. LTD.
4/19 Asaf Ali Road,
New Delhi-110 002 (INDIA)
e-mail: prabhatbooks@gmail.com

ISBN 978-93-5521-164-4
MAHARANAS: A Thousand Year War For *Dharma*
by Shri Omendra Ratnu

Edition
2026

Price
₹ 600.00 (Rupees Six Hundred only)

Printed at
R-Tech Offset Printers, Delhi

**Dedicated to
the unknown, unsung
Bhils, Rajputs and all
Hindu ancestors of Mewar,
who sacrificed livelihood and life
and yet stood like a rock with
their Maharanas for one thousand years.**

Mewar Insignia

जो दृढ़ राखे धर्म को,
तिही रखे करतार
One who bears Dharma steadfastly,
is protected by the Divine.

Preface

"The East bow'd low before the blast
In patient deep disdain;
She let the legions thunder past,
And plunged in thought again..."

Mathew Arnold, a British poet, wrote these lines about the Hindus of Bharat. This is the crux of the core narrative embedded in the consciousness of this besieged nation, for the past 300 years. This is especially ingrained in our academic and literary discourse during the past seven decades of unopposed Leftist-Christlamic onslaught on our history. The crux being that Hindus are a meek race, indulging only in commercial or spiritual pursuits, and are no match for the muscular Islamic invaders who had been ravaging the subcontinent unceasingly.

Then, a couple of years ago, while meandering on Twitter, I chanced upon a tweet by Sanjay Dixit (former bureaucrat, author and thinker) mentioning the Battle of Dewair, where Maharana Pratap Singh of Mewar conclusively defeated Akbar's army in September, CE 1583.

Initially, out of my intellectual arrogance and sloth, I brushed it aside as an exaggerated fantasy of right-wing Hindus to idolise Pratap. I then contacted my friend, Shatrunjay Singh of Devgadh, who introduced me to a very pious *soul,* Shri Narayan Upadhyaya of Devgadh. Narayan-*sa* took me to Dewair and the areas around it to point out the physical evidence of the battle that took place in Dewair on Vijayadashami Day of CE 1583.

Memorial of the fallen soldiers at Dewair

I saw the memorials of *jauhar,* practiced by the brave Hindu women in Dewair, besides the ancient, paved pathways used for the movement of Mewar's armies which were dotted with resting places and water holes to nourish man and beast alike. He took me to Rajsamand where the history of the royal clan of Mewar, penned by Telugu historian, Ranchod Bhatt Tailang, is engraved in stone and clearly mentions the battle of Dewair in detail. I saw the hoof

700 year old pathways of Mewar army

marks stubbornly engraved on five-century-old pathways refusing to fade with time.

Ancient Water hole or Bawri

I personally interviewed reputed historians of Mohanlal Sukhadia University at Udaipur. Senior historians like Prof. K.C. Gupta and younger ones like Dr. Manish Shrimali endorsed the happenings and significance of Dewair.

I saw innumerable references in books by reliable authors who testified to the validity of the crucial battle of Dewair, which established the freedom of Mewar from the clutches of the Mughal ruler, Akbar.

While digging up the facts around Dewair, two books that were critical in substantiating the facts of the battle were *Annals and Antiquities of Rajasthan* by James Tod and *Veer Vinod* by Shyamaldas[1]. Flipping through the pages of these books, I chanced upon the life and deeds of the entire Sisodiya dynasty of Mewar and was baffled to learn about the life and deeds of the Maharanas of Mewar, and what these great kings of Mewar achieved with so little in hand.

I was thrilled to read about these amazing characters and incidents woven around the lives of these great kings of Mewar. It filled me with immeasurable pride that with such limited resources they could defeat these ruthless murderers.

Unfortunately we find very few written records of these Maharanas. Three primary sources have been referred to by almost all historians and authors while penning the history of Mewar: engraved stone carvings in and around the Hindu temples and forts; *vanshaawali* (family tree) records and *khyaati* (records of deeds) of Mewar's royal dynasty; and *lokashruti* (local folklore) woven around the lives of the Maharanas.

1. *Annals & Antiquities of Rajasthan* by James Tod, p. 278; *Veer Vinod*, p. 158; *Veer Shiromani Maharana Pratap* by G.H. Ojha, p. 27; *Mewar ke Maharana aur Shahanshah Akbar* by Rajendra Shankar Bhatt, p. 291 and *War Strategy of Maharana Pratap* by Dr. L.P. Mathur, p. 146.

During the thousand-year-old struggle of Mewar against Islam, the barbarism of the Islamic invaders put the custodians of the history of Bharat at a disadvantage because of the desecration of Hindu temples and destruction of literature and books as part of the campaigns and religious beliefs of Islamic invaders.

Bakhtiyar Khilji, in the 13th century, sacked and destroyed the University of Nalanda, a great centre of learning. It is recorded that Nalanda kept burning for months before all the books and manuscripts kept in the library were reduced to ashes. The number of Hindu temples destroyed by the Islamic marauders runs into thousands. These twin factors led to the loss of a sizeable portion of the treasures of Hindu history and heritage in the subcontinent.

The excessive reliance of modern Indian historians on Islamic chroniclers like Ferishta, Abul Fazl, Al Badayuni and Mughal emperors like Babur, Jehangir and Aurangzeb is an unfortunate reality of penning history of the subcontinent with defeatist narratives and falsehoods striking roots in the consciousness of our great civilisation.

This is one of the many reasons why only lies are unearthed when we try to delve deep into the history of the 10,000-year-old Hindu civilisation.

And yet, when I read the history of the Maharanas of Mewar by James Tod and Shyamaldas in *Veer Vinod*[2], I was amazed to discover the truth of the glorious resistance put up by one single family

Sh. Shyamaldas Dadhwadiya

Col. James Tod
(1782-1835 CE)

2. Sita Ram Goel and Shyamaldas.

against the Islamic invaders for an uninterrupted thousand years! To the best of my knowledge, there is no known example of such a fierce, sustained and victorious resistance against treacherous, violent and merciless assaults by Islamists on another faith in ***entire human history***.

Logic and factual information made me realise the scale of lies perpetrated by the court-historians of our unfortunate nation in belittling the valour of the great kings of Mewar and eulogising the role of the invaders. After cheating their own conscience and knowledge so shamelessly, how these so-called historians are able to live with themselves is a question only they can answer.

But Hindu society has a right to find out the true motives of these so-called historians.

Why is Akbar, the murderer of 40,000 innocent Hindus of Chittor in a single day, called Akbar the Great? Why are Mughal marauders depicted as benefactors of our great land and people? Why are the murderous assaults on Hindu ethos given the appearance of some routine rivalry between two kings?

Why was the civilisational battle between Hinduism and Islam camouflaged under the cloak of imperialism and power struggle between kings?

During a thousand years of assaults, all that these Islamic invaders could build in Bharat were three buildings—the Red Fort, Taj Mahal and Qutub Minar (these too are contested). Don't the thousands of forts, sculptures, cave carvings, palaces, paintings, etc. that survived despite their plunder, count for anything in the eyes and intellect of our so-called historians?

The worst treachery committed by these so-called historians of this nation was to completely erase the names of the valiant Maharanas of Mewar, whose deeds were nothing short of a revolution at that time.

Bappa Rawal, the founder of the Mewar dynasty and the mighty King of Mewar, who is recorded to have defeated the first Arab Islamic invaders of Bharat, has been completely erased from our history books while plunderers and murderers have been eulogised as the Delhi Sultanate, which itself is a phony construct by Leftist and Islamic academicians.

The Hindu kingdoms of Maharana Sanga, Kumbha and Hammir Singh of Mewar were several times the size of the so-called Delhi Sultanate. They find no mention in our curriculum, while raiders of various clans like the Tughlaqs, Khiljis and Lodhis, ruling a few hundred square kilometres around Delhi, are depicted as mighty Sultans.

Besides propagating the myth of the Delhi Sultanate, another lie that was busted during my reading of Mewar's history is the utter falsehood of a 'thousand years of Hindu slavery'. When all of Mewar was not defeated even for a single day by Islamic invaders, why refer to Hindus as slaves? And why only Mewar? The Shahiya dynasty of Punjab fought Mahmud of Ghazni and such Islamic marauders from the 10th to 12th century CE; the great Lalitaditya Muktapida of Kashmir was instrumental in halting the Islamic invasion into north and central India in the 8th century; the Gurjara Pratihara kings of central India were dreaded by Arab invaders and a Pratihara King finds mention in Arab history as the 'King of Jurz' who was described thus: "Among the princes of India, there is no greater foe of the Mohammedan faith than he"; the Jats of Sindh who destroyed Mahmud Ghazni's retreating army after the latter had plundered the Somnath temple, and the great Mularaja of the Chalukyas who defeated Muhammad Ghori in CE 1178. The Kakatiyas, Ahoms, Kalinga, Hindu kings of Bengal, the Cholas, the Rashtrakutas, and countless such Hindu kingdoms have been the victims of this selective amnesia and were erased too.

Some Western historians like John Mill and Richard Eaton, started this tradition of creating a larger-than-life image of Islamic plunderers and belittling or completely obliterating the names of Hindu kings who resisted Islamic invasion throughout the history of the Indian subcontinent.

Most Hindu historians actively participated in popularising this completely false version of Indian history without investing enough time and effort in chronicling the correct history of the Hindu-Muslim conflict in the subcontinent, possibly out of design or by default.

Some did it in the false belief that by ignoring the muscular

Hindu resistance to Islam, they could prove the superiority of India's 'spiritual culture' over the 'materialistic culture' of the West and the Middle Eastern invaders.

It is also an index of the intellectual sloth, mediocrity and a certain degree of capitulation of the Hindu leadership and Hindu elite, that these lies went on unopposed in the textbooks and the civic life of this nation.

The Christian missionaries gladly joined in this effort to reap the windfall benefits with their obsession of proselytising gullible, deracinated Hindus.

The transfer of power on the 15th of August 1947, from the fair-skinned *Gora* Sahibs to the indigenous, dark-skinned, Brown Sahibs of the Congress, Leftists, Islamists and Marxists, the Brown Sahibs masquerading as historians and academicians, completed the job of British historians and missionaries.

Missionaries, Marxists, and Mullahs find the defeatist version of Hindu history very convenient for the advancement of their expansionist agenda. Later, the media and *Macaulayputras*, or the anglicised Hindus too joined the chorus and tried to overwhelm the academic milieu of this nation.

The mystery is that the Leftist-Jehadi combine did this in clear worldview and weren't ever questioned.

After World War-II, the German establishment was divided into two hostile camps: one wanted to negate the holocaust, the other wanted the future generations to know the truth. The latter stated that the purpose of history is to let the future generations know the mistakes of their ancestors, so that a repetition would not occur. Fortunately, this camp prevailed. Diametrically opposite to this approach was adopted by the Indian state. It persistently negated the worst kind of atrocities that were perpetrated by Islamic kings on our ancestors.

To understand the extent of this state-sponsored negationism, one example will suffice.

In 1989, the West Bengal Board of Secondary Education issued a circular stating that "Muslim rule should never attract any criticism. Destruction of temples by Muslim rulers and invaders should not be mentioned." A detailed two-column table was attached with the circular. The first column contained the prevalent content that was based on historical facts and the second carried the changes required to be made. The first column was titled *Ashuddo* (faulty, impure) and the second *Shuddho* (correct, pure). The circular was sent to the publishers and the authors of books. The instructions were explicit and authoritarian.

The publishers and authors "are being requested to incorporate the amendments if books published by them have these *ashuddho* in all subsequent editions and paste a corrigendum in books which have already been published. A copy of the book with corrigendum should be deposited with the syllabus office."

For the sake of brevity, we are just quoting one example:

On p. 89 - *Ashuddho* - Sultan Mahmud used force for widespread murder, loot, destruction and conversion.

Shuddo - There was widespread destruction and loot by Mahmud.

The irony is that these facts have been taken from Mahmud Ghaznavi's memoirs.

Had Indian state and her self-appointed custodians been honest like post World War-II Germans, the people responsible for these lies would have been imprisoned[3].

And yet, truth has myriad ways of sprouting out like a tiny sapling striking roots even in hard rock. Honest historians, like Robert Orme and James Tod in the 18th and 19th centuries respectively, very laboriously chronicled the historical facts on Aurangzeb and the Mewar dynasty. Maharana Raj Singh of Mewar appointed the Telugu historian Ranchod Bhatt to etch in stone edicts, the history of the kings of Mewar. In the 19th century, Maharana Sajjan Singh of Mewar funded the detailed research of Mewar's history by Shri Shyamaldas and thus *Veer Vinod* was penned.

Great historians like R.C. Majumdar, Sir Jadunath Sarkar, Gaurishankar Heerachand Ojha, Rajendra Shankar Bhat, Dr. Ram Gopal Mishra, Dr. Shri Krishna Jugnu, etc., tried to write a neutral account of the history of India but were completely ignored by the

---

3. *Eminent historians* by Arun Shourie, Third impression, 2007, p. 63-65. Contributed by Sh.Neeraj Atri.

state and in the absence of marketing and adequate recognition of their scholarly works, were made to fade away from Hindu consciousness into oblivion.

This book is a limited attempt to rewrite the history of the great Maharanas of Mewar with a prime focus on Maharana Pratap Singh and his successful campaign against Akbar. This book also questions the premise of two historical lies created around a non-existent Delhi Sultanate and an equally spurious label of Hindu slavery.

I have tried to narrate the stories of these Maharanas with whatever information I could lay hands on from the written records of *Veer Vinod* and James Tod, to the records kept in various royal houses, to local folklore. This book is an attempt at dismantling the white lies woven around 1,400 years of Hindu-Muslim conflict in the subcontinent and rekindling the self-respect and honour of the Hindus on this globe as we look back at the amazing stories of these great Maharanas.

I can only hope that young Hindus take up similar endeavours all across Bharat and do alternative research and bring forth the truth about the Hindu resistance to Islamic invaders. Be it the Kakatiyas of Andhra, Gowdas of Karnataka, Ahoms of Assam, Jats of Sindh and Rajasthan and Uttar Pradesh, Chalukyas, Gurjar Pratiharas, Rashtrakutas, Prithviraj Chauhan of Delhi, the Vijayanagar kingdom, the invincible Marathas and dozens of such kingdoms that faced Islamic invaders squarely. Every dynasty's history and sacrifice must be brought into public domain as a mark of gratitude to our great ancestors.

It is also my endeavour that this book should be able to jolt our sensibilities and sensitivities alike. Hindus must realise the scale of lies that have been spoken to them and the degree of cover-up of the erasure of this amazing Hindu resistance to Islamic expansionism.

I hope one day an independent commission of enquiry is set up to investigate this matter and those historians and academicians guilty of spreading these lies and erasing the truth, get punished for their deeds.

In brief, the bottom line of this book is:

Islam came to subjugate us.
Our great ancestors didn't let that happen.

The Arabs were conclusively defeated and pushed back for 500 years continuously by Hindu kings. Then came the Afghans, the Uzbeks, and the Turks—each gaining partial success in the northern and north-western areas of India.

But all through these unrelenting attacks by predatory Islamists, one saffron flag of resistance stood unbent and flying high, rooted in the pious land of Rajasthan for a thousand years, striking fear in the hearts of these marauders: **The Sisodiya Rajputs of Mewar.**

It is true that all Hindus irrespective of their *varna* fought alongside these great kings but the critical mass, the leadership, the fortitude and the first blow was always braved on their chests by the glorious Rajputs of Mewar. Leadership is everything in human existence. Without leadership, men are rudderless and anarchic group of individuals.

It was the Sisodiya Maharanas of Mewar who provided leadership to the Hindus of this besieged nation region through their heroic resistance to Islamic imperialism. These amazing Maharanas were fully aware of the death and suffering that would befall them for fighting Islamic invaders; yet not one of them even contemplated compromising with the barbarians.

Like many other Hindu kings who aligned with the invaders, the Mewar kings too could have boozed, womanised and lived off the blood of the people of Mewar; instead, they chose to resist, suffer, kill and die for the honour and preservation of Hindu *dharma*.

Hindus were often heavily outnumbered, outmanoeuvred and ill-equipped against the well-oiled, well-funded, ruthless, immoral killing machine of *jihad* by Islamists, who had mastered the art of purchasing the loyalties of Hindus and had no moral compulsion in pursuance of their singular obsession of the total annihilation of Hindus and whatever they valued.

These amazing Maharanas spent their entire lives on horseback or in the jungles, sleeping on beds of leaves and stones, resisting this murderous mafia. They stood for an uninterrupted thousand years against all assaults on the freedom and prosperity of Hindus. These Maharanas endured all kinds of treachery and deceit but never allowed the Islamic invaders to pollute the soul of the land of *Bharatvarsha*.

The Maharanas did not sheath their swords, bend their spears, relax their bows, or let their arrows be blunted even when death and despair danced all around them.

These amazing *devapurushas* (celestial beings) are living embodiments of *kshatriya dharma* which teaches us to stand fearlessly against all adversity to protect our women and deities.

In their lives, deeds and death, the Maharanas proved that Hindus are not a bunch of wimps wallowing in cowardice, but a lion-hearted people, capable of fighting steel with steel, fire with fire and blood with blood.

The two Maharanas who stand out in this long lineage of great Sisodiyas are Maharana Hammir Singh and Maharana Pratap Singh. Both inherited a shattered and wounded Mewar, and yet, by sheer grit and meticulous planning, recovered the kingdom from the brink of total collapse. Both taught us through their life and actions that freedom and *dharma* are non-negotiable: no price is too high for the preservation of both; no sacrifice too costly and no suffering intimidating enough to forsake freedom or *dharma*.

Had the kingdom of Mewar splintered under the weight of Islamic tyranny, our northern and western borders would have been overrun and within decades, we would have become another Afghanistan. There was no other hope for Hindus at that time except to look up to Hammir and Pratap, who raised the banner of *dharma* singlehandedly.

And that is the reason both of these *devapurushas* must be venerated, because if we are Hindus today, it is solely because of them. Both gave hope to the Hindus—Hammir against the Tughlaqs and Pratap against Akbar.

All Hindus of north-west and northern sub-continent and even fellow Hindu kings looked to them for leadership. These

Maharishi Sita Ram Goel

amazing Maharanas rallied Hindus from under the saffron flag and destroyed the Islamic invaders of their times. Both paid a heavy price in terms of their personal lives and suffered hugely before regaining their respective kingdoms. Both also proved to be critical links in the unending chain of the Sisodiya Maharanas of Mewar.

The great thinker and a modern *maharshi* (great sage) of our times, Shri Sita Ram Goel writes[4]:

"Rich plunder functioned as a good supplement to the religious zeal of the Muslims. The Muslim practice of dividing the spoils of war between the leader and the soldiers might have encouraged the soldiers to follow their leaders through thick and thin. The Hindu soldiery had no such incentive. Hindu religion and culture forbade such beastly motives for bravery. But this was the very basis on which Muslim brotherhood had been organised from the very beginning. In its behaviour towards non-Muslim societies, it has always been a brotherhood of bandits."

When we look back 14 centuries in hindsight, it dawns upon us that both these Maharanas of Mewar and their people realised the truth about this 'brotherhood of bandits' and treated them accordingly and kept fighting them ceaselessly.

That Bhama Shah, the main War General of Pratap was an Oswal Jain and Dayal Shah, a General of Maharana Raj Singh during the time of Aurangzeb, another Jain,[5] adequately demonstrates that the teachings of *ahimsa* (non-violence) did not confuse the people of Mewar. While they venerated Bhagwan Mahavir and entire Mewar is littered with Jain temples, they also picked up the sword to fight the 'brotherhood of bandits' that threatened their very survival.

Can there be a bigger example than that by the Jains and

4. *Heroic Hindu Resistance to Muslim invaders,* p. 44.
5. *Tod erroneously refers as a Brahmin.*

Brahmins of Mewar who displayed that the principle of *ahimsa* is relative and not absolute?

The Maharanas and the people of Mewar did not carry any baggage of pseudo-morality to camouflage the cowardice that plagues a lot of Hindus today. And amazingly, these Maharanas were not merely warriors or killing machines. They were writers, poets, architects, patrons of art, builders, musicians and protectors of all that is beautiful in life.

This book is a very humble offering at the feet of these great *devapurushas*, who I believe, had descended from heaven to save us from a murderous assault by an evil ideology. How else could they have fought and defeated armies three to four times their size?

Unfortunately, not much has changed in the past 1,400 years for the Hindus except the shrinking of geographical space through loss of territories in the formerly Hindu territories of Afghanistan, Pakistan and Bangladesh. The same threat of Islamic expansionism looms large on the Hindus of today, albeit in a morphed form. Today, it comes disguised as Sufism, humanism, Communism, Liberalism, Wokeism, etc., but the end game is always the same: **Islamisation of the Indian subcontinent.**

All these will be duly resisted by Hindus at various levels. But let us revisit our history with a fresh perspective and re-look at the lives of the great Maharanas who kept fighting a very muscular, ruthless and predatory religious force and kept it in check.

They fought and they won. They defeated the most immoral expansionist force mankind has ever seen. They defeated this vile and hideous ideology while still adhering to the sublime philosophy of Hinduism. They defeated the mighty and deceptive force of *jihad* with a determined *dharmic* army of Hindus who trusted and followed their Maharanas to victory or death.

They delivered us from slavery and passed on the mantle of freedom won by their sheer sacrifice and consecrated in their blood. It is up to us now to honour and cherish their tradition and pass on the same freedom to our children. Only then will we be worthy of being called sons and daughters of these *mahapurushas* (great men) of Mewar.

Only then will we rise to reclaim our lost confidence and glory.

Only then will we be doing justice to the legacy of the Maharanas of Mewar.

Only then will we prove that people like Matthew Arnold were wrong to assert that Islamic invasion of this *Vedic* land was a walkover on us.

Only then will we shatter the web of lies created by *panchamakāras* (five crooks) to confuse Hindus into inaction and submission.

Only then, will we establish the supremacy of the Sanatana Hindu thought that war and peace always co-exist.

The surest way to peace is to be ever ready to go to war. Only then will Hindus be left alone by predatory conversion mafias.

Only then will the end game of Abrahamic religions to overrun Bharat be conclusively defeated.

Har Har Mahadev!

—Omendra Ratnu

Acknowledgements

Gratitude is a very inadequate word for what I feel for my dadosa, Thakur Akshay Singh Ratnu, who filled me with *Sanskaras* of Santana Hindu Dharma. Grandma groomed us all with unconditional love and care. Papa, Dr. Karni Singh Ratnu would have been the happiest person on this globe to see this book penned.

Elder brother Shivendra, who taugth me lessons on dignity and honour, watches me from Swargas.

My mother, Smt. Anand Kanwar, filled me with extreme sense of honour and commitment to Hindu dharma and I place this book at her lotus feet.

I am very grateful to Sri Sanjay Dixit for planting this seed in my being and advising me at every juncture.

Beloved friend, philosopher and guide, Dr. Pariksith Singh is the reason behind writing this book. Before this, I was writing random articles. It was Pariksith who encouraged me to take the plunge.

I cannot express my gratitude in words to beloved Partho Sanyal Dada, who helped me at every step to give shape to this work.

Neeraj Atri, Sandeep Deo and Dr. Gyaneshwar Khurana were very kind in responding to every call for help that I made to them.

Heartfelt gratitude to my dear friend Makarand Paranjape for giving valuable inputs to me from time to time.

A special thanks is due to Shri Pushpendra Kulshreshtha and Ms. Madhu Kishwar for giving wise counsel whenever approached.

The one man who laboured as much as me in penning down

this book is Sri Narayan Upadhyay of Devgadh. Countelss phone calls, half a dozen travels through Mewar, digging out old archives from friends and indifferent owners, lending all his books to me to consult and refer to, this book is a brain child of Narayan Sa. He embodies the real spirit of the glorious people of Mewar who just stood for their freedom and dignity alongside their Maharanas, expecting nothing in return.

I am indebted to Sri Shatrunjay Singh of the royal family of Devgadh for not only connecting me to Narayan sa, but also giving me valuable inputs on the history of glorious Mewar.

Gratitude to Shri Pushkar Naraniya of Chittorgarh who has been very prompt in any help needed locally.

And there is Jai Ahuja. In him, I have found a brother, friend, co-traveller, teacher and a true blue blood warrior. He is the result of the *Punyas* of my previous births. He not only encouraged me to write the book, but also understood my every demand and fulfilled it without ever bothering about his own comfort or business. His level of understanding and relating to the content of this book is truly amazing.

There are two ladies for whom I am struggling to find words for, to express my gratitude. These two women showered me with their *Shakti* and never let me be bogged down by the hurdles that came up from time to time.

Uma Deshbhotla typed this book for me on the computer since my eyes were tired of looking at the computer screen. Inspite of being a working woman, with so many family responsibilities, she helped me out with the most difficult part of this book. It is a surreal coincidence that like Ranchod Bhatt Tailang, who wrote Mewar history three hundred years ago, Uma too is of Telugu origin. Mewar and Andhra connection lives on.

Richa Gautam. I have always believed internet to be a blessing of Mahadev in fighting Abrahamics. Nothing enforces my belief more than Richa. We met through the net and became friends instantly. For the past two years, she has been with me in every micro or macro decision about the book, besides being there for me in the running of Nimittekam and DFI, the NGOs to help Hindus and Sikhs in Pakistan. That she did all this at a huge personal and professional cost gives me hope that with women like Richa standing for *Dharma*, Hinduism has a bright future.

I will not belittle the love and support of Uma and Richa by thanking them to have suffered a maverick like me all these years.

I only wish that every Hindu man finds such source of *Shakti* in his life too.

My family is my anchor around which I dance and play. Maneesha, Sarthak, Ananya—all contributed in their sweetest ways to this book. My brother Bhupendra and his wife Neeti too deserve my gratitude along with their girls, Nayanika and Lakshika who listened to the stories of Mewar patiently.

Love to Dushyant Ratnu and Manju Bhabhi for being there.

I am deeply indebted to Prof. K.S. Gupta and Dr. Manish Shrimali for their prompt help in penning down the facts about the history of Mewar.

Thanks are also due to Shri Narayan Singh Dewal and Shri Avind Shaktawat for relevant inputs.

A word of thanks is due to Sejal Thakur and Geetanjali Ahuja for intial editing with the book.

The creatives and the cover of this book were done by my chidlhood buddy Melven Castelino and I am so proud of his work.

My special thanks are due to Diwakar Acharya for helping me translate the English content into Hindi and thus speeding up things. He has been very prompt and professional in his work.

May Mahadev guide the path of recovery of Hindu *Dharma* under the illuminated life and deeds of the great Maharanas of Mewar.

Contents

Part-III

Part-I

"That audacious armada of the religion of Hijaz
Whose insignia reached every corner of the world
Which learnt no obstruction from any fear
Which felt no hesitation in Persian Gulf or faltered in the Red Sea
Which valiantly crossed all the seven oceans
Oh, drowned was that armada (of Islam), when it reached the mouth of Ganga!"

—Mawlana Khwaja Altaf Husain Hali

1

Bappa Rawal: Conqueror of Arabia
(approx CE 728-758)[6]

Fathered by Nagadit and mothered by Kamlavati, Bappa Rawal was born as a direct descendant of the Guhilote dynasty. He was named Kalabhoja at birth. Later, he was called Bappa, meaning 'father,' as a form of endearment by the people of Mewar.

The Guhilote dynasty traces its lineage to Luv, the son of Shri Rama. It later went on to become the mighty Sisodiya dynasty that ruled Mewar for an uninterrupted 1,400 years and adorns the royal line and throne of Udaipur even today.

Bappa Rawal had a tormented and deprived childhood. He was taken by his mother to the safety of the jungles of Bhinder in Mewar, where he was protected by the Bhils of Yadu descent. The Bhil king, Mandalik protected Bappa during his childhood. This was the beginning of the Bhils' association with the royal lineage of Mewar—an association that continues even today.

Bappa is said to have met a Shaiva mystic, Harit *sadhu,* who

6. Historians differ on the exact dates of the rules and events around the lives of these Maharanas. The author has tried to deduce the dates after consulting various books and put them together as correctly as possible.

revealed to him the mysteries of the *Shaiva Tantra*, principles of morality and lessons in warfare along with a plan to lead Hindu resistance to Islam by winning back Chittor and re-establishing Rajput control over Mewar. As it happens with many ancient figures, Bappa's history is replete with anecdotes of many miracles, which are not a matter of focus for the writer.

Bappa and Harit Rishi

Being with the mystic *sadhu,* Bappa developed a deep devotion to Bhagwan Eklingji, an *avatar* of Shiva and the presiding deity of the Mewar royal house till date. Bappa had vision of Goddess Bhawani, who blessed him and instructed him to serve the Mori dynasty of Chittor, which was the most powerful centre of sovereign India at the time.

Bappa was received well at Chittor by the Mori king, Manmori, the then ruler of Chittor. Bappa was designated as a *samant* and granted a suitable estate. It was at this time that arms of Islam for the first time, crossed the Indus through Sindh and entered Bharatvarsha.

Raja Dahir Sen of Sindh
(663-712 CE)

Mohammad Bin Qasim
(695-715 CE)

In 712 CE, at the age of 17, Mohammad Bin Qasim of Arabia attacked Raja Dahir Sen of Sindh. Several attempts by Qasim were repulsed by Dahir and his valorous brother. Then the Buddhists of Sindh, who were alienated from Dahir, joined hands with Qasim. At Nerun, the Buddhist head of the town, Bhandarkar Samani, not only helped Qasim to cross Sindhu river, but also supplied enough food to meet the needs of an army. Thus, the traitors gave Qasim entry to the Hindu king's garrison resulting in the defeat of Dahir's army at the Battle of Aror[7]. Besides the Buddhists, local 'Med' tribe also supported Qasim and added to his numbers. Dahir's forces and his sons and brothers fought a fierce battle but were finally defeated because of treachery by the locals. Consequently, Qasim beheaded Dahir and his brother, captured Dahir's daughters and forcibly carried them off to Baghdad, to offer to the then Caliph of Arabia, the cruel Hajjaj Bin Yusuf, as sex slaves.

Qasim, armed with the loot of the riches of Sindh, was able to raise an army of mercenaries and moved eastwards to attack Mewar. Tod writes that the slain Raja Dahir's son escaped to Chittor and informed Bappa about the fall of Sindh and how women were being abducted as sex slaves.

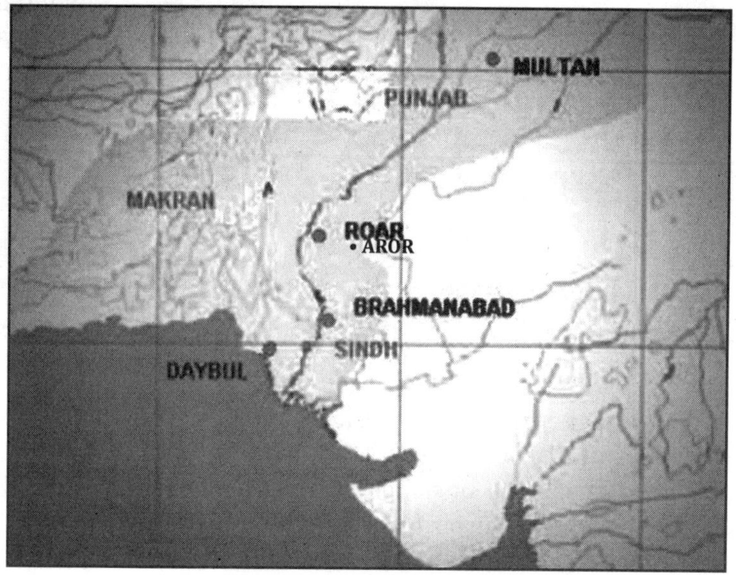

Initial success of Arabs in Sindh

7. Mishra p. 23.

Sex slavery was unheard of in Hindu civic and military life at the time.

Before the arrival of Islamic invaders, Hindu kings too fought against each other to acquire territory and power. The rules of engagement for the armies were clearly laid down and none would ever violate those norms. Two armies of Hindu kings would fight each other and the victorious king would take over the defeated kingdom, either appointing the defeated king as a vassal or driving him out of the kingdom. But the citizenry, peasantry, mercantile class and artisans would never be touched. Everyday life would carry on as usual with the transfer of power only at the monarch's level. To capture womenfolk of the royal house or even the citizenry was inconceivable in the Hindu ethos.

Islamic zealots brought with them this evil of physically subjugating and violating women of this great Vedic *bhoomi* (land) and thus, the greatest living civilisation of all times was infected in thought and action by the misogynistic belief system from the lands of Arabia.

Hindu girls and women for sale in Arab markets

Bappa was enraged when he learnt of the treatment of women by Qasim but also understood the need for a combined Hindu alliance to check the onslaught of these murderers from alien lands. He readied himself for a long haul as he anticipated that these attacks by the *mlechchhas* (those with evil intent) would go on ceaselessly and a continuous struggle would be required if the land and *dharma* of Hindus were to be saved[8].

Bappa Rawal, leading the Mewar army, struck alliance with the brave Nagabhatta1 of the Gurjara-Pratihara dynasty ruling the Malwa region, in today's Madhya Pradesh. Bappa also allied with Pulakesiraja and Jayabhatta of Gujarat and the joint Rajput forces fought the Arab Muslim invaders in the crucial Battle of Rajasthan. Nagabhatta approached Chalukya King Jai Simha Varman of South India who sent his son Pulkesiraja to assist the Hindu formation.

It was Juniad Al Marri who led the Arabs and had been partially successful in southern Gujarat, Malwa and southern Rajasthan. In CE 738, somewhere around Jodhpur of present-day Marwar, this decisive battle was fought between 5,000 to 6,000 Hindu troops against 60,000 Arabs. The Arabs were comprehensively routed and Junaid was killed. Thus, the Umaiyyad dynasty of Arabia was sent a clear message by the Hindus to stay away from this pious land[9].

What the Arabs were able to achieve in a few decades in Middle East, Persia, Mesopotamia, Surya (Syria), North Africa, was denied vehemently on our land by the triple alliance led by Bappa Rawal.

This act of Bappa had huge implications not only for western India, but the entire world, as the advent of militant Islam was halted on the western frontiers of our nation and the Far East and China were saved by default.

We can only imagine the consequences of an Arab victory over the Hindus. Plush with money and manpower of our great land, Islam would have become unstoppable by any army of the world.

The writer doesn't believe that a nation can have a father, but if at all such a pedestal needs to be granted to a mortal, it should be reserved for Bappa Rawal who saved Hinduism from a darkness that would have irreversibly engulfed us.

Sans Bappa, India would have become a part of Islamic Caliphate and economic doom and slavery would have engulfed

8. Tod, vol. 1, p. 185-86.

9. https://military-history.fandom.com/wiki/ Battle_of_Rajasthan

the citizens. There would have been no Vedic culture or Sanatana Dharma left just as everything un-Islamic was destroyed in the Caliphate.

Hindus must also be deeply grateful to Pratihara King Nagabhatta and Pulakesiraja, who pre-empted the Islamic threat and aligned with Bappa to repel the invasion on our *dharma*.

If these glorious ancestors of ours could defeat the marauders from Arabia during those difficult times, what prevents the modern-day Hindus to repeat the feat?

We will be worthy descendants of Bappa only and only when all Hindus unite to defeat Islamic imperialism.

Bappa was a fierce warrior with a deep understanding of the human mind. He also understood the nature of the threat posed by Qasim's invasion when Raja Dahir's son escaped Qasim's attack on Sindh and took refuge in Mewar, informing Bappa of the religious fanaticism and cruelty of the Arabs. The Arabs were decimated in the battle of Rajasthan and chased back up to Iran by Bappa. According to Tod, Arab historians themselves wrote: "Not a place of refuge could be found against the Hindu fury[10]."

Bappa's way of swearing secrecy and loyalty from his companions is still preserved in Mewar. Digging a small pit and taking a pebble in his hand, he would roar, "Swear secrecy and obedience to me in good and evil; that you will reveal all to me that you hear, and failing that, the good deeds of your forefathers may, like this pebble (dropping the pebble into the pit), fall into the washerman's well." All his followers willingly took the oath.

The Arab mercenaries were decimated by Bappa and his allies, forcing them to flee to their native lands via Gujarat, Saurashtra and Sindh. Bappa did not relent and continued to chase the Arab invader up to Iran. He found the city of Ghazni in Afghanistan, in possession of one Salim.[11]

Bappa defeated and captured Salim and married his daughter. He also put his nephew in charge of the city and thus secured Afghanistan as a Hindu kingdom for a few centuries to come. He

10. Goel, p. 12.
11. Tod, vol 1, p. 185.

erected check-posts at regular intervals on his way back from Arabia. These were instrumental in halting further invasions by Islamic armies for the next four hundred years.

Muhammad Bin Qasim's *karma* caught up with him in Baghdad.

The Chachnama, a 13th century Persian manuscript written by Hamid bin Abu Bakr Kufi, narrates an incident in which Qasim's demise is attributed to the daughters of Dahir.

Upon capture, the two daughters of Dahir—Surya Devi and Premala Devi, were sent over to fill the Caliph, Al-Hajjaj ibn Yusuf's harem in Baghdad. The account relates that the girls then tricked the Caliph into believing that Qasim had violated them before sending them over. This subterfuge enraged the Caliph and Qasim was wrapped and stitched in oxen hides, and despatched to Syria. In CE 715, Muhammad Bin Qasim died en route from suffocation. Thus, the Hindu girls secured retribution for their father's death and informed the Caliph that they had lied to him to punish Qasim. This revelation filled the Caliph with remorse and rage and eventually he ordered the sisters to be buried alive in a wall.

That two helpless Hindu girls could use their intelligence to extract a revenge for the murder of their father should be a source of inspiration for all Hindu women. Anyone who harms our family and rapes innocent girls, should face retribution as per the principle of natural justice.

Thousands of miles from home, surrounded by medieval barbarians, scarred by the decimation of their family, how those delicate princesses maintained their mental balance and devised the story to incite Hajjaj against Qasim is something that will fill our hearts with respect and gratitude for those brave girls.

The sacrifice of these two princesses should find place in Hindu history with reverence and pride.

Bappa's triumphant Arab campaign catapulted him to the status of a miraculous warrior and he annexed Chittor from the Mori dynasty in CE 726 to establish the present-day Mewar dynasty, proclaiming himself as 'Maharao' Bappa Rawal. It is difficult to establish whether Bappa killed or exiled Manmori to annex Chittor. *Amarkavyam* states that Manmori was killed by Bappa[12].

According to the chronicles available in Chittor, "Bappa took Chittor from Mori and himself became the *mor* (crown) of the land." Bappa was also named the 'Sun of the Hindus' (*Hinda Sooraj*) and protector of princes (*raj guru*), titles which are attached to the royal family of Mewar even today[13].

The title of Rawal was given to Bappa by his Bhil army and friends. '*Ra*' stands for rajya or state, '*wa*' stand for varatva or blessings, 'L' stands for *laxmi* or wealth[14].

Bappa's campaign had another positive effect on the Hindu kingdoms of Lahore and Peshawar. In CE 761, the Afghans of Kirman and Peshawar, which were originally a Coptic colony of Egypt, crossed the Indus to travel eastwards and attack the Hindu ruler of Lahore. Within five months of this event, seventy battles were fought with varied outcomes. In the last one, the Rajput Hindu prince of Lahore carried his army to Peshawar and a truce was signed.

Thus happened a union of interests and all of Kohistan, west of the Indus, was ceded to them on the condition of guarding this barrier into Hindustan against any invasion. The Rajputs erected the fortress of Khyber in the chief pass of Daman-e-Koh. For two long centuries after this, peace prevailed in what is known as upper Sindh and Punjab today, and India was rendered accessible only through southern Sindh, thus narrowing the chances of Islamic invaders to attack Hindustan.

Bappa Rawal thus sowed the seeds of Hindu resistance to Muslim invasions for his future generations by clearly identifying the alien nature of Islamic invaders vis-à-vis Hinduism and laid down a policy of non-reconciliation with the barbaric values of Islamists, as a norm for his progeny to follow. He thus laid the ground for armed resistance against the designs of the Islamic imperialists.

What Bappa Rawal did was to recognise the vile nature of Arab theological expansionism and forged alliances with fellow-

12. *Amarkavyam* p. 99.
13. *Annals & Antiquities of Rajasthan*, James Tod, vol. 1, p. 186.
14. *Rajprashasti* by Ranchod Tailang.

Hindu kingdoms to not only conclusively defeat the invaders, but make such arrangements so that Islamic invaders could not defeat Hindu kings for the next three centuries.

Bappa's reach up to Afghanistan and Iran and forging matrimonial bonds with the locals there meant the continuance of Hinduism in these regions for centuries to come. The impact of Bappa's victorious campaign can be assessed by the fact that despite relentless attacks by Arabs and Turks for the next fourteen centuries, Hindus are found living even in today's Afghanistan and Pakistan. Though heavily depleted in numbers, the fire of Hinduism could not be fully extinguished by the Islamic invaders because of the confidence and loyalty that warriors like Bappa established in the hearts and minds of the Hindu populations. Approximately one Crore Hindus and Sikhs still live in Pakistan.

The single biggest statement of Bappa Rawal's reach beyond the western frontiers of Rajasthan is that even today, the capital of the Islamic Republic of Pakistan is the twin cities of Islamabad and Rawalpindi. Despite decades of hatred against Hindus, Pakistan, even now has its main cantonment city named after a Hindu emperor who was loved and cherished by the people of that land. Considering the meticulous execution of his victorious campaign against Arabs, it wouldn't be an exaggeration to state that Bappa Rawal is the only reason that Vedic civilisation still pulsates in the Indian subcontinent.

According to Tod, Bappa defeated dozens of small Muslim kingdoms west of Sindhu River and married the daughters of their kings. As many as 130 sons were born to him from these women and after the return of Bappa to Mewar, these sons were identified according to the clans of their mothers. Today, these people are referred to as Naushera Pathans.

It would be prudent here, to glance at other Hindu kings and kingdoms who resisted Arab invasions into Bharatvarsha, briefly.

Dr. Ram Gopal Mishra has authored the book, *Indian Resistance to Early Muslim Invaders up to 1206 CE*, where he has meticulously researched and documented Hindu resistance in a relatively obscure period of Indian history. Although we shall restrict ourselves to the lives and work of Mewar's Maharanas, it is important that the names of kings and people who resisted the initial Islamic invasions be mentioned here.

Gurjara-Pratihara king, Nagabhatta I, the founder of the dynasty, ruled Avanti (Malwa) around CE 725. An inscription in Gwalior tells us that he defeated the army of a powerful Arab Islamic ruler who invaded his dominions[15].

The Gurjara-Pratiharas were known by Arab historians as 'kings of Jurz'. Referring to one such king, the Arabs wrote, *"Among the princes of India, there is no greater foe of the Mohammedan faith than he."*

Another king worthy of mention here, a contemporary of Bappa, was Lalitaditya Muktapida (AD 724-760). He allied with Yashovarman of central India. Lalitaditya was merciless in his slaughter of Arabs and ordered that half of the Islamists' foreheads be shaved off as a mark of their submission. The Jats in Sindh also handed a crushing defeat to later Arab invasions and so did the Pratihara kings in Multan[16].

Thus, we see that Arab imperialist thugs, who took less than ten years to completely devour Persia, Mesopotamia and Egypt, were not only halted by Bappa Rawal and his confederacy but chased back to the lands of their origin. The pan-India resistance to the Arab onslaught resulted in the conclusive defeat of Arab imperialists, best worded by an Arab historian Al Baladhuri himself: *"The people of India returned to idolatry with the exception of the inhabitants of Qasbah. A place of refuge to which the Moslems might flee was not to be found, so he [Arab governor] built on the further side of the lake, where it borders on al-Hind, a city which he named Al-Mahfuzah [the protected] establishing it as a place of refuge for them, where they should be secure and making it a capital[17]."*

The Arab invasions of Sindh have been described thus by Wolsley Haig: *"A mere episode in the history of India, which affected only a fringe of that vast country... The tide of Islam, having*

15. Indian Resistance to Early Muslim Invaders upto 1206, Dr. Ram Gopal Mishra, p. 87.
16. *Heroic Hindu Resistance to Muslim Invaders*, Sita Ram Goel, p. 12.
17. Mishra p. 30.

overflowed Sindh and the lower Punjab, ebbed, leaving some jetsam on the strand[18]."

It took brave and visionary leaders like Maharao Bappa Rawal and his Hindu alliances to defeat the barbarians and keep the light of *dharma* burning in India. No Hindu king has influenced the course of Islamic invasions as profoundly as Bappa. If Bappa Rawal could do it 1,400 years ago, what stops us from fighting for the sake of *dharma* when we are so well-equipped today? That is the question to which every Hindu must find an answer to.

Bappa Rawal, after ruling Mewar from Chittor for 27 years, heeded to his spiritual call and went off to the jungles around the Eklingji temple, 30 kms north of modern-day Udaipur and lived the life of an ascetic, till his death at the age of 100 years.

CV Vaidya in his book,' Medieval Hindu India' compares Bappa's life with that of Charles Martel of France. Just like Bappa, Charles Martel rose from being a nobody to sieze power in Paris. Just like Bappa defeated the Arabs, Chales Martel too defeated Abd al-Rahman al-Ghafiqi of the Ummaiyad Dynasty.[19]

Martel's son Pepin continued the dynasty for few generations. Bappa on the other hand started the Sisodiya Dynasty which has gone on uninterrupted for the past 1400 years and the sons of glorious Bappa Rawal still adorn the royal seat of Udaipur.

Bappa Rawal was succeeded by various rulers of Mewar for the next five hundred years, among whom Shakti Kumar, Khuman I, Khuman II and Khuman III continued the expansion of the kingdom of Mewar. Khuman II and his victory in warding off another onslaught by the Islamists on Mewar will be covered in the subsequent chapters.

Bappa attained *moksha* (liberation) as an anonymous *saadhak* (spiritual seeker) at Kailash Puri near the Eklingji temple in Mewar. Even today, there is a Shiva temple and Bappa's life-size statue, as his *samadhi* is believed to be here.

Tragically, the name of this greatest Hindu king of the 8th century has been erased from our historical consciousness. It is a matter of profound sadness and mystery that not only Bappa

18. *Cambridge History of India*, vol. 3, p. 10.
19. Vaidya, p.73-74

Rawal's name, but the entire failure of Arab Islam to penetrate into Indian subcontinent has been wiped away by the Leftist historians of our unfortunate nation.

Erasure of an event as crucial as this from our consciousness also demonstrates the mediocrity of Hindu thinkers and leadership. Islamists and Leftists did what they had to; but, what were we doing? The intellectual sloth of Hindu intelligentsia is appalling to say the least. What paralysed the Hindu society and leadership into such indifference to such virulent assaults on the history of Hindu *dharma*? What paralyzed our thought processes that the very greats who saved our *dharma* and land were pushed into oblivion?

All that was infected by the religious intolerance of the Arabic invaders was destroyed. The pathetic condition of those societies conveys a singular message to us Hindus—if Arabs hadn't been defeated by Bappa Rawal and giants like him, we would neither have Hindu *dharma* nor a nation today.

For five hundred uninterrupted years, Arab Islam was not allowed to cross the Indus River by our glorious ancestors. Thus, this not only saved the Hindus, but also the entire free world and the global consciousness from subjugation and slavery.

Now it is solely upon us to revive the name, life and deeds of this great Hindu son who laid the foundation for a thousand-year-long struggle against Islamic imperialism.

□

2

Rawal Khuman II: Devourer of Arab Invaders

(CE 820-860)

Khuman was a direct descendant of the great Bappa Rawal after a gap of four to five generations between them. There have been three recorded Khumans in Mewar between the 8th and 10th centuries and all three were instrumental in defeating Arabs during their time. The most remarkable and courageous were the battles of Khuman II. The recorded historical details of the times of Khuman are very patchy and whatever little we know about the great ruler comes from a great literary creation, *Khuman Raso* containing 5,000 couplets in the Rajasthani language and its various dialects available in the Devnagari script, giving a detailed description of the war of Khuman with the Arab invaders.

A Jain *muni* (saint), Dalpati Vijay, is credited with the creation of *Khuman Raso* but there is a dispute about the exact time when the *muni* penned it. We shall leave that debate to historians and focus on what is largely agreed upon by most historians as the life and work of Khuman II.

Khuman II's reign is believed to have lasted from CE 820 to 860. Though different historians calculate the years slightly differently from each other, but largely there is a consensus on this.

When the news of Bappa's death reached Arabia, the then Caliph sent Hashim to invade India. Hashim came to India via Gujarat's sea-route and continued northwards through Rajasthan where he achieved some initial successes. But Nagabhatta, the King of Bhinmal, a principality southwest of Chittor, and Khuman II entered into an alliance to take on Hashim. They were regularly informed about Hashim's movements by their spies and a major battle ensued, in which the Arabs were crushed and driven away for a few decades.

It was during Khuman's reign that massive infighting was rampant among the Arab tribes regarding the claims to the Islamic Caliphate. Around this time, a General of Caliph, Al-Ma'mun by the name of Mahmud, son of Khurasan, raided India. He was different from Mahmud of Ghazni, and constituted a major act of vandalism committed by the Arabs on India.

The chief objective of *Khuman Raso* is to celebrate the resistance put up on the occasion of Mahmud's invasion of India with a massive army. *Khuman Raso* chronicles the princes who aided Khuman, the bulwark of Hindu faith. The composer of Raso depicts Khuman as a defender of the crimson standard[20] of Mewar who treats Mahmud's demand for tribute with utter contempt. After a ferocious onslaught, in which the barbarian is pursued, driven back and discomfited in the plains, he returns triumphant with Mahmud held captive.

The greatest tribute to Khuman is his leadership, which united forty royal houses, from Kashmir to Rameswaram, and who unitedly defeated the formidable Arab army. Never in the history of India had such a formidable and large union of armies materialised as under Khuman II.

Col. James Tod describes all these houses in detail in his book *Annals and Antiquities of Rajasthan*. He writes:

"From Ghazni came the Gehlotes; the Tak from Aser; from Madolye the Chauhans; the Chaluk from Rahirgadh; from Set-

20. Term used by Tod to mean *bhagwa dhwaj.*

Binder the Jiskera; Khairavi from Mundore; from Mongrol the Makwanas; Kachchawas from Narwar; Kalum from Sanchore; Gaurs from Ajmer; Tanwars from Delhi; from Patun, the Chawura; Deoras from Sirohi; from Jalore, the Sonigurra; from Gagraun, the Kheechi; the Jadoo from Junagadh; from Kanauj, the Rathore."

Tod described the lineage and reign of each of these royal houses with whatever information he could gain access to, reading through inscriptions and the recorded Hindu annals. The Islamic records of these times are virtually non-existent, though Dr. Ram Gopal Mishra has tried to dig out the truth of Hindu resistance to Islam from CE 6th to the12th century in a meticulous manner.

Amarkavyam describes Khuman's army in the following words: "One lakh Rawats, thirty lakh horsemen, seven lakh infantry, nine thousand elephants and a thousand drums were assembled under Khuman." There is little doubt that this is a grossly exaggerated version of the numbers, but it can be said safely that it was a huge army that took on the Arabs[21].

Unfortunately, Islamic marauders destroyed the two most important means of recording history by Hindu historians and kings. All books in universities like Nalanda and Takshashila were burnt and the pillar and stone inscriptions were lost along with the plunder of Hindu temples. The mindless hatred of these imperialists against civilisation has almost completely blacked out the records of the crucial era from the CE 7th to 12th century.

Most of the old cities and dwellings have become extinct now with time, due to temporal decay or incessant Islamic invasions. Yet, the fact that armies from entire Bharatvarsha assembled under Khuman to fight Arabs belies the belief that Hindus never fought unitedly. Within 100 years of Bappa, Hindus were again ready to unitedly halt the march of Islamic bigotry.

Khuman's defeat of Mahmud was conclusive and since it was the army of the Caliphate of Islam, it completely demoralised the Arab invaders. Mahmud was held captive under very humiliating conditions by Khuman. He was let go after extracting heavy penalties from Arabs[22].

---

21. *Amarkavyam*, p. 106.
22. Tod: *Annals & Antiquities of Rajasthan*, vol 2, p. 197.

Khuman is documented to have fought twenty-four battles all over northern and western India to destroy Arab garrisons and uproot all remnants of Islamic invaders up to Iran and Afghanistan. It is a sad reflection on the lack of pride and enterprise in the modern Hindu community that a leader as important as Khuman has been almost erased from the history of our great civilisation. It is because of kings like Khuman that the Hindus constitute the most ancient race existing in the world today.

British historian and thinker, Sir Arnold Toynbee had worked extensively on ancient civilisations and documents, recording that approximately twenty-five ancient civilisations have become extinct and lie buried under the sands of time. Among the four surviving, viz. Western, Islamic, Hindu and Far Eastern, the oldest living civilisation is the Hindu civilisation[23].

We cannot be grateful enough to kings like Khuman II that we are still thriving and form 15 per cent of the global population today.

Khuman put an end to Arab invasions permanently and thus saved even the Far East and China from the marauders of radical Islam. One can only imagine the global consequences of an Arab victory in India. If India had capitulated to Islam, there is little doubt that the entire world would have been Islamised.

This fear of Islam reaching China and Far East is documented in the *Travels* of the Chinese Ou Kong, who refers to Lalitaditya Muktapida of Kashmir and says that Mungti (Muktapida) was in alliance with the ruler of central India, (Yasovarman) and together they blocked the five passes leading to Tibet[24].

It is well documented that the Arab caliphate had to divide their forces into two main streams to attack Europe towards the west and India towards the east. If Bharat was to be overrun by Islamic marauders, the Caliphs could have singularly focussed on the Western invasions. It would have been only a matter of time before the West would have been subjugated too.

While the entire world is aware of and celebrates the Battle of Tours fought in CE 732 between Charles Martel and the Ummayyad Caliphate, we have ourselves relegated our heroes like

23. Arnold Toynbee: *A Study of History*, vol. 1-6.
24. Cited by R.S. Tripathi: *History of Kannauj*, 1950, p. 203; Mishra, p. 29.

Khuman and Bappa Rawal into oblivion.

While there are innumerable movies made on the crucial role played by Joan of Arc, Richard the Lionhearted and Pelagius of Spain in stalling westward onslaught of Islam just as books and literature have been written to keep their memory burning in the human psyche, it is grossly unfair and tragic that heroes like Khuman have almost been erased from our history, though their contributions are as critical, if not greater than their European counterparts in saving mankind.

It is also a commentary on the poor maintenance of records on the part of Hindu scholars that such great legends do not even own a recorded history in their name. It was only a British officer, Col. James Tod, who wrote his exhaustive book on the history of Rajasthan, to whom we owe the memory of Khuman.

Though it must be said in all fairness to the foresight and perseverance of Hindu kings and priests throughout the ages, the original script of *Khuman Raso* is still kept in the original at Poona Museum as of today[25].

The Hindus owe it to their great forefathers who fought the *asuras* and *mlechchas* (reference to invaders in ancient Rajasthani

Samadhi of Khuman near Nagda

25. *Hindi Sahitya ka Itihas*, Ramchandra Shukl.pdf/%6.

literature) so valiantly as to be recorded in the Hindu annals. We must never forget the sacrifices of these great kings and instead, keep this history alive through research and meticulous documentation of the stories of these great monarchs.

During his time, Khuman became a household name in Rajasthan, like that of Caesar in Rome. In Mewar, even today, if you take a false step, or even sneeze, you will hear someone exclaim, *"May Khuman help you!"*

Royal rulers have to battle many contradictions in governing a state. Khuman was advised by the advisors in his court to hand over the reins of Mewar to his younger brother Jograj towards the end of his reign. But Jograj proved to be a greedy and myopic ruler. Khuman had to come back from his retirement to dethrone him and banish him from his kingdom. Khuman slew all the advisors of Jograj who had advised him to make the move in the first place. Years later, Khuman was murdered by his son Mangal. Mangal was evicted from the kingdom by his chieftains, but he managed to establish a separate kingdom later.

Bharthari Bhatt succeeded Khuman with the consent of the *samants* and during his reign, Mewar's territory added vast expanses. Bharthari Bhatt had thirteen sons and each of them was settled in Malwa and Gujarat with independent possessions. They came to be known as Bhatewada Gehlots.

Thus, the Mewar Rawals kept fighting and defeating Islamic imperialism for 500 consecutive years from the 7th to the 12th centuries, though this important epoch has been erased from the collective memory of Hindus.

The biggest defeat of Arab Islamic imperialism happened here in Bharatvarsha. Our intelligent ancestors recognized the true nature of these rapists and murderers and fought them tooth and nail. After five hundred years of failed attempts by Arabs at converting Hindus to Islam, the Afghans, Turks and Central Asian tribes like Uzbeks, Kazakhs, Tatars, started invading Bharat. These were certainly more brutal and immoral than Arabs. The resistance to these offshoots of Arabic Islam is an altogether different story.

Great kings like Khuman were the only reason why Arabs had

to face defeat in Bharatvarsha. We would do well to remember that a period of five hundred years of relative tranquility passed from 7-12th century, when Hindu kings slaughtered the Arabs at regular intervals.

To forget such greats like Khuman, is not only unfair to them but also demonstrates our pathetic ingratitude.

To bring alive his memory in the Hindu consciousness will be true homage to Rawal Khuman.

□

3

Rawal Jaitra Singh: Destruction of Nagda & Defeat of Iltutmish

(CE 1213-1253)

The life and work of Rawal Jaitra Singh is critical for three reasons. First, Rawal Jaitra Singh forms a vital link in the saga of Hindu resistance to Turkish and Afghan invaders in the 13th century. He thus provides a crucial continuity to the victorious saga of Bappa, Khuman and Shakti Kumar against the Islamic invaders. Second, Jaitra Singh's battles provide the perfect response in exposing the lie called Delhi Sultanate. Jaitra Singh waged a protracted conflict with slave ruler Shams-ud-Din Iltutmish lasting for ten years from CE 1224 to 1234.

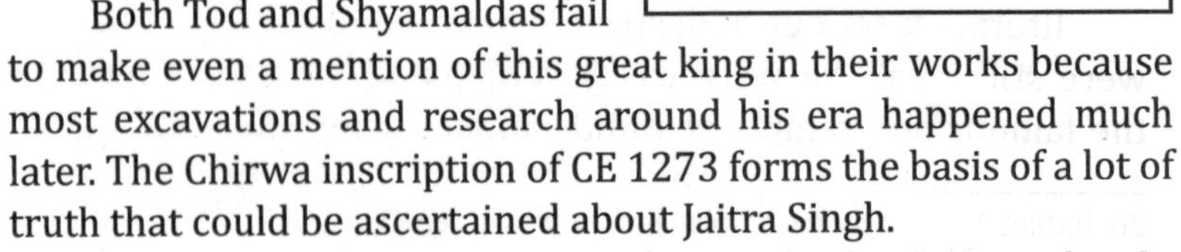

The third and most important reason:

Both Tod and Shyamaldas fail to make even a mention of this great king in their works because most excavations and research around his era happened much later. The Chirwa inscription of CE 1273 forms the basis of a lot of truth that could be ascertained about Jaitra Singh.

Dr. Gopinath Sharma has mentioned in his book, *Rajasthan ke*

Itihas ke Srot (1983, p. 110) an inscription, located at the outer gate of a new temple located 8 miles north of Udaipur in the Pratapgarh *tehsil* of Chittorgarh, giving important information about the descendants of Bappa Rawal: Padma Simha, Jaitra Simha, Tej Simha and Samar Simha. It is now known as Chirwa inscription.

In the *Vienna Oriental and Indian Antiquary* journals, articles are published regarding the Chirwa and Mount Abu inscriptions providing valuable details about Jaitra Simha[26].

Based on these sources, we try to tell the story of this great Rawal of Mewar.

At the second battle of Tarain, in CE 1192, the first significant defeat of Hindu king Prithviraj Chauhan happened at the cruel hands of Muhammad Ghori. This changed the contours of the Hindu-Muslim conflict in Bharat irreversibly.

Ghori killed Prithviraj and appointed Qutb-ud-Din Aibak as a Governor in northern India.

Aibak was a slave General with Ghori, since Ghori had only a daughter as his child. Aibak died in CE 1210 while playing polo and Shams-ud-Din Iltutmish became the new ruler of Aibak's territory.

Iltutmish was a ruthless Islamist who amassed a huge army and started destroying Hindu kingdoms of Ranthambore and Mandore.

He also destroyed many educational institutions in Rajasthan and turned towards Mewar. He was confronted by Rawal Jaitra Singh of Mewar, who was ruling a beautiful temple-city of Nagda at that time. Nagda was situated 20 kms north of present-day Udaipur and it was also one of the twin capitals of Mewar; the other being Chittor.

Legend has it that Nagda had 999 Shaiva, Vaishnava and Jain temples at that time. During Jaitra Singh's reign, Mewar also became an important centre for trade in silver.

Iltutmish set out to destroy Mewar via Ajmer. The Chauhans were still weak, so were easily subjugated. Iltutmish destroyed the famous sun temple at Nandeshma. During those times, Mug

26. Indian Antiquary, Vol. 57 also has an article regarding Chirwa inscription and Jaitra Simha. https://www.rajputcommunity.in/t/rawal-jaitrasmha-and-the-forgotten-battle-of-bhutalghati/981

Brahmins were known as great astrologers and used to build these sun temples to predict events of the year and these temples were great education centres for astrology.

It is said that Nandeshma Sun Temple was the first temple of Mewar to be destroyed.

The Mewar forces of Jaitra Singh, led by Pamraj Tanter attacked Iltutmish in the valley connecting Gogunda with Nagda in CE 1229. This is also known as the battle of Bhutala. It was one of the fiercest battles of Rajasthan in which thousands from either side were killed. Tanter died defending his king but succeeded in salvaging Jaitra Singh from the Islamic army. Jaitra Singh took refuge in a house in Nagda and Iltutmish burnt down the entire city of Nagda, razing each and every temple to the ground.

Many Chauhans, Solankis, Parmars, Charans and tribal Bhils wrought havoc on the Muslim army.

Jaitra Singh was surrounded but escaped unhurt. Iltutmish's army too was nearly decimated and he was forced to retreat.

The destruction of Nagda is one of the most brutal and yet the most neglected assault of Islamists on Hinduism in the subcontinent. Each and every idol was ordered to be broken in a way that it couldn't be rebuilt.

There is a famous saying in Mewar which bears witness to this mindless plunder:

अल्त्या रे मस मूरताऊं बाथ्यां आवै,
जैत नीं पावै तो नागदो हलगावै।

(Soldiers of Iltutmish can only fight with idols. When they couldn't find Jaitra Singh, they burnt down Nagda.)

Invaluable sculptures and historical inscriptions were lost in Iltutmish's mad desire to destroy Hindu temples. The ruins of Nagda today are mute reminders of the bruised soul of Mewar at the hands of the Muslim looters. The sheer beauty and magnanimity of these ruins is enough to enlighten what majestic structures had been lost to this evil mafia. Jaitra Singh got the Baghela pond constructed in the memory of the martyrs of Bhutala. Eminent historian, Dr. Shri Krishan Jugnu too has described this battle and its aftermath in his book.

Pillaged temples and pillars at Nagda

Partially destroyed Sahastra Bahu temple at Nagda

Almost all Leftist and *jihadi* historians have blunted their pens writing lies about the benevolence of Muslim invaders and spreading the lie that the destruction of Hindu temples is exaggerated by awakened Hindus. Some day the Leftist thugs masquerading as historians should be taken on a tour of the ruins of Nagda to witness the scale of plunder that the followers of Islam had unleashed on Hindus. Maybe some amount of shame would make them see the lies they have been peddling as history to the masses of this nation in stupor.

At that time, Gujarat was under the Solanki king, Bhimdev, who was also referred to as Bhola Bhim, meaning naive Bhim, because of his young age and later, his indifferent rule. The real power centres were the father-son duo of Baghel Rajputs—Rana Lavanprasad and his son Veerdhawal. Gujarat was a declining power at that time and Iltutmish had his eyes set on Gujarat. Veerdhawal had reached out to Jaitra Singh of Mewar and Som Singh, Udai Singh and Dharawarsh of Marwar for a military alliance before the destruction of Nagda.

Shams-ud-Din Iltutmish : The slave who destroyed Nagda

Mewar's Rawal Samant Singh had been defeated by Gujarat's Kitu Chauhan, four generations ago and Mewar had been reduced to being a vassal of Gujarat during the subsequent reigns of Kumar Singh and Padam Singh.

Jaitra Singh had shaken off the allegiance to Gujarat during the earlier years of his reign and hence he turned down the request for alliance.[27]

Meanwhile, Iltutmish had amassed wealth from his loot of Rajasthan and started engaging even Hindu soldiers to his side in order to become a formidable force.

27. https://www.jstor.org/stable/44303995 Rawal Jaitra singh of Mewar: A survey of his foreign policy. Author: ML Mathur, Source: Proceedings of the Indian History Congress , 1951, Vol.14, pp. 343-352 . Published by Indian History Congress.

Jaitra Singh miscalculated the strength of Iltutmish and was defeated. He lost many valuable Rajputs and Nagda was completely destroyed.

Jaitra Singh retreated to Chittor and sent emissaries to Veerdhawal to fight Iltutmish jointly. The Hindus finally regrouped and attacked Iltutmish at an unknown place in Mewar and defeated him in CE 1234. Iltutmish died shortly after this defeat in CE 1236.

This was the first defeat of the so-called 'Delhi Sultanate' by a king of Mewar. The Chirwa inscription describes this victory in the words: *'Jaitra Simha protected the earth and proved Agastya to the sea of Turushka armies.'*

The inscription is referring to the Hindu sage, Agastya who is believed to have drunk an entire ocean.

Jaitra Singh thus managed to save the silver trade of Mewar and recovered his kingdom from the brink of annihilation. Nagda was, however, lost permanently and Jaitra Singh was prompted to declare Chittor as the capital of Mewar.

Jaitra Singh is also recorded to have defeated a Muslim army of Sindh. The Abu inscription describes this victory in these words: *'The ghosts of Mewar army, intoxicated by drinking blood the army of Sindh, praised the strength of Jaitra Singh'.* G.H. Ojha dug up Persian annals and believes that this Sindh army belonged to Jalaluddin, who defeated a Hindu king, Jai Singh of Thatta in Sindh, and invaded Gujarat. Jaitra Singh intercepted him en route to Gujarat and looted his wealth.

The final battle by Jaitra Singh was with Nasiruddin Mahmud of Delhi in CE 1248. The fighting lasted eight months and Nasiruddin was forced to return to Delhi.

Besides fighting the Islamic invaders, Jaitra Singh also subjugated Tribhuvanpal of Gujarat in CE 1242 as also the Chauhans of Nadaul, Parmars of Malwa and other smaller kingdoms surrounding Mewar before restoring the authority of his family.

This great king was the ruler of Mewar for a very long time and relinquished the throne to his son Tej Singh within his life-time. Jaitra Singh died somewhere between CE 1253-61 due to natural causes at a ripe old age.

Tej Singh was an equally aggressive king and continued expansion of Mewar. He humbled Visaldev of Gujarat.

Tej Singh ruled till 1273 and then his glorious son, Samar Singh ruled Mewar for nearly thirty years. Samar Singh joined hands with rulers of Gujarat and defeated the Slave ruler, Ghiyasuddin Balban, pushing him back to Delhi.

Chirwa inscription describes Samar Singh thus: *'He was like a lion in annihilating enemies—extremely courageous, luminous like moon, focussed on his karma and intensely aware of his dharma.'*

Samar Singh died in CE 1303 when Ratan Singh became the ruler of Mewar. The most vicious and sustained attack on Chittor was to be endured by young Ratan Singh whose resistance to Allauddin Khilji has been forever etched into the history of Hindu-Muslim conflicts in the subcontinent.

We thus come to the end of this extremely crucial phase of resistance to Islam by the Hindus.

With Prithviraj's murder, Islamic rule was established in the northern parts of Bharat by the Afghan and Turk slaves. Arab invasions were by now a thing of the past. Islam had well and truly arrived into the subcontinent after incessant onslaughts for 500 years. Mewar still managed to fend off this entrenched Islamic rule from Chittor, but couldn't do much beyond her borders. In the rest of the nation, Islamic states mushroomed in Sindh, Bengal, Bihar, etc. The Rathores from Kannauj were forced to seek newer pastures in Marwar of Rajasthan and the Rajputs of Gwalior were driven out to seek shelter in the Kachchawa kingdom of Amer.

Rawal Samar Singh (1272-1303 CE)

Thus, the three clans of Amer, Marwar and Mewar combined in Rajasthan to take on the Islamic invaders for the next 400 years, from CE 1300-1700.

Rawal Jaitra Singh and

Samar Singh, who became legends in the folklore of Rajasthan, continued to inspire resistance to Islamic invaders.

The writer has immense satisfaction in penning this section on Rawal Jaitra Singh whom Hindus have all but forgotten. Without Jaitra Singh, the Slave dynasty would have rapidly Islamised our nation and for which, we must look back with a lot of pride and gratitude that in spite of the reverses, the great Maharanas rose back from the ashes of their destruction to defeat the Islamic zealots.

If the creed of Islam had produced hordes of pillagers hell-bent on destroying civilizations and converting the Hindus by sword and jihad, then Hinduism too nurtured these glorious Mewar Kings who rose to that challenge with passionate zeal and love for Dharma, pushing back these marauders for a relentless thousand years.

□

4

Rawal Ratan Singh: Maharani Padmini, Assault of Khilji & the First Saka-Jauhar (CE 1303)

Rawal Ratan Singh was the son of Rawal Samar Singh, who himself was an exceptional king. Much has been written and speculated about this era of Ratan Singh because of his beautiful wife Padmini and Allauddin Khilji's lustful efforts to woo the queen of Mewar, resulting in the first siege and *jauhar-saka* of Chittor.

A lot of confusion around this era springs out of relying on the poetic leverages of Malik Muhammad Jayasi (1477-1542) who penned an imaginary ballad around Ratan Singh and Padmini, but historically, Jayasi's account is unreliable. Hence, it is being quoted only to dispel some myths around Rani Padmini and Ratan Singh.

Firstly, there was no queen by the name of Padmavati; it is a fictional character Jayasi created for his work, albeit inspired by Rani Padmini. Hence, all efforts and designs to refer to the great queen of Chittor—Rani Padmini as Padmavati—must be refuted. An imaginary person cannot be allowed to replace one of the greatest queens of Hindu history, as she made one of the greatest sacrifices for her honour and *dharma*.

Secondly, Jayasi penned *Padmavati* a good 250 years after the actual siege of Chittor. Hence, his poetic work cannot be a basis for a historical recreation of events at that time.

Allauddin Khilji was born in CE 1267 and was raised by his uncle Jalaluddin, who ruled over a small area around Delhi.

Jalaluddin started his career as an officer in the Mamluk or the Slave dynasty and took over control after the death of the last slave ruler, Muizuddin Qaiqabad. Jalaluddin was seventy-years old at the time of his ascension. His daughter was married to Allauddin.

Allauddin Khilji (1296-1316 CE)

Allauddin murdered Jalaluddin and took control of Delhi in CE 1296 when he started destroying Hindu kingdoms in North India.

He was single-handedly responsible for putting an end to several Hindu dynasties, including the Parmaras, Vaghelas, Chahamanas (Chauhans) and also the Rawals of Mewar.

His infamous eunuch-slave General Malik Kafur, was the first Muslim General to cross the Vindhyas and wreak havoc on the South Indian kingdoms of Yadavas, Kakatiyas and Hosyalas.

Kafur was born a Hindu but was purchased as a slave by Allaudin's General Nusrat Khan in CE 1299[28].

We will restrict ourselves to destructions caused by Allauddin in Rajasthan to Ranthambhore and Chittor.

In CE 1297, two of Allauddin's best Generals, Ulugh Khan and

28. Kishori Saran Lal, 1950, *History of the Khaljis*, p.86.

Nusrat Khan, looted and plundered Rudra Mahalaya and Somnath temple and rushed to carry the broken pieces of the Shiva *lingam* to Allauddin. The Jalore prince, Kanhad Dev Songara, assisted by a neo-Muslim convert, Muhammad Shah, confronted and defeated Khilji's army. Kanhad Dev installed the broken Shiva *lingam* at five temples in Prabhas Patan, Bagada, Abu, Jalore and his personal garden[29].

Kanhad Dev fell out with Muhammad Shah and his soldiers because they consumed beef and Muhammad Shah with another General, Kabhru, approached Hammir Dev to seek refuge from Allauddin. Hammir provided them shelter with the intent of using them against Allauddin.

Allauddin laid siege on the Ranthambore fort of Rajasthan and eventually seized it in CE 1301.

Most of the historical accounts talk of the 'victory' of Allauddin over the then Chauhan ruler of Ranthambhore, Hammir Dev Chauhan, but the local folklore tells an entirely different story about this mysterious saga of valour and treachery.

The writer roamed around the fort, talking to locals and guides for days, to find an alternate version, but all were consistent in their account of the events that unfolded in the war between Khilji and Hammir. This story is being narrated only to stress the evil nature of Khilji and how the written history of today is a distortion of facts to suit the narrative of 'breaking India' forces.

In the year CE 1300, Allauddin sent two of his ablest Generals, Nusrat Khan and Ulugh Khan, to lay siege on Ranthambhore. Nearby 80,000 Muslim troops of Allauddin attacked Hammir's troops, but the Muslims were completely routed in this battle. Nusrat was hit by a manjaniq stone and killed. Hammir came out of the fort and destroyed the Muslim army[30].

Ulugh Khan survived and continued the siege by bringing in reinforcements, while Khilji himself joined him in CE 1301.

Struck by famine due to the long siege, the Rajputs had no option left but to open the gates and fight in the open. Assisted by

29. Dasharatha Sharma, 1959, *Early Chauhān Dynasties*, p. 162.
30. Banarsi Prasad Saksena, *A Comprehensive History of India*: *The Delhi Sultanate*, 1992, p. 342.

Virama, Jaja and Muhammad Shah, Hammir took on Khilji close to the fort. It was decided that if the Rajputs lost, the women and children would commit *jauhar.*

Hammir defeated Khilji and Ulugh in the frontal battle and dispatched Ranmall, one of his Generals to convey the good news to the residents of the fort. Little did Hammir know that Ranmall had been bought over by Khilji with a promise that if Hammir was killed, he (Ranmall) would be given the reign of Ranthambhore.

Padamala pond in the Ranthambhore fort

The symbolic head of Ranmall, the traitor of Ranthambhore

Ranmall and his associate Ratanpal told the queens and residents that the battle had been lost. In the meanwhile, Ranmall asked his men to open the rear gates of the fort to let Khilji's men enter surreptitiously.

The family of Hammir, chief queen Ranga Devi, all other queens and children committed *jauhar* on hearing the false news about the defeat. Hammir's daughter named Padmala tied herself to boulders and sank herself in a pond inside the fort. It was the first incident of *jal jauhar* anywhere in India. The Padmala *Taalaab* (pond) located in the Ranthambhore Fort bears witness to that ultimate sacrifice of Princess Padmala. Hammir rushed into the fort on seeing smoke and embers rising from the pyres of *jauhar.* He was devastated to learn about the treachery of Ranmall and his associates. Hammir publicly beheaded Ranmall and Ratanpal and then beheaded himself at the local Shiva temple. The loyal Rajputs kept on fighting without their leader till the last of them fell. Thus, Khilji captured the vital fort of Ranthambhore due to the treachery of a Hindu vassal of Hammir.

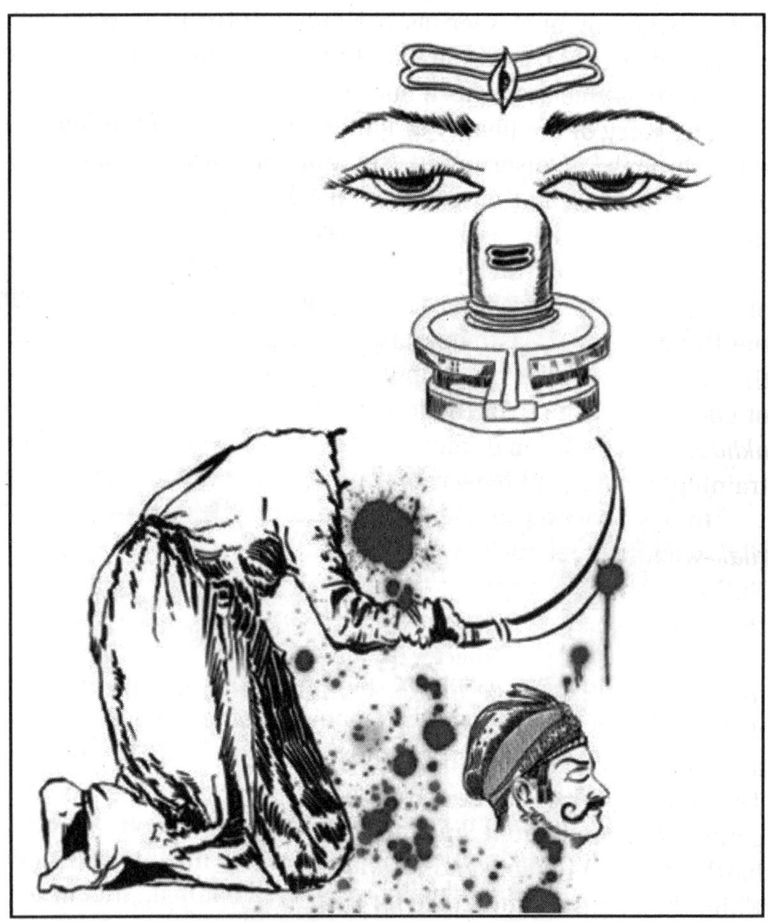

Hammir Dev Chauhan gives himself to Shiva

The victory at Ranthambhore was a major morale booster for Khilji and he sold it to his army of mercenaries as a 'gift of Allah to the pious'.

Malik Kafur amassed huge amounts of wealth from his raids in South India and sent it to Allauddin. Gradually amassing wealth and hiring an army of mercenaries, Allauddin set his eyes on Chittor since it was the seat of Hindu power in northern India. Allauddin eventually wanted to invade South India for its riches, but Chittor stood in the way, both metaphorically and literally. Chittor was not only seen as a Hindu centre of power, but it controlled critical trade routes to the South and Gujarat, both on its eastern as well as western borders.

The story of the beauty of Rani Padmini reached Allauddin's ears through a disgruntled servant of Mewar—Raghunath, who was a bard and entertainer in Rawal Ratan Singh's court. He has been falsely and notoriously portrayed as a Brahmin priest in Bollywood movies and trashy literature, with the aim of demeaning the priestly class as debauched traitors. In reality, the Brahmins of Rajasthan were the most committed Hindus as they not only tutored the Rajputs on Hindu scriptures and values of *dharma*, but many of them were warriors themselves and ran *akhaadaas* (traditional monasteries for physical and military training) throughout Mewar to train Hindu youth in warfare.

In a Bollywood movie, Raghunath has been shown to be a *tilak*-wielding debauch, who was sexually drawn to Padmini. Nothing except demeaning the great Brahmin teachers could be the motive of such a false portrayal.

Plush with the successes of Ranthambore and Shivana forts, Khilji laid a siege on Chittor fort in CE 1302. He laid the dishonourable condition for the surrender of Rajputs and acquisition of Padmini for himself in lieu of lifting the siege. Thousands of Rajputs and Hindus from surrounding kingdoms gathered around Ratan Singh to fight the *jihadi* invader. A bloody battle ensued and thousands of warriors on both sides were killed. Khilji then made an overture for peace to Ratan Singh and asked for an audience with the Rana. A lot of stories have been going around that Khilji asked for Padmini's face to be seen through a reflection in a mirror, but this hasn't been substantiated by any recorded account. Going by the history of the Mewar dynasty, it is extremely unlikely that Rajputs would have yielded to Khilji's demand and the meeting was merely agreed to, in order to discuss the terms of a treaty between the warring kings.

Maharani Padmini, an artist's impression

Padmini Mahal in Chittor

Khilji, true to the faith of his co-religionists, sweet-talked Ratan Singh and agreed to lift the siege in lieu of a few gifts. Ratan Singh, in his simplicity, escorted Khilji down the fort, where Khilji revealed his true colours and abducted Ratan Singh. The only condition laid down by Khilji for Ratan Singh's return was the surrender of Padmini. He knew very well that Rajputs would never give up their queen and that he would easily be able to defeat a leaderless, demoralised army.

Gora and Badal

But Khilji was in for a nasty surprise. The beautiful queen was not mere beauty, but brains and will of a fierce warrior and a master planner herself. She planned an extrication of Ratan Singh with the Mewar nobles led by her uncle Gora and her nephew, Badal. Badal was very young, but the Rajputs were expected to take on the enemy even at that tender age and Badal lived up to the call of honour. Khilji was informed that the day he withdrew his troops from the trenches surrounding Chittor, Queen Padmini would be sent, but would be accompanied by her handmaids. Strict demands were made by the Rajputs to prevent any violation of the sanctity of the female decorum and privacy.

More than 700 palanquins were covered and dispatched to Khilji's camp. Each palanquin was occupied by one of the best warriors of Mewar and was to be carried by six armed men disguised as palanquin-bearers. Half an hour was granted for the audience between Ratan Singh and Padmini.

Ratan Singh and Padmini escaped in the palanquins for a few kilometres where a fleet of horses awaited them. They safely reached their fort, while 5,000 Hindu troops took positions at the outer gate to prevent Khilji's army from entering into the fort of Chittor.

Armed with the noblest sentiments, committed to the safety of their king Ratan Singh, and with their hearts burning with the sole desire to protect the honour of their queen, Gora and Badal wrought havoc on Khilji's troops. Thousands were killed in this battle of mutual destruction, but Mewar warriors managed to beat back the invaders comprehensively.

Allauddin Khilji was thus defeated in his objective and perceiving the havoc wrought by the Rajput army, he was forced to end his siege and retreat to Delhi.

Gora made the supreme sacrifice at the gates of Chittor and very few Hindu warriors survived to make it back to the safety of the fort, including the mortally-wounded boy-warrior Badal. Below is an account of the conversation between Badal and his aunt, Gora's valiant wife.

James Tod quotes this conversation from the epic *Khuman Raso*:

'The aunt asks Badal as to how did her lord conduct himself ere she joins him.

The stripling replied: "He was the reaper of the harvest of battle; I followed his steps as the humble gleaner of his sword.

On the gory bed of honour, he spread a carpet of the slain; a barbarian prince his pillow, he laid him down, and sleeps surrounded by the foe."

Again, she said: "Tell me, Badal, how did my lord behave?"

"Oh, mother! How further to describe his deeds when he left no foe to dread or admire him?"

She smiled farewell to the boy and adding, "My lord will chide my delay," sprung into the flame.

Such were the sacrifices made by our ancestors in keeping the Islamic forces at bay[31].

Allauddin replenished his resources by plundering the rest of Rajasthan and returned to Chittor two years later. Mewar had not yet recovered from her loss of many of her sons and Khilji carried out his attacks more ruthlessly this time. After months of siege, Khilji managed to obtain the hill at the southern point, where he entrenched himself.

The poetic annals point to a vision that Ratan Singh saw and in which the presiding deity of Chittor came to him and said that the continuance of Rajput control over Chittor needed regal blood.

31. *Annals & Antiquities of Rajasthan*, James Tod, vol. 1, p. 214.

Hence, twelve, who wear the diadem, must bleed for Chittor, else the land would pass from the line.

Goddess Durga

Ratan Singh convened a midnight council of his nobles and announced his intention to carry out the advice of the divine vision. Twelve sons and nephews of Ratan Singh were lined up and it was decided that each of them would lead the final assault, one by one. Eleven princes, including the eldest Ari Singh, were martyred thus in three days of Mewar's frontal assault on Khilji. On the third night, Ratan Singh's favourite son, Karan Singh, was made to escape from the northern gates to the safety of Kailwada. On the fourth day, Ratan Singh proclaimed, *"I give myself to Chittor now."*

But with that proclamation, a horror was to be unleashed on the soul of Bharat. In CE 1303, the beautiful Padmini along with thousands of brave women entrenched inside Chittor were to perform *jauhar* by giving themselves to the *agni* or fire to escape captivity by the *mlechchhas*.

The funeral pyre was lit within the great subterranean retreat in chambers impervious to light. The defenders of Chittor beheld with a strong heart the procession of queens, their own wives and daughters walking to their *moksha*.

Husbands put *sindoor* on the foreheads of their wives one last time.

The women in whose embrace men had scaled heights of love and ecstasy, looked at each other one last time.

Every man was helpless and yet, free.

Helpless that he wouldn't be able to save his family.

Free, that at least his family would not be enslaved by stinking barbarians.

Fathers would have kissed the foreheads of their tender daughters. For the last time their being would have reverberated with the scent of their beloved girls.

Young children would have looked quizzingly at their fathers when they were being tied to their mothers.

Every Hindu woman would have taken blessings from priests, Gurus and Charans so that courage doesn't desert them in that moment of trial.

The men and Gurus would have emptied their faces of all signs of weakness, lest the last journey of their beloved and their children be painful.

Not hundred, two or three hundred, thousands of men and their families were undergoing this horrific ordeal.

In the lust for freedom and self respect... life, relations, compassion, love, attachment, all was rendered insignificant and meaningless.

The fair Padmini closed the throng, augmented by every female beauty or youth that could be tainted by the vicious Tatar lust. The glorious women of Mewar entered the cavern, to be devoured by fire, thus saving them from dishonour by the invaders, as they burned in the sacred flames. Instead of surrendering to brute lust, our amazing ancestors chose to be permanently destroyed in the safety of the rising flames of jauhar that day.

To give one's body to the fury of fire is not an easy choice by any standards. What age, and wear and tear would have worn out anyway, was wilfully surrendered to fire on that glorious day of *jauhar*. The beautiful Queen Padmini chose the extremely painful path of turning her fair skin into blisters of blood by self-immolation because the barbarian from Afghanistan had left her no choice in the matter.

It was the feminine audacity of a woman with a steely resolve to refuse submission to the Tatar invader; a woman who denied him the option of laying eyes even on her dead body. That is why the great Queen Padmini of Chittor, along with 20,000 of her loyal maids, friends and ordinary citizens of Chittor, chose to close the doors in the face of a ruthless debaucher who had no value for the delicate and the pristine.

In those subterranean retreats in the rocks of Chittor fort, the Hindu women of Mewar conveyed the clearest and most direct message to the Islamic invaders and fellow-Hindus—that honour and freedom are non-negotiable. By that one act of *jauhar*, Maharani Padmini ossified the Hindu-Muslim struggle in the subcontinent and all chances of co-existence with alien forces were put to flames in those embers rising out of the *jauhar*.

Maharani Padmini dissolves herself

If the Tatars wanted to subjugate our will by force, that was not going to happen. The onus of fighting this bunch of marauders was passed on to the successive generations by that singular act of jauhar on that glorious day when Queen Padmini rose to the pedestal of *amaratva* or immortality. Maharani Padmini of Chittor will remain alive in the hearts of the great people of this land till the last Hindu is alive.

Allauddin Khilji, finding nothing but the ashes of the object of his lust, went berserk with rage and ordered a general plunder and slaughter of Chittor. Thirty thousand civilians and soldiers were killed on 26th August CE 1303[32].

Thus, after withstanding the Islamic heat for 600 years, fell the greatest seat of Hindu resistance to the Islamic invaders in CE 1303, to the most merciless and cold-blooded invader this nation had ever witnessed.

Khilji bore a striking resemblance to Aurangzeb, both in success and the bigoted zeal to spread his religion by force. He named himself *Sikander-e-Sani* or the second Alexander and even minted coins, using this title.

Khilji plundered every building and temple of grandeur that stood in Chittor over the next few days. Having committed every act of barbarity and wanton destruction, overthrowing every temple and monument of art, he handed over the fort to his son Khijr Khan and left to ravage the rest of Rajasthan.

32. *The Delhi Sultanate*, R.C. Majumdar, p. 26.

The proud Ahulwara, the ancient Dhar and Avanti, Mandore and Deogir—the seats of Solankis, Paramars and Pratiharas, the entire Agnikul races were overturned forever by Allauddin Khilji. Jaisalmer, Gagron, Boondi, Jalore suffered the horrors of assault from this foe of Hindus[33].

It was only because of the resilience and inner grit of the Rajputs that within decades of being ravaged so brutally by an enemy like Khilji, almost all of them rose again to fight the evil forces of Islamic imperialism. Khilji had taught the Rajputs bitter lessons in warfare and religious hatred. The soft-hearted, just and virtuous principles of war were of no use against this killing machine of *jihad*, and as the coming centuries would prove, Rajputs learnt their lessons well. As the hordes of invaders kept pouring into India from the western border, the Hindus of India, led by the Maharanas of Mewar kept fighting and defeating them.

The northern and north-western frontiers of our land faced onslaughts from invaders of all hues, ranging from Khiljis to Tughlaqs and Syeds to Lodhis to Mughals. Each one encountered overwhelming resistance from the royal house of Mewar under the Sisodia family, always standing tall, raising the saffron flag and their insurmountable spirit of freedom. It was the supreme act of wilful sacrifice by the great Queen Padmini and her cohorts in Chittor that provided fuel to the children of Mewar to never give in to the brute force of the invaders.

Karan Singh, the son of Ratan Singh, found refuge in the hills of Kailwarra and started building an army to regain Chittor. Karan had two sons, Rahap and Mahap. The elder, Mahap went to Doongarpur and annexed it. The younger Rahap was a fierce warrior and settled in the village Sisod, hence the name Sisodias for the descendants of his clan. Rahap, along with his father Karan, was killed in the war to reclaim Chittor.

But the fight for Chittor never ended. Nine generations of Sisodias were lost in a short span of three decades in an attempt to reclaim Chittor. The torch was passed on from one generation

33. Col. James Tod.

to the next until Chittor was ultimately regained by Bhuwan Singh after a fierce fight[34].

Thus ends the story of the first takeover of Chittor by the death cult of the desert, the sacrifices to reclaim it and how it was regained by the valorous sons of Mewar. The memory, facts and truth of this siege have kindled many imaginary tales of valour and romance in the folklores of Rajasthan over the centuries, but none can deny the fact that there was a fair, beautiful, intelligent, and valorous Queen Padmini who committed the first recorded *jauhar* in the history of Rajputs.

She thus laid the grounds for an irreconcilable conflict between the Islamic design of capturing *kafir* women and the Hindu design to remain free, for centuries to come.

A conflict which is well and truly on, even to this day, albeit in a different context and with myriad connotations. *Maharani* Padmini still embodies that undying Hindu spirit to not yield to force, in matters of honour and freedom. We are truly blessed to be heirs and bearers of the legacy of that amazing queen and her brave king, Rawal Ratan Singh.

It is now up to us to continue that struggle kindled by the supreme sacrifice of Queen Padmini who threw herself to the flames, to never ever capitulate to molesters and murderers.

□

34. Ojha vol. 1, p. 187.

5

Maharana Hammir Singh: Recoverer of Chittor & Destructor of Tughlaqs (CE 1326-1364)

The story of this great Maharana reinforces the observation that how bizarre the saga of survival and ascendance of kings to the throne of Mewar in the Sisodia dynasty had been. How fate intervened to impose defeat from near-certain victories of Mewar or conversely, saved the Maharanas and their armies from the very brink of annihilation, by a stroke of luck. It makes the most compelling read ever recorded in human history.

Sometimes, one is forced to believe that there was a divine power audaciously determined to keep the Hindu resistance alive in the subcontinent; otherwise, how was it possible for one single house to continue ruling Mewar and be the centre of resistance to unceasing Islamic attacks for one thousand years?

Friends turned foes, affluence turned to abject poverty, gaiety to unimaginable sorrow, dance of celebration to dance of death, all creativity of Mewar architecture built over centuries plundered in days by Islamic marauders. Hindu customs and traditions crushed and banned with an iron will, cities destroyed and entire population slaughtered for singular wish of the Islamic invaders—convert to Islam or die.

What was that singular thread, except an amazing understanding of the ethos and values of Hindu *dharma*, which made not only the Maharanas stand against *jihad* but the entire population of Mewar and at times, all of Rajasthan, unite with their kings?

One is baffled at the fortitude of these amazing kings who were outnumbered, outwitted, and out-resolved in the fight against Islam and yet, they stood firm, in opposing the designs of all these murderous assaults on Hinduism.

After Ratan Singh was killed by Allauddin Khilji, Chittor was taken over by Islamic forces for the first time and every *haveli*, temple and structure of consequence was either desecrated or destroyed. Khilji continued to plunder Chittor for about a fortnight and then gave the fort to his son, Khijr Khan, who named the city Khijrabad.

Before going out for the final battle or *Saka*[35] at Chittor, Ratan Singh instructed his sons and brothers to escape from the rear gate of Chittor at night. He ordered them to fight the Muslims and regain the fort at an opportune time.

Almost nine generations of Ratan Singh died trying to regain Chittor, but finally, Bhuwan Singh recovered the fort. Many great warriors like Rahap, Mahap, Karan Singh sacrificed their lives trying to regain their ancestral place in a short span of three decades.

Bhuwan Singh was succeeded by Laxman Singh, while in Delhi, the power had shifted from the Khiljis to the Tughlaqs. Muhammad Bin Tughlaq attacked Chittor, and Laxman Singh along with his son Ari Singh, died defending Chittor. Chittor was lost once more. The younger son of Laxman, Ajay Singh, escaped with severe injuries and built his capital at Kailwada where he was sheltered and healed by Jain *munis.* Laxman Singh had two sons, Ajay Singh and his elder brother Ari Singh.

Before the attack by Tughlaq, Ari Singh went out to hunt

35. *Final assault on enemies after the women in the fort had given themselves to fire. More in the chapter on Saka-Jauhar.*

boars in the jungles of Kailwada and came across a local lass in the village of Oondwa. She confronted him when he wanted to enter a cornfield while chasing a wounded boar. The girl asked Ari Singh not to ruin the farm and wait for her to return with the game. To Ari Singh's utter amazement, the girl came back with the carcass of the animal. Then, the girl politely asked Ari Singh to cook the boar in the village and enjoy his meal.

As they were walking back, Ari Singh, already impressed with her, noticed how carrying a milk pitcher on her head, she was also effortlessly dragging two buffaloes. Ari Singh contemplated, 'If I were to have a son from her, he would be a very powerful man indeed.'

Ari Singh inquired about the family, who happened to be Chandana Rajputs and asked for her hand from her father. Ari Singh married the girl, Urmila, but because she was no royalty, the marriage was kept a secret. He kept visiting the girl regularly and a boy was born to the Chandana girl. The boy was named Hammir Singh. In the meantime, Muhammed Bin Tughlaq attacked Chittor and acquired it after killing Laxman Singh and Ari Singh[36].

Ajay Singh, the other son of Laxman Singh, escaped from the war with Tughlaq and settled at Kailwada. He had two sons, Sajjan Singh and Kshem Singh, both of whom were weak and ineffective. Ajay Singh was constantly challenged by a local mountain chief, Moonja Balocha, but was too old to fight him. Then, some *samants* loyal to Ari Singh told Ajay Singh about Hammir Singh, who was beckoned from his village Oondwa, at the age of thirteen.

Hammir set up his men and learnt that Moonja would be coming to Semari village to attend an event.

Hammir attacked him and beheaded him, carrying back Moonja's head on his saddlebow. Ajay Singh kissed his nephew, applied a *teeka* on Hammir's forehead with Moonja's blood. Thus, Hammir Singh became the king of Mewar, overcoming his circumstances through his extreme valour and twist of fate around CE 1326[37].

---

36. *Veer Vinod*, vol. 1, p. 290-91.
37. Somānī, Rāmavallabha 1976, *History of Mewar, from Earliest Times to CE 1751 India*, p. 105.

From Rawal to Rana

Another very significant change that occurred with the coronation of Hammir was the change of title of Mewar kings from Rawal to Rana.

Two different theories have been proposed to explain this.

First, as we talked in the end of the chapter on Rawal Ratan Singh, the Mewar royal house was divided into two between Karan's two sons, Rahap and Mahap. The descendants of the younger Rahap were named Sisodias after the village Sisod where Rahap ruled. Seeing the loss of Chittor as a sign from the divine forces, Rahap proposed that henceforth the kings of Mewar would cease to be kings and be mere Dewans, or caretakers of Mewar. Eklingji, an *avatar* of Shiva, would henceforth be the king of Mewar.

This was a remarkable shift at the level of human consciousness. The arrogance of kings was to be replaced by humbling them as servants of Mahadev. This is one of the reasons why Sisodias always remained the most rooted kings in entire Bharatvarsha. They practised true democracy via the *samants* and *jagirdars* of Mewar, in consultations and tax collections. They mingled freely with the ordinary people of the state and wined and dined with them. This was the reason that the ordinary people of Mewar willingly endured the hardships and plunder that fell upon the great Maharanas. They remained aloof from personal sufferings, living like *mahayogis*, but staying focussed on protecting their people, land and deities.

Without doubt, these great Ranas became the living embodiment of the aphorism; humility is the very essence of human existence.

The second reason for the nomenclature of Rana is believed to be etymological. If we break up the word Maharana in Sanskrit, it yields, *maha* + *arnav*, literally meaning 'great warrior.'

Shyamaldas gives one more explanation, saying that after the first loss of Chittor, Karan Singh escaped to Kailwada. He was challenged there by Rana Mokal Padiyar of Mandovar. Karan's younger son Rahap defeated Padiyar and brought him to Karan. Karan took away the title of Rana from Mokal and granted it to

Rahap. Be that as it may, Hammir Singh became the first Maharana of Mewar.

× × ×

Ajay Singh's sons, Sajjan Singh and Kshem Singh were exiled by their father to prevent a civil war in the family. Sajjan Singh went to the Deccan where his progeny was destined to fight the wrongs done to Hindustan by the then Mughal ruler Aurangzeb in Delhi. Sajjan Singh was the ancestor of the great Chhatrapati Shivaji Maharaj, the founder of Satara throne. This lineage is also recorded in the chronicles of Mewar[38].

Hammir made Kailwada his residence and his first plan of action was to order the people of Mewar to vacate the plains and climb up the hills according to the 'scorched earth policy' of Mewar. This policy was made to render the plains of Mewar barren and useless for the enemy and create such hardships that they would starve in the absence of local farming and other commodities required for sustenance. This evacuation of the plains and shifting the entire population to the hills was a movement that was carried out by successive Maharanas of Mewar, to counter Islamic invaders.

It was quite an amazing feat to achieve and even communicate such a message to the entire state in those challenging times. Even more baffling was the total trust the population had in their king to have joyously followed their Rana to a life of extreme hardship and adversity.

One can only look back in awe at such trust and love showered by the entire population on their ruler and it is difficult to decide whose sacrifice among the two was greater—the Maharanas, who chose to famish the entire commerce of their state and live a life of a warrior or the people of Mewar, who followed the Maharanas to poverty and deprivation.

We will see this practice of evacuating plains for the Aravallis, in the lives of other Ranas of Mewar as well. But the most remarkable example of this practice and the resulting victory of Mewar was seen twice—once with Maharana Hammir and then two centuries later with Maharana Pratap.

---

38. Tod, vol. 1, p. 217.

However, it was not an easy journey for Hammir. Even after putting his people through all these hardships and destroying all local commerce, Hammir did not gain much military success. A time came when he did not even have the money to pay the salaries of his army.

In the meantime, Tughlaq went back to Delhi, leaving Chittor in the hands of Maldeo Songara of Jalore as his vassal. Maldeo protected it fiercely and nursed the ambition of ruling the whole of Mewar some day. Maldeo was informed of the moves of Hammir Singh, but he considered Hammir a weak and spent force.

Although Kailwada provided the perfect refuge from the plains, the repeated failures at regaining Chittor began to tire out the *samants* and friends of the royal house. The entire campaign to free Chittor began to disintegrate.

Hammir, dejected and defeated, abandoned his home and retreated to Dwarka in Gujarat. En route to Dwarka, he camped at night in a village called Khod, which was a settlement of the local Charan community.

Here Hammir had a chance meeting with a female mystic Barwadi Devi, daughter of Chakhda Charan, to whom he narrated his misfortunes. This encounter and her advice not only changed his life, but also the dimensions of entire Hindu-Muslim conflict in the subcontinent irreversibly.

Barwadi looked at Hammir and proclaimed, *"O brave brother, go back to Kailwada! You will get Chittor and when you get a matrimonial offer from the most unexpected place, don't reject it; accept it. That offer will be instrumental in getting back your lost kingdom."*

Hammir replied, *"Bai (sister), how will I get Chittor back? I don't have a horse to ride, nor men to fight for me and no money even to feed my family."*

Barwadi told Hammir that her son Baru would come to Kailwada with a caravan of 500 horses and enough wealth to help him build an army with them and then pay her back when he had enough[39].

Hammir was inspired by Mata Barwadi's words and

39. *Veer Vinod*, vol. 1, p. 294.

contemplated following her advice. In any case, he did not have anything to lose by following the Charan lady's assurances.

Hammir came back to Kailwada and waited. As promised by Mata Barwadi, within weeks, Baru followed him with his 500 horses and money. Hammir saddled all of them and Baru was honoured as the *raj kavi* of Mewar. Many villages were given to him as grants. Baru's descendants inhabit these villages even today. Once again, the Bhils of Mewar rose to support the Rajputs of Mewar and provided Hammir with thousands of warriors and bowmen and furnished information about the movements of the enemy troops.

Then, through a strange turn of events, Maldeo, who was entrusted with Chittor by Muhammed Bin Tughlaq, was advised by his well-wishers to give a daughter to Hammir as they thought that, it would truly expand their frontiers. Though, without doubt, Maldeo merely wanted to use matrimony to augment his own power, little did he know of the fate that awaited him.

From Hammir's perspective, this offer was unacceptable, but Hammir was convinced about Mata Barwadi's prophecy and considered accepting it.

The priests from Maldeo approached Hammir and told him about the traditional friendship between Jalore and Mewar. The priests also told him that Hammir's forefathers were killed by Mohammedans, not Maldeo or his family.

Whether Maldeo's offer was meant to entrap Hammir or was wielded as an insult, worried the latter. He calculated all possibilities and scouted for possible dangers in his mind. In the end, his trust in the female mystic and his obsession to retake Chittor made him accept the offer.

He told his assistants, *"The coconut may be retained!"* He is supposed to have uttered: *"My feet shall at least tread on the rocky steps on which my ancestors have walked. A Rajput should always be prepared for adversity—one day to abandon his abode covered with wounds and the next to reascend with the crown on his head."*

Thus, Hammir undertook the most daring adventure of his life, walking straight into the arms of the enemy with nothing except courage and faith in the Charani mystic's words at his disposal.

The marriage took place at Chittor and the Songara princess won Hammir's heart on their very first night. The Songara princess fell instantly in love with Hammir and laid out a plan for him to win back Chittor. She advised Hammir to ask for Maldeo's servant Mauji Ram, to which the bride's father Maldeo, consented.

Mauji Ram came to Kailwada with the newlyweds and immediately approached Hammir, *"Now is the time to make your move, for which you had sought my loyalties from Maldeo."*

Hammir followed Mauji Ram, who took Hammir and his small army to Chittor on the pretext of hunting. At midnight, since the gatekeepers recognised Mauji Ram, the gates of Chittor were opened and Hammir seized Chittor, slaughtering whatever little resistance he faced. Maldeo's son Jaita was exiled from Chittor.

All remnants of the Islamic takeover were obliterated within weeks by Hammir and any memory naming Chittor as Khijrabad was erased. In any case, the glorious people of Mewar had never accepted the name Khijrabad for Chittor as evidenced by the revenue records of that time.

Maldeo was furious when he learnt of this and gathered his army to attack Chittor. Maldeo had five sons, who fought for him. Hammir gathered all his former chieftains and repelled the attack of the Jalore army.

Maldeo approached Tughlaq and the joint forces of Muhammed bin Tughlaq and Jalore came to attack Chittor. In the meantime, as the people of Mewar learnt about Hammir's ascendance to the throne of Mewar and the pride of Hindwa Sooraj reinstated, they poured in streams from the western highlands and the valley of Kumbalgarh to cheer their king. The glory of Chittor being restored was a signal for the people to return to their ancient abodes in the plains from the hills and other hideouts.

Battle of Singoli

Every Hindu chief, who wished to uproot the barbarian occupying his motherland, rejoiced at the possibility of throwing off the barbaric yoke of the marauders once more. Armed with such zeal and fervour of the people and the *samant* of Mewar,

Hammir collected a vast army and instead of waiting for Tughlaq to attack him, decided to march towards him and meet him at a place and time of his choice.

There are three routes to approach Mewar—the western route through Marwar, the central route through Dewair and eastern route through the plateaus of Aravallis.

Mohammad Bin Tughlaq

Tughlaq captive of Maharana Hammir Singh

Tughlaq was ill-advised by his counsellors to approach through the east where his superior numbers were rendered useless by the intricacies of the narrow passes of Mewar. Tughlaq was resting with his army of 70,000 cavalry and 20,000 infantries on the banks of Chambal River, at the village of Singoli. In CE 1336, Hammir attacked Tughlaq with an army of 20,000 cavalry, slaughtered his army, killed most of his Generals and also killed Maldeo's grandson Haridas, in one-to-one combat, and took Tughlaq as a prisoner[40].

Hammir's destruction of the combined Tughlaq and Jalore forces should educate us about the so-called 'Delhi Sultanate,' which finds such eulogistic references in our history textbooks, when in reality they were mere occupations of a few hundred square kilometres by Muslim gangsters. All the so-called greatness of Delhi Sultanate is thrust down our throats as history, while even a passing reference to Maharana Hammir and his critical

40. R.C. Majumdar, 1960, *The History and Culture of the Indian People: The Delhi Sultante* (2nd ed.), p. 70.

victory over these robbers from Delhi has been erased from our textbooks and civic life.

A note must be made that most of the Indian historians relied on Persian or Arabic record-keepers for digging out the truth about medieval India. One such writer has been Ferishta who has been quoted extensively by Indian historians. When Ferishta, himself being loyal to his faith, completely obliterates even the mention of this battle of Singoli. Only a few inscriptions from Jain temples of the time and the return of Mewar to her lost splendour direct us to the truth recorded in the annals and *khyatis* of Mewar.

It is a matter of shame for academicians and historians of modern India that they participated in this conning of Indian history, the motives of which only they can tell.

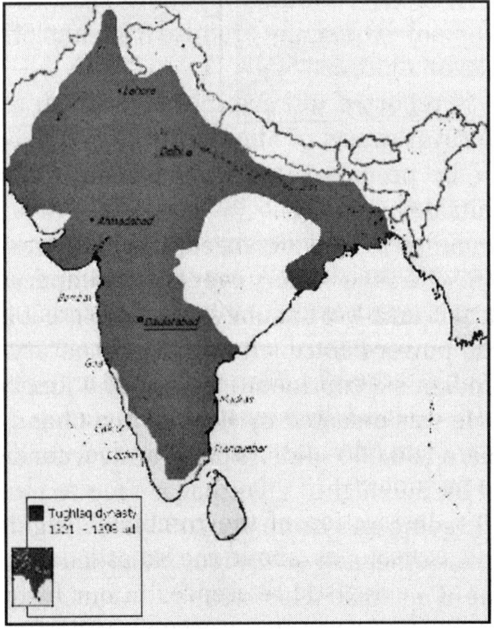

Tughlaq's reign falsely shown on internet.
Hammir's kingdom missing from the map

If teachers and record-keepers start concealing the truth and peddling white lies in society, then total destruction of such a society is inevitable.

Credit goes to the local history-keepers of Mewar and the folklore singers and storytellers who kept the truth of Hammir Singh alive in the consciousness of the local population. Hammir took Tughlaq to Chittor and kept him prisoner for three months. The mighty Delhi Sultanate's ruler was kept captive like a dog in the ordinary prison of Chittor, but not one soul from 'Delhi Sultanate' dared to lead an attack on Chittor to free him from the clutches of Hammir. Thus, it can be safely deduced what the real power centre of Bharatvarsha was in the 14th century CE.

It was Mewar, for sure.

Tughlaq was forced to surrender Ajmer, Ranthambore, Nagamand and Shivpuri to Hammir, besides giving Rs. 50 lakh as fine and one hundred war elephants as a penalty[41].

Hammir was so confident by now that while releasing Tughlaq, he did not extract any promise from him of launching no further attacks on Chittor.

Hammir is reported to have said to Tughlaq as he stood in chains in the royal courts of Mewar: "If you were ever to attack Chittor again, be prepared that I will defend Chittor, not from within, but outside her walls."

Thus, humiliated, and defanged, Tughlaq was released by Hammir and this decisive victory over Islamic imperialists remains one of the most crucial yet unsung stories of a great king who was the sole Hindu power-centre left in the 14th century. Tughlaq ran around the Indian subcontinent in quest of a kingdom he could never build. He was defeated by Raja Prithvi Chand of Kangra in Himachal where 100,000 soldiers of his army were killed. Tughlaq was defeated by the mighty Vijayanagar Empire too after Singoli and died while going on a campaign to Thatta in Sindh in CE 1351.

Banbeer, the other son of Maldeo, joined Hammir and went on to become one of his trusted lieutenants. Hammir is quoted to have told Banbeer, when granting him the *jagirs* of Neemach, Ratanpur and Kairar: *"Eat, serve and be faithful. You were once the servant of a Turk, but now of a Hindu, of your own faith. For I have taken back my own, the rock moistened by the blood of my ancestors, the gift of the deity I adore, and who will maintain me in it; nor shall I*

41. *Annals & Antiquities of Rajasthan*, James Tod. vol. 1, p. 220.

endanger it by the worship of a fair face, as did my predecessor."

Maldeo died of old age in Jalore. Banbeer was a Songara prince and this alliance of the Sisodias with the Songaras proved critical for the survival of the Sisodias as we witness in the ascent of Maharana Pratap to the throne, and his relentless fight against the imperialist Turk, Akbar.

Hammir became the sole prince of power in north-west, surrounded by the Muslim states of Delhi, Malwa and Gujarat, but capable of expelling all three.

The state of incessant conflict in and around Delhi was very favourable to Mewar, when the Khiljis, Tughlaqs, Sayyeds, Lodhis and Suris kept deposing and murdering each other for two centuries. The power of Mewar was so well consolidated by Hammir that for the next six generations spanning two centuries, Mewar not only repelled armies from her territory, but carried the war abroad, leaving tokens of victory at Nagore, Malwa, Saurashtra and up to the walls of Delhi. The Hindu chiefs of Marwar, Ajmer, Boondi, Gwalior, Chanderi, Raesen, Sipri, Calpi, Abu, etc. brought their levies and paid homage to the prince of Chittor. Mewar saw unprecedented wealth and prosperity in the times of Hammir. The trade routes flourished and the people of Mewar became the richest in India. The architecture and the scale of the buildings, columns and temples of those times bear witness to this unprecedented prosperity[42].

Creating a false narrative around a non-existent Delhi Sultanate and erasing the name and deeds of Maharana Hammir Singh of Mewar is a sin committed by modern Indian historians for which responsibility should be fixed and people named and shamed for these acts of commission and omission.

Hammir invited Mata Barwadi from Khod in Gujarat and hosted her in Chittor with full honour and affluence. He even constructed a temple in her memory, called the Annapoorna temple. It stands at the fort of Chittor even today.

Hammir's story from birth to death is a surreal saga of what Sisodia princes endured in medieval India to keep themselves free from Islamic invaders and maintain Hindu *dharma* at the core of their lives.

---

42. *Udaipur ka Itihas*, Gaurishankar Heerachand Ojha, vol.1, p. 220.

Annapoorna temple made in memory of Barwadi Mata, in the Chittor fort

That Mewar came back from the brink of extinction by the miraculous intervention of Mata Barwadi is a well-documented incident of Mewar's rich history. The descendants of Baru Barhat still inhabit the villages around Chittor as bearers of this timeless truth[43].

It not only demonstrates the deep influence of Charans on the Sisodia clan but also that they were well-wishers and even protectors and providers of this brave clan of Rajputs when all had abandoned them. Why else would a mystic lady of Gujarat rebuild Mewar's kingdom from scratch, investing her goodwill and resources, risking enmity not only with Islamic imperialists but also other houses of Rajasthan?

It was only out of her unflinching love and trust that the great Sisodias of Mewar were the only hope for Hindu survival in the subcontinent.

Hammir's conquest of the Delhi Sultanate and imprisonment of Muhammed bin Tughlaq was a dagger into the heart of Islamists who were dreaming of Islamising the nation after capturing Chittor and Ranthambhore and attempting near

43. *Veer Vinod*, vol. 2, p. 293-96.

decimation of the Sisodia Rajput clan of Mewar.

Hammir ruled uninterruptedly for almost fifty years, rebuilt Hindu temples all over the region up to Gaya and Benaras, and died at a ripe age due to natural reasons. He left behind a name venerated in Mewar, as one of the wisest, most gallant and invincible unbeatable kings of Mewar, bequeathing a well-established and extensive Hindu kingdom to his sons.

□

6

Maharana Lakshya Singh (Lakha): Protector of Hindus

(CE 1382 -1421)

After Hammir, his son, Kshetra Singh, also known as Maharana Kheta, became the king of Mewar and ruled from CE 1365-82. Kheta was as brave and aggressive as his father. He conquered Ajmer, Mandalgarh, Dussore and the whole of Chuppun and merged them into Mewar.

According to the inscriptions around temples in Gogunda, Kheta captured a Muslim invader by the name of Ami Shah and imprisoned him. R.C. Majumdar thinks that this was Dilawar Khan of Malwa, while *Veer Vinod* names this person as a Tughlaq. G.H. Ojha concludes from three different souces, viz. the Shringi inscription, the book called *Eklingmahatmya* and the Kumbhalgarh inscription that Ami Shah was indeed the ruler of Malwa.

The Kumbhalgarh inscription says, 'The Malwa ruler used to have nightmares of Kheta. Kheta caught Ami Shah like a snake catches a toad.'[44]

---

44. *Udaipur Rajya ka Itihas*, G.H. Ojha, vol. 1, p. 226.

This inscription is another evidence of Mewar's superiority over the so-called Delhi Sultanate and their vassals.

Kheta is also known in Mewar as the originator of guerrilla warfare when he used to lure his enemy into the passes of Mewar and then trap them on both sides and slaughter an army many times larger in size.[45]

Maharana Kshetra Singh. (1364-1382 CE)

Kheta was very attached to Baru Barhat, who had helped his father Hammir win Chittor. Once, when Baru was insulted by the Hada Rajputs of Boondi, Maharana Kheta was killed in the brawl that ensued with the Hadas. Thus, a promising life was yet again abruptly terminated due to needless infighting amongst the Rajput clans.

Maharana Lakha

Lakshya Singh, also known as Lakha, was beyond his age when he became the king of Mewar under turbulent circumstances. This great Maharana of Mewar was the grandson of Maharana Hammir and his life and work are crucial to the history of Mewar for three reasons:

1. It was Lakha who defeated the Tughlaq ruler of Delhi at Badnore, chased him out of Mewar and raided Muslim looters up to Gaya in today's Bihar and liberated it from the clutches of the Islamic invaders.
2. The silver and lead mines of Jawar were discovered and made productive during his time and they proved critical to Mewar's economic lifeline in fighting the Islamic invaders.
3. The amazing story of Choonda, his son, who is also referred to as the Bhishma of Rajasthan, brings alive the amazing sacrifice of a son for his father.

45. Mathur, p. 13.

Let us briefly touch upon each one of the aforementioned points.

Wars with Tughlaqs and Freeing of Gaya

One of the first acts of Lakha as the king was to forgive the Hadas of Boondi for the death of his father and cement a treaty of friendship with them by granting them 24 villages as *jagir*. Ojha narrates an incident where the Bundi fort was reconstructed in sand and then destroyed by Lakha to symbolically take revenge for his father's death[46].

Lakha then set out to conquer the regions of Marwar and perform the destruction of Beratgadh when he built the new city of Badnore. It was at Badnore that Lakha defeated a Tughlaq king and chased him out of Mewar.

Tughlaq used to tax the Hindu pilgrims in Gaya. Lakha captured Tughlaq and let him go after extracting heavy penalties from him and forcing him to withdraw the tax levied on Hindus of Kashi, Gaya and Prayagraj.

There are conflicting records by various authors about which Tughlaq was defeated and chased away by Lakha.

Tod refers to a Mohammed Lodhi, but the Lodhi dynasty started a good 20 years after Lakha's *moksha*. *Veer Vinod* says that it was Ghiyasuddin Tughlaq, but Ghiyasuddin ruled much before Lakha became king.

Besides, Rana Hammir is well documented to have defeated Muhammed bin Tughlaq, Ghiyasuddin's son at Singoli, so this seems improbable.

In all likelihood, it was the great grandson of Ghiyasuddin by the name of Ghiyat-ud-Din Tughlaq as pointed out by Shyamandas[47].

It could also be a local Muslim lord of Uttar Pradesh and/or Bihar to be defeated by Lakha and forced to withdraw the said penalties imposed on Hindu pilgrims.

The route from Mewar to Dwarika was under pressure by another band of dacoits, the Kabas, who once surrounded a small

46. Mitti ki bundi, Ojha, P.239
47. *Veer Vinod*, vol. 1, p. 305.

army of Mewar that was escorting Lakha's mother to Dwarika for pilgrimage.

That small army was assisted by Rao Singh Dodia of Sardulgadh. A fight ensued where Rao Singh, along with his two sons Kalu and Dhawal, fought valiantly for Mewar. Rao Singh sacrificed his life protecting the Rajmata and finally defeating the Kabas.

Kalu and Dhawal escorted the Rajmata to the borders of Mewar and went back. Lakha rewarded the two brothers with Ratangadh, Nandrai and Masuda as *jagirs* and the Dodias were made permanent allies of Mewar. The Dodias played a significant role in the lives of the subsequent Maharanas of Mewar, as we will find out through the lives of Sanga and Pratap.

On the next pilgrimage to Gaya, Dhawal accompanied the Rajmata and Mewar's contingent was attacked by a local chief of Chappar, Sher Khan. He was defeated, imprisoned and all his wealth was taken to Mewar.

Lakha fought many such wars with Islamic marauders and kept the Hindus free from their tyranny.

The second crucial event that happened during Lakha's regime was the discovery of silver and lead at Jawar. Lakha worked on them and metals like silver, tin, lead, copper and antimony were mined in abundance.

The mines provided a continuous supply of money to the Maharanas of Mewar for centuries. Lakha used the money from the mines to build several forts around Mewar and to renovate Chittor. A Brahma temple was constructed by him in the fort along with magnificent palaces. Lakha continued the works of his grandfather Hammir too.

The Amazing Saga of Choonda

The third point that is especially important in Lakha's life is an interesting story laced with emotion, honour and loyalty.

Lakha's oldest son, Choonda, was a worthy prince destined to rule Mewar after him.

Rinmull of Marwar sent a coconut (a symbol of establishing

matrimonial ties) for fixing his sister's marriage with Choonda. The emissary was received by Lakha in the Mewar court since Choonda was not around. Lakha informed the emissary that Choonda would soon return and accept the offer.

Rawat Choonda : The Bhishma of Mewar

Lakha added in a lighter vein: *"I don't suppose you send such playthings to an old grey-beard like me."*

Choonda heard of this and refused the offer of Rinmull, saying that even if in jest, his father desired this alliance for himself, so there was no question of his (Choonda) accepting the offer.

Rinmull was appalled at the thought of giving his sister to old Lakha and refused the proposal. Choonda asked for a Charan to act as a mediator from the Marwar group. So Chandan Charan was brought in to negotiate.

Chandan Charan said to Choonda that the Maharana was old and if they gave their daughter to him, the son born to them would be serving them all their life. What was the point of such a deal!

Choonda replied, *"I relinquish my right to rule Chittor. I will serve the son of Maharana all my life."*

Chandan rebutted, *"What about your sons, O Choonda?"*

Choonda replied, *"I take the oath of Eklingji that none of my offspring will ever claim the throne. They will have to face me before they can touch the yet unborn king of Mewar."*

Chandan went to Rinmull and convinced him, saying, *"Choonda is a man of honour. He has renounced his right to Mewar. If our daughter were to bear a son from Lakha, he will be the heir. This opportunity should not be missed. Also, remember O king, an old sandal (sandalwood) is better than a new block."*

Thus, Lakha was married to Hans Bai, the princess of Marwar. She gave birth to a son after thirteen months of marriage. The son, Mokal, went on to become a very just and brave ruler of Mewar[48].

Can we ever fathom the level of sacrifice made by Choonda for the sake of his father's subtle desire made in jest?

While we see Hindus fighting real brothers for a few inches of land, can we even comprehend the love and sacrifice of Choonda?

What would be the moral fibre of a man who could give up not only his own but also his children's right to rule Mewar? What spiritual quotient would dictate such indifference to power when confronted by a moral dilemma?

The only event of equivalence to Choonda's sacrifice is found in the *Mahabharata* when Bhishma forsook his right to rule when faced with a similar predicament regarding his father Shantanu.

However, Choonda's sacrifice surpasses that of Bhishma, since Choonda also renounced the right of all his future generations to claim the throne of Chittor. And what can be written of the great descendants of Choonda who remained loyal to a promise of their ancestor?

The Rajputs of Mewar were the greatest amongst all warriors that Hindu *dharma* had ever produced, but within the Sisodias, if there were any true Spartans, the real bearers of the Kshatriya spirit, then it was the descendants of Choonda, known as Choondawats.

Choonda served Mokal all his life and protected him from external and internal enemies like a true brother would.

Later, when Hans Bai (Mokal's mother) doubted Choonda's loyalty and asked him to leave, Choonda left Mewar with his brothers without a whimper and settled at Begu, outside the limits of Mewar.

Soon after Choonda had left Chittor, Mokal was murdered by his cousins and Kumbha ascended the throne. By this time, Mewar was practically under the control of Rao Rinmull, the brother of his grandmother. The same Rinmull who had married his sister to Rana Lakha.

The Sisodia Rajputs and the loyal *samants* resented this

48. *Veer Vinod*, vol. 1, p. 307.

control of Rathores over the affairs of Mewar. One night, a servant of Kumbha named Ikka was crying silently when his tear drop fell on Kumbha's feet. When Kumbha questioned him, he replied, *"Chittor is infested with Marwaris. If the Sisodias lose Mewar, Rathores will own it. That's why I weep."*

Kumbha consulted his mother Saubhagyawati, since he could not trust anyone else. It was decided that Choonda would be recalled for help. Choonda immediately responded and arrived at Chittor with his troops.

It was decided that Rinmull had to be eliminated.

A dancer was to lure Rinmull and get him intoxicated one night, to lay a trap to kill him. The dancer did her job and tied an inebriated Rinmull to the bed. Rinmull was an exceptional fighter in spite of his advanced age. When eight to ten swordsmen attacked Rinmull who was tied and unarmed, the latter managed to extricate one hand and using a metal pitcher, killed three attackers before he was overpowered and killed.

Rinmull had a premonition of the attack on him and had sent his son, Jodha out of Chittor before the attack. Jodha escaped to Marwar on hearing of his father's murder.

Choonda was despatched to kill Jodha. Choonda with his sons conquered Mandovar, but Jodha escaped.

After some time, Kumbha was advised by his mother and grandmother to forgive Jodha. Kumbha recalled Choonda to Mewar.

Like Bhishma, Choonda too attained a ripe age. Unfortunately, not much is known about where, and under what circumstances, this valorous, unsung son of Mewar attained his *moksha*.

Men of Choonda's calibre and loyalty are like the pillars of a foundation as they are neither noticed nor praised. They are the invisible bearers of *dharma*. Such giants silently accept their destiny and save *dharma* in turbulent times before riding into oblivion.

Choonda is the greatest living embodiment of detachment from power and riches. Unassuming love for father, immeasurable patriotism and a personality that transcended pain and pleasure, victory and defeat. Honourable men like Choonda are worthy examples to emulate in modern times.

Choonda's children came to be called Choondawats and helped Mewar in the coming generations. Choondawats were critical in the future wars and stood with Maharana Sanga and Maharana Pratap in their war campaigns. Choondawats remained loyal to Chittor's throne for generations and were always a part of the Harawal group in the Mewar army. Choondawats remain a remarkably successful and proud community even today and are scattered around the globe.

Besides the unthinkable sacrifice made by Choonda, this amazing story of Rawat Choonda and his successors teaches us two very crucial lessons: first, how high Rajputs used to hold the value of a promise. Without any paperwork, the true worth of the spoken word was demonstrated by our ancestors. If we look around, what is the singular physical faculty that separates man from animals? It is speech.

A man is worthy of being called a man only as long he honours his word, otherwise he is just an animal.

The extent to which Hindu society has tied itself in a web of lies can only be reversed if we learn some lesson from the life of Rawat Choonda.

A promise is the very premise of commerce, relationships, decency, family and civilised conduct in society. Only those societies that honour and value a promise reach the pinnacles of civilisation. A society that lives and conducts it's affairs around lies ends up with a hollowness that affects every sphere of life. Such a society can never be affluent or happy. In this respect, the Japanese and most of the Western world are far ahead of Hindus.

These societies value a promise to such an extent that even major business deals are sealed on oral assurances.

Another lesson to be learnt from Choonda's life is the immense respect that was given to elders. Without any exception, Choonda's promise was sustained by all his subsequent generations. It is difficult to find a comparable example in human history where a promise was kept by the progeny of a man for 500 continuous years.

Choondawats never ever eyed the throne of Mewar and never participated in any conspiracy against any Maharana. Unattached to worldly possessions, free of avarice, these glorious people continued to serve the Ranas without expecting anything in return. This was true *karma yoga*[49].

A huge share of the glory of Mewar's victories goes to these brave sons of *dharma*, for giving their life and limb for the sake of a promise.

Treachery and personal ambitions were unknown to this clan of Rajputs.

The day Hindu society realises the value of this fidelity to one's honor and *dharma*, that will be the day when we will start our recovery as human beings.

Loyalty is everything.

Loyalty is humanity.

Loyalty is worship.

Loyalty is prayer.

Loyalty is life itself.

Choonda's glorious story also gives us a glimpse of the dark crevices of human mind where lust still lurks, unmindful of age, love or even social disgrace.

How can a father be so overwhelmed by his sexual urge to trample his own son's well-deserved rights?

Choonda has been immortalised by his act of love and sacrifice for his father, but this episode will always be a blot on the otherwise fair life of Maharana Lakha.

Choonda's sacrifice was infinitely greater than Bhishma's. A person can still let go of his personal rights, but to forsake the rights of all his future generations is something unheard of.

The country paid a huge price for the lust of Shantanu in the form of the *Mahabharata* war which would never have happened if Bhishma hadn't taken the oath of celibacy.

We will never know what would have happened if Choonda was to succeed Lakha.

When the mindless lust of a man takes possession of his mind, how he forgets all sense of justice and love, even for his progeny, is a lesson for all of us to learn.

---

49. A principle elucidated by Shri Krishna in *Gita* where he explains the purity of an action when performed without expectation of the fruit for it.

Sans Choonda's episode, Maharana Lakha was a worthy Sisodia king.

Rana Lakha in his old age set out to visit the eastern parts of India to keep Hindu pilgrimage sites free from the *mlechhas* and died in one of the skirmishes. It was an amazing tradition in Mewar when a king in the *vanaprastha* stage of his life would willingly renounce the throne and go to unknown frontiers with a few chosen warriors to randomly fight the Islamic forces harassing Hindu pilgrims anywhere in India.

Thus, a very eventful and turbulent life, which was to leave an impression on all coming generations of the Maharanas of Mewar, came to an honourable end—an end befitting the Mewar lineage known for defending the Hindu *dharma* against Islamic marauders.

□

7

Maharana Kumbhakarna Singh (Kumbha): The Invincible Genius

(CE 1433-1468)

After Maharana Lakha, his son Mokal, who was born when Lakha was of advanced age, became the Maharana of Mewar. Mokal was equally aggressive and wise as his father Maharana Lakha and expanded the frontiers of Mewar while fighting and defeating the neighbouring Muslim states of Malwa and Gujarat, and also a huge army of the Delhi Sultanate.

It is certain that Mokal defeated a ruler of Delhi according to the inscriptions found at Chittor and Eklingji[50].

If we match the timelines of Tughlaqs and Mewar, it could be Ghiyathuddin Tughlaq or Mohammad Shah that was defeated by Mokal at Jaavar.

Unfortunately, Mokal's rising career was abruptly cut off by his distant cousins Chaacha and Mera, who were instigated by an unintended satire by Mokal and killed him in his sleep. Before this tragic end, Mokal was an active king—fighting the Islamic forces and expanding Mewar's borders. He had multiple wives and two of his queens got pregnant almost simultaneously.

50. *Udaipur Rajya ka Itihas*, G.H. Ojha, vol. 1, p. 244.

According to folklore, the younger queen, jealous of the elder one, performed some *tantric* trick on the elder queen due to which the elder one went past the gestation period but did not enter labour. The *tantric* spell was performed through an earthen pitcher that was kept by the younger queen to be effective.

Maharana Mokal (1421-1433 CE)

When royal well-wishers heard of the queen not delivering past the gestation period, they travelled to Ramdeora in Marwar desert to a living deity, Baba Ramdeo for help. Baba Ramdeo had already decided to leave his body and was in *samadhi*. He advised the Mewar chiefs to go to Dharmaswaroopji, who was Baba Ramdeo's uncle and had been bestowed with similar metaphysical powers as him.

Dharmaswaroop consented to help and marched towards Mewar. He is supposed to have performed multiple miracles enroute and even today, his temples stand and various congregational *melas* are organised to commemorate his help to the house of Mewar. But all his efforts to break the spell that was cast on the queen and induce childbirth, failed. Then, Dharmaswaroop told the *samants* to falsely announce the birth of a son by playing drums and distributing sweets.

It is said that when the younger queen heard the noise of *nagadas* (large drums), she broke the pitcher which was the edifice of the spell on the elder queen, in a state of fury.

The elder queen immediately went into labour and a son was born to her in CE 1417. The child had been in-utero for ten months, a full one month over the normal human gestation period.

An earthen pitcher is called *kumbha* in Sanskrit, so the new-born child was named Kumbhakarna and lovingly called Maharana Kumbha in Mewar.

Kumbha was to inherit a vast kingdom of Mewar—well preserved and plush with funds and riches collected by his past three generations.

Kumbha went on to become one of the most successful

kings of Mewar. He is considered to belong to the class of all-time great kings that ever ruled Bharat by a lot of contemporary historians. He is placed in the same category as Ashoka, Harsha, Samudragupta, or Chandragupta Vikramaditya[51].

Chamunda temple at Madariya, where Kumbha used to worship. The priests of this 800 year old temple are local Bhils

Kumbha inherited a royal house which was at war with itself because of the conflicting loyalties between Rathores and Sisodias. The Sisodias resented the control of Rathores on day-to-day affairs of the state, especially under Rinmull Rathore, the maternal grandfather of Kumbha. Along with his wise mother, the Rathore grandmother (who was married to Kumbha's grandfather

51. *Delhi Sultanate*, Majumdar, p. 336.

Lakha), maternal grandfather, Rao Rinmull Rathore and his other chieftains with conflicting loyalties, Kumbha set out to first put his own house in order.

It is not in the domain of this book to take the reader through the internal strife and manipulations of the Mewar family and hence, the focus remains on the military campaigns, fortification of Mewar and the art and architecture during Kumbha's reign.

All of these scaled unparalleled heights during Kumbha's four-decade-long rule over Mewar. We will briefly talk about Kumbha's personality that left irreplaceable marks on the trajectory of the Mewar dynasty. We will also detail how Kumbha spent his life, destroying the combined forces of the Islamic states of Malwa, Gujarat and Nagaur.

It has rarely happened in human history for one state to have possessed so many energetic and successful princes as Mewar did, for several centuries.

Mewar was now in the middle of its glorious rise built on the ashes of its brave sons and daughters who laid down their lives in protecting it from the Arab and Turk assassins. A century had elapsed since the dance of death by Allauddin Khilji at Chittor where he destroyed every Hindu temple and building of consequence and dishonoured women leading to self-immolation by Padmini and her companions. Mewar had bounced back with a vengeance of her own. Chittor had recovered from the murderous assaults of the Khiljis and the Tughlaqs and new defenders of Hinduism had sprung up all around Mewar.

As James Tod writes beautifully about the impending Turk invasion led by Babur: *"All that was wanting to augment her resources against the storms that were brewing on the brows of Caucuses and the banks of Oxus and were destined to burst on the head of his grandson Sanga, was affected by Maharana Kumbha."*

Tod is referring to the impending clash between Kumbha's grandson Sanga and Babur in CE 1527 at Khanwa.

Kumbha possessed Hammir's energy and Lakha's fortitude and taste for the arts. With this genius combination, Kumbha succeeded in every venture he undertook, raising once again the crimson banner (bhagwa dhwaj) of Mewar on the banks of Ghaggar, where a Mewar prince had laid down his life fighting alongside the great Prithviraj Chauhan against Mohammad Ghori. It is a noteworthy fact that after Prithviraj's defeat by Mohammad Ghori, Delhi was ravaged by infighting among various Muslim invaders ranging from Turks to Afghans to Uzbeks and Islamic slaves.

The barbaric power struggle in Delhi mimicked the violent conflicts of the Caliphate in Arabia. It speaks volumes of the anarchy in Delhi, where twenty five monarchs ruled through assassination, rebellion, subterfuge and dethronement in rapid succession. In the same time period, less than half that number, i.e. eleven Ranas donned the Mewar crown, some of them having died defending their faith from the invaders. Needless to say, the longevity of the Maharanas' tenure and continuity of lineage ensured a stable and just rule for the citizenry in Mewar. There needs to be a detailed study on the impact of the contrasting power-hungry Delhi invaders on governance.

× × ×

The bloodbath in Delhi which continued for another three centuries is a statement of the kind of social and regal hierarchy that Islam brings to a society. The incessant assaults of Islamic invasions showcase how a barbaric and unethical aggression could annihilate long standing civilizations as it did in Persia, Mesopotamia and Egypt. However, it also showcases that if the defenders of that civilization have the steely grit and resolve to fight the mindless slaughter, they could emerge victorious, as done by the Mewar Maharanas..

The Delhi Sultanate was already made to bite the dust by Rawal Jaitra Singh, Hammir Singh, Rana Lakha and Rana Mokal. There was no ruler of consequence in Delhi at the time of Kumbha. The Islamic seed though had spread its tentacles towards central and western Bharat while the vast and strong kingdom of Mewar stood as a bulwark against the Islamic invaders.

According to folklore and annals of Mewar, Kumbha fought fifty-six wars in his lifetime and did not lose even one. That makes Kumbha a warrior par excellence and a master strategist who anticipated every move of his enemies and beat them at it. We will cover four such campaigns of Kumbha.

Kumbha defeated and subjugated the Muslim kingdoms of Malwa, Gujarat and Nagaur; he won a small battle in Marwar to capture Mandore; and he merged Marwar into Mewar, a feat no other king had achieved before him.

Conquest of Malwa

Malwa was ruled by a powerful Sultan, Mahmud Khilji, who usurped the throne of Malwa by killing his father-in-law Hoshang Shah. Mahmud was an audacious opponent of Mewar, cunning, battle-hardened and a religious zealot. Kumbha's first encounter with Mahmud happened around CE 1437 at Sarangpur in Malwa where Kumbha defeated him. It is said that Kumbha led a force of 1,00,000 horsemen and 1,400 elephants in this major battle[52].

It is mindboggling that the kingdom of Mewar had the resources to finance such a vast army.

Mahmud retreated to the fort of Mandu, but Kumbha chased him and captured him there. Mahmud was brought to Chittor and kept prisoner for six months.

Unlike Hammir's treatment of Tughlaq in similar circumstances, Kumbha treated Mahmud in a dignified manner and released him honourably, albeit after extracting heavy penalties from him in terms of money, war horses and elephants. This capture of Mahmud has been documented by Abul Fazl too and he praised Kumbha for the dignified treatment he gave to a Muslim king.

The mistake of misplaced magnanimity

This trait of Hindu kings of not terminating their Islamic enemies defies logic and has been one of the reasons for the Islamic invaders not being weeded out of our vedic motherland, for good, forever.

Tod also wonders at this trait of Hindu kings like Prithviraj, Hammir, Kumbha and Sanga and writes: *"Such is the character of the Hindu: a mixture of arrogance, political blindness, pride and generosity. To spare a prostrating foe is the creed of the Hindu cavalier and he carries all such maxims to excess[53]."*

52. Ojha, vol. 1, p. 255.
53. Tod, vol. 1, p. 231.

Although it is simplistic and unfair to examine the great Maharanas from posterity, but when we see a pattern of forgiveness for the vilest and most dangerous enemies of Hindu *dharma* and their people, one cannot help but ponder as to why the Maharanas of Mewar kept repeating such blunders!

It was these gestures of pseudo-magnanimity that not only allowed the Islamic invaders to be left alive to re-group and continue attacking India, but also made a mockery of all the hardships endured by the people and Mewar in fighting and subjugating these Islamic marauders. It also sent a wrong message to the invaders that even if they were to lose, they would not be killed, and this knowledge emboldened them to repeatedly attack India.

Let us briefly review what the forgiveness of Ghori, Tughlaq and Khilji cost us as a nation and *dharma*.

The consequence of Prithviraj's leaving Ghori alive after the first battle of Tarain was that a vengeful Ghori attacked India again. This time, the Afghan invader won and blinded Prithviraj before killing him.

Prithviraj's brother-in-law, a Rawal of Mewar, too was killed in this battle, as were thousands of brave Rajputs because of Prithiviraj forgiving a murderer.

Ghori wrote letters to Prithivraj that if he was to convert to Islam, there would be no war between them. One wonders why the Brahmin teachers and other advisors of Prithivraj did not see the streak of blind religious bigotry in Ghori and why they did not advise him to kill Ghori when he was defeated the first time.

Dr. R.G. Mishra writes about the first victory of Prithviraj Chauhan, *"Prithviraj could now have easily consummated his victory by chasing and annihilating his routed enemy. Instead, he allowed the defeated Muslim army to return unmolested. This magnanimity, though in accordance with Hindu Shastras, was completely unsuitable against a ruthless enemy who recognised no morals or ideological scruples in the attainment of victory. The Hindus lacked the capacity to comprehend the real nature of their ruthless adversaries and the new tactics needed to encounter their challenge to Indian independence[54]."*

54. Mishra, p. 118.

Islam, which had been prevented from entering India for 500 years due to hard-fought battles by Bappa Rawal, Khuman, Jaitra Singh, Nagabhatta, Lalitaditya, Anangpal and dozens of Hindu kings, gained entry into the heart of India because of one major blunder by Prithviraj.

India has not recovered from that defeat of Prithviraj in CE 1192 till date.

Ghori appointed Qutub-ud-Din Aibak as his Governor at Ajmer and thus the first resident-Islamist secured a foothold on the sacred land of Hindus.

Prithivaraj's folly of not killing Ghori after the first battle of Tarain was still a minor issue, since he was not the first one to forgive an Islamic invader. He was the first one to be killed though. What is baffling is the same blunder was being repeated by all Hindu kings when they had Pritiviraj's example in front of them!

Hammir's forgiveness of Tughlaq made him escape to Delhi, regroup and attack the Deccan kingdoms in south. To the great fortune of the Hindus, the Vijayanagar Empire in the south arose about the same time and conclusively defeated Tughlaq.

As we go ahead, we will find that in Kumbha's case too, Mahmud Khilji took no cognisance of Kumbha's benevolence and attacked Mewar at least six more times in his lifetime[55]. Although he was defeated by Kumbha each time, but at what cost to the treasury? Why was there this needless loss of lives? Why the risk to the entire future of Mewar through such an act of stupid chivalry?

Maharana Sanga's forgiving of his enemies led to a total disaster and we will deal with it in the coming pages.

These acts of Hindu kings only demonstrate a distinct lack of understanding of *dharma* and statecraft as taught by Kautilya.

Shri Krishna offered no such mercy to the Kauravas. At the end of the *Mahabharata* war, even when Duryodhana was the only one left alive in the Kaurava camp, Shri Krishna finished the job of complete extermination of *adharma*. Can we forget the end in *Mahabharata*, when Bhima in his anger forgot to hit Duryodhana on his weak part—the thighs?

Shri Krishna, standing witness to this duel between Bhima

---

55. *Udaipur Rajya ka Itihas*, G.H. Ojha, vol. 2, p. 267.

and Duryodhana, struck his own thigh to remind Bhima of what he had to do to finish Duryodhana.

When Bhima struck Duryodhana and he fell, Yudhishthira looked at Shri Krishna, puzzled.

Shri Krishna smiled and walked away from the scene uttering these immortal words, '*Mayawi mayayaa vadhya satyametad yudhishthira*,' meaning, 'Kill the deceitful by deceit, that is the only truth O' Yudhishthira.[56]'

Similar message echoes in the epic *Ramayana* too.

It says, '*Poorvapkarinam hatva na hyadharmen yujyate.*'

It means: '*it is no sin to slay the unrighteous*[57].'

Kautilya too had nowhere advised mercy to the enemy of the state.

The forgiving acts of Hindu kings can only be explained based on *sattvic ahamkara*, where ego comes wearing the cloak of *satva*—forgiving murderous plunders was an act of individual glory for which coming centuries of Hindus and even their progenies would pay heavily with their blood. Veer Savarkar calls it '*sadgun vikruti*[58],' meaning a distortion borne out of good temper.

A note must also be made of the priests and *samants* of Mewar, none of whom is supposed to have advised these kings against such suicidal acts.

The Hindu ethos of the times perhaps allowed these acts of magnanimity, but when both Hammir and Kumbha had the example of Prithviraj in front of them, they should have been more *dharmic* in their understanding and made the enemies rootless.

To the great relief of Hindu socicty, Pratap never suffered from this disease of excessive magnanimity, as we will see in the chapter on Dewair. Pratap slaughtered everyone who stood in his way when eradicating the Turks from Mewar. Pratap outshines everyone not only as a warrior but also as a visionary, who learnt from his ancestors and executed the plans to eradicate the enemies of his *dharma* with clinical acumen.

---

56. *Mahabharata*, 9.30.6.
57. *Ramayana*, 2.96.24.
58. When Hindu kings show tolerance, unmindful of the times and circumstances and thus bring huge suffering and pain to themselves and their people.

Conquest of Gujarat

Let us now turn to Kumbha's encounters with Qutub-ud-din, the ruler of Gujarat.

Kumbha's army used to regularly charge heavy duties from trade caravans passing through Mewar to Surat in Gujarat and the Islamic rulers of Gujarat had wanted to defeat Mewar for a long time now. Kumbha had also merged the powerful kingdoms of Sirohi and Boondi into Mewar because he knew that these neighbouring states of Mewar could align with Gujarat anytime and become an irritant, and Sirohi and Boondi were critical to controlling the western trade routes to Gujarat.

Kumbha also annexed Gagraun, Ajmer, Chaksu and even far-flung places like Sambhar near Jaipur, to Mewar.

Mahmud Khilji's messenger Taj Khan, approached Qutub and said that because of disunity amongst us, *kafirs* were living peacefully and that they should join hands to crush the Hindus.

Qutub agreed and the Muslim rulers of Malwa and Gujarat forged an Islamic alliance against Kumbha in 1456, at Champaner in Gujarat. A treaty was signed between the two Muslim rulers to jointly attack Mewar and finish Kumbha once and for all[59].

The objectives of the treaty of Champaner described by Muslim historians were as follows: "To direct their efforts against Rana Kumbha, Mahmud Khilji would attack him from one side and Qutub-ud-din from the other. They would utterly destroy him... divide his region between them...all the towns lying contiguous to Gujarat were to be attached to the kingdom of Qutub and districts of Mewar and Aheerwara would be retained by Malwa forces[60]."

Mewar was totally besieged at this time, as one of Kumbha's brothers, Kshema had rebelled and picked arms against Kumbha. In the winter of 1456–57, Muslim armies attacked Mewar simultaneously. Qutub entered via the southwest in Sirohi and plundered Kumbhalmer district and then turned to Chittor. Kumbha came out to fight a battle with Qutub and defeated him. Although all Muslim records say that Rana offered money to Qutub to retreat to Gujarat, it does not add up and seems incorrect. Why would a

59. Ojha, vol. 1, p. 269.

60. R.C. Majumdar, *Delhi Sultanate*, p. 335.

winning Qutub settle for peanuts when according to the treaty at Champaner, the entire southwest of Mewar was to be his domain!

While Rana was engaged in defeating Qutub and pushing him back to Gujarat, Mahmud of Malwa devastated parts of northeast Mewar and attacked Ajmer. He was repulsed by local chiefs of the Rana. Mahmud retreated to Mandalgarh and was attacked there by Kumbha.

The Muslim annals by Ferishta describe the result of battle thus: *"The Malwa officers persuaded their king of the necessity of retiring on account of their reduced numbers and the wretched state of the camp equipment. The Sultan was induced to return to Mandu."*

As Col. Briggs, the British scholar who translated Ferishta's works. writes: *"The drawn battle mentioned must be deemed a defeat*[61]*."*

The Islamic forces were very comprehensively defeated by Kumbha, and Qutub was forced back to Gujarat. The Maharana, however, was relentless and during the years 1457–58, he attacked both these rulers at a time and turf of his choice, recovering every inch of the lost territory. Mahmud Khilji made at least six attempts to capture Mewar in the coming years before dying in CE 1469.

Conquest of Nagaur

The third conquest of consequence by Kumbha was Nagaur. At that time, the Jodhpur kingdom had not come into existence. Nagaur was under the rule of one Mujahid Khan. Mujahid's brother, Shams Khan, wanted to be the king and approached Kumbha for help. Kumbha had long cherished expanding the borders of Mewar into Marwar. Kumbha came with a large army and defeated Mujahid to crown Shams Khan as the king of Nagaur.

Kumbha extracted two promises from Shams before returning to Mewar:

1. Shams was to demolish all battlements at the fort of Nagaur.
2. The Hindu population of Nagaur was not to be harassed by Muslim religious zealots.

61. R.C. Majumdar, *Delhi Sultanate*, p. 336.

Shams did not keep either of his promises. He started building new battlements at the fort and promoted the slaughtering of cows publicly to humiliate the Hindus. Kumbha came back with 50,000 troops and defeated him. Shams ran to Qutub-ul-Din, the Sultan of Gujarat who dispatched a huge army under one of his Generals, Imad-ul-Mulk, who was a hopeless alcoholic, to fight Kumbha in Nagaur. Kumbha waited patiently in Nagaur and when Gujarat's forces reached Nagaur, they were slaughtered by Kumbha's army.

The Kirti Stambha inscription reads thus on Kumbha's victory: 'Kumbhkaran mocked the Sultan of Gujarat and took Nagaur, burnt the *masjid* built by Firoz, broke the fort, snatched all elephants, arrested Muslim women, punished *Yavanas*, liberated cows, burnt all masjids in the city and turned Nagaur into a gochar[62] and looted the entire wealth of Shams Khan[63].

Shams and Qutub never returned to Nagaur after that. Nagaur was annexed along with Sambhar and Khandela and a Hindu vassal was appointed by Kumbha at Nagaur.

Kumbha personally oversaw the demolition of all battlements of the Nagaur fort and took the mighty gates of the fort and an idol of Hanuman back to Kumbhalgarh. The gates and idols were installed and they exist till date on the gate, known as Hanuman Pol.

Mandore

The last conquest of Kumbha was of Mandore, the erstwhile capital of Marwar. In a long and convoluted saga of intra-family rivalry, which we briefly touched upon when discussing the life of Rana Lakha, Kumbha was forced to chase his cousin and uncle Jodha to Mandore.

Rawat Choonda, who was Kumbha's uncle, was the main protagonist in Kumbha's quest for Marwar. Choonda won Mandore and kept his sons in charge of the fort. In the meantime, Kumbha's grandmother convinced him to go soft on the Rathores of Marwar as they were blood relatives and both had a common enemy in Islamic invaders.

62. Pasture for grazing cows.
63. Ojha, vol. 1, p. 268.

Kumbha relented and let Jodha capture Mandore from Choonda's sons.

Jodha went on to set up the city of Jodhpur, which became the second power-centre for Rajputs after Mewar. Jodhpur was to prove crucial in containing the Mughal invasion and the eventual front in the war between Ajit Singh and Veer Durga Das Rathore against Aurangzeb.

Kumbha's benevolence towards Jodha and the Rathores proved fortuitous. It laid the foundation for a formidable union that would last generations—a union that would come to the aid of Kumbha's grandson, the great Rana Sanga to establish a mighty kingdom of Mewar and to fight the Islamic invasion led by Babur.

It was this association between the Sisodias and the Rathores that eventually defeated Aurangzeb during the reign of Raj Singh in Mewar. Thus, we can say that Kumbha's foresight and magnanimity laid the grounds for unity amongst the Rajput clans and was critical in uprooting the Mughal dynasty from the brow of the land.

Kumbha: Art and Architecture

We now turn to the architectural prowess of Kumbha. Of the eighty forts that are spread across the landscape of Mewar today, thirty-two were built by Kumbha alone. Can we imagine the amount of money involved, the mobilisation of resources, logistics, manpower and Kumbha's undying creativity to have achieved this in a reign of forty years?

Amongst these forts, the one that stands out singularly is the fort of Kumbhalgarh, which was to become the capital of Mewar later. Legend has it that the fort was originally built by Samprati Raja, a Jain prince who was a descendant of Chandragupta. Kumbha raised Kumbhalgarh in such a manner that it became not only an architectural wonder but also impregnable to any invading army.

Built in the Aravallis at a height of 1,100 m (3,600 ft) above sea-level, the fort has a perimeter of 36 km, making it one of the longest walls in the world, surpassed only by the Great Wall of China. The frontal walls are 15 feet thick. There are seven fortified gateways. The fort boasts of 360 temples, 300 of which are of Jain heritage. Kumbhalgarh sits at a vantage point that separates

A view of the great wall of Kumbhalgarh

Solid fortification of Kumbhalgarh

Mewar and Marwar and was used to keep an eye on both these regions. Kumbhalgarh fort is not only a formidable testament of Rajput architecture but also an insight into the strategic prowess of the Rajputs in building such invincible fortifications. The citadel proved to be a shelter and safe refuge for all of Mewar when Islamic attacks besieged Chittor. Kumbhalgarh was attacked repeatedly by Qutub and Mahmud Khilji during Kumbha's reign but could never be won.

The temple of the presiding deity, Baan Mata, located at some distance from the fort, was destroyed by Mahmud of Malwa in frustration at his defeats by Kumbha.

While laying an unsuccessful siege on Kumbhalgarh, Khilji attacked the temple in CE 1442. Kumbha had kept a valiant Rajput, Deep Singh, with a few hundred troops to protect the temple. Deep Singh and his men fought so bravely that they didn't let the entire army of Malwa breach the strong walls of the temple for a full seven days. Mahmud then surrounded the walls with wood and set it to fire in order to weaken the wall. After suffering heavy losses, Mahmud breached the temple and after killing all the warriors defending the temple, set it to fire[64].

He turned the centuries-old idol of the deity to powder and forced the locals to eat that dust in betel leaves. He did all this while Kumbha was engaged in other campaigns on his eastern front. Kumbha took quick retribution for this heinous act of Mahmud and defeated him crushingly. Mahmud escaped to Mandu with his life. Had Kumbha killed Mahmud during the first attack, Mewar would not have lost the magnificent temple or a brave warrior like Deep Singh to the *jihadis*.

Kumbhalgarh fell to Shahbaz Khan, a General of Akbar in CE 1578, during Akbar's reign for a brief period of five years. Kumbhalgarh was taken back by Pratap in 1583 during the Dewair campaign. These five years was the only time when Kumbhalgarh was in enemy hands in the entire history of Mewar-Muslim conflict[65].

Vijay Stambha

Besides Kumbhalgarh, Maharana Kumbha erected the citadels of Achalgarh and Vasantgarh in the hills of Abu, within the fortress of the ancient Paramars. He fortified the passes between the western passes and Abu. He erected the fort of Vasanti at Sirohi and Macheend to defend Deogarh from the local Mairs[66] of Aravallis who were dacoits. He re-established Ahore and many smaller forts to keep a watch over the troublesome Bhils of Jalore and Panora and defined the boundaries of Marwar and Mewar.

Kumbha repaired the entire fort of Chittor as if in anticipation of the assaults it was to withstand in the future from the firepower

64. *Veer Vinod*, vol. 1, p. 325.
65. Mathur, p. 138.
66. forest dwellers of areas around Deogarh and Dewair.

of Mughals. He constructed the Vijay Stambha, a nine-storey tower to commemorate his victory over Mahmud Khilji of Malwa. Vijay Stambha is an architectural marvel that impresses any modern-day architect too. Made as a tribute to Bhagwan Vishnu, this 122-feet tall tower was completed in CE 1448. This amazing structure was designed by Jaitaji and his three sons—Napa, Pooja and Pema, under the guidance of Kumbha himself. He constructed innumerable Hindu and Jain temples around Mewar, including the Laxminath temple at Chittor, the Eklingji temple and Ranakpur Jain temple in Godwar. Under his patronage, his chief architect Mandana wrote several books on iconography, house building and house decoration.

Thus, while the Muslim rulers were constantly making plans to overcome Kumbha and Mewar through mindless murder and mayhem, the Hindu ethos of leading a beautiful life woven around art and music carried on during Kumbha's reign. It is unbelievable that a king, who was consistently travelling and fighting, built all these structures during forty years of his reign.

Kumbha was also a great singer, *veena* player and an exhaustive writer. His literary work on Hindustani *ragas* and *raginis*, known as *Sangeet Raga*, is one of the longest text written on music. One of his works was on Carnatic music, demonstrating how we were connected as a nation throughout history and how the North-South divide was a manufactured myth perpetrated by the British. Kumbha penned four plays in Marathi, Carnatic and Mewari dialects. It is not known how Kumbha could speak and write in Marathi[67].

He penned the *Sood Prabandh* on realpolitik and *Sangeeta Mimaansa* on music, *Chandi Shatak* on Mother Goddess, *Kamraj Ratisar* on love and indulgence and a commentary on *Geet Govindam*.

67. Ojha, vol. 1, p. 278.

It is said that Kumbha ordered presentation, translation and commentaries on 1,800 different Hindu scriptures at his time and invited Vedic scholars from all over India for it. He used to shower riches on poets and Brahmins lavishly. He loved organising religious debates and music festivals.

Temples like Kumbhaswami and Adivaraha were constructed. A destroyed portion of Eklingji temple was reconstructed and named *Kumbha-mandapa*. Beautiful Jain temples at Ranakpur, Sirohi and Sringar Chauri temple at Chittor were built by him.

So, while the Leftists are busy painting Rajputs as 'fighting animals', the truth is that the Maharanas of Mewar gave supreme patronage to art and architecture.

Now we can realise that it isn't without reason that Kumbha was equated with Harsha, Vikramaditya and such great kings of the time. His holistic persona and extreme commitment to Hindu *dharma* truly make him the *Hindwa Soorya* of all times.

It is tragic that such a great king has almost been erased from our history books, while his contemporary looters of Delhi Sultanate have dedicated chapters in their names.

Trouble with Charans and Death of Kumbha

Kumbha had entered the sixth decade of his life and was still very actively ruling Mewar.

Earlier in life, a fortune-teller had told him that Kumbha would be killed by a Charan; hence, Kumbha banished all Charans from Mewar. All *jagirs* of Charan chieftains were confiscated.

This was a major reversal of fortunes for Charans who were enjoying the fruits of state patronage since the times of Rana Hammir, who owed his life and success to a Charani woman named Mata Barwadi.

Be that as it may, around CE 1468, Kumbha went to Eklingji temple where a cow ranted loudly. From that day onwards, Kumbha was obsessed by that incident and he kept repeating a half-sentence, '*Kamadhenu taandav kariya*', meaning that the *Kamadhenu* cow dances furiously.

The Mewar chieftains and the royal family were baffled at this behaviour of the Rana and the eldest son Raimal (father of

Sanga) even asked him what the meaning of his utterances was. Kumbha lost his temper and exiled Raimal for being indecent. Raimal retreated to Idar, his in-laws' abode.

Then a Charan approached one of the *samants* of Mewar and claimed to know how to complete the incomplete line of the *chhand* that Ranaji uttered to free him from his obsession.

The Charan composed a *chhand*, such that the line uttered by Kumbha was incorporated in it and made perfect sense. Kumbha was delighted and said to the Charan that though he claimed to be a Rajput, only a Charan could compose such poetry. The Charan bowed to Kumbha and revealed his identity. Kumbha forgave him and reversed his order of confiscating Charans' properties. Thus, by the creative talents of a poet, a broken relationship was restored.

On a tragic morning of CE 1468, while bathing in the pond of Mamdev in the northern ramparts of Kumbhalgarh, Kumbha was attacked and beheaded by his own son, Udai Singh, who was also known as 'Ooda'[68].

Thus ended the life of one of the wisest, gallant and visionary kings of Mewar at the hands of his own progeny, all at the age of fifty-one years.

Kumbha's murder is one of the darkest blots in the history of Mewar. For once, Hindu royals displayed the streak prevalent only in the Islamic rulers of the time to kill and usurp power from their own relatives at any cost.

Ooda ruled for four years after murdering his father, when the *samants* of Mewar revolted against him. A *samant* of Mewar, Rawat Kaandhal planned the overthrow of Ooda. He visited Raimal, the eldest son of Kumbha and convinced him to come back from Idar, and when Ooda was out on a hunting expedition, Raimal was taken instead of allured inside and the gate of Kumbhalgarh closed on Ooda.

Ooda joined the Sultan of Malwa. One day, Ooda was hit by lightning and killed instantaneously—a fair retribution by divine intervention to an act of extreme cowardice by a traitor. This settled the feud in favour of Raimal.

68. VV, vol. 1, p. 334.

Mamdev Shiva temple where Kumbha was murdered

There are a lot of fantastic stories about Kumbha which the people of Mewar believe in and which are related to Kumbha's life. Those are not of interest to us.

There is no doubt though that Kumbha's conquests and amassing of immense wealth were critical for his future generations to fight further Islamic invasions of Mewar, as will be demonstrated through the life of Sanga and Pratap. But for Kumbha's victories and amassing of immense wealth, the resistance of the Mewar Maharanas to Islamic invasions would never have been possible.

We, as Hindus, must be eternally grateful to Kumbha, the *mahapurusha* (great soul) for playing his role in keeping us free from the horrors of Islamic slavery in the subcontinent.

It is as though the three decades of success and prosperity of Kumbha were a fitting interlude for securing Mewar against the forthcoming Islamic invasions.

A mighty king, a visionary military strategist, an architect and builder, a singer and composer, a musician, a prolific writer, an accomplished dancer and a devout Hindu *bhakta* of Durga and

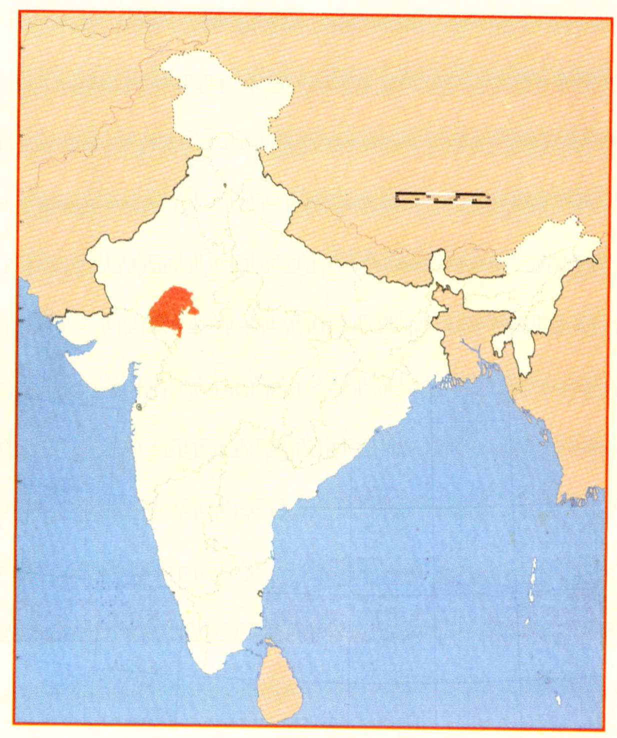

Mewar in Map of India

Mewar in Map of Rajasthan

Writer with Shri Narayan Upadhyaya at Dewair Memorial

Hoof marks on 500 year old pathways around Dewair

Dewair Memorial

The Sacred Valley of Dewair

Bappa Rawal : The real father of Hindusthan

Ancient Hindu Watch Tower in today's Khyber region of Pakistan

Temple at the Samadhi of Bappa Rawal; idols of Bappa and Harit Muni around a Shivlingam

The magnificent Sahasrabahu Temple at Nagda amidst the ruins

Unbelievable stone carving in the ruins of Nagda

Aanapoorna Mata and Baan Mata Temples in Chittor Fort

Kumbha overlooking Mewar at Madariya

Panorama at Madariya

Writer at the feet of Maharana Kumbha at Madariya

Shiva Temple at Kumbhalgarh where Kumbha used to worship

Writer with the Bhil priest of Chamunda Temple, Mangu Ba Bhil at Madariya

Destroyed Temples in Kumbhalgarh. Sad thing is that the restoration efforts by ASI are in Islamic architecture instead of the original Hindu style

Kumbhalgarh : the invincible Citadel of Hinduism

The thick walls protecting Kumbhalgarh

Kumbhalgarh overlooking Mewar and Marwar

Keerti Stambh and Jain Temple at Chittor

Wonderful Vijay Stambha made by Kumbha at Chittor

Mamdev Shiva Temple at Kumbhalgarh where Kumbha was murdered

Sanga—the name is enough

Marks of pellets and shrapnels at the memorial of Khanwa. Some dispute this claim

The Memorial at Khanwa near Bharatpur

Writer at Khanwa Memorial

Hindu chhatri on the battlefield at Khanwa

The ruins of the Somnath Temple

The rebuilt Somnath Temple—a symbol of Hindu resilience

Shri Krishna could teach a lesson or two to our modern generation in multitasking.

While the world celebrates the great Italian Leonardo Da Vinci as the greatest genius ever to be born, Kumbha too must find his place in the league of kings as the greatest genius-king of all times.

R.C. Majumdar writes on Kumbha that when the records of his reign, that lie scattered in more than sixty inscriptions and numerous other sources, have been fully worked out in a comprehensive and connected account, Kumbha will certainly be proclaimed as the greatest ruler, at least of medieval India[69].

Kumbha was a genius who blessed the land of Rajasthan with his foresight and creativity. He was

- a master strategist who did not lose a single war.
- a passionate person who loved all good things in life.
- a true king who will be remembered for all times to come.
- a king who has earned his place in Hindu history and it is time we restore that place to this great son of the land.

□

69. *The Delhi Sultanate*, R.C. Majumdar, p. 330.

8

Maharana Sangram Singh (Sanga): The Spiritual Warrior

(CE 1508-1528)

Raimal became the king of Mewar after Kumbha's murder and continued the work of his father. Raimal was a worthy son of his father and continued the expansion of Mewar kingdom. Giyasuddin, the Sultan of Malwa, attacked Raimal but was defeated by the latter at Chittor. Giyasuddin reassembled his forces and again attacked Mewar, and this time, Prithviraj, the eldest son of Raimal, fought Giyasuddin and arrested him after a stealth attack on Malwa camp. Giyasuddin was kept a prisoner in Chittor for one month and let free after extracting heavy penalties. Raimal died in CE 1508, passing on a flourishing kingdom suffused with money and resources to his son, Sangram Singh.

The third child of Maharana Raimal, Maharana Sangram Singh, fondly known as Maharana Sanga, ascended the throne of Mewar. His subsequent struggles and victories are perhaps the most intriguing saga ever to be found around a king anywhere in human history.

Raimal had thirteen sons, with Prithviraj and Jaimal being the eldest, followed by Sanga. One day, the three brothers went to consult a fortune-teller, who predicted that Sanga would be the one to adorn the throne of Mewar. Prithviraj lost his temper and hit Sanga's right eye with the rear of his sword. This ruptured Sanga's eye and left him blind in one eye. Both the elder brothers attacked Sanga to kill him, but Sanga was saved by Surajmall, brother of King Raimal.

Rana Raimal (1473-1509 CE)

After a few months, the question bothered the elder brothers again and they took Sanga along with their uncle to a Charan girl, a mystic named Biri Bai, who was supposed to be Shakti incarnate (Mother Goddess).

Biri Bai had arranged for a throne and a carpet made of tiger hide in the temple of the goddess. Prithviraj and Jaimal sat on the throne while Sanga and his uncle sat on the ground, on the carpet. When the older brothers asked Biri Bai who would ascend the throne of Mewar, she replied, *"The decision has been made. This tiger hide was meant to be for the king of Mewar. Since Sanga sits on it, he will rule Mewar after Raimal. The other two brothers will be killed in a war with the enemies of Mewar."*

The two brothers attacked Sanga, determined to kill him there and then. But Surajmall intervened again and fought them, allowing Sanga to escape with his life.

Jaimal chased Sanga, who ended up in a village called Sevantri. An old friend of the Mewar family, Rao Beeda was at the Roop Narayan temple at Sevantri. Beeda took Sanga under his protection and administered first-aid to his wounds. Jaimal arrived soon afterwards. Beeda fought with him and his forces, and sacrificed his life, thus giving enough time and rest to Sanga to escape further westwards to Marudhara, Marwar.

Upon hearing of the internecine feud among the brothers, Rana Raimal exiled Prithviraj and Jaimal. Sanga, on the other hand, gave up his horse and became a shepherd in Srinagar near Ajmer, at the house of a Rajput named Thakur Karamchand Panwar.

As foretold by the mystic, Jaimal was killed by a fellow Rajput, Ratan Singh. Prithviraj too was poisoned by his brother-in-law and cremated at Kumbhalgarh. Raimal was deeply aggrieved at the loss of both his elder sons until he learnt that Sanga was alive.

Raimal summoned Sanga and showered Thakur Karamchand with *jagirs* for protecting his heir for all these years. With Raimal's death in CE 1508, Sanga became the ruler of Mewar.

The deep impact of astrology and divine incarnates on the Hindu psyche and life is aptly demonstrated at the prediction about Sanga's life by the fortune-teller and Biri Bai. The Hindu society has, through the ages, been guided by these metaphysical domains. It is not the author's intent to speak for or against the practice. The idea is to merely present an aspect of social life throughout the ages as it had such a profound influence on royal families. We can only imagine how the ordinary citizens of Mewar yielded to these occult practices.

The practice of polygamy affecting the history of Mewar so adversely also deserves a mention. It is not only a relic for barbarism and primeval necessity but gave birth to many trajectories of family feuds that it became impossible to so contain them. While the Islamic marauders were menacing at the doors of the land, every queen of the Maharana was engaged in conspiracies to annoint her son the crown ruler of Mewar. The argument that matrimonial bonds were forced to augment the economic and military might of royal dynasties does hold some merit but if we weigh the cost-benefit ratio, the cost of polygamy in royal families far outweighs the benefits of this practice.

The turbulent childhood and violent ascent of Sanga to Mewar's throne also tells us how adversity shapes the persona of a royal warrior. It also tell us how he eventually overcomes all handicaps that life and fate throw at him and rises to the pinnacle of not only the kingdom of Mewar, but to become one of the greatest Hindu kings ever.

We will come across more such examples on studying the lives of Maharana Pratap and Maharana Amar Singh too.

Prima facie, it appears that Prithviraj, the elder brother of Sanga, was of a foul temperament. Though he had the skills to become the next king of Mewar, his uncontrollable anger and myopic pursuit of his ambition, led to his untimely death when he was killed by his own brother-in-law over a petty dispute.

Sanga appears to be a timid and reclusive person in his youth. Although fit and muscular, he did not fight his brothers aggressively and even endured the loss of an eye with a certain degree of indifference. His naivete' in trusting his jealous siblings also shows in his conduct during his youth when he goes to Biri Bai for the same question even after losing an eye to Prithviraj. But for his uncle, Surajmall, Sanga would have been killed at the temple itself. We can only imagine the consequences if such a disaster had befallen mewar.

Sanga's *agyaatvaas* (incognito stay) at Thakur Karamchand's place in Ajmer underlines his aloof persona, which was resigned to a life of anonymity without much agitation. But we also witness the metamorphosis of the same mundane and disinterested person into one of the most aggressive warrior kings to have ever ruled not only Mewar, but a substantial portion of the country at the time. Sanga's expansion of the kingdom matched that of Rana Kumbha's even though he inherited a war-torn house of Mewar.

It establishes Sanga as a deeply spiritual and fiercely loyal servant of Mewar, as he, though uninterested in the throne, rose to the occasion and responded wholeheartedly when beckoned to war. As we travel further through the life of this amazing Maharana who defeated the mighty Lodhis of Delhi and numerous other kings and Sultans, we shall realise in him the steely resolve, military acumen and leadership skills of the highest quality seen anywhere.

What must be underlined here is the fact that courageous and fearless Sanga did not fight his brothers. Both the times he was attacked, he chose to escape instead of confronting his brothers.

Maybe we can learn a very valuable lesson from Sanga that even if all is at stake, one never attacks his own family.

Inspite of losing an eye to his brother, Sanga forgives Prithviraj. Yet the same Sanga transforms into a ferocious warrior when confronted by Islamists and other enemies of Mewar.

Maharana Sanga's life is a tale of how a beaten-up prince overcame his physical and psychological handicaps and rose from a state of pathos and abasement to the highest pedestal.

The central message of Sanga's life is that no defeat is final, no handicap crippling enough, no hardship severe enough if one's spirit and inner resolve remain unbent to external adversities.

Man has infinite capacity to recover from every setback in life.

Once on the throne, Sanga immediately got down to the business of governing and expanding the borders of Mewar. After the Chauhans, Delhi witnessed an incessant civil war, unleashed successively by the dynasties of Ghori, Khilji, Slave and Lodhi.

Rana Sanga set out with 80,000 horses, seven Rajas of the highest ranks, nine Raos, and 104 chieftains bearing the titles of Rawal and Rawat, along with 500 war elephants to conquer the vast territories of northern, central and western India[70].

The prince of Amer, Prithiviraj Kachchawa and Rao Gaanga of Marwar paid homage to him; the Raos of Ajmer, Gwalior, Sipri, Raesen, Kalpi, Chanderi, Boondi, Gagroun, Rampura and Abu served him as tributaries and held him as their chief.

Sanga gave Karamchand Parwar, the Thakur who had sheltered him, the grant of Ajmer and the title of Rao for his son, Jugmal. It is quite remarkable that a prince, who had so meekly surrendered his right as the heir of Mewar and was resigned to live a life of anonymity, rose to become one of the strongest rulers of Mewar under whom the expanse of Mewar resembled that of Rana Kumbha's reign.

Strange are the ways of life.

A meek person who would otherwise have been relegated to the dustbin of history became the king of Mewar and took its glory to amazing heights.

Sanga's ambition was countered by the surrounding Muslim kingdoms of Delhi, Malwa and Gujarat.

Conquest of Malwa

Malwa was a rich kingdom to the east of Mewar and was ruled by Nasir-ud-din. Nasir died shortly after Sanga's ascent and Mahmud Khilji II became the ruler of Malwa, assisted by a Rajput chieftain, Medini Rai.

Medini Rai was an ambitious General and soon his writ ran large over the affairs of Malwa. It was merely a matter of time

70. *Annals & Antiquities of Rajasthan*, James Tod, vol. 1, p. 240.

before Mahmud and Medini fell apart. Medini took control of Malwa and exiled Mahmud. Mahmud ran away to Gujarat and appealed to Muzaffar of Gujarat to help him get rid of Medini Rai.

Medini turned to Sanga for help and appealed that there was no man better than him and that if he did not assist his own race, who else would do so?

Sanga consented to help Medini and attacked Mahmud Khilji II at Gagraun in CE 1519.

The Muslim historians themselves maintain that as many as thirty army Generals and thousands of soldiers of Khilji were slaughtered and Mahmud himself was captured alive and taken to Chittor. Sanga took care of him and released him honourably on three conditions:

1. Reparations for all the expenses of the wars fought between Mewar and Malwa.
2. Surrender of a precious gold cap and belt belonging to the Malwa family.
3. A son of Mahmud Khilji would be stationed in Mewar court as a pledge for good relations[71].

One cannot fathom the motive behind Sanga's act of leaving Mahmud Khilji alive because, though Khilji could never damage Mewar directly, but for the rest of his life, he kept joining the enemies of Mewar, thereby causing loss of life and property to Mewar.

Mahmud never showed any gratitude towards Sanga for sparing his life. It must also be remembered that Mahmud Khilji's co-religionist Allauddin Khilji was responsible for the first *saka* of Chittor when thousands of Hindu women committed *jauhar* due to Allauddin's siege and when Rawal Ratan Singh perished fighting the Khiljis.

Mahmud Khilji stayed loyal to the *Ummah* or Muslim brotherhood and viewed Sanga as a perennial Hindu rival. This malaise of forgiving captured Muslim rulers by Hindu benevolence was eradicated only with Rana Pratap mercilessly slaughtering his enemies instead of yielding to fake morality and individual glory at the cost of the safety of Mewar.

---

71. *The Delhi Sultanate*, R.C. Majumdar, p. 341.

The main protagonist of the battle against Khilji was a Charan general called Haridas Mahiyariya, a very close friend of Sanga. Sanga was so pleased with Haridas that he offered him the fort of Chittor. Haridas being a loyal friend, refused the fort and settled for 12 villages as Jagir for himself. Such was the simplicity of Sanga and such was the loyalty he inspired in friends like Haridas.

Campaign against Gujarat

Muzaffar Khan, the Nawab of Gujarat, was another enemy that Sanga vanquished while expanding the borders of Mewar.

Muzaffar nominated Mubariz-ul-Mulk as the Governor of Idar. Mubariz kept a pet dog at his door by the name of Sanga. When news of this act of Mubariz reached Sanga, he attacked Mubariz-ul-Mulk with an army of 40,000 troops and totally routed them at Idar. The Muslim army escaped to the fort of Ahmednagar and locked themselves up in the fort. Muzaffar was livid with Mubariz for insulting Sanga and refused to offer any help.

Spikes on Gates of Forts

A Rajput warrior, Dungar Singh, showed exemplary fighting skills in this siege and slaughtered a lot of enemies.

Dungar lost most of his sons and brothers in this battle. One of his sons, Kanha, performed an unbelievable feat. The gates of the fort had sharp spikes on them to prevent elephants from breaking the gates open. Kanha stood in front of the spikes and ordered the *mahout* to let the animal loose on the gates. Though, Kanha's body was crushed but the elephant managed to break the gate of the fort.

Sanga's army slaughtered the Muslim army, though Mubariz escaped with a few of his aides[72].

Muzaffar then sent a force of one lakh cavalry and 100 elephants under Malik Ayaz and Imad-ul-Mulk to defeat Rana Sanga. Mahmud of Malwa too joined them and the huge army laid siege on the fort of Mandsaur, which was protected by a vassal

72. *Veer Vinod*, Shyamaldas, vol. 1, p. 359.

of Sanga, Ashok Mal Rajput. Sanga too assembled an army of one lakh and came to the village, Nandsa, near Mandsaur.

Salhadi Tanwar of Raisen was the main General for Sanga in this battle.

Ayaz was totally routed by Sanga and he escaped to Gujarat. Mahmud of Malwa approached Sanga to get his son released from Sanga's captivity in lieu of meeting all the expenses of the war.

Treachery of Bahadur Shah

After his defeat, Muzaffar stayed in Gujarat and didn't bother Sanga. But Gujarat was destined to play another sinister plot in Sanga's life.

The second son of Muzaffar, Bahadur Shah, left Gujarat and took shelter with Sanga. In reality, he was nursing grudges against Sanga for his slaughter of the Muslim army of Gujarat at Ahmednagar.

Sanga's mother adopted Bahadur Shah as her son, who later became the king of Gujarat.

After Sanga's murder in CE 1528, Bahadur attacked Chittor in CE 1535 and destroyed it. The second Saka of Chittor happened because of the siege laid by Bahadur Shah.

Sanga's simplicity and large heartedness bred a snake, like Bahadur Shah to have disastrous consequences for Mewar.

On one hand this incident shows the naiveté of Sanga and his mother, on the other, it also demonstrates the value system of a *jihadi* like Bahadur Shah.

He had all the right to nurse a grudge against Sanga for the slaughter at Ahmednagar, but to seek shelter and create a place in the heart of the family of the enemy and then cause total destruction of that family adequately demonstrates that *jihadi* value system has no place for loyalty and friendship over the commitment to spread and victory of Islam.

The story of Bahadur Shah needs to be told only to underline the failure of Hindu royalty to understand this amoral and opportunistic behaviour of Islamists.

Bahadur Shah had an Islamic teacher, Sheikh Jiyu, as his master. Bahadur told Sheikh about his desire to destroy Chittor as a revenge for Sanga slaughtering Muslims.

Sheikh replied, *"With the destruction of Chittor, you too shall be destroyed."*

Bahadur replied, *"I don't care."*

Bahadur went to Sanga as a refugee and was accepted by him and his mother, the Jhali queen.

Once, a nephew of Sanga had invited Bahadur for dinner. Bahadur was attracted to one of the dancers. Seeing this, the nephew of Sanga mockingly said, *"This damsel was taken in the loot of Ahmednagar."*

Bahadur lost his cool and cut the nephew into two pieces there and then. Rajputs leapt upon Bahadur for revenge but the queen mother took out her dagger and proclaimed, *"If anyone was to harm my son Bahadur, I will stab myself*[73]*."*

This disease of hyper sentimentality has infected Hindus for centuries. Even after seeing his true colours, the Hindu king and his family were blind to the truth about Bahadur. Rest has been told.

Bahadur had his revenge and destroyed Chittor when his time came.

Annihilation of 'Delhi Sultanate'

Sanga also recaptured the prestigious and impregnable Ranthambore from the imperialist General Ali and killed him.

Sanga reached the Afghan city of Ghazni twice during his victory campaigns. He slew Firoz Shah Pathan to annex Nagaur.

Thus, during Sanga's time, Mewar extended from *Peela-Khal* (yellow rivulet) near Bayana in the north to Malwa and Gujarat in the south; up to the Sindhu River in the west, while the Aravallis formed the eastern boundary.

Eighteen pitched battles were fought between Mewar and the forces of Delhi and Malwa, where two battles were fought frontally, between Sanga and Ibrahim Lodhi at Bakrole and Khatauli.

At Khatauli, in CE 1517, Lodhi's army was slaughtered and his son was held captive. It was at Khatauli that Sanga lost one of his hands in combat and because of an arrow injury, his one leg too was compromised.

---

73. *Veer Vinod*, vol. 1, p. 361; Ojha, vol. 1, p. 317.

Sanga took Ibrahim Lodhi's son to Chittor and released him after extracting heavy reparations.

In CE 1518, Lodhi again attacked Sanga at Bakrole, near Dholpur, with a much larger force and was routed by Rana conclusively. Lodhi's army, led by Miyan Makhan comprised of 30,000 infantry and 300 elephants but Rajputs slaughtered them and a huge catch of elephants, horses and riches came their way.

Sanga was now in the vicinity of Agra and itching to release the heart of northern region from the clutches of *mlechchas*.

The victory over Ibrahim Lodhi was the crowning glory of Sanga's life. Rana Sanga was now the claimant to the heart of Bharat and Mewar's imperial ambitions were unstoppable. Sanga materialised this ambition both by diplomatic means and military efforts[74].

It was at this time of the might and expanse of Mewar's Rana Sanga that the Chugtai Uzbek, Babur, invaded India's north-west frontiers.

A big misconception that has been circulated in the history teaching of our nation is that Sanga invited Babur to invade India with the idea of defeating Ibrahim Lodhi unitedly. It defies logic that Sanga would have invited Babur to defeat Ibrahim Lodhi whom Sanga had singlehandedly defeated already at Bakrole, Khatauli and Dholpur. There is no reference to such a letter by Tod, Shyamaldas, Rajendra Bhatt or any prominent historian in their works. In fact, R.C. Majumdar quotes Ferishta in his book that the Sultan of Gujarat, Muzaffar Khan's General, Imad-ul-Mulk sent such a letter of help to Babur.

This letter was intercepted by the ruler of Dungarpur, who was a vassal of Sanga. Sanga sealed a treaty with the Gujarat Sultan and thus, instead of a Gujarat-Mughal treaty, a Gujarat-Mewar treaty was signed[75].

Conflict with Babur & Battle of Khanwa

The stage was thus set for the final march of Sanga as the resurgent Hindu claimant for liberating the heartland from the

74. Majumdar.

75. *The Delhi Sultanate*, R.C. Majumdar, p. 345.

Muslim robbers sitting in and around Delhi.

Babur defeated a weak and depleted Ibrahim Lodhi in the First Battle of Panipat in 1526, where Ibrahim Lodhi was slain and his army destroyed.

Zahiruddin Mohammad Babur; Plundered Bharat between 1528-1530 CE after murdering Sanga by poisoning

Babur was a fanatic Islamist and always credited his victories to his Prophet and thus inspired the confidence of his troops. He is supposed to have remarked after the First Battle of Panipat, "Not to me, oh God! But to thee, be the victory."

On 21st February 1527, Sanga met the Turk-Afghan forces at the town of Bayana on the north-eastern border of Rajasthan. The advanced parties of Sanga's armed forces slaughtered 1,500 of Babur's forces in a skirmish when Babur made a hasty retreat. The Muslim Generals sang praises for Rajput warriors and Babur's army was completely demoralised.

A Mughal General, Mansur Barlas is quoted as saying: *"The Rajputs have indomitable courage. They are personification of azrail (death). Unlike our troops, they do not abandon the field."*

The Afghans in Babur's army began to leave. The Turks started complaining about defending a land that they hated. They even requested Babur to return to Kabul.

Babur himself writes, *"No manly word or brave counsel was heard from anyone whatsoever."*

Babur meditated upon his loss and made peace overtures to Sanga to which Sanga responded initially, but the talks broke down when Sanga insisted that Babur pay yearly taxes to Mewar.

Babur was fully aware of the sunken morale of his troops.

So, he appealed to the theological affinity of his troops and gave very passionate speeches to his men to fight and kill the infidels in the name of Islam. Even when an Afghan astrologer Muhammad Sharif predicted defeat, Babur did not back off.

There is a folktale that Babur asked the fortune-teller to predict how long he (the astrologer) was going to live. The fortune-teller replied with a date few decades hence. Babur beheaded the fortune-teller there and then and proclaimed, *"Just like his forecast of his own age has been falsified, so will be his prediction of the defeat of Allah's army."*

According to *Baburnama*, this is just a folktale as Babur forgave this astrologer later, but forbade him from making any more predictions[76].

Additionally, Babur publicly vowed to never touch wine and women and never shave his beard or tax a Muslim again.

Thus, stirring Islamic passion and zeal in his army of mostly Turkish, Uzbek, Tatar, Afghan and Mongol mercenaries, Babur prepared for the final showdown with the Hindu forces.

Here is a portion of the speech given by Babur, as written in his own biography, *Baburnama*:

"Noblemen and soldiers and every man that comes into the world is subject to dissolution.

Only Allah is everlasting.

Whoever comes to the feast of life must, before it is over, drink from the cup of death.

How much better it is to die with honour than to live with infamy!

With fame, even if I die, I am contented;

Let fame be mine, since my body is death's.

If we win, we will be the Ghazis; if we lose, we will be shaheed; either way, riches await us.

Let us then, with one accord, swear on Allah's holy name that none of us will even think of turning his face from this warfare, nor desert from the battle and the slaughter that ensures, till his soul is separated from his body[77]."

76. *Baburnama*, p. 394.

77. *Baburnama*, p. 383-84.

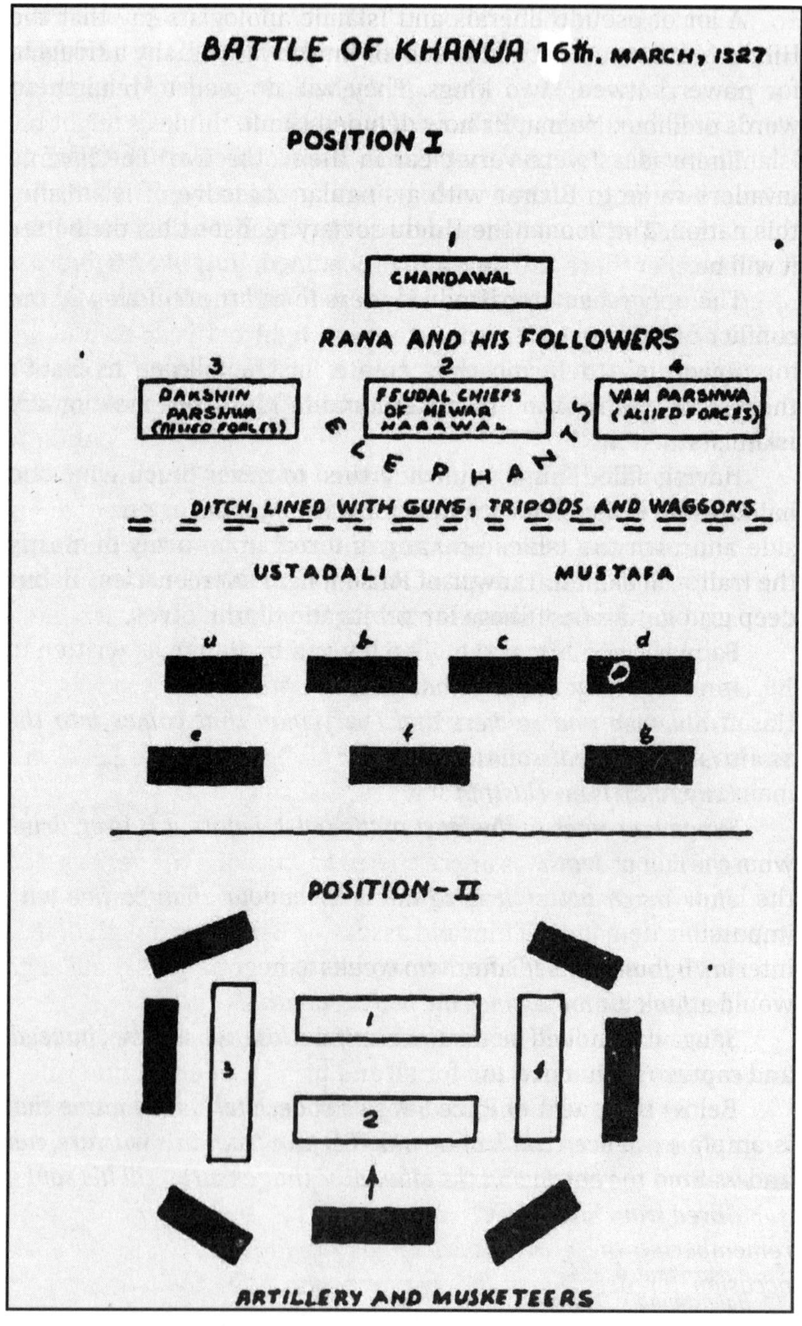
BATTLE OF KHANUA 16th. MARCH, 1527
POSITION I
1
CHANDAWAL
RANA AND HIS FOLLOWERS
3
2
4
DAKSHIN PARSHWA (ALLIED FORCES)
FEUDAL CHIEFS OF MEWAR HARAWAL
VAM PARSHWA (ALLIED FORCES)
ELEPHANTS
DITCH, LINED WITH GUNS, TRIPODS AND WAGGONS
USTADALI
MUSTAFA
a
b
c
d
e
f
g
POSITION-II
1
2
3
4
ARTILLERY AND MUSKETEERS

A lot of pseudo liberals and Islamic apologists say that the Hindu-Muslim conflict in this subcontinent was actually a struggle for power between two kings. They will do well to read these words of Babur. No matter how deluded Hindu thinkers might be, Islamic invaders were very clear in their objective. The Islamic invaders came to Bharat with a singular objective of Islamising this nation. The sooner the Hindu society realises this, the better it will be.

The only reason for Hindu leaders to call the Hindu- Muslim conflict of this subcontinent as a mere fight between two kings for power, is a delusion they create for themselves to justify their sloth and inaction in understanding the true intentions of Islamists.

Having filled his army with this religious fervour, Babur hatched the evil conspiracy to bribe a Hindu *kafir* to defect to his side and turn the tables on Sanga's formidable army. He found the traitor in Salhadi Tanwar of Raisen, near Gwalior. Tanwar had deep grudges against Sanga for subjugating him a few years ago.

Babur bribed him and fuelled his anger against Sanga.

In the meanwhile, a local Rajput, who had converted to Islam, Hasan Khan Mewati, joined Rana Sanga with 10,000 horsemen as also many subordinates of Ibrahim Lodhi joined the Rana, the main amongst them being Mohammed Khan Lodhi.

Sanga had realised the evil nature of the new invader, Babur, whose religious zeal was unparalleled in attacking the very *soul* of the land. Sanga kept engaging Babur in superficial talks, making impossible demands of him and assessing Babur's strength in that interim. Babur realised after two weeks of negotiations that Sanga would attack him.

Sanga had indeed made up his mind to fight the Uzbek invader and capture Delhi once and for all and bring it under Hindu rule.

Below is the text of Rana Sanga's speech to his troops, which is ample evidence that Sanga was fed up with Islamic invasions and wanted to rout the Turks forever:

"Everyone must act according to the warrior's code remembering the brave deeds of our forefathers. This is the final occasion for destroying the invaders who have tainted our holy

land for centuries. Once we seize this opportunity, they will never be able to raise their heads again, and the flag of Hindu padpadshahi (suzerainty of Hindu king) will fly over the entire country."

On 16th March 1527, the forces of Mewar and Babur clashed in the legendary Battle of Khanwa.

Khanwa is indeed the most decisive battle to have been fought between Hindus and Muslims in the subcontinent.

Sanga led an army of two lakh against 90,000 of Babur.

The battle began early in the morning.

A very lethal and smart war tactic surprise awaited Sanga and his forces in the form of Mughal cannons equipped with their firepower. The Rajputs were totally bewildered by the might and effects of gunpowder. Thousands of Sanga's forces collapsed and the horses and elephants rampaged backward on his own army.

Then, the Rajputs came up with a mind-numbing solution to the cannons.

Rajput soldiers and chieftains sunk their heads into the blazing cannons, thus rendering them useless by studding them with meat and blood. The Mughals were astounded to see this extreme act of valour by Sanga's army and the tide started turning in favour of the Mewar army.

A very lethal war tactic amongst Muslim invaders was to depute dozens of their best archers, secured by guards, to search for the enemy king or leader and bombard him with a barrage of arrows to incapacitate him or eliminate him.

Muslim rulers never exposed themselves to the Hindu armies and stayed behind their ranks and file. Hindu kings, on the other hand, led from the front as an act of valour and leadership.

This was an act of naïveté which cost Hindus a lot in their wars against Islamists.

Babur had deputed his best archers to identify Sanga and hit him singularly with the barrage of arrows. One arrow hit him hard on his skull and Sanga lost consciousness. He was taken away from the battlefield by his lieutenants. This caused a lull in the war for an hour or so.

Babur writes in his memoirs, *"The accursed infidels remained confounded for an hour."*

Then Ajja Jhaala of Halwad wore the royal dress himself and pretended to be Sanga to keep the morale of his troops high. The trick worked and the Hindu army resumed fighting the Turks ferociously.

Around mid-noon, Salhadi Tanwar, along with his 35,000 horsemen, defected to the army of Babur.

Sanga's chieftains regrouped and resumed their attack even after this treachery, but kept dying one after the other.

By evening, every single chief of any consequence had laid down his life to save their *dharma*.

Manik Chand Chauhan, Rawal Udai Singh of Vagad, Ratan Singh Choondawat of Merta, Chandrabhan Chauhan, Jhala Ajja, Ramdas Songara, Gokul Das Parmar, Raimal Rathore, Khet Singh, Hasan Khan Mewati and Muhammad Lodhi were all slain fighting for their Rana.

Both sides suffered heavy losses, though the numerical loss of Hindus was significantly higher because of the use of cannons and muskets by the Muslims. The roads to Delhi, Agra, Bayana and Alwar were littered with limbs and bodies of soldiers from both sides. The war continued well into the night with only a few thousand warriors left on each side. Leaderless, the Hindu army retreated to their camps and were relieved to find that their king was still alive. The Muslims stayed huddled in the night for fear of a retaliatory attack by Rajputs.

Rao Gaanga of Marwar, Medini Rai and Raja Prithviraj Kachchawa of Amer protected Sanga as he recovered from his wound.

Babur proclaimed Khanwa as his victory and writes,

"For the sake of Islam, I became a wanderer;
I battled infidels and Hindus.
I determined to become a martyr.
Thank God, I became a holy warrior[78]."

In almost all recorded history, Khanwa has been documented as a loss for Sanga and a decisive victory for Babur.

We attempt to present an alternate version based on the following facts and arguments;

78. *Baburnama*, p. 394.

1. The fundamental question that arises is that if Khanwa was indeed a victory for Muslims, then why wasn't Rana Sanga killed?

Babur killed Ibrahim Lodhi at Panipat. Throughout his war campaigns in Afghanistan and Bharat, it was the norm for him to kill the enemy. Then what prevented him from doing the same to Sanga?

The only reason for this could be that Sanga had inflicted enough damage on Babur at Khanwa to immobilise him. Besides, with the powerful kings of Jodhpur, Amer, Sirohi and Chanderi still at his side, Sanga was still a formidable force.

2. Another question that arises is that if Khanwa was lost by Sanga, why wasn't Sanga chased even a few kilometres?

In fact, Babur writes in *Baburnama, "When I had gone 2 miles towards the pagan's camp, I turned back because it was late in the day. I came to our camp at the bed-time prayer*[79]*."*

Sanga survived almost one year after Khanwa, but Babur was unable to touch him. How?

3. There are three independent sources of Mewar history that talk of Khanwa as a victory for Sanga after a fierce battle. Ranchod Bhatt, in his book, *Amarkavyam,* writes of a meeting between Babur and Sanga after Khanwa. *Chittor Paatnama* too mentions a similar meeting after Khanwa[80,81]. Surajmal Misran writes in his epic work *'Vansh Bhaskar'* about the conclusive victory of Sanga at Khanwa. This is a very significant change from the narrative set by Muslim historians who mention nothing of such a meeting.

4. The writer travelled to Khanwa and was astonished to see Hindu style Chhatris littered around Khanwa even today. Such Chhatris were only built in memory of Hindu kings and chiefs. If Khanwa was lost, then how did Rajputs make these Chhatris for their fallen kings and leaders? These are big structures, that would have taken months to build. There are at least nine such Chhatris in and around Khanwa which are in an extremely vulnerable state. 500 years after Khanwa, these Chhatris standing are ample evidence that Khanwa was a victory for Sanga.

---

79. *Baburnama*, p. 372.
80. *Amarkavyam*, p. 193-94.
81. *Chittor Patnama*, p. 165-66.

5. If indeed Khanwa was lost by Sanga, why was Humayun, Babur's son, sent to Kabul instead of being stationed somewhere in India? Why wasn't Humayun given an area to govern in Bharat, if Babur had conclusively defeated all his enemies?

After completely destroying Lodhis, and defeating the Rajputs, who was Babur afraid of?

These are some fundamental questions that must be investigated and answered.

6. If we look at this from the other side, the only premise for claiming Khanwa as a Mughal victory are the memoirs of Babur. If there is any independent source that calls Khanwa as Babur's victory, at least this writer hasn't been able to lay his hands on it.

The basic rule of historiography is that the claims of victory by any party are not accepted on their face value unless corroborated by neutral sources or from the opposite camp. If no other version is available, then the claim is not considered final.

Just like the story of Sanga's letter to Babur is a total lie, why couldn't this story of one-sided Mughal victory be a lie perpetrated by Babur?

These dacoits were known to spread lies and falsehood as a legitimate weapon of war. On what basis have the memoirs of a religious zealot been taken as gospel truth? Why has no critical analysis and research of this crucial battle been done till date? One can only hope that some day thorough research on Khanwa will be done and truth of this battle will be discovered and documented.

7. It is very interesting to note that Babur writes things with very meticulous details in his memoirs. He describes people, places, events and wars in quite sufficient detail.

Why is Babur completely silent on Sanga's death?

For one full year after Khanwa, Sanga was roaming in the same territories as Babur, but Sanga finds no mention by Babur. This is very inconsistent with Babur's style of writing, unless he was deliberately downplaying Sanga's murder.

8. Even if we were to accept that Sanga lost at Khanwa, why is it that Sanga is erased from history instead of establishing the truth about him? Babur's loss at Bayana is merely a setback, but Sanga's so-called loss at Khanwa is final?

The Hindu chatris standing even today at Khanwa

Ruins of a Hindu temple in the battlefield of Khanwa.

This is a very biased view of history which must be exposed and opposed with arguments and evidence.

Some historians say that Babur's encampment was on the water source to Fatehpur Sikri which was very close to the battlefield and he poisoned the water source that fed Sanga and his troops. This needs further investigation by archaeologists and historians, instead of sitting with a one-sided verdict on Khanwa as being a loss for Sanga.

The facts simply don't add up.

Babur has himself written in his memoirs that he was constantly under fear of being attacked by Rajputs, especially when he was travelling. Who was he afraid of, if not Sanga and his army!

Khanwa was not just another battle between Hindus and Muslims. Khanwa changed the course of the sub-continent's history irreversibly. Very meticulous investigation and research needs to be put into this vital event, before declaring it a victory for Babur.

If Sanga didn't lose Khanwa, then it can be said with a reasonable certainty that Sanga was indeed poisoned by Babur.

That means all the talk of the muscular Muslims defeating meek Hindus are smokescreens created to cover up for the treachery of a bunch of rapists and looters.

Sanga's poisoning by Babur means that the very premise of

the so-called Mughal empire was not manly combat, but deceit and murder.

To even compare these treacherous murderers with chivalrous Rajputs is a blasphemy of humongous proportions.

Since the Hindu Muslim conflict of this besieged nation is far from over, we will do well to find out the truth of these villains of history.

Back in the Hindu camp, Rao Gaanga of Marwar, Medini Rai and Raja Prithviraj Kachchawa of Amer protected Sanga as he recovered from his wound. Sanga was furious with his nobles for removing him from the battlefield. The Maharana told his chiefs that without defeating Babur, there was no question of his going back to Chittor. Sanga retreated to the safety of Ranthambhore and started regrouping his men to attack Babur. Unfortunately, within months of Khanwa, Sanga's trusted friend, Prithviraj Kachchawa of Amer died mysteriously.

Another lie propagated about Sanga's death is that he was poisoned by his own *samants* who were tired of fighting under him. This is as absurd an argument as it is pedestrian.

The pathetic state of the Samadhi of Maharana Sangram Singh at Baswa

Why would the *samants* who had been fighting loyally under Sanga for twenty years and had tasted success in nearly 100 battles under him, suddenly be tired of fighting? And tired to such an extent that they would poison their own Maharana!

Only fake historians, who have no idea of the value of honour and loyalty, can come up with such a churlish argument.

The Mughals were known to poison their enemies and it seems more plausible that Babur bribed someone in Sanga's camp to poison him. Since there are records of peace talks between

Sanga and Babur, it is quite possible that Sanga was poisoned in one of these meetings by Babur.

More intense research and investigation is needed to draw fair conclusions on this turbulent but decisive phase of history of the subcontinent.

In the absence of any written record besides Babur's, it is quite possible that Khanwa was either a victory for Sanga or a stalemate. If the Hindu victory of Bayana is not considered final, why should Khanwa be considered a final Mughal victory?

After Khanwa, Sanga and Babur kept fighting each other for full one year and this ended with the murder of Sanga by poisoning.

On 30th January of CE 1528, one of the bravest, visionary Hindu king was tragically murdered by his enemies at the young age of forty-five years.

Confusion has also been spread about the place of death of Sanga. Most historians agree it was at Kalpi, though some say that Sanga died at Chittor. That his *samadhi* is at Baswa in northeast Rajasthan close to Kalpi, should settle this issue in favour of Kalpi.

The writer visited the Samadhi of Sanga at Baswa. The gross neglect of that pious place is a measure of the ingratitude of Hindus to one of the greatest defenders of Hinduism. What should be a pilgrimage centre for Hindus lies in such gross neglect speaks volumes about our priorities.

Thus, the life of one of the most courageous and visionary Hindu kings that ever ruled Bharat *bhoomi* came to a tragic end at the hands of a treacherous and immoral enemy. A king who had fought all adversity with such nonchalant bravery could only have been murdered by such deceit, since even death was scared to confront him frontally.

With Sanga's murder, the dream of a Rajput kingship over Bharatvarsha was destroyed.

The Mughals got an opportunity to entrench themselves in this land.

Centuries have to pay the price of the follies of moments.

Mir Baqi, one of the Generals of Babur went on to destroy the Ram temple at Ayodhya and construct the Babri mosque on it. It was the biggest centre of Hindu reverence for which lakhs of Hindus and Sikhs have kept fighting and dying incessantly for 500 years.

In these 500 years, most were times of deep despair—the occupying force was so brutal, the occupation so one-sided, that any hope looked unreal and unimaginable. Not only the alien murderers, but the political dispensation and leading historians of the nascent nation-state were also inimical to the Hindu belief that Bhagwan Shri Ram was born on this *punyabhoomi.* In such adversity and against every nefarious trick in the communist book, how the Hindus stubbornly ploughed on, is a tale of courage and perseverance, that must be told to the entire humankind.

What was this insistence? What was this audacity of Hindus? How did they manage to keep the embers smouldering in the threatening storms?

Many years ago, I had gone with my elder brother, Sh. R.P. Singh a Major at that time, to the Army cantonment. A middle-aged soldier saluted him sharply with a "Ram-Ram saab".

It shocked me in a good way.

The upper officers of the forces, their wives and children—all conversed in English, but the ordinary soldier had kept Ram's name alive with a forceful insistence. Even if the marauders managed to raze the temple of Shri Ram, they could not wipe Him and His name out of our collective consciousness.

What we lost as Ram Janmabhoomi and the temple, we imbued in our souls and spirits as the '*tatva*' of Shri Ram.

Ram became our cry, a refrain that was repeated on every occasion a Hindu could find—from the holy songs at birth to the holy nuptials, to when we give *agni* the mortal remains to whom we hold most dear. Our ancestors knew that no attack in the world could wipe out Shri Ram from our hearts.

The Islamic invaders desecrated thousands of temples and erected mosques over them, but our *rishis*, the *mathadheeshas*, the *gurus* did not let time fade the memories of Shiva's Kashi, Mathura of Krishna's and Ayodhya of Ram's *janmabhoomi*.

They're not *just* land masses for Hindus; they're the nerve centres of *dharma* itself.

For the Ram Janmabhoomi, thousands of Hindus and Sikhs toiled on. Goswami Tulsidas and other Bhakti saints and poets kept his memory alive. No Hindu, of any caste or creed, ever gave up on Shri Ram and his birthplace, because they knew in their hearts that Shri Ram and His Name are what keeps the *Dharma* of Hindus alive. No Ram, No *Dharma*.

After an incessant struggle, countless sacrifices, innumerable martyrs and in the face of glaring archaeological evidences, the Indian Supreme court on 9 November, 2019 ruled in favor of constructing a Ram Janambhoomi temple on the disputed site.

The model of the proposed Ram temple

The day, doors of this Mandir are thrown open, what the world would witness is not just a structure of stone and cement. They will see a monument to the indomitable spirit of humanity in the face of the worst religious persecution.

It'll tell one and all that the past glories and legacy can be recovered.

Sanga's amazing sacrifices were not in vain. Hindus reclaimed what was rightfully theirs. That is the fittest tribute to the memory of the great Maharana Sangram Singh of Mewar.

Khanwa might have witnessed a stalemate, but Babur has been defeated with the resolve and sacrifices of the Hindu community.

Let us return to the battle and its analysis now.

It will be a worthy exercise to look into the reasons for this stalemate at Khanwa by a Hindu army twice the size of invaders to understand the military shortcomings of Hindus:

1. The Hindu army was a collection of various kings and chieftains joining Sanga in times of war against an external invader.

   They did not practise war with each other and hence, even the chain of command was not established as we witness in the commotion in the Hindu army at Khanwa.
2. The cannons dealt the first mortal blow to the Hindus who were ill-prepared to deal with it. Hindus, therefore, paid a heavy price for being outsmarted in war technology.
3. The Muslims devised very effective war tactics such as *tulughma* and *araba.* These new war tactics were introduced by Babur.

Tulughma meant dividing the whole army into various units, viz. the left, the right and the centre. The left and right divisions were further subdivided into forward and rear divisions. Through this, a small army could be used to surround the enemy from all sides in no time. The centre forward division was then provided with carts (*araba*) which were placed in rows facing the enemy and tied to each other with animal-hide ropes. Behind them were placed cannons which were protected and supported by mantelets used to easily manoeuvre the cannons.

These two tactics made Babur's artillery lethal.

The guns and cannons could be fired without any fear of being hit as they were shielded by the bullock carts, which were held in place due to the hide ropes holding them together. Hindus consider cattle sacred but not the Islamists. The Muslim mercenaries were safe behind them. Additionally, the nozzle of the heavy cannons could also be easily changed as they could be manoeuvred by the mantelets which were provided with wheels. Such organised use of fire power and artillery meant heavy losses for a relatively less organised Hindu army.

4. The treachery of Salhadi Tanwar is hotly contested by some people who deny this claim. However, reliable history sources have endorsed this act of Salhadi and it is in the interest of documentation that Salhadi's treachery finds mention in this book. The idea is not to offend anyone. Khanwa was the turning point in the military conflicts between Hindu-Muslim tussles in the subcontinent, and we will be doing a great disservice to ourselves if we do not record the truth, howsoever discomforting it might be.

The disgrace of Salhadi's action was erased within one generation of Tanwars. Gwalior's king, the great Ram Shah Tanwar was defeated by Akbar, but instead of choosing suzerainty of Akbar, Ram Shah joined Sanga's son Udai Singh at Chittor. Ram Shah Tanwar went on to become the chief of Mewar Army. He and his family were immortalised by their contribution at the battle of Haldi Ghati.

5. The rules of engagement by Hindu troops remained humane against an enemy who had scant regard for such values, blinded by the singular pursuit of victory. Sanga could have chased Babur and finished him at the Battle of Bayana itself, but perhaps due to a false sense of benevolence or Hindu chivalry, or even as a tactical move, Babur was let off. That blunder cost Hindus a battle as decisive as Khanwa. Based on a superior morale and greater numbers, Khanwa should have been a one-sided victory for Sanga.

Destiny had other plans for Hindus perhaps and by superior military tactics, Babur was able to halt Sanga that fateful day.

Babur had lost almost all of his artillery and his cannons had been rendered useless. Most significantly, Babur had to witness the ferocity and extreme valour of the Hindus in defending their king and land, and hence, did not chase Sanga.

Sanga kept tormenting Babur for one year after Khanwa through surprise attacks on him. Babur writes in *Baburnama* that he was terrorised to travel around Agra and Delhi since Rajputs could attack him any time. Babur could only relax after Sanga had been murdered.

Babur too died on 27th December 1530, within two years of Sanga's murder. Thus, he could not take any significant advantage from Sanga's demise except causing plunder in north India and Bengal. He is said to have been poisoned by Ibrahim Lodhi's mother.

All the stories about Babur offering his life to the divine above, in lieu of the life of Humayun, are just that—stories. At least the writer didn't find any evidence for this concocted tale. In fact, the only reason for this concoction could be to show these psychotic murderers as humane and civilised.

Back in Mewar, Sanga's murder proved to be the downward turning point in Rajput dominance, not only in Mewar, but in entire Bharatvarsha.

The consequences of Sanga's murder were even more devastating for Hindus than the loss at the Battle of Tarain by Prithviraj Chauhan in CE 1192.

1. The Rajput confederation was completely destroyed and Rajputs could never assemble under one roof after Sanga. Neither did Rajputs get a statesman of the stature of Sanga, nor could Mewar become the pivot of Rajput unity again.
2. A loose Muslim rule was established in the heart of Bharat and a whole lot of foreign mercenaries were lured to come and raid our holy land. The entire Hindu society suffered the scourge of these murderers for the next 150 years.

3. Mewar got so depleted after Sanga, that it could no longer halt the march of Islamic forces into the heart of Bharat. A weak and directionless Mewar soon descended into a civil war within its royal line and the *samants*.
4. With the death of Prithviraj Kachchawa of Amer after a few months of Khanwa, Rajputs of Rajasthan were left in abject disarray. Mewar witnessed the murderous attack by Bahadur Shah on Chittor. The second *Saka-jauhar* of Chittor happened with Rani Karmawati, the widow of Sanga, committing *jauhar* with 13,000 other women and 32,000 Hindu warriors were martyred while defending Chittor. This is the same queen around whom the lie of her letter to Humayun for help has been woven.

   The fact of the matter is that no such thread of *rakhi* was ever sent by the queen. Humayun watched the destruction of Chittor from a safe distance leisurely.
5. After Khanwa, Islamic invaders brazenly pitched Hindu kings against each other and furthered their assault on Hindus with relative ease. Before Khanwa, Hindus had rarely allied with Islamic invaders.

Sanga was one-eyed, one-armed and one-footed with eighty-four wounds of metal on his body, but his *prana* (spirit) remained untouched by physical trauma and he never let his physical handicap overpower his inner resolve. It is quite remarkable that a king possessing such a wrecked body inspired such confidence in his troops, that they followed him to victory and death likewise.

Once Sanga won a battle and was invited by Samants to sit on the throne of the annexed kingdom. Sanga refused. He said that just like a mutilated idol can not adorn a temple, a handicapped king must not sit on the throne too. Such was the humility of Sanga. The Samants then said that since Sanga had been handicapped in fighting wars, this was not a fair comparison. Sanga sat on the throne reluctantly.

Can we even imagine a lame king with a damaged eye mounting a horse with some help, leading his armies up to Afghanistan, Bengal, Maharashtra, and Delhi without ever evoking doubt, weakness, or pity on his physical frame? Instead, he evoked such confidence in his Generals and army that he single-handedly created the largest Hindu kingdom of medieval India!

Death is an inevitability in this fragile world.

But before leaving his mortal body, Sanga, in life as in death, had sowed the seeds of wisdom, valour, and supreme sacrifice for generations to come.

A generation that saw a warrior-king like Pratap who singlehandedly withstood the Turkish invasion, when all hope had been lost.

Sanga taught the warriors of Mewar that against Islam, they were fighting an existential conflict in which there could be no relenting.

Ever since Bappa Rawal's time, Islamic invaders had continued to attack Hindustan and were not going to stop with a war or two. It was going to be an unending conflict till one of the two was completely annihilated.

Sanga not only continued the tradition of the amazing Maharanas of Mewar but took the qualities of audacious valour and steely resolution to new standards, inspired by which, the royal line of Mewar could never be enslaved by the Turk invaders and remained the *Hindwa Sooraj* as the apex guardian and protector of Hindu *dharma* for centuries to come.

□

Part-II

"'Undaunted heroism, inflexible fortitude, that which "keeps honour bright", perseverance, with fidelity no nation can boast, were the materials opposed to a soaring ambition, commanding talents, unlimited means and the fervour of religious zeal; all, however, insufficient to contend with one unconquerable mind.

"There is not a pass in the alpine Aravallis that is not sanctioned by some deed of Pratap—some brilliant victory or, oftener, more glorious defeat.

"Haldighati is the Thermopylae of Mewar; the fields of Dewair her Marathon."

—Col. James Tod

9

Pratap: Childhood and Youth (CE 1572-1597)

As narrated in the chapter on Rana Sanga, Mewar descended into a near civil war after the murder of Sanga due to infighting amongst the claimants to the Mewar throne.

This struggle is being mentioned briefly only to underline how critical it is to protect leadership and how difficult it was for Pratap to revive a sunken Mewar from such despair. When civilisations or nations lose a leader of stature, chaos and mayhem follow. Civilisations and nations take years, if not decades, to recover from such losses.

All social order and peaceful existence are so fragile, that one man's presence can save a sinking civilisation, or his absence can lead to complete collapse of the social order.

Such is the nature of human societies.

After Sanga's murder in 1528, Ratan Singh II, his third son became the Maharana and defeated the Sultan of Malwa. Ratan Singh was an able king but was killed in a duel with his maternal uncle, Suraj Mall, in CE 1531.

Suraj Mall was the brother of Sanga's favourite wife Karmawati, who had her own ambition of making one of her son's king of Mewar.

Karmawati got her chance after Ratan Singh's death and her son Vikramaditya ascended the throne. Vikramaditya proved to be a very poor ruler. He indulged in meaningless sport and insulted the brave *samants* constantly. The *samants* left the corridors of Chittor and Bahadur Shah[82] of Gujarat attacked Chittor to annex Mewar.

It is important to expose the lie of a letter and the thread of *rakhi* from Rani Karmawati to Humayun, who was ruling Delhi at the time. According to *Veer Vinod*, it were a few *samants* of Vikramaditya who approached Humayun for help. Humayun even started for Chittor but around Gwalior, he received a letter from Bahadur Shah which read: *"I am on jihad. If you help Vikramaditya, with what face will you stand in front of Allah?"* Humayun aborted his mission and stayed on at Gwalior[83].G.H. Ojha quotes Ferishta endorsing Veer Vinod.

Seeing Bahadur Shah's imminent attack, Karmawati pleaded to the loyal *samants* of Mewar to save Chittor.

She wrote to the *samants*, *"Till now, Chittor has been with the Rajputs, but it appears time has come for it to be lost to Muslims. I leave this fort to you. Keep it or let it go to the enemy. Even if the present king is incompetent, the royal house of Sisodias is yours by traditon. If Chittor falls, it will bring a lot of infamy to you all too[84]."*

The loyal *samants* responded to the call of their besieged queen and under the leadership of Rawat Bagh Singh, Arjun Hada, Rao Satta, Mala Songara, Dodiya Bhan, Bhairav Das Solanki, Jhala Sajja and dozens of such warriors stood guard to defend Chittor against Bahadur Shah. With superior firepower and a disintegrated Hindu leadership, Bahadur managed to defeat the Mewar warriors in CE 1534. 32,000 Rajputs laid their lives defending Chittor and Rani Karmawati committed *jauhar* with 13,000 other women.

Vikramaditya escaped with a few soldiers. Bahadur then

82. Same Bahadur Shah who was sheltered by Sanga at Chittor.
83. Ojha, vol. 1, p. 344.
84. Both *Veer Vinod* and G.H. Ojha quote this letter.

had to fight Humayun at Mandsore in Malwa, where he was defeated. Bahadur went on to ally with the Portuguese against Humayun but was killed by the Portuguese in CE 1537, at the age of thirty-one, and his body thrown into Arabian Sea.

Banbeer Murdering Child Chandan

The words of Bahadur's spiritual teacher Sheikh Jiyu were proven right[85].

Mewar's *samants* recaptured Chittor as Bahadur's forces deserted the fort and Vikramaditya was restored as king.

If we recollect Sanga's youth, he had an elder brother Prithviraj, who had a son Banbeer from his mistress. Banbeer was an ill-mannered person who was exiled by Sanga. Seeing a weak Vikramaditya, Banbeer returned to Chittor and killed Vikramaditya by deceit. Banbeer then went to the quarters of the younger prince, Udai Singh.

The palace where Panna Dhaay sacrificed her son, Chandan

85. Refer to page 116.

Panna Dhaay escaping with the child Udai Singh to Kumbhalgarh

Here we witness the greatest sacrifice imaginable by the foster mother of Udai Singh. Panna Dhaay (foster mother) placed her son Chandan in place of Udai Singh and Banbeer slashed the child into two, thinking him to be Udai Singh.

Panna was a Gurjar lady who used to breast feed little Uday Singh when he was a toddler. This is another example of the social cohesion amongst Hindus of Mewar. The royal ladies used to keep ladies from all jaatis to breast feed the princes as foster mothers.

These ladies were referred to as Dhaay Maa and were respected in the royal houses as good as real mothers of the kings for life. As seen here, Panna lived upto that demand of motherhood.

Panna started weeping, uttering the name of Udai Singh so that Banbeer wouldn't find out the truth. Panna stayed back to ensure the funeral of her son and then took the boy Udai Singh to Kumbhalgarh without letting anyone know the truth. At Kumbhalgarh, she went to Asha Devpura, a Maheshwari businessman whom Sanga had appointed as the keeper of Kumbhalgarh. Asha decided to protect the child Udai Singh and soon all the *samants* of Mewar were beckoned and the truth was revealed to them.

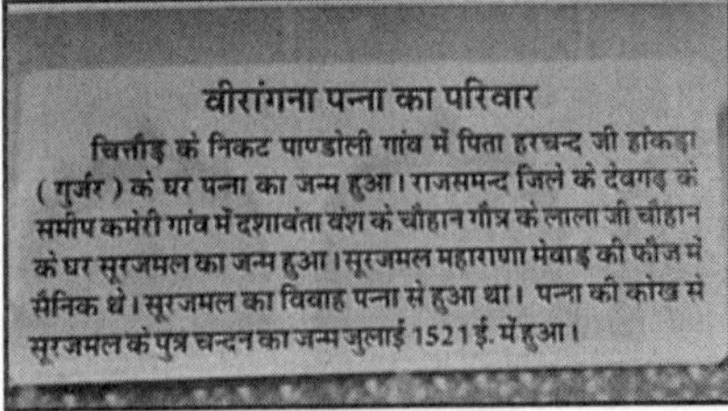

Board at the panorama for Panna Dhaay in Kameri Village

Udai Singh accompanied by his loyal *samants* attacked Banbeer and defeated and killed him in the Battle of Mawli.

The history of Mewar is replete with episodes of extreme sacrifice and loyalty shown by ordinary men and women under extraordinary circumstances. The commitment, courage and sacrifice of Panna Dhaay is etched in the legends of India and is narrated as part of folklore, passed down to every generation. Can we feel the resolve and pain of a mother who sacrificed her own child for the sake of protecting the royal line?

It was through such unimaginable sacrifices that Mewar kept the little lamp of resistance to Islamic invasions burning with the very blood of its citizens serving as the oil in that lamp.

If Udai Singh had been killed by Banbeer that night, there would have been no Maharana Pratap. Without Maharana Pratap, Akbar would have swallowed our entire nation and there would have been no Hinduism left. That's how delicately civilisations are poised in human existence. That is how significant is the ultimate sacrifice of Panna Dhaay in keeping the fire of *dharma* alive in the subcontinent.

Udai Singh became the Maharana of Mewar in CE 1540 and in the same year, on 9th May, from his eldest queen, Jaywanta Bai Songara, was born his first son, Pratap Singh, at Kumbhalgarh.

Our story in the next six chapters will revolve around the life and deeds of Pratap, the greatest king of Hindus in medieval India.

Childhood

Pratap was the eldest son of Udai Singh, the Maharana of Mewar and grandson to the great Maharana Sanga. Mothered by the Songara princess Jaywanta Bai, Pratap was a very well-built and courageous child. Right from his childhood, he was coached by his mother to be true to his Rajput lineage and committed to the land of Mewar. Jaywanta Bai also instructed Pratap to always carry twin swords for himself as a bearer of the royal flag. This was a promise he kept all his life, and this image became uniquely associated with Pratap.

Pratap's father, Udai Singh, was enamoured by Pratap's stepmother, the Bhatiyani queen. Udai Singh had another son, Jagmal from the Bhatiyani queen, on whom the queen doted and groomed to be the heir to Mewar's throne.

Child Pratap at the feet of his mother

It is not clear when and in what moment of weakness Udai Singh yielded to the Bhatiyani queen's wicked design, but when the child Pratap came to Udaipur from his birthplace, Kumbhalgarh, Udai Singh did not accommodate Pratap and his mother in the Chittor palace but in a village called Kunwarpada (कुंवरपदा) or the residence of the prince, at the foothills of Chittor.

'Kunwarpada' at the foothills of the Chittor fort

Only ten armed guards were assigned for the safety of Pratap and his mother, and food was sent from the fort daily to feed the royal prince and his mother in the most humiliating way. No royal prince had ever been treated in Mewar in this manner, but Pratap converted his deprivation into an opportunity. He was large-hearted even as a child and established a tradition of the food *peti* or box that used to come every day from the fort above, by sitting on the ground and eating his meals with the guards. This was something unheard of and it earned Pratap the unflinching loyalty and love of his entire army as the news of this gesture reached everyone. The tradition of sitting on the ground in a line and eating his meals with the army continued as long as Pratap lived. His amazing humility endeared him to ordinary soldiers and enabled him to forge an extremely strong bond with his armed forces[86].

Pratap's deprived childhood also presented an opportunity for the kingdom of Mewar—one that would prove instrumental in his final victory over Mughal imperial forces. This deserves an elaborate explanation.

Mewar has always been inhabited by the mountain-dwelling Bhils. The Bhils lived in the jungles of Mewar, disconnected from royalty and the rest of the subjects in terms of food, customs and language.

Though Bappa Rawal's life was initially saved by Bhils and the tradition of the Rajput-Bhil alliance dates back to the 7th century, the bond cemented by Pratap was unprecedented in its scale and emotion. The influence it had on the wars that Mewar fought with Mughal imperialists in the coming centuries was unlike anything else. Pratap dissolved all boundaries between the royalty and its subjects. Living amongst the Bhils, Pratap integrated Mewar on an unprecedented scale. Here was a prince who ate, drank, slept, moved and lived with his poorest of subjects most nonchalantly. An attitude and behaviour hitherto unheard of in traditional Rajasthan.

As a child, Pratap wandered in the jungles around Chittor, made friends with Bhil children of his age and learned the tricks of hunting and survival in the Aravalli mountains and passes of Mewar.

---

86. *Amarkavyam*, p. 239-40.

The Bhils began referring to the child Pratap as *Keeka*, which means 'little son' in the Bhil lingo. It also means that the womenfolk had a special bond with the child Pratap, else the name Keeka wouldn't have found its roots in the consciousness of Bhil society.

Many historians of Mewar and annals record this amazing occurrence and the deep friendship Pratap maintained with the Bhils. Bhils referred to Pratap as 'Rana Keeka' even after Pratap ascended the throne of Mewar. Pratap, in turn, very affectionately accepted this title from his Bhil subjects.

Very rarely in human history do we find such examples where the royal prince of one of the richest and most powerful kingdoms of the land had such an intimate connection with his masses that all distinction of kinghood and his people was lost, and a unique oneness was achieved at the civilisational plane.

While many critics of medieval Rajasthani civic life blame the caste hierarchy and shed crocodile tears for its sufferers, none glorifies this 1,400-year-old alliance of the princely class with the simplest of Mewar's children, the Bhils. The Mewar insignia (see preface) where the Bhils and Rajputs are seen standing together to protect Mewar, establishes a much more equal relationship among the diverse population of the region, compared to the colonial narrative.

Bhils were also critical to the survival of ordinary citizenry in the hills of Aravallis when the Mewar Maharanas would ask their populations to shift from the plains to the hills to enforce the 'scorched earth policy'. It was the Bhils of Mewar who provided for entire populations for years together. Thus, the contribution of these courageous hill people in saving Hindu *dharma* was as much, if not more than the great Rajputs.

The Bhils taught Pratap the intricate networks of the passes connecting various parts of the Aravallis. They also taught him the art of surviving in the jungle, feeding oneself and saving oneself from wild animals and poisonous plants and animals.

Bhils were inculcated into the Mewar army on Pratap's insistence and were taught military skills. They formed the core team of Pratap for his entire life and stayed loyal to him as well as to his later generations. During the most difficult period of Pratap's life, from the Battle of Haldighati to the Battle of Dewair, it was the Bhils who provided the security cordon around Mewar and never let Mughals come near Pratap for an entire period of eight years.

The glory of Bhils will be highlighted again in the chapters where we discuss the preparation for the Battles of Haldighati and Dewair.

Modern psychology clearly emphasises the importance of childhood experiences in shaping a person. The following events from Pratap's childhood are being described in that light. To sum up his childhood, we may safely deduce that though being the eldest in the royal family of Mewar, Pratap encountered hardships and adversity very early on in life.

Instead of succumbing to the dark alleys of victimhood, he forged his way around them with a deep understanding of human relationships, both within the family and the outer world.

This was an understanding that was the result of his own *sanchit karma* (accumulated deeds), the spartan tutelage of his mother, along with a spiritual streak in his personality. These factors made Pratap look beyond the mundane and focus on his education, war training and love for his family and people. Instead of looking at the world through a gaze of desire, he accepted what life gave him, made the best use of it in his formative years and grew up to be a young man, deeply committed to the honour of his family and *dharma*.

Youth

Pratap grew up to be a fine young man with a tall and heavy build, with beautiful large eyes and a well-kept, thick *Rajputi* moustache adorning his round face. Though there are a lot of unbelievable stories woven around Pratap's physical build but after consulting more than a dozen books, all these turned out to be rumours.

Even Google records Pratap at 7 feet and 5 inches, but no written evidence suggests that to be true. However, one look at his armour kept in the city Palace of Udaipur can safely deduce that Pratap was a very strongly built man with a height between 6 to

7 feet. His twin swords, his spear, his gun and his metal armour easily weighed around 80-100 kgs. To wear such weight and wage war required immense strength and fitness. There is no doubt that Pratap had both.

Child Pratap training with Jaimal Rathore

Pratap was fierce with his sword in training with the ablest swordsmen of Mewar, but the weapon of choice for Pratap was the spear, as was the tradition with most of Mewar's warriors. Pratap's overall weapon training was looked after by Jaimal Rathore and Rawat Krishnadas Choondawat.

The spear was the default weapon of choice for the Mewar army because Mewar's wars were mostly fought in hilly terrains and the throw of the spear, along with its long reach, made spear warfare easy for Mewar's warriors.

This was also the time Pratap was taught by his teachers to never forsake three things—one's horse, one's sword and one's women.

Imbibing these lessons in valour and conduct, Pratap immersed himself in hunting adventures. Hunting was a very crucial event in Mewar, both as a form of ritual as well as training in the use of weapons like spears, swords and daggers.

It was referred to as *teekadaud* (टीकादौड़) and every Mewar prince was supposed to pursue it as a matter of honour as well as a test of valour. Pratap however, simply loved hunting.

It is a strange coincidence that even on the day of his

turbulent coronation, Pratap could not desist from going on a hunting expedition. Tragically, Pratap was also injured in a hunting accident that eventually led to his *moksha* in CE 1597, at the young age of fifty-seven years.

Pratap was also an exceptional wrestler and would indulge in one-to-one duels with his friends.

Very soon, the adulation for Pratap's persona and conduct spread deep and wide to the ordinary masses of Mewar and they saw great hope in their young prince. Pratap was well aware of his father's wish to bypass him and name Jagmal as the heir, but kept aloof from such manoeuvres and focused on governing Mewar, helping his father in day-to-day affairs.

Pratap had a deep sense of family loyalty.

Once, during the monsoon season, the royal family was at the southern banks of the Pichola Lake and Rana Udai Singh was resting at the city palace with his queens when one night, heavy rains flooded the palace. Pratap was on the other side of Pichola. He weathered the rain, manoeuvred boats to reach the palace and rescued his father and the rest of the family[87].

Every evening, Pratap would descend from the palace of Chittor to be with his mother, like any ordinary chieftain serving the crown of Mewar and stayed with her and the locals, mingling freely with them.

Pratap's intellect and indulgence in the affairs of state and his respectful conduct with his Generals and counsellors endeared him to the *samants* (vassals) of Mewar, who watched him closely.

All *samants* and chieftains of Mewar from places like Deogadh, Saloombar, Amet, Bhainsrodgadh, etc., would liaise with Pratap over matters of the state and it was this bond that earned Pratap their lifelong loyalty to him—an occurrence that proved crucial in his ascendance to the throne of Mewar and finally, his successful reign over Mewar.

With the help of these *samants*, Pratap delved into the goal of expanding Mewar's boundaries even though he was just a prince. He defeated Karam Singh Chauhan and annexed Bagad from him. He subjugated the Rathores of Saloombar and won the area of

87. *Amarkavyam*, p. 216.

Chappan. He also annexed Godwar and merged it with Mewar. These victories brought him closer to the hitherto demoralized armed forces of Mewar and they all rejoiced when, after decades of Udai Singh's uninspiring leadership, they had finally found an aggressive prince to lead them.

Another aspect that needs underlining here is Pratap's training in Hindu *dharma* and his understanding of the resistance of his forefathers to Islamic imperialists. Pratap had immense respect for Hindu *sadhus* and Brahmin teachers of Mewar from whom he imbibed deep devotion for the *ishta dev* (personal deity) of the Mewar dynasty, Eklingji, a form of Shiva. Pratap's formal training into Hindu *dharma* was under Acharya Raghavendra. His commitment to Hindu *dharma* and its core values would provide Pratap's lifelong resolve to resist the imposition of Islam on the people of India. Two incidents of Pratap's youth are noteworthy here.

First, while roaming around the jungles of Mewar with his Bhil friends, Pratap encountered *muni* Roopnathji, an ascetic belonging to the Naath *sampradaya* (sect) of Hinduism. Pratap was deeply influenced by him. Roopnathji not only initiated Pratap into the moral and spiritual practices of Sanatana Dharma but also gave lessons in politics, warfare and statecraft.

Pratap with Muni Roopnath

The traditions of the Naaths as a stream of Hindu monks go back to the great Matsyendra Nath (also known as Machchandar Nath) and Guru Gorakh Nath, who were spiritual warriors of the highest degree. It is no coincidence that in recent times,

Mahant Avaidyanathji of Gorakhpur and his disciple *Mahant* Shri Adityanathji (who currently rules Uttar Pradesh as its chief minister) are heirs to the same Nath traditions that have protected and guided Hindu values in the subcontinent for centuries, not only with wisdom and spiritual energy but also guiding the kings militarily when it became difficult to preserve and practise *dharma* in the subcontinent. Mahant Avaidyanath's Guru, Mahant Digvijaynathji, was born a Sisodia Rajput before renouncing this world.

Pratap's bond with Roopnathji continued all through his life and it was *muni* Roopnathji who instructed Pratap to choose Dewair as the final place to take on the Mughals and defeat them permanently.

The second incident of Pratap's youth that left a deep impact on his psyche concerns a hunting incident around Chittor when he entered into an argument with his younger brother, Shakti Singh, over a petty claim to the fruits of hunting on that fateful day.

Shakti Singh, also known as Shakta in Mewar, was very similar in temperament to Pratap for being brave and fearless. When he was all of five-years old, Shakta was sitting with his father when an armourer brought a dagger to demonstrate its edge by the usual proof of splitting thinly spread cotton. The child Shakta asked the Rana, *"Is this dagger not intended to cut bones and flesh?"* Seizing the dagger, the child tried it on his own little hand. As blood gushed onto the carpet, the child showed no signs of pain, fear, or surprise.

Shakti Singh

Pratap and Shakta lived amicably under the watchful eyes of Mewar's teachers and masters of warfare. That fateful day, Pratap lost his composure during that argument over the game and challenged Shakta to end the quarrel by single combat. Shakta responded, *"Do you begin?"*

Standing in front of each other, spears pointed at each other, the fury of Rajput blood was directed at each other. Fate would have struck a deadly blow to the house of Mewar that day in the form of death or injury to either of the princes. At that moment, some wise and loyal soldiers rushed to the fort and brought the head priest of the royal family, Purohit Narayan Paliwal to the scene to drill some sense into the blood-thirsty princes.

The priest tried every conceivable argument to disentangle the brothers, but both were unrelenting. The *purohit* feverishly implored the brothers not to ruin the future of the house. When neither of the two responded to his pleas, Paliwal performed the ultimate act of sacrifice for the sake of the royal house. He took out his dagger and stabbed himself to the utter disbelief of the fighting brothers. The dying priest said to Pratap, *"Should you still choose to fight, the curse of brahmahatya (murder of a Brahmin) will be on you."*

Such was the degree of sacrifice and wisdom of the gurus of Mewar. Paliwal understood that day that the untamed youth of the princes was beyond logic and both were incapable of seeing the consequences of their infatuated aim. The Mewar house would be permanently divided with infighting if either of the princes was injured or killed.

Paliwal made the highest sacrifice in the service of the motherland that day to break the spell of anger and ignorance that had gripped the warring princes. We Hindus owe as much to the teachers of Mewar like Paliwal as we do to Pratap and other Maharanas.

Pratap banished Shakti Singh from Mewar after this incident and Shakti went to the court of Akbar. Throughout his life though, Shakti remained loyal to Pratap and Mewar and kept Mewar informed of Akbar's plans well ahead of time.

While on a campaign with Akbar, near Dholpur in Rajasthan, Shakti Singh learned of Akbar's designs to lay siege to Chittor and forewarned Udai Singh and Pratap, thus saving their lives. It was Shakti again, who saved Pratap during his escape from Haldighati and finally broke ranks with Akbar in CE 1580 to join Pratap formally and fight from Mewar in the decisive battle of Dewair in CE 1583.

Thus, the personality and trajectory of this great Maharana were shaped by the events of his childhood and youth and these hold vital lessons for all of us, even today.

- how to be large-hearted amidst all the glaring unfairness even from family and relatives;
- how to be singularly focussed on one's *kartavya karma* (action ordained by duty) as the prince of a state that was the beacon of freedom and *dharma*;
- how to give one's complete attention and time to prepare oneself as a warrior through *tapa* and *niyama*;
- how to be loyal to one's mother, motherland and people like a true son;
- how to be utterly fearless in pursuit of *dharma*;
- how to be ego-less and free of hollow arrogance of princedom and instead reach out to and mingle with the ordinary folks of one's land;
- how to be loyal to the family and serve them without expecting anything, even praise, in return.
- how to be singularly focussed on your goal and not get distracted by trivialities.

The aforementioned are the lessons one can learn from the Maharana's eventful life.

Men rise and fall like the winter wheat, but if Pratap rules our hearts and minds even today, more than four centuries later, it is because he was an extraordinary human being who fulfilled his *karma* of saving Mewar and Hinduism from annihilation.

If Pratap lives on in the Hindu consciousness today, it is because he embodied the *kshatra dharma*.

Pratap gives us the hope that if a lone king could take on the mightiest ruler of the time, we too can take on and defeat the designs of the 'breaking India' forces.

Pratap will live on as long as there is the last Hindu living on this globe, because the likes of Pratap never die. They etch their place in history in fiery metal. Not because they want to, but because they raised human values to such heights of loyalty, valour and love for their motherland, that history is forced to make way for that greatness.

□

10

The Third *Saka* of Chittor: Akbar, the Carnage & Chittor Scarred (25th February, CE 1568)

When the world breaks free from the spell of pseudo-secularism and appeasement of murderous mafias who have attacked Hindus in the Indian subcontinent for 1,400 relentless years, it is the people of Rajasthan who will stand out in their resolve to fight Islamic imperialism.

Of course, the people were led by magnificent kings like the Sisodias of Mewar, Chauhans of Ajmer and Ranthambore, Songaras of Jalore, Bhatis of Jaisalmer, etc., yet, it was the ordinary people of Rajasthan who silently supported their kings and even rose to the highest level of sacrifice to defend Hindu *dharma*.

Saka is a term used in Rajasthan to describe the time when Hindus were surrounded by Islamic invaders. *Saka* never happened in the pre-Islamic era because the rules of military engagement were humane, civilised and limited to the armed men in conflict. The very idea of harming unarmed citizens, businessmen, priests, artisans, farmers, and above all, women and children, was unthinkable. Being the most prosperous and evolved society on the globe, Bharat had been attacked by invaders for 2,500 years now. Huns, Saks, Kushans, Greeks and even Mongols came up to the Indus to attack us, but never in the pre-Islamic history did we witness the horror of *Saka-jauhar* being performed by Hindu women in Bharatvarsha.

There is not a single recorded incident of women being captured as sex slaves by Hindu armies fighting each other before the 8th century, when Mohammad bin Qasim attacked Raja Dahir of Sindh.

It was Mohammad Qasim who abducted two daughters of Raja Dahir as sex slaves back to his Caliph, Hajjaj bin Yusuf in Arabia. Hindu women were made to serve food and wine to Islamic murderers, without clothes on them, and the mercenaries were free to violate Hindu women of Sindh at will. After Dahir's murder, one queen of Dahir, Rani Bai, fought Qasim from the fort of Ror. When surrounded from all sides, the queen committed *jauhar*. This is perhaps the first act of *jauhar* in written record of history. It also means that the news of sex slavery and necrophilia had reached Rani's ears too.

Slavery was unheard of among Hindus and when the son of Raja Dahir took refuge with Bappa Rawal of Mewar, Bappa immediately realised the true nature of these Islamic marauders from the deserts of Arabia and forged formidable alliances with neighbouring Hindu kingdoms to fight this new evil jointly. Bappa's detailed life and struggles have been presented in this book in relevant chapters.

Hindus the world over owe much to Bappa and his warriors for chasing Arab invaders back to Arabia, recapturing Afghanistan and Sindh from Arabs and installing Hindu vassals in their place. Bappa knew that future invasions by Islamists were going to happen only through Sindh. Therefore, on his way back from Iran, Bappa erected Rajput outposts every hundred kilometres or so to stop further invasions by forewarning the kings of Mewar, Punjab and Sindh.

Bappa's foresight and arrangements kept India safe from Islamic invasions for the next 500 years, before Mohammad Ghori

Muhammad Ghori (1173-1202 CE)

defeated Prithviraj Chauhan through deceit in CE 1192. With all the modern technologies at our disposal, it is still a tall order for mankind today to protect the land and people from murderous invasions. Bappa achieved this feat 1,400 years ago. One can only look back with utter amazement and awe at these great warriors who understood the value of protecting the Hindu way of life from a bunch of mindless, invaders who coveted the property and women of *kuffars* (infidels), all in the name of religion.

The second assault on Hindu life happened when Mahmud of Ghazni attacked Bharat repeatedly around the turn of 10th century. Mahmud was resisted by Jayapala, Anandapala and Trilochanpala of the Shahiya dynasty in today's western Punjab. Later, the Chandellas of central India too resisted Mahmud. In 1026, Mahmud attacked and destroyed the Somnath temple after killing 50,000 Hindu warriors who tried to defend the temple. According to Dr. Ram Gopal Mishra, Mahmud was chased out by the Chalukya king, Bhimadeva I. Dr. Mishra quotes Islamic historian Ghardizi: *"Mahmud returned in haste. For Param Dev, Badshah of Hindus, stood in his path. Mahmud decided to leave in fear, lest his victory was turned into defeat. He left by the way of Mansura to Multan. His soldiers suffered many hardships, partly on account of water and partly on account of the Jats of Sindh. Many soldiers of Islam lost their lives in this way."*[88]

The Jats of Sindh harassed and molested Mahmud's army during his retreat from Somnath. But it became known to the Hindus that these marauders were not content merely with looting Hindu wealth, but were also out to destroy our faith and use every means to impose their religion upon the Hindus.

The third assault that Hindus witnessed after Qasim's treatment of women in Sindh was the way Hindu women, especially, Sanyogita, the beautiful queen of Prithviraj Chauhan was treated by Shahabuddin Ghori's army. She eventually killed herself to save her honour.

Ghori's Muslim armies subjected Hindu women to mass rape

88. Mishra, p. 66

and sex slavery. What moral compass would make human beings behave in this manner is something for psychologists to ponder, but we can only look back, at what our ancestors endured, with utter reverence and sadness in our heart.

The fourth trauma that affected the Hindu psyche was the plunder and rape ordinary Muslim armies resorted to, even without war. The whole idea of the attempted Islamic conquest of the Indian subcontinent was to convert the Hindus to Islam by muscular subjugation.

This rape and murder of the citizenry by Muslims was not a mindless pursuit. It was a design to capitalise on the weakness of the human mind.

Fear paralyses the mind into inaction. For centuries, the Hindus who were converted and kings who surrendered without a fight was a consequence of this fear. The tyranny of slaughter is too obvious to be ignored by all. Thus, they could easily enslave societies that capitulated.

Fear works like a hypnosis. A hypnosis where an individual or society can only think of its survival. A hypnosis which leads to loss of all memory and rationality. Thus, a man is reduced to a subhuman level of intellect. Such a man or society can be enslaved very easily.

If we look at the Islamic expansion in the Middle East, it took them merely some decades to overrun Mesopotamia and Persia of Sassanid Empire to convert them into Iraq and Iran, respectively. Similarly, the Byzantine and Egyptian civilisations were plundered and the inhabitants forcibly converted[89].

The westward advance of Islamists was halted by the courageous Christians, while its eastward spread was halted by Hindus. The repeated waves of Turks, Arabs, Uzbeks, Afghans, Kazakhs and Tatars into India were fiercely resisted by Hindu kings at every inch of their attempted conquest. Frustrated by the solid Hindu resistance and as a part of their theological doctrines, Islamic armies would slaughter even non-combatant Hindus residing in villages.

Rape has been a legitimate tool used by Islamic invaders

89. Mishra, p. 7.

and conquerors to suppress and humiliate the people they had conquered throughout history. Sex slavery has unfortunately found legitimacy in Islamic history with women being categorised as war booty. This practice, unfortunately, is still advocated by certain extremist elements within Islam. For the Hindus, Buddhists and Jains of the subcontinent, this was something unheard of and hence, as a society, they had to evolve a response to this gory practice.

Another evil practice during Islamic invasions was necrophilia[90].

Hindus of the subcontinent were horrified to witness the murderous invaders indulging in intercourse with and dishonouring the dead bodies of Hindu women and children.

The only way to break the hypnosis of this fear, or '*dahshat*' was to invoke a higher realm of intelligence. That realm was the will to sacrifice oneself at the altar of freedom. A person or society that is ready to die to protect its freedom, becomes free of fear. The consciousness of such people transcends the physical realm to a higher plane of existence. This was the state of being of the men and women who committed Saka-Jauhar. This was the spiritual premise of Saka-Jauhar.

From the 7th to the 17th century, for one thousand years, the lands of Rajasthan continuously faced the onslaught of Islamic invaders and kept the flag of Hinduism and freedom flying high. The kings and people of Rajasthan had to evolve a defensive technique that could not only save their honour but also send a message to fellow Hindus that even in death, there was no chance for these barbarians to defeat us.

It is through the deepest spiritual insight of the Hindus of Rajasthan that the unique practice of *saka-jauhar* was devised in response to the incessant Islamic invasions.

Saka is the name given to the practice by Hindu warriors to open the gates of the citadels and forts after tying saffron bands to their foreheads and die fighting the enemy, till the last man had fallen.

---

90. https://www.businessinsider.com/egypt-necrophilia-farewell-intercourse-2012-4?amp.

Jauhar was the practice of Hindu women and young children immolating themselves willingly so that the enemies could not defile their dead bodies. Ashes and bones were all that the enemy could lay hands on.

Some writers have mischievously equated *jauhar* with *sati*. It demonstrates a distinct motive to malign the supreme sacrifice made by the Hindus in the face of an imminent defeat by Islamists. The practice and concept of *sati* needs its own historical and cultural exploration in another book perhaps. It is not only ignorance to equate *jauhar* and *sati*, but the fact that that *saka* is not mentioned along with *Jauhar* also demonstrates a distinct motive to undermine the supreme sacrifice of the Hindus in the face of imminent slavery by Islamists. *Saka* and *Jauhar* mentioned together implies that the whole family chose death over dishonour.

Many friends have raised questions on the reason for choosing such a painful death when there are easier ways to kill oneself, like consuming poison and/or stabbing oneself. There are two reasons for choosing fire as the weapon of dissolution of the human body by our glorious mothers of yore.

First, *jauhar* was a message of the resolve of Hindus to fight Islam and a message that we will continue fighting it even when our physical body is dissolved.

We can only imagine the mushrooming smoke clouds smelling of *ghee* and Sandal rising from the forts of Rajasthan and being seen by the citizens of the land for miles on end. We can only imagine the impact on ordinary citizens of the knowledge of this supreme sacrifice by their queens and warriors for *dharma*.

We can only imagine the resolve of the ordinary people witnessing the rising embers of fire from the forts of Rajasthan, signalling the ultimate sacrifice made by the womenfolk and families of the determined warriors of Rajasthan.

We can only imagine the mental shock on hearing the cries and shrieks of the women immolating themselves to save their honour, on the minds and psyche of the people below witnessing it.

We can only imagine the effect of the smell of *ghee* and sandal mixed with smoke which the sad winds of Rajasthan would scatter for miles around the site of *jauhar*, on the residents of the state which endured the barbarity of Islamic marauders. Nowhere in the world can we find such an extreme act of self-sacrifice when faced with certain death and humiliation by the enemy as in *jauhar* and *saka*.

It was an ultimate act of defiance by an extremely proud people who rendered any victory of Islamic invaders hollow and turned their own defeat into an act that would reverberate across the consciousness of the entire nation, inspiring every Hindu never to yield to aggressors, whatever be the cost.

The second reason has already been covered under necrophilia. Hindu women refused to give even their dead bodies to the barbarians. Can we imagine scenes of dead Hindu queens being raped on the streets of Rajasthan? Our forefathers were fully aware of the devastating effect it would have on the psyche of ordinary citizens. *Jauhar* denied the Islamic rapists any possibility to indulge in this naked dance of medieval barbarism.

Although Rajasthan witnessed more than a dozen *saka-jauhars* in the thousand-year opposition to Islamic invaders, the cruelest and most graphic was the third *saka-jauhar* of Chittor on 25th February 1568, when Akbar besieged the fort.

By the sheer scale of the slaughter of Hindus by Mughals and because we have a lot of historic records available from both Hindu as well as Islamic authors, we shall talk about the third *saka-jauhar* of Chittorgadh in detail and try to recreate the sequence of events leading to that ill-fated day for Hindus of Chittorgadh.

It was the third *saka-jauhar* of Chittor that changed the course of Mewar's history. Rajasthan and the people of this great nation saw the real face of Islamic barbarism and its capacity to slaughter fellow human beings in the name of religion.

The third *saka* also had an everlasting impact on the psyche of Pratap, who vowed to avenge the murder of innocent Hindus at the hands of mindless murderers. It is estimated that Pratap lost more than 500 close and distant relatives in the slaughter of the third *saka*.

Let us briefly talk about the build-up to the siege of Chittor by Akbar, as well as the other events leading to the third *saka-jauhar* of Chittor. As has been narrated in the chapter on Pratap's youth,

Pratap's brother Shakti Singh was exiled from Mewar for being overly ambitious and temperamental.

Shakti Singh joined Akbar's court, but his heart was always with Mewar. If we look at his life and its events, we can even conjecture that Shakti Singh was actually a spy planted by Pratap to keep Mewar forewarned of Akbar's designs. There are enough pieces of evidence to connect the dots of this proposition as discussed elsewhere in this book.

In 1567, accompanying Akbar on one of his campaigns around central India at Dhaulpur, Akbar mockingly looked at Shakti Singh and said, "All Hindu kings have surrendered to me, except Udai Singh of Mewar. I plan to attack him now. Will you help me in doing that?" Shakti Singh understood that Akbar planned to lay siege to Chittor. One night, Shakti left for Chittor along with his trusted aides. He approached his father Udai Singh and informed him of the imminent attack by Akbar and his 80,000 troops.

Jaimal Rathore and Patta Choondawat

The war council of Mewar huddled and discussed the threat. *Samants* of Mewar knew that in the battles with Gujarat's Bahadur Shah, the army and resources of Mewar had depleted significantly. Chittor had barely regained from Bahadur's forays.

Akbar was a formidable foe, but half his troops were Hindu Rajputs led by Bhagwan Das, hence no significant harm could come to Chittor.

It was decided that Maharana Udai Singh, along with Pratap, would leave Chittor for the hills around southern Mewar, while 8,000 troops would be left to protect the 40,000 residents of the fort of Chittor under the leadership of Jaimal Rathore and Patta Choondawat. Jaimal Rathore was sixty-one years old at that time.

Chittor was fortified and reinforced by the Mewar army and its people. On 15th October 1567, Akbar camped at Nagri village, 6 miles from Chittor and laid siege on this most important centre of Hindu resistance to Islamic invaders. The two main warriors representing the Rajputs were Jaimal Rathore and Patta Choondawat; the others who were holding fort inside were Saidas Rawat, Ballu Solanki, Thakur Saanda, Shaliwahan Tanwar and Isardas Chauhan.

Akbar used his cannons to blast the walls of Chittor, but this ancient vanguard of Hinduism stood unyielding. Finding the walls of the Chittor fort impregnable to Mughal firepower, Akbar ordered two underground tunnels leading to the walls of the fort to be blown up with explosives.

Mughals had little experience of fort warfare and how to conduct a successful siege. It was the two Hindu advisors of Akbar, Bhagwan Das of Amer and Todar Mal, who planned the siege for Akbar.

The crucial idea for breaching the walls of the fort was to dig trenches to reach up to the walls by lines of labourers, called *sabat*.

One silver coin was paid to the local labourers for a bucket filled with sand. The labourers who dug the tunnels were killed by the Rajputs from within the fort with arrows and gunshots. Almost 200 Mughal soldiers and labourers were killed by the Mewar army every day by bullets and arrows[91]. The Mughals were ready to pay that price for Chittor. Besides, the bodies of dead soldiers and labourers were used to build walls around *sabats*, under the cover of which the Mughals would keep digging.

After three months, the warriors inside the fort living on frugal resources, decided to raise the white flag and send a peace overture to Akbar. So, Thakur Saanda of Dodiya and Isardas Chauhan were deputed to descend from the fort and talk to Akbar. Thakur Saanda spoke thus to Akbar, *"We are ready to give you gifts and acknowledge your greatness in lieu of lifting the siege and ending this conflict."*

Akbar replied, *"I am a king and I will receive gifts only from a king. Udai Singh has to come and surrender, else there will be no end to the siege. You are a brave and loyal servant of your master; ask anything of me except lifting the siege."*

Saanda replied, *"Mewar's Maharana will never bow to you, O*

91. Abul Fazl.

Akbar. If war is inevitable, my only demand is that the corpses of Hindu warriors be cremated in Hindu tradition."

Akbar accepted this glorious demand of the Rajput with appreciation and respect. Akbar was so impressed with Isardas Chauhan's loyalty and valour that he even offered him to defect to his side. Isardas of course declined politely.

When departing, Bhagwan Das, the king of Jaipur serving Akbar, confronted Isardas Chauhan, saying, *"You didn't do mujra (salutations) to the emperor."*

Isardas Chauhan replied, *"I will do my mujra to him on the battlefield, for he is not my emperor."*

It should be noted here that all hopes of Mewar warriors of getting even diplomatic help from Bhagwand Das or Todar Mal were quashed on witnessing the slavish conduct of these Hindu kings in front of Akbar.

A painting showing the explosion during Chittor siege

Akbar blasted the northern walls of the fort with 4,800 kilograms[92] of explosives but the warriors inside repulsed the attack by the Mughals and repaired the wall overnight.

The southern wall was similarly blasted on 17th December 1567, but it ended only in killing some of the best Mughal soldiers when a fuse went off accidentally. Mughal historian, Al Badayuni writes in his *Muntakhab-ul-Tawarikh*: *"The fuse blew the tower and both friends and foes were killed. The soldiers of Islam (Muslims) were buried under stones, some weighing 4,000 kilograms and the stone-hearted infidels (Hindus)*

92. *Veer Vinod*, vol .2, p. 78.

flew about like 'moths in that flood of fire'. This stream flowed to paradise and hell. (Muslims going to paradise and Hindus to hell) Though the blood of Guebre and an unbeliever—both flowed at one place and was a happy day for vultures and crows."

Akbar began a frontal attack on the fort with cannons damaging the walls of the fort here and there, but the Mughals still couldn't breach the walls of the impregnable fort of Chittor. They used to take the cover of the broken stones and fire with guns towards the parapets of the fort.

One fateful day, Akbar aimed his gun called Sangram at a very active figure inside the fort and shot at him. It was Jaimal Rathore whose hip bone got broken by the bullet. This was a decisive blow to the troops inside the fort and lowered the morale of Mewar's army considerably.

The spot where Jaimal Rathore was shot in his hip

Nizam-ud-din Bakshi, an Islamic chronicler, writes in *Tabaqat-e-Akbari*: *"The garrison was disheartened by the fall of their leader and each man hurried to his home. They collected their wives and children. The property and effects were assembled in a place and burnt. This proceeding, in the language of infidels of Hind, is called jauhar."*

The Jauhar sites of various communities around Bhim Taal in Chittor fort

Jaimal called the chiefs and counselled that the resources of the Mewar army were limited and with rations running out, it was time to open the gates and slaughter as many Mughals as one could and then ascend to their *devas*.

The women were, of course, asked to commit *jauhar*, as has been discussed at the beginning of this chapter, where huge wooden pyres would be lit and women and children less than 10 years of age would give themselves up to the fire.

Bhim Taal , which witnessed maximum Jauhar pyres

Abul Fazl describes *jauhar* in these words, *"Akbar expressed his happiness at shooting down Jaimal Rathore, to Shuja't Khan and Raja Bhagwan Das. An hour had passed when Jabbar Quli reported that the enemy had all but disappeared. Just at that time, fire broke out in several places in the fort. Raja Bhagwan Das represented that this was the fire of jauhar".*

"A pile is made of sandalwood, aloes, etc., as large as possible, and firewood and oil is added to this. Then they leave hard-hearted confidants in charge of their women. As soon as it is certain that there has been a defeat and that the men have been killed, these stubborn ones reduce the innocent women to ashes."

The marks of the palms of the Hindu women who committed Jauhar

Old painting showing Jauhar

The confidants who used to support the Rajput women were Charans. Charans kept telling stories of valour to the women and children and finally on getting the signal, would light the pyre with their hands and watch their queens and children being consumed alive by fire. These great Charans had to witness and carry out the most gruesome act imaginable to the very queens whom they had taught and groomed like their own daughters. These Charans would then tie saffron scarfs on their heads and go to battle to kill and die alongside their friends and masters.

All for the sake of freedom and *dharma*.

Contrast this with the moral compass of a brain-dead *jihadi* like Abul Fazl, who calls Rajputs stone-hearted and Charans as 'stubborn ones'.

Following is the list of some of the royal ladies who committed *jauhar* that fateful day:

1. Rani Sajjan Bai Songara, mother of Patta
2. Rani Jiwa Bai Solanki - Patta's wife who died fighting.
3. Rani Bhagwati Devi Chauhan - daughter of Isardas Chauhan
4. Rani Madalsa Bai Kachchwahi, daughter of Sahasmall
5. Rani Padmavati Bai Jhala
6. Rani Ratan Bai Rathore
7. Rani Balesa Bai Chauhan
8. Rani Bagdi Bai Chauhan, daughter of Dungar Singh Parmar
9. Rani Asha Bai Parmar
10. Two sons and five daughters of Patta Choondawat.

Wouldn't earth have been torn that day?
Wouldn't the skies have melted that day?
Wouldn't the throne of *Indra* have been shaken that day?
Wouldn't the Gods have wept witnessing so much pain?
Wouldn't *Brahma* have wondered on the purpose of existence?
Wouldn't Budhha have been shaken that day?
Wouldn't Krishna's equanimity be rudely ruffled that day?
Wouldn't Kali's hands have tremored that day?
Wouldn't Shiva's trance have been shattered that day?

For most of us, death tiptoes her ways around us and engulfs us unnoticed.

The glorious Hindus of Mewar turned the pages of their destiny to choose the time and mode of the evaporation of their bodies by fire and steel.

What kind of resolve and fortitude would make thousands of Hindus undergo such an ordeal is beyond the writer's capacity to imagine and describe.

The first fires to rise to the skies were from the palaces of Jaimal Rathore and Patta Choondawat. Soon, the entire fort was lit with funeral pyres.

A royal site for Jauhar pyre

The Haveli of Jaimal Rathore

Seeing the smoke and embers rise into the sky, when Mughals could not make sense of the events, the king of Amer, Bhagwan Das, fighting for Akbar, warned the Mughal army that the final attack by Mewar's warriors was imminent.

Thus, all tender bonds of love and concern for the safety of the family were consigned to fire and the Mewar warriors gave each other the last *beera* (betel leaf) and put on saffron robes to ride to *veergati* (the warrior's death).

The next morning, the gates of Chittor were opened.

It was not a war for survival or any outcome. It was a war for honour. It was about repaying the debt of their mothers whom they had put to fire with their own hands. It was about taking down as many foreigners *yawanas* as one could, in this last act of life.

Hails of 'Har, Har Mahadev' and 'Jai Eklingji' the clash of cymbals, the thumping of terrible war drums, along with shrieks and screams of men hungry for revenge, reverberated the skies.

Abul Fazl writes: *"No one has ever seen such a battle, nor had ever heard of such from experienced ones. What shall I say of this battle and engagement! I cannot even describe one item out of a hundred thousand."*

The Samadhi of Kalla Rathore at the place where he fell

The Samadhi of Jaimal Rathore in Chittor fort where he fell

Jaimal couldn't walk, hence, his brother Kalla Rathore, made him sit on his shoulder so that Jaimal could fulfil his last wish of slaughtering as many Mughals as he could.

The final act of Jaimal and Kalla Rathore

Kalla is reported to have said to his brother, *"Sit on my shoulders brother and quench the thirst of your sword with the blood of mlechchhas."*

Both were martyred after killing dozens of Mughal soldiers between Hanuman Gate and Bhairav Gate of the fort. Akbar personally beheaded Jaimal, after Jaimal had already died of a bullet wound, as documented by the Mughal historian Abul Fazal.

Dodiya Saanda descended with his horsemen and died fighting the Mughals on the banks of Gambhiri river.

The Eastern route out of Chittor where Dodiya Sanda descended with his cavalry

By noon, Akbar pushed his elephants into attacking the Mewar army. About 300 war-elephants were unleashed. The main elephants used were Madhukar, Jangiya, Sabdiliya and Kadira. The Rajputs too, took the elephants head on. Isardas Chauhan climbed up an elephant named Madhukar and asked for the name of the *mahout*. Chauhan then sliced the trunk of the elephant saying to the *mahout, "Give my mujra (salutations) to the appreciator of merit, Akbar."*

Thus, Isardas kept his promise he made to Bhagwan Das in the meeting held for peace at the foothills of Chittor.

Isardas Chauhan was crushed by Madhukar before the animal fell and died. The number of trunks of Mughal elephants cut off by Rajputs was so great that Abul Fazl writes thus: *"Snakes were raining from the skies."*

This was a sight which made even Akbar wonder at the fighting capacity of Mewar's men. Another elephant, Jangiya, killed a total of 45 men before dying of bleeding. After three hours of this bloodbath, Akbar entered the fort, surrounded by his elephant army. Patta Choondawat was to deliver the final onslaught on Mughal forces once Chittor was breached. Patta was wounded by an elephant while defending the temple of Govind Shyam, and was brought to Akbar, carried by the elephant in his trunk. Akbar beheaded the wounded Patta at the Ram Gate of Chittor fort.

The Samadhi of Patta Choondawat. Akbar beheaded Patta here

Mughal historians themselves write about the valour and fearless assault by the Mewar warriors on the Mughal army: *"When one Rajput was beckoned, ten would rush to help him. They attacked our elephants like bees. When one would fall, the other would start stabbing the elephant. And they were fair warriors. Every single fighter of Mewar fought one on one with Mughals and kept dying[93]."*

One young man ran towards Akbar himself and challenged him. Akbar fought him in single combat and refused all help. After a long duel, the wounded young man was overpowered by the stocky Akbar and was beheaded. Akbar kept on asking his name, but the boy did not respond and continued attacking him. Despite all efforts, Akbar could not find out the name of the warrior who fought him so courageously.

After slaying 8,000 warriors, Akbar had to face the resistance from 30,000 residents at the fort. There were artisans, labourers, mahouts, horse keepers, barbers, blacksmiths, all of whom picked up swords, fought the Mughal army and were brutally killed by Akbar's henchmen.

British historian James Tod writes: *"Akbar measured his success by the quantity of cordons (janeu or sacred thread) taken from the necks of the slain Hindus."*

Seventy-four-and-a-half *muns* is the amount recorded. A *mun* is 40 kilograms and thus 2,980 kilograms was the weight of the threads of *janeus* on the Hindus killed on that dreary day. Seven-and-a-half bundles of this sacred thread were carried to Agra to demonstrate that the Hindu hegemony over Mewar had been finally broken.

To eternalise the memory of this disaster, the numeral '74 ½' is accursed till date in Mewar.

Marked on the banker's letter in Rajasthan, it is the strongest of seals. For the sin of the slaughter of Chittor, it is thereby invoked on all who violate a letter under the safeguard of this mysterious number. So long as '74 ½' shall remain recorded, some good will result from the calamity of *saka-jauhar*, and may survive when the event that caused it, is buried in oblivion.

---

93. Badayuni.

Even today, if a letter is marked with the digits '74½' in Mewar, no unauthorised person can open that letter lest that person suffers the sin of the slaughter at Chittor[94].

On the afternoon of 25th February, 1568, after a siege that lasted four months, Akbar seized the fort of Chittor and raised the Mughal flag over it.

This day is known as one of the darkest days of Hindu resistance to Islamic invaders in our history, when approximately 10,000 women and toddlers committed *jauhar* while 20,000 unarmed civilians and 8,000 warriors were killed by Akbar mercilessly.

Eminent historian K.S. Lal writes about the massacre of Hindus on that fateful day: *"Akbar entered the citadel in a mood of ruthlessness."*

Taimur Lung, the Turk-Mongol invader-murderer, unsheathed his sword on 17th December of CE 1398 and asked his army to slaughter Hindus of Delhi who had been fighting him. One lakh Hindus were slaughtered in a day.

Taimur Lung (1336-1405 CE)

Akbar too unsheathed his sword and ordered a general massacre of non-combatant civilians till he was to sheath the sword. The slaughter continued for nine-and-half hours with unimaginable brutality.

Innocent Hindu men, women, and children were put to the sword, lance, or hatchet to the accompaniment of shouts in praise of Allah. Even babies were not spared. Many were roasted alive in the name of vengeance; many were crushed to pulp under the feet of war elephants. Abul

94. Tod, vol. 1, p. 263.

Fazl estimates that over 40,000 Hindus *"wallowed in the dust in repentance of the crimes against the imperial army."*

Akbar kept brandishing his diamond-studded sword in exultation and urged his Generals to ensure that no trace of the tribe that dared to defy him be left behind. He wanted even the birds of Chittor to be slaughtered for the sin of having breathed the same air as the one that gave life to the defenders of the citadel[95].

Let it be known to the world that Bhagwan Das, Todar Mal and the Hindu soldiers of Amer, stood petrified on witnessing this slaughter and pillage of Hindu temples right in front of their eyes, not knowing how to halt this butchery. Todar Mal approached Akbar, who had gone into a trance standing on the ramparts of Chittor, to deploy skilful phrases to soften the Mughal, but in vain.

Ruins of a Hindu temple destroyed in Chittor

Akbar was standing with his eyes closed as if in communion with some occult source and said: *"I am in no mood to listen to the sound of good words. My ears are only attuned to enjoy the clang of the sword. Leave me alone. I am in communion with Amir."*

"Send me a good reciter. Ask him to read from chapters 7–12 of

95. K.S. Lal quoted in http://mariam-uz-zamani.blogspot.com/2015/07/mughal-rajput-war-jauhar-saka-massacre-at-3rd-siege-of-chittor-pt6.html.

Shahnama. The story of kingly wisdom stored in those pages cannot be surpassed for its depth and beauty. Blood, not nectar, holds the key to the success of a sovereign. Give me war. Peace is of no avail to me."

Having said this, Akbar fell back into his trance and only occasionally opened his eyes or uttered something unintelligible with a smirk on his face. For nine hours he stood like this, while the helpless Hindus kept dying at the swords of the murderers.

In an interesting turn, about few dozen musketeers of Mewar army mingled with the 1,000 odd artisans of Mewar and escaped the war unhurt. The Gwalior prince, Shaliwahan Tanwar, too escaped by concealing his true identity. This brave son of Gwalior was not allowed to do *saka* by Jaimal because he was a guest of Mewar. Shaliwahan was the only Hindu warrior of some consequence to have escaped alive from this slaughter. Shaliwahan was to give vital clues to Pratap about the army of Akbar and was finally to lay down his life defending Mewar in the Battle of Haldighati.

This was the darkest day in the history of Mewar when so many of its sons were slain defending it; a day that was to have repercussions on every future conflict of Mewar with Mughals; a day which can never be forgotten for the sheer bravery of the sons of Mewar paralleled with the barbarism of its enemy.

But this day is also a glorious reminder that Mewar's forefathers chose death over surrender, that Hindu *dharma* was dearer to them than to convert to an alien faith, that they stayed loyal to their ancestors even when brutal death stared them in the face.

What was that *tattva* (element) that made the women and children of Chittor enter funeral pyres willingly?

What was the reason that starting with the *jauhar* of Maharani Padmini, Hindus continued this act of supreme sacrifice for centuries at regular intervals, but never yielded their freedom and *dharma*?

What kind of steely resolve would a man possess to allow his wife and little children to enter funeral pyres rather than forsake their *dharma*?

What would a man be possessed with, to throw himself in

front of a mighty, enraged elephant!!

What was the hope that drove the hopelessly outnumbered Hindus to die fighting than to convert to Islam?

What was the spiritual quotient of these amazing people who rose to face death with such grace, only because they were sure that their Maharana was safe somewhere and would continue fighting the Turkish murderers?

If we can muster up even a fraction of that courage, hope, and fortitude, we may be able to withstand and overcome the conflicts we are caught up in, even today.

If we can keep the memory of '74 ½' alive in our civic life, in our families and spiritual discourse, that day of the greatest sacrifice of Hindus will go down in history as a glorious testimony of a people who stared death in the eyes and didn't blink.

The real question that should haunt Hindus and the academicians of this nation is whether an imperialist foreign murderer, who ravaged a docile population needlessly on this scale, should be taught in our schools as Akbar the Great? Should Bollywood be making movies on a man so evil that he ordered his troops to behead and burn 40,000 innocent civilians and children only on the suspicion that they had helped the Mewar army? Hindu Samaj should ask itself whether to remember this evil man with fondness or with utter contempt as a devourer of our amazing ancestors?

These are the questions we need to ask ourselves as Hindus, because if we continue eulogising Akbar as a great king, we will be mocking the memory of the great sons and daughters of Mewar.

The past is never dead. It is not even past.

If the flames of *jauhar* reverberate through our beings today, the past is the present.

If the clash of metal and the insurmountable courage of our glorious ancestors can be heard even today from the warring citadel of Chittor, the past is the present.

If the resolve of Hindus to not allow the *mlechchhas* touch their women and gods as long as they are alive, can touch our beings, the past is the present.

As long as the wails and shrieks of the women and children burning alive in fire haunt our beings, the past is the present.

The Mughals were vanquished and a spent force within three generations of Akbar, as natural justice would have it.

But the Hindus who stood firm against the marauding armies and often fought with nothing but their bare hands and raw guts, still live on.

The people who gave their families to the purity of fire and themselves to the purity of swords, live on in our memories even today—the people because of whom we are Hindus today, as the heirs of the oldest *dharma* thriving on this globe.

As long as mother earth is rotating on her axis, the immortal sacrifice of *Saka-Jauhar* will be alive in the heart of Hindus.

As long as sun sprinkles its warmth of life on earth, those immortals will be alive in our hearts.

As long as the *Punyas* of this earth don't get depleted such that Hindu Dharma itself ceases to exist, those immortals will stay alive in our hearts.

Dharma is the *Tatva,* that bears us. On that fateful day of 25th February, 1568, 40,000 Hindus of Chittor bore Dharma on their bare chests.

What remains to be seen is whether Hindus have the strength, courage and fidelity in us to bear our Dharma and do justice to the memory of those immortals.

That bearance alone will be true homage to our glorious forefathers and foremothers.

□

11

Maharana Pratap Singh: Ascendance to the Throne and Fortification of Mewar

Rana Udai Singh died at the age of fifty, at Gogunda, four years after the loss of Chittor. He left behind twenty-five sons, all of royal blood and thus, laid a fertile ground for infighting in the state of Mewar.

Udai Singh's last act could have actually triggered this civil war when he nominated Jagmal, the son of Dheer Bai and the Bhati queen, as the heir of Mewar. It is to the immense credit of the democratic traditions of Mewar and the foresight of the *samants* (vassals) who immediately gathered to discuss this grave injustice committed by Udai Singh.

Maharana Udai Singh (1540-1572 CE)

The following is the account of how the events unfolded since Udai Singh's death to Pratap's ascendance.

In Mewar, there is no interregnum—the last rites of the departed king and the *rajyabhishek* (coronation) of the new king are done simultaneously at the same priest's house; hence, Pratap was to be crowned the king of Mewar at Gogunda itself. While his brothers and other nobles attended the funeral of the departed Rana, Jagmal was coronated as the king in a separate ceremony

Pratap's maternal grandfather, the Songara king and Jalore Rao, both confronted Kistna the 'great ancient' of Mewar and the leader of Choondawats and asked him to explain how he agreed to sanction the injustice of Jagmal's ascension!

"When a sick man has reached the last extreme and asks for milk, why refuse it?" replied Kistna, adding, *"But Songara's nephew is my choice and I stand by Pratap."*

The nobles gathered and heated and concerned discussions ensued amongst them.

Akshay Raj Songara is recorded to have said to Rawat Krishnadas of Saloombar and Rawat Sanga of Devgadh that if Jagmal was to be the king, it had to happen with their consent. *"On one hand, we have a formidable enemy like Akbar. Chittor is gone. Mewar is becoming barren. If the royal house sinks into infighting, then Mewar is sure to be ruined and enslaved,"* mused the *samants.*

Both the nobles consented, with Songara asking for which fault should the eldest son Pratap, worthy and brave, be rejected?

Pratap did not want a bloodbath in the family and was reconciled to his fate. He was saddling his horse Chetak to ride away to his solitude in some corner of Sindh, when the *samants* approached him and informed him of their decision to name him the king of Mewar.

Pratap was reluctant to dishonour his father's wish, but he saw the doom of Mewar if Jagmal was to remain the king.

With a heavy heart, Pratap consented.

Rawat Kistna and Akshay Raj along with Ram Shah Tanwar of Gwalior took the arms of Jagmal and with minimal force, removed him from the throne.

Kistna remarked, *"You have made a mistake Maharaj; that place belongs to your brother."*

Then, girding Pratap with a sword, thrice touching the ground, Kistna hailed him the next king of Mewar.

Jagmal being forced down by the samants of Mewar

Is there any way Hindus can repay the debt of these unknown *samants* of Mewar? These greats, who did the unthinkable at that time to defy the royal decree for the sake of the motherland!

Had these brave and intelligent *samants* of Mewar been gripped with weakness or indifference that fateful day, we would have lost Pratap forever. Losing Pratap meant only one thing—slavery of Hindus.

These divine souls saved Hinduism and our great nation by their foresight and courage that day.

Pratap's strange ascendance to the throne also proves the deep democratic principles that have governed Hindu society for millennia. Although elsewhere in Bharat, the king is supposed to be a representative of Bhagwan Vishnu, but in Mewar, a Maharana is merely the custodian of the kingdom of Bhagwan Shiva. And thus, he has no scope of deviating from the path of *dharma*, even if he is the king.

Not yielding to cheap sentimentality or hollow loyalty to the throne, the *samants* of Mewar stood firm against a myopic decision of their Maharana and thus saved *dharma* and nation from total destruction.

The place of Pratap's coronation at Gogunda

The second coronation of Pratap, with all the ceremonies was done a few days later at Kumbhalgarh. Maharana Pratap Singh became the ruler of Mewar at the age of thirty-two, in the midst of the gravest existential crisis faced by the Sisodia clan and the people of Mewar.

Pratap's ascendance to the throne is a strange mix of human weakness and strength in the most trying times. Udai Singh's traumatic childhood and precarious journey to kingship had made him a weak, insecure and indecisive person who perpetually dwelt on his victimhood and yielded to sycophants, thus leading to poor judgements in his life. Pratap, on the other hand, turned similar insults and the trauma of his childhood into his strengths and overcame all insecurities to rise as a towering figure in Mewar and a worthy leader of the great clan of the Sisodias.

Pratap's turbulent life began with his childhood itself, but because of his iron will and a deeper understanding premised on spiritual guidance by his teachers, he did not sway from his goal of serving his motherland to his utmost capacity.

To quote Col. Tod: *"Pratap was often heard to exclaim, "Had Dajirajsa (Udai Singh) never been, or none intervened between him and Rana Sanga, no Turk could have ever given laws to Rajasthan[96]."*

Tod writes, stressing the rise of Sanga:

"Hindu society had assumed a new form in the century preceding. The wrecks of dominion from Ganga and Jamuna had been silently growing into importance. Amer and Marwar had gained such power that the latter single-handedly coped with the mighty imperialist Sher Shah[97].

A prince of commanding genius alone wanted to snatch the sceptre of dominion from the Islamist. They found in Sanga such

96. Tod, vol. 1, p. 266.
97. Battle of Giri-Sumel: Sher Shah Suri attacked Maldeo Rathore of Marwar in 1543 with 80,000 troops. Maldeo responded with 50,000 and forced Sher Shah to fortify his camps at every step. Facing shortage of Water and food, Sher Shah wrote a forged letter indicating that trusted lieutenants of Maldeo were assisting him. The copies of the letter were strategcally made to reach Maldeo. The trick worked and suspicious Maldeo left the battle-field with majority of his troops on 4th Jan.1544 CE. Two Generals of Maldeo, Jaita and Koompa Rathore, decided to fight Sher Shah with their residual 12,000 troops. Thousands of Afghans were killed before they overpowered the small force of Rajputs and martyred Jaita and Koompa. The Rajput army came so close to victory that Sher Shah remarked, *"I almost lost Hindustan for a handful of millets."*

a leader, who possessed every quality that extorts spontaneous obedience and the superiority of whose birth, as well as dignity, were admitted without cavil by Hindus.

These states had powerful motives to obey such a leader in the absence of whom their ancient patrimony was lost, and such they would have found in Sanga's grandson, Pratap, had Udai Singh not existed or had a less gifted sovereign than Akbar been his contemporary."

Fate had presented Pratap with the most difficult predicament any Hindu king could face at his time. The interim between Pratap and Sanga was marked by massive infighting in the Mewar household with weak and ineffective kings, like Ratan Singh II, Vikramaditya, the usurper Banbeer and Udai Singh ruling Mewar in quick successions, causing the economic and military decay of Mewar.

Pratap had the task of not only unifying his own clan and *samants,* but take on one of the mightiest invaders of that time—Akbar. That Pratap achieved both these objectives successfully demonstrates the foresight, large heartedness and vision of Pratap as a true heir of the glorious Mewar.

After his humiliation, Jagmal left Mewar for Delhi and prostrated to the arch enemy of the house, Akbar, proving the decision of Mewar's *samants* to be right. Jagmal was a petty prince, who aspired for a position of power he did not deserve in the first place.

Hindus will be forever indebted to the foresight of Mewar's chieftains, who saw this and defied the wish of their king to replace him with Pratap.

Jagmal was granted the *jagir* of Jahajpur in Bhilwara by Akbar. He was married to the daughter of Sirohi's king, Man Singh, who died without an heir in 1571. Jagmal approached Akbar to help him annex Sirohi from Surtan, the royal nominee of Sirohi. Akbar sent two of his Generals and the royal army to assist Jagmal in annexing Sirohi.

On 17th October 1583, Jagmal attacked Abu, where Surtan was fortified and one of the most ferocious battles of Rajasthan was fought. Here the invading army of Akbar was crushingly defeated by a relatively smaller army. The two Rajput Generals, Rai Singh and Koli Singh, along with Jagmal, were killed by Surtan, making Surtan the undisputed king of Sirohi. Thus was destroyed a threat to Pratap and Mewar, which could otherwise have complicated Pratap's resistance to Islamic imperialist aggressors.

Pratap became king of Mewar and succeeded to the titles and renown of an illustrious house, but also to a kingdom without capital, a clan without resources, samants dispirited by reverses and subjects demoralized by losses. Yet equipped with the noble spirit of his race and a steely resolve to overcome the immense challenge ahead of him, Pratap contemplated the recovery of Chittor and the vindication of the pride of Rajputs.

Akbar, though unstable in Delhi, was gaining strength and allies rapidly. The houses of Amer, Bikaner and Boondi forged alliances with Akbar and thus Pratap had to reconcile with the fact that he was going to fight, not only the Turks, but also his own brothers in faith and blood. This fact would weigh very heavily on the mind of Pratap in the subsequent war he was to fight with the Turks.

One of his brothers, Sagar, also deserted him and allied with the Turks.

The scars of the third *saka* of Chittor had ravaged the consciousness of Mewar, and its entire population was dejected and demoralised.

Pratap inherited a wounded Mewar but was also nobly supported by old friends, like the sons of Jaimal Rathore and Patta Choondawat. The houses of Saloombara, Deogarh, Amer, etc. declared their total loyalty to Pratap. The erstwhile chief of Gwalior, Ram Shah Tanwar, became his main Army General and the chief of Dailwara became the king's right hand.

Bhama Shah, the Oswal Jain[98] cashier of the royal house was an even fiercer and greater warrior than he was a finance manager. Bhama Shah and his brave brother Tarachand swore loyalty to Pratap and were instrumental in funding and strategy for the two epoch making wars of Mewar against the Turks, viz. Haldighati and Dewair.

98. Followers of *Jain dharma*, were mostly rich traders.

Bhama Shah (1547-1600 CE)

A Painting showing Pratap and Shakti Singh praying together at Ban Mata temple

A special mention of Shakti Singh is required—the estranged brother who played a critical role in Pratap's life and which has been detailed elsewhere in this book. Shakti Singh's sons came to be known as Shaktawats and went on to become fierce loyalists and warriors for Pratap and Mewar.

From the time of his ascendance to the throne in 1572, until the year of his moksha in 1597, Pratap was king for 25 years and he single handedly withstood the might of the Mughals, and ultimately defeated it. Some of his own people deserted him for greener pastures but Pratap stood his ground alone in this wilderness.

Fighting wars, killing his enemies ruthlessly, losing friends and allies to death and deceit, flying from one rock to another, carrying out destruction from the plains to guerrilla warfare in the mountain passes, feeding his family and army with the fruits of the native hills and rearing the nursling hero, Amar Singh, amidst savage beasts and savage men, Pratap energised his people and army with his amazing leadership and resolve to continue fighting the Turk imperialists.

The magnitude of the perils he faced only affirmed his fortitude with the vow 'to make his mother's milk resplendent.'

The mere idea that the son of Bappa Rawal should bow to

a mortal was unsustainable. It is to the immense credit of the *samants* and the general population of Mewar, who stood by their king through unimaginable suffering, death and poverty.

Mewar had witnessed the destruction caused by Akbar at Chittor on 25th February 1568 at the third *saka* and yet it rose to defend her freedom and honour from the ashes of *jauhar* at Chittor. Mewar rose to become the beacon of Hindu hope in the region solely because of one man—Maharana Pratap Singh, the greatest Hindu warrior-king of all times.

One man, who altered the entire saga of the attempted Islamic subjugation of the Indian sub-continent by his insurmountable grit and determination.

One man, who was not a reckless, self-serving, indulgent monarch, sucking the blood and money of his people, but a *mahayogi*, who donned the mantle of a warrior to free the motherland and banish the dark clouds of slavery that loomed on the Hindus of the region.

One man, who gave up all comforts and riches that a Maharana could have enjoyed. Refusing to compromise with the Turk imperialist, he chose instead a life of hardship because honour was dearer to him than a few years of a wretched life.

A true leader who respected the counsel of his wise and loyal *samants* as well as groomed the youth to lead the future of Mewar.

A true Spartan, who chose to sleep with his spear as his pillow than to rest his head on velvet at night.

The following were the four vows that Pratap took upon becoming the king of Mewar. They became a part of the folklore of Mewar and stirred the most insignificant and remote subject of Mewar to take on the Mughal marauder:

- All articles of luxury and pomp were to be abandoned until Chittor was reclaimed.
- The gold and silver dishes were laid aside for *pattals* or plates and utensils made out of leaves.
- The beds of cloth and soft velvet were replaced with straw and leaves.
- The martial *nagadas* (drums) which used to lead royal processions were placed at the rear to mark and remember the fallen fortunes of Mewar and stimulate its recovery.

Ascendance to the Throne: Initial Fortification

Pratap commenced the duties of governing and generating revenues immediately. New grants were issued to the nobles, with regulations defining the services required. Kumbhalgarh was declared the capital and strengthened. Similarly, Gogunda and other mountain fortresses were strengthened and fortified. Unable to keep the plains, Pratap reverted to the ancient system of his ancestors, commanding his subjects to retreat to the mountains.

Pratap prepared himself for the impending protracted war with the Turk imperialist with meticulous implementation and unrelenting severity to enforce the compliance of his edicts.

The fertile area between Banas and Beris was to be evacuated and left *be-chiraag*, i.e. without a lamp. The idea was to burden the Mughals with carrying their supplies whenever they were to attack Mewar. There would be no local supply of any kind and no slaughter of ordinary citizens, which was the practice of the Turks at that time.

Pratap would personally enforce strict rules on the people of Mewar.

Once, accompanied by a few horsemen, Pratap set out to invigilate the obeisance of his commands. The silence of the deserts prevailed in the once green pastures of Mewar; jungle grass replaced the fields of corn; the highways were choked with thorny *babool*; beasts of prey inhabited the deserted villages.

The shepherd defying state orders is hanged

In the midst of this wilderness, a lone shepherd took out his flock to the remnants of vegetation in the once luxurious meadows of Ontalla, on the banks of River Banas. After a brief enquiry, the shepherd was put to death and his corpse hung high on a tree to send a message across to the violators of Pratap's plan of fighting the Turks.

To quote Tod:

'By such patriotic severity, Pratap rendered 'the garden of Rajasthan' of no value to the conqueror, and the commerce established between the Mughal courts and Europe, conveyed through Mewar from Surat and other ports, was intercepted and plundered[99].'

We can only imagine the resolve and determination of the people of Mewar who rallied behind Pratap in following his plans to make life hell for the invading Turk forces. All farming communities moved out of Mewar between 1572 and 1583, when Mewar was won again..

Ordinary citizens relocated into the hills of Aravallis and thus, thousands of new villages came into existence. This also resulted in close contact between the people of Mewar and the mountain-dwelling Bhils. The Bhils welcomed them with open arms, fed an entire population on fruits and protected them by accommodating them in the safety of the jungles.

The Bhils were instrumental in this movement of population from plains to the hills and this community has had the distinction of adorning the royal insignia of Mewar for centuries now. Bhils were also the mainstay of the armed resistance by Mewar, as will be detailed in the subsequent chapters.

Pratap prepares Bhils for war *Rana Punja*

99. Tod, p. 266, vol. 1.

Inspired by Pratap, the *samants* and the chieftains became liberal with regard to tax collection from their impoverished subjects. The love and trust the people of Mewar showered on Pratap is unparalleled in the history of mankind. Armies fight wars and soldiers die and kill for honour and riches, but never had an entire population fortified itself against a foreign invader as it happened in Mewar under Pratap.

If any other king were to pass such edicts, Mewar would have been littered with traitors and revolts, making it ungovernable. Yet Pratap was extraordinary in leading by example in forebearance and fortitude, anticipating the hardships and preparing his people. He thus proved himself an able leader, an excellent war strategist, a compassionate king and a farsighted and intelligent ruler.

The love showered by the people of Mewar on Pratap is unparalleled.

Not only did he plan the campaign against the Turk aggressor, but very effectively communicated it to the last of his subjects.

The wars of Haldighati in 1576, the seven years of interim and the final victory at Dewair, were to prove the effectiveness of Pratap's genius in pushing the Turk invader away for as long as he lived.

Pratap learnt from his grandfather Sanga's mistakes of exposing themselves to Mughal firepower and chose guerrilla warfare to inflict damage on the Turks. He learned from the third *saka* that the enemy was a ruthless marauder, who would pitch Rajputs against Rajputs and mercilessly slaughter Hindus.

Pratap saw how fellow-Hindu kings, like Bhagwan Das of Amer, stood as meek witnesses to the slaughter of Hindus at Chittor and he knew he would have to fight a solitary fight to retain Mewar's freedom and honour.

Pratap understood the vile and hideous nature of the Islamic imperialists and knew two facts, one that coexistence with these amoral barbarians was impossible and secondly, war was an inevitablity. Hence, he devised a long term campaign to defeat Akbar and weed him out of Mewar permanently.

He struck alliances, subjugated rebellions, purchased the loyalty of fence-sitters, created a socially cohesive alliance of all communities in Mewar and implemented the campaign with clinical precision.

One more misinformation that needs to be countered is that Pratap lived a life of penury in jungles. This is a totally false narrative built by Hindu poets and writers themselves to dramatise Pratap's war of independence. A king from the line of Sanga and Kumbha couldn't have been without money and resources to take on a strong opponent like Akbar. A fully equipped army of Mewar comprising of tens of thousands of soldiers, along with cavalry and elephants is a matter of record.

The '*Ghaas ki roti*' metaphor may appeal to the poetic creativity of our times, but it doesn't resonate with the reality of Mewar.

Pratap was a simple man, unattached to luxuries and he also wanted to set an example for the Mewar subjects to follow. Pratap was an affluent king of a rich kingdom. His spartan life style was his choice, not his compulsion.

The Hindus haven't truly understood and recognised the military genius and supreme sacrifice of Maharana Pratap Singh.

When the Leftist-*jihadi* historians could not erase the life and deeds of Pratap, they concocted and spread the lies of Pratap being a mindless rebel with little understanding of military strategy. Pratap was shown to be an impractical hothead, who rose against Akbar without realising his strengths and weaknesses objectively.

The scale of lies is so humongous yet spurious, that they fall apart even on a cursory examination of facts.

If Muslims were to retreat, it was a tactical move; if a Hindu king retreated, he was an escapist.

If Muslims lost a battle, it was a mere setback; if Hindus lost a battle, it was final.

If Muslims fight guerrilla warfare, it was a masterstroke; if Hindus fight it, it was a compulsion.

If Muslims raped Hindu women, it was their religious duty; if Hindus returned Muslim women unmolested, silence.

If Muslims offer treaty, it was strategic wisdom; if Hindus did the same, it was capitulation.

If Muslims slaughtered innocents, the pretext was religion; if

Hindus slaughtered non-combatants, it was murder.

If Muslim wins a war, he is Ghazi; if Hindu wins a war, it's a stroke of luck.

The direct consequence of these lies is that the whole saga of the glorious Hindu resistance to Islamic invasions has been completely derailed.

While the intelligentsia of the Hindu society and the entire globe should have been examining what Islamic invaders brought to the table, the entire focus was shifted to the lies woven around the stiff Hindu resistance to Islam.

Instead of the global community being grateful to Hindus for halting the march of a dark force that offered nothing to human civilisation except blind faith, false theories were floated and perpetrated endlessly.

All this was done so that Islam as a thought, as a way of life escapes scrutiny, while the world is engaged in the noise and glitter around the Hindu resistance to Islam. Thus, the acidic damage being caused by Islamic invasions to Bharat were glossed over in these lies. Writer—Historian Ivan Austin writes in his book, '*Mewar: The World's Longest Serving Dynasty*' that if Bappa, Khuman and Pratap had not stopped the tide of Islam, entire world would've been Islamised.

To call Pratap an escapist is akin to calling a lion escaping from a jackal.

Death was no deterrence to a man like Pratap who had faced it frontally numerous times in his life. Pratap fought every war with the wise counsel of Mewar's war council and his trusted lieutenants. To run away from war was unknown to him. Of course, if one is surrounded by enemies from all sides, what is the point of dying needlessly!

Pratap used the geographical advantage of Mewar to the hilt and defeated Mughals comprehensively.

He treated friends with respect and kindness, and enemies with merciless slaughter.

Pratap single-handedly shaped the contours of the Hindu-Muslim conflict with unparalleled ferocity towards Islamic imperialists and established *dharma* so effectively into the psyche of a dying Hindu society that dozens of kingdoms rose against the Mughals.

Within three generations of Akbar, the Mughals were finished, while Mewar in all its glory stands even today. Not as a relic of its turbulent past, but as a glorious reminder of its power, sacrifice and fortitude.

Pratap carried the highest principles of morality and honourable conduct on his lone chest all his life. Pratap passed on to us a legacy worth living for, worth fighting for, worth dying for. We are indeed the luckiest people on this globe to be the heirs of this sublime legacy.

□

12

Pratap and Akbar: Two World Views

The defining feature of Maharana Pratap's life and work has been his incessant struggle against the Turk-Mughal invader, Akbar.

It was a royal family feud of a very unique kind. Babur had fought Pratap's grandfather Rana Sanga and Babur's grandson Akbar and Pratap continued the tradition of their families.

Mohammad Jalaluddin Akbar (1556-1605 CE)

In the interim, both the families were led by weak kings, Humayun and Udai Singh, both of whom did not leave much impact on history except raising their sons, both of whom altered the history of the land of the Hindus permanently in their own ways.

Mewar was recovering from Rana Sanga's murder and Udai Singh's turbulent rise to the throne of Mewar.

Pratap witnessed all this as a child and a young man.

Udai Singh was a relatively weak ruler of an aloof nature and an indecisive mind.

Akbar inherited a turbulent Delhi from his father Humayun and most of the affairs of the state were managed by his caretaker, Bahram Khan.

In 1556, the Second Battle of Panipat was won by Akbar who defeated the Hindu king, Hemu Vikramaditya. With that defeat of Hemu, Hindu opposition to Akbar considerably weakened. But Akbar and Bahram Khan got a taste of Hindu fury at Panipat, where Akbar won the war merely by an act of deceit and luck.

On 5th November, 1556, when Hemu's huge army descended upon an army of Akbar five times smaller in size, it was thought that it was just a matter of time before Hindus would crush the Turks. But the old tactic of Islamic invaders to deploy a team of the best archers to identify and go for the Hindu king worked once again. It was as though Hindus refused to learn anything from history and were hell-bent on repeating the same mistakes.

Chivalry has little place when confronted with a deceitful enemy—a reality that Hindu kings refused to learn.

At Khanwa, Akbar's grandfather Babur had similarly injured Sanga by employing a team of archers hitting him. The same tactic was repeated at Panipat by Akbar, where Hemu was hit and mortally wounded by the Mughal archers. The Hindu kings repeated the same mistake of leading from the front while Islamic sultans or *badshahs* always kept themselves concealed at the rear.

After Hemu had been beheaded, his old father was asked to convert to Islam, and he too was beheaded when he refused to do so. Akbar understood that Hindus could not be subjugated and converted by force. He therefore put up the mask of tolerance and started employing Hindu ministers. This portrayal of softness worked to his advantage and Hindu kings softened to Akbar's ambitions.

Akbar looked back at the last 350 years of incessant conflict and understood that the only way for Islamic rule to find roots on the Hindu soil was by aligning with the Rajputs.

It is worth noting that between 12th and 16th century, for almost 350 years since the 2nd battle of Tarain (1192) when Ghori defeated Prithviraj Chauhan of Delhi, no Islamic invader could establish himself in Delhi. This was partly due to their rabid zeal for Jihad, to plunder and force conversion which was resisted with a do or die attitude by Hindu kings. It was also partly due to extensive infighting among the Invaders who were largely looters and not from a civilisational ruling class.

Until 1556 CE, the so called Delhi Sultanate was nothing but an unending saga of assassinations, dethronements, treachery and barbaric lust for power. No work of consequence was ever erected by these so called sultans, as all their lives were spent in quelling internal rebellions and fighting local rulers.

With Akbar's rise, Hindus faced a new kind of enemy who cunningly changed tactics and would pitch Hindus against Hindus, using the internal rivalry and the insatiable greed of some Hindu monarchs for power to his advantage.

As Akbar was intensely engaged in expanding his kingdom, he focussed all his energies on Rajasthan as he knew that Rajputs in general and especially the Sisodias of Chittor would be very difficult to contain or subdue. Akbar therefore befriended the Kachchawas of Amer (Jaipur) and extended his hand for matrimonial relationship. Babur had made similar offers to Amer's Rajputs but had been rebuffed by Jaipur's Rajputs.

A lot has been written about the alignment of Amer Rajputs to Akbar and especially the marriage of Harkhu Bai (erroneously known as Jodha), the daughter of Raja Bhar Mal of Amer with Akbar.

Let us try to do a dispassionate assessment of the circumstances in which the Amer Rajputs decided to align with Akbar.

First, Jaipur as a state is largely made up of plains, unlike Mewar, which is protected by the Aravallis all around. If Amer (Jaipur) had decided to fight with a strong Akbar, they would not have been a match for the religious zeal of the Turks and the massive firepower they wielded in the plains of northern Rajasthan. Fighting a guerrilla war was not even an option for Jaipur.

Second, there was no Rajput confederation or a leader of any stature to unite the Rajput kings of Rajasthan after Sanga had been poisoned and killed by Babur. Mewar, the beacon of Hindu resistance was in disarray and each royal house was left to fend for itself. Jaipur alone was incapable of leading a fight against a powerful Akbar, especially after the defeat of Raja Hemchandra Vikramaditya.

Third, inter-house rivalry also played a role in those times. The house of Jaipur was always subservient to Mewar for centuries. Although there is no documentation of Mewar's princetons belittling fellow-Rajputs but off and on, some skirmishes would take place. It cannot be ruled out that Bharmal, his son Bhagwan Das and his son Man Singh nursed some grudges against the house of Mewar.

Fourth, poet Shyamaldas records in his exhaustive book, *Veer Vinod*, that when Mughals offered matrimonial bonds to them, the chiefs and the priests of Amer decided that to implement peace, Jaipur might give its daughters but to accept Mughal daughters would eventually lead to Islamisation of the Jaipur royal house[100].

Thus, accepting Mughal women into the Rajput clan was politely declined.

This was a very wise move that prevented conversions within the Jaipur royalty as giving a daughter, albeit with a heavy heart was easier than bringing a Muslim daughter into the royal house as it would result in a dilution of Hindu Dharma and customs in Jaipur's Rajputs and their progeny, and possible Islamization.

Fifth, is financial reasons. In 1616 CE even the mighty Mewar under Amar Singh had to sign instead of barter a peace treaty with Jehangir after Pratap's moksha(passing into immortality). As Mewar faced a financial crunch and inability to pay salaries to its army, the fear of impending revolt loomed large.

As such, Amar Singh sent his son Karan Singh as an emissary to Jehangir's court and bought interim peace with the Mughals. If this fate befell the mighty house of Mewar, Jaipur would possibly have similar reasons for their treaty with Akbar, given the times.

Sixth, and very importantly, Jaipur had always been a very strong ally of the Mewar house and their fight against Islamic invaders.

In the 1000 year war for Dharma, Jaipur left Mewar's side only and about 108 years between 1562 and 1670 to align with Akbar, Jehangir and ShahJahan.

We should not forget that Prithviraj Kachchawa was Sanga's trusted friend and allied with him against Babar at Khanwa. Kachchawa warriors aligning with Raj Singh against Aurangzeb is also a well documented historical fact.

Seventh, Jaipur's Rajputs forming a sizeable army of Mughals implied that there would be no plunder and slaughter of the local Hindu population. This is why during the reign of Akbar, Jehangir, and Shahjahan, we see no mass-scale destruction of Hindu temples and/or forceful conversions of Hindu population. When Aurangzeb began destroying Hindu temples and forcibly converting Hindus, the Jaipur Rajputs rebelled and many of them aligned with Mewar and Marwar, deserting their Mughal posts.

100. *Veer Vinod*, vol. 2, p. 170.

It is due to this rebellion that Mughal rule crumbled as soon as Aurangzeb died in CE 1707.

Eighth, innumerable Hindu temples were built by Jaipur's kings in Mathura, Vrindavan and Kashi. The Jaipur royal house provided patronage to most Hindu schools of thought where Vedic teachings were kept alive. Man Singh was instrumental in protecting and patronising Goswami Tulsidas, who penned the epic *Ramcharitmanas* during that time.

Kashi Vishwanath temple and the corridor around it, along with a major *ghat* on Ganga at Benaras was built by Man Singh. Later, Mirza Raja Jai Singh protected the Sanskrit Vidyapeeth at Benaras and educated his son Ram Singh over there.

Ninth, even in direct combat, there are innumerable instances when Jaipur's Rajputs helped fellow-Rajputs escape. In Haldighati, when Pratap had been surrounded by Mughals and most of his ablest Generals were dead, it seems theoretically impossible for Pratap to have escaped if Man Singh and other Rajputs hadn't gone soft on Pratap. Abul Fazl, the Muslim historian at Haldighati records that the Muslim Generals asked Man Singh to chase and finish off Pratap, but Man Singh ignored him. It was Asif Khan, the Mughal, who sent two Mughal officers to chase Pratap but they were eventually killed by Pratap's brother Shakti Singh.

At the battle of Mohi in CE 1577, Pratap slaughtered 1,000 Mughals while Man Singh was a few kilometres away and didn't lend help to the Mughals. Man Singh did the same with Amar Singh too. After Pratap's *moksha*, Man Singh kept postponing the attack on Amar Singh. Akbar was very unhappy with Man Singh for his softness towards Pratap and Amar Singh, but Man Singh was too powerful for Akbar to be subjugated into compliance.

Tenth, amidst all the criticism of Man Singh for fighting Pratap at Haldighati, historians and Hindu opinion makers overlook the war pursuits of Man Singh elsewhere in the region. Man Singh led Mughal forces against Afghan rebels and crushed the Afghans mercilessly.

Shouldn't Hindus be grateful to Man Singh for arranging the slaughter of one Muslim army by another? A Mughal-Afghan alliance would have surely Islamised entire Bharat.

Had Man Singh not crushed Afghans using Mughal war machinery and Afghans had marched to the western fronts of the land, can we even imagine the consequences of a truce between Mughals and Afghans?

Man Singh undertook similar campaigns in the rest of Bharatvarsha, especially Bengal, where he again pitched one Muslim army against another.

Hindus should be grateful to, instead of being contemptuous of this great Rajput king of Jaipur.

Yes, his attack on Pratap at Haldighati evokes revulsion, but kings and nobles bear huge paradoxes on their shoulders and we should look back at them with compassion instead of judging them with a one-sided worldview.

Lastly, many stories have been floating around about the real identity of Harkhu Bai, daughter of Jaipur's king, Bhar Mal. Some say that she was not actually the daughter of the king but a maid's child whose true lineage was found once married to Akbar. On hearing about the marriage of an inconsequential girl to Akbar,

Mariam-ul-Zamani also known as Harkhu Bai. Falsely called Jodha Bai

Raja Bharmal of Jaipur. The first to align with Akbar

the fourth Sikh guru Shri Ram Das is supposed to have said in jest, *"Rajputs too have learned the art of politics."*

Some even say that she was a Portuguese slave purchased by Jaipur royals and passed on to Akbar.

This particular account does not stand the test of logic and record, as there are no records of such a slave in Jaipur's annals. Secondly, all his life, Man Singh's loyalty to this queen of Akbar implies that she must have been a relative of some consequence.

But one last thing must be mentioned about this episode of Harkhu marrying Akbar. Harkhu was converted to Mariam-ul-Zamani at the time of marriage itself, hence, those scenes of Akbar celebrating Janmashtami in the Bollywood movie *Jodha Akbar* and *Mughal-e-Azam* are lies perpetrated to influence gullible Hindus into believing the mirage of a 'Ganga-Jamuni *tehzeeb*', when no such culture ever existed.

Akbar was *Khooni-e-Azam* who was prevented from Islamising our glorious Vedic *bhoomi* by the great Maharana Pratap Singh of Mewar.

All that can be said for Jaipur Rajputs is that life does not always grant us the luxury of choices. We have to make the best out of a given situation.

Prima facie, what looks like an alliance of the Rajputs of Jaipur with Islamic invaders might actually have been just a stop-gap arrangement to tide over the difficult fortunes of Hindus at the time.

One may agree or disagree with what the Jaipur Rajputs did, but none can doubt the commitment of Jaipur's royal house to Sanatan Dharma.

During the subsequent wars with Mewar, though Jaipur sided with Akbar because of the reasons mentioned above, we find numerous incidents during the war and in Akbar's court where Man Singh helped fellow-Rajputs of Mewar, directly or indirectly. These incidents will be mentioned when we discuss the battles in the chapters that follow.

We must remember that Jaipur's Rajputs claim direct descent from Kush, the second son of Bhagwan Shri Ram. Given this background, it can be reasonably inferred that the alignment of Jaipur with the Turks for a brief interim was a mix of the geo-political situation prevailing in those times and also the vulnerability of Jaipur being in close proximity to Delhi.

But above all, Hindus must remain eternally grateful to the Rajputs and the people of Jaipur for never having thought of converting to Islam. Though we have examples of a Sisodia chief, the nephew of Pratap, son of his brother Sagar, converting to Islam and becoming Mohabbat Khan or a Rathore from Nagore converting to Islam, there is not a single instance of a Kachchawa Rajput of some consequence, converting to Islam.

Mirza Raja Jai Singh : Saviour of Hindus

Inspite of matrimonial bonds with Islamists, there is no mention of even a small chieftain of Amer converting to Islam. This must have taken an extraordinarily strong resolve, and deep committment to Sanatan values.

By no means is this a small achievement considering the aggressive proselytising nature of Islam and how this ideology devoured the entire Middle East in a few decades. Jaipur, however, stood like a bulwark against conversions. Its alliance with Mughals was thus, a temporary compromise for the Jaipur house to tide over the crest of the Turk fortunes. Jaipur's kings clearly laid down the condition to Mughals that the temples and forts of Hindus would not be destroyed in lieu of their services.

Aurangzeb broke this truce by ordering the destruction of Hindu temples and obtained the revolt of Jaipur's and Jodhpur's Rajputs in return.

At the time of Aurangzeb, Jaipur's Mirza Raja Jai Singh formally distanced the Jaipur Rajputs from Mughals. Jai Singh was despatched by Aurangzeb to fight and capture Chhatrapati Shivaji Maharaj. In CE 1665, Jai Singh concluded the treaty of Purandar and sent Shivaji Maharaj to Aurangzeb's court on personal guarantee. Jai Singh wrote a letter to his son Ram Singh that should Aurangzeb break his promise and ill-treat Shivaji, Ram Singh should arrange his escape from Agra.

Jai Singh's suspicion proved correct. Aurangzeb arrested Shivaji and put him in Ram Singh's palace. Ram Singh arranged Shivaji Maharaj's escape in a fruit basket and ensured his safe passage back to his kingdom. Aurangzeb held Jai Singh responsible for Shivaji's escape. On 16th July in CE 1667, Jai Singh was poisoned in Burhanpur by a maid on instructions from Aurangzeb. This has been adequately recorded in Jaipur annals and quoted by Shyamaldas in *Veer Vinod.*

Thus, Jaipur's royal house sacrificed their king to keep the fire of freedom alive in South India. The murder of Jai Singh has been described in detail in the chapter on Raj Singh as well.

The only permanent blot on the name of the Amer house is the third *saka* of Chittor in CE 1568. Bhagwan Das of Amer not only fought for Akbar and mercilessly wiped out a tiny army of 8,000 Mewar warriors, but also stood as a meek witness to the slaughter of 30,000 innocent civilians by the Turkish barbarians. There is no rationale for Bhagwan Das witnessing the murder of fellow-Hindus silently.

Jaipur's Rajputs should have revolted and laid down their lives fighting the *mlechchhas* instead of impotently watching their brothers and sisters being butchered on that fateful day. The Hindu army of Jaipur should have revolted on witnessing the desecration of their gods and temples.

Though it should be noted that there is not a single mention by Abul Fazl, Badayuni, Ferishta, or any Muslim historian about slaughter of Hindus by Rajputs of Jaipur.

It is possible that the Rajput army of Jaipur wasn't allowed to enter the fort that fateful day, else there would have been revolt by Rajputs on witnessing the desecration of their temples.

All said and done, the blot of the third *saka-jauhar* will remain forever on the ancestors of the Rajputs of Jaipur.

Akbar was a very shrewd man with an equally cunning advisor in Bahram Khan, who knew that Hindus could not be subjugated in a frontal attack.

Akbar very smartly observed and capitalised on the fault-lines of Hindu kingdoms, especially the Rajput kingdoms of Amer, Marwar and Mewar. After defeating and beheading Raja Hemchandra in the second Battle of Panipat, Akbar organised the northern states around Delhi, with the Malwa sultan pledging allegiance to him. Raja Bhar Mal of Amer was the first one to capitulate and give his daughter Harku Bai to Akbar in matrimony.

Minarets of Hindu heads raised by 'Akbar the great' after second Battle of Panipat in 1556 CE

Bhar Mal's son Bhagwan Das became the main General of Akbar's army and was with him during the siege of Chittor in 1567–68.

Akbar's insistence on subjugating Mewar arose from his understanding that the house of Mewar was the one that stood against the Islamic plunderers. He knew that as long as Mewar was unconquered, his dream of Islamisation of the region could not be achieved. Akbar also knew that Mewar was significantly weakened after Sanga's demise and that Udai Singh was a weak king. Akbar hadn't encountered Pratap until then, though he had heard stories of the amazing strength and valour of this prince of Mewar.

Pratap was a first-hand witness to the slaughter of Chittor by Akbar and the *saka* and *jauhar* of 1568 was stuck in his heart like a thorn. Pratap had lost more than 500 close relatives in the *saka-jauhar*, hence, he made the vows of penance which have been detailed in the chapter on 'Ascendance of Pratap to the Throne of Mewar'.

Pratap was deeply scarred by the loss of Chittor. The once invincible fort of the Sisodias was rendered indefensible against an army of marauding mercenaries. The abode of regality that had reared her head above all cities of the land became the refuge for wild beasts. Pratap was a strong believer in Hindu unity against the Turks and the act of Bhar Mal marrying off his daughter to them deeply disturbed him. He saw through the cunning move of Akbar to infiltrate the royal Rajput bloodline and chose to resist it tooth and nail. In many of the couplets and poems of those times, Pratap is quoted to have said that whatever fate befalls Mewar, no Sisodia daughter will warm the bed of a Turk.

Maharana Pratap Singh :
The Greatest Hindu king of all times

Once, Akbar, frustrated at Pratap's belligerence and continued resistance, spread a rumour in Delhi court that Pratap had sent an emissary to talk of surrender. A prince of Bikaner, Prithviraj, though serving Akbar, was proud of Pratap in his heart and wrote the following couplets to Pratap:

"If Pratap is going to refer to Akbar as an emperor, then the sun might as well rise from West.

Tell me O mighty Pratap, shall I continue twirling my moustache or kill myself with my sword?"

Pratap replied thus:

तुरक कहाशी मुखपतौ इण मुख सू एकलिंग,
ऊगै जयाँ ही ऊगशी प्राची बीच पतंग।

"I will refer to Akbar as a 'Turk' as long as there is life in this body.

The sun will rise from the East only.

As long as my sword is on the neck of yavanas, keep twirling your moustache.

Pratap will bear every blow on his head; may you be victorious in this battle of words with the Turk[101]."

So, despite Pratap's vision and desire for Hindu unity, Akbar's cunning moves forced Pratap to travel the path of frontal adversity with him and his Hindu vassals. But Pratap kept humouring fellow-Rajputs and never belittled them for aligning with Akbar.

101. Ojha, p. 29-30.

The Rajputs and Charan (bard) courtiers of Akbar also provided him with vital information about Akbar's moves from time to time.

Pratap knew that every Hindu courtier serving Akbar was actually with him (Pratap) and he alone was the hope of Hindu revival in the region. He therefore kept enduring the hardships of mountain warfare and in doing so, kept hope alive in every Hindu heart.

It is easy for us to look back at the events that unfolded 500 years ago and analyse how Akbar's reign was singularly responsible for the destruction of Hindu ethos, culture and social system; but for a contemporary Pratap to witness and anticipate this damage is an amazing feat that aptly demonstrates his foresight and vision.

Pratap also witnessed Akbar luring and helping the rebels and enemies of Mewar, and this only deepened his enmity with Akbar. But most importantly, if we look at the entire history of the royal lives of Mewar, from Bappa Rawal to Udai Singh, it can be easily deduced that Pratap perfectly understood the plan of Islamists and found Akbar to be the epicentre of that plan.

This included instigating infighting among Hindu kings, inviting foreign mercenaries like Bahlol Khan from Uzbekistan, and creating a fully armed wing of hired killers, suppressing and killing his own loyalists ruthlessly, for example, chasing and capturing his main benefactor Bahram Khan and marrying his wife.

All Islamic invaders were treacherous, amoral and obsessed with a lust for power. It is a fact we have established in this book but the Mughals took it to the next level.

Babur himself talks of using poison as a tool of war in his memoirs. Humayun ran around the north and north-west to save himself so we will never know about his love for poisons.

Akbar is documented to be a collector of various kinds of poisons. He had an officer appointed to monitor and deliver the desired poison when asked for. Akbar had specifically designed long robes, known as *khilats,* with their collars and arms laced with poison.

He used to give these *khilats* to his enemies and thus

eliminate them. Rajendra Shankar Bhatt quotes Italian physician, traveller Manucci, *"Akbar killed a lot of kings and nobles whom he considered a threat to his rule."* Manucchi visited India during the reign of Shahjahan and Aurangzeb and writes, *"This concealed way of killing people was widely prevalent when I was in the Mughal courts*[102]*."*

Akbar had poison tablets for his enemies. It is said that Akbar himself died by consuming one such tablet accidentally[103].

Aurangzeb was a master in this craft of using poison. He first eliminated Prithivraj, the gallant son of Jodhpur king, Maharaja Jaswant Singh. He then eliminated Jaswant Singh himself by poisoning. Aurangzeb then poisoned Mirza Raja Jai Singh of Jaipur and Maharana Raj Singh of Mewar. Both these murders have been dealt in the chapter on Raj Singh.

So according to the *dhimmi*[104]-Leftist-*jihadi* cabal occupying the intellectual space of this nation, a person and a dynasty which murdered people in this manner, were great people whose examples we should all follow. I leave it to the judgement of the reader whether they agree with this cabal or think otherwise.

Another very evil and humiliating practice deserves mention here as it was a cornerstone of Pratap's hatred for Akbar. It was the practice of Navroza, meaning nine days, not to be confused with the Persian festival of Nauroz. Akbar used to hold a nine-day fair in Agra where only women were allowed. Akbar would attend this fair in disguise to pick women who caught his eye. Once, Akbar is supposed to have passed an edict that every newly married Rajput princess would have to spend the first nine days of her marriage in Akbar's harem. The Rajputs of course, revolted and Akbar was forced to withdraw this humiliating *farman* (edict) after a few weeks.

The official records[105] of Navroza are patchy and inconsistent but a lot of local literature of Rajasthan endorses this demeaning practice being promulgated by Akbar. Perhaps, news of this practice

102. Bhatt, p. 167
103. Italian traveller Niccolao Manucci
104. Dhimmi–A non Muslim in an Islamic rule who justifies Islamic practises
105. This is a popular folklore amongst the Charans of Rajasthan, bards and history-keepers of Rajputs

reached Pratap and his resolve to fight Akbar only strengthened. Navroza was one of the main reasons besides the *saka-jauhar* of Chittor, for Pratap's hatred for Akbar and his resolve to never even contemplate surrender or alignment with Akbar.

Even today, in Rajasthan, a folk-song '*Jala*' is sung in marriages and ignorant Hindus dance to this song of slavery of Hindus. Set tune to the original folk-song 'Panihari', this song describes the marriage procession of Akbar. The writer has personally witnessed this blind indulgence of ignorant Hindus. This is a song that should be forever removed from the social space of Hindu society.

Italian writer and traveller Niccolao Manucci, in his book *Storia do Mogur* or History of the Moghul Dynasty in India described Akbar's harem as follows: *"A policy that he employed.... was to contract in marriage with the Rajas' princesses. By means of these maliometan women, he embroiled the Rajas in perpetual wars with one another."* Manucci, who has professed to writing only that which he had seen with his own eyes during the Mughal era, also wrote about how Meena Bazaar served as a platform to recruit Hindu women into the Mughal harem. Though Meena Bazaar was supposed to be a woman-only affair, Akbar was said to have disguised as a woman and entered the fair (Abul Fazl). The writer's interest in quoting this horrible practice is only to show the power of Rajput kings who forced Akbar to withdraw this demeaning *farman*.

To contrast this Islamic trait of Akbar of exploiting enemy womenfolk with Pratap's *dharmic* value system, an incident is quoteworthy.

In 1585 CE, Akbar despatched Abdul Raheem Khankhana to defeat and arrest Pratap.

When Khankhana was camping near Abu, Kunwar Amar Singh, managed to lay hands on the daughter and a few other women of Khankhana's family.

Amar Singh captured and brought them to Pratap.

Pratap was furious at Amar Singh and said, *"What is the difference between us and that mlelchcha Akbar if we also start attacking women in war? Is this the way of Hindus? Let Khankhana's daughter tie a rakhi thread to your wrist and make you her brother. Then personally go and drop them to Khankhana's camp."*

Pratap returns the womenfolk of Abdul Raheem Khankhana

Amar Singh apologised, got a thread tied to his wrist and dropped off the women to Khankhana's camp himself.

Khankhana was a deeply spiritual person. He later renounced Islam and became a Krishna devotee.

Khankhana was a Shia Muslim and son of Bahram Khan, Akbar's mentor. He was deeply moved by Pratap's gesture and returned to Agra without attacking Pratap. When Akbar questioned him why he didn't fight with Pratap, he gave a reply that has been written in golden words in history. He replied, *"One can fight with mortals, one can't fight with angels."*

Have we ever paused and wondered about the contrasting moral compasses of Akbar and Pratap?

What is the code of conduct for a civilised society to follow? Pratap's or Akbar's?

The Leftists and pseudo-liberals inhabiting this nation, who continue to teach our children that Akbar was a great ruler, must be compelled to realise the dangers of their false claims.

Do we want our children to follow Akbar's footsteps or Pratap's?

Hindu society has to look deeply into this question and come up with an answer. This amalgam of diffuse morality cannot be allowed to confuse our children anymore.

Either the dignity of a sister or a daughter is a non-negotiable entity as in Hindu *dharma*, or women-folk of a society are mere objects to be bartered or crushed by brutes in the mad desire of a faith to overpower this world.

Either women are goddesses who bless us with life and joy as in Hindu *dharma*, or they are commodities to be used and thrown.

If we glorify the vices of a rapist Akbar to our children, we will have to witness the degradation of Sanatan Dharma into a misogynistic cult.

On the other hand, if Pratap's truth is taught in our schools, our children will be dignified and honourable citizens of our great nation.

A nation cannot have two ideals. If Akbar is indeed great, then let us forget Pratap. If Pratap is great, then Akbar must be thrown into the dustbin.

This massive schizophrenia of Hindus accommodating two antagonistic worldviews has resulted in supreme confusion and stupefied our society into inertia and inaction.

If we do not stand for our principles, we are not even human beings.

Hindus have to decide now. Who will rule the psyche of Hindus, Pratap or Akbar? Answer to that question will decide if we will perish or prosper in coming years.

Akbar was a cunning debauch who exploited Hindu women regularly and slaughtered Hindus without mercy. What did he contribute to the ethos of this great nation that he is adorned with such laudatory adjectives?

Akbar was a cold-blooded murderer who pursued his

ambition of Islamising the Indians in the subcontinent with unmatched passion and fervour.

Pratap knew that he alone stood between Akbar and his design of Islamisation of Hindustan.

Pratap knew, that without him standing, the Hindus of this great land would be forced to convert or die piecemeal.

Without doubt, if we are Hindus today, it is largely due to that one man—Maharana Pratap Singh of Mewar.

This awareness itself should be sufficient for us to raise Pratap to a level of a *mahapurusha* (great being) and bow our heads in reverence to the amazing resistance that he put up and took to its logical end, all on his lonely shoulders.

□

13

Battle of Haldighati: The First Win against Akbar

Much has been written about this battle between Mewar's forces led by Maharana Pratap Singh and the Islamic imperialist Akbar's forces led by Man Singh of Jaipur and Mughal General, Asif Khan.

We will attempt a slightly different approach to this battle than hitherto attempted by various self-appointed custodians of history and based on that, draw a picture of what happened on that glorious day.

Pratap had ascended the throne of Mewar at the ripe age of thirty-two and was fully educated in the war strategies of the Mewar army and the long history of the struggle of his forefathers with the Islamic invaders of various hues. He had witnessed the extreme barbarity of Akbar in the third *saka* of Chittor where Akbar had slaughtered 40,000 innocent civilians in a day.

Pratap was well aware of the firepower at the command of the Mughals that had turned the tides in favour of the Turks in previous battles. He also knew of Akbar's cunningness in bribing and causing defections amongst the Rajputs.

Maharana Pratap was fully conscious of Akbar's determination to annex Mewar and that Akbar would be relentless in the pursuit of his goal of devouring Mewar at any cost.

Most importantly, Pratap was fully aware of the huge responsibility that had fallen on his solitary shoulders to lead the resistance against this powerful foe. Most Hindu kings had either allied with Akbar, or had been killed, like Raja Hemchandra or driven out of their kingdoms, like Ram Shah Tanwar of Gwalior.

He was fully informed and cognizant of his and his army's limitations in numbers and weaponry as much as he was aware of his strengths—the loyalty of his friends, the support of his population including the Bhils and his thorough knowledge of Mewar's topography, his quick mobility and choice of vantage points to fight the Turks.

Against this background of Pratap's predicament, we can say that he planned Haldighati as the beginning of his armed conflict with Akbar to regain Mewar. Pratap was in for the long haul as demonstrated by his choice of Army Generals and the place of conflict itself.

From 1572, since occupying the Mewar throne to June 1576, we see Pratap forging alliances with other Rajput houses, gathering resources, creating perfect hideouts, scattering a brilliant espionage network of Bhils, entering into dialogue with multiple delegations sent by Akbar for negotiating peace (thus buying time for his preparation), and constant discussions with *samants* and chieftains on strategic and tactical matters.

When we examine Pratap's moves from 1572 to 1583, it can be amply demonstrated that Pratap was a visionary leader and a master strategist, besides being a fearless warrior who had played out every possibility in his mind. He kept spaces for unexpected moves and losses and implemented his plans with such meticulous precision that one can't help but be in awe of this great king of Mewar.

Let us examine a few points that help us establish this understanding that Haldighati was not a battle that was declared at the spur of a moment but was rather the first point of interface between Pratap and Akbar. This was where Pratap learnt his lessons and implemented his plans to finally uproot the Mughal invaders from Mewar in 1583 at Dewair.

In almost all history books of post-independent India, Pratap's moment of glory has been falsely depicted as Haldighati. The subsequent references to Pratap show him to be a helpless absconder, whereas the truth is that Pratap lived to be a free king, who regained all of Mewar from the Mughals, except the fort of Chittor. Pratap died a free man, leaving a rich and powerful kingdom of an affluent Mewar to his son Amar Singh in 1597, after a brief illness due to a hunting accident.

Akbar's Peace Overtures

Let us briefly take an account of the attempts of Akbar and his coterie to reach out for peace agreements with Pratap between 1572 and 1576. These attempts help us peek into Pratap's resolve to not surrender and his diplomatic acumen in postponing the confrontation till he was ready.

The first delegation to Pratap was led by Jalal Khan Korchi in August 1572, but Jalal Khan was ignored by Pratap and he returned to Akbar two months later, reporting the failure of his talks.

The famous peace proposal by Man Singh happened in April 1573, and this incident reflects the real character of Pratap. Man Singh was all twenty-three years of age when he came to Mewar. He came to Mewar from the southern side via Dungarpur where he overcame Rawal Askaran, killing his forces and destroying the city. Askaran escaped to the hills. The Bhil spies of Pratap constantly updated him regarding Man Singh's troops marching towards Mewar.

Pratap sent two of his spies, Purbia Dursa and Sisodia Neta, to gain advanced knowledge of Man Singh's inclinations and designs. Man Singh was received by the *jagirdar* of Saloombar on being instructed by Pratap. Both the spies and the *jagirdar* informed Pratap that the behaviour and thinking of Man Singh were hugely influenced by the Turks and that nothing Man Singh said could be trusted[106].

---

106. Mathur, p. 83.

It can be safely presumed that in his heart, Pratap was aiming to rekindle Man Singh's Rajput pride and hoping to find an ally in him. It must be noted that Man Singh's grandfather Bharmal used to serve the kingdom of Mewar till Pratap's father Udai Singh ruled Mewar.

Facing attack from Mewat's Nawab Mirza Muhammad and a weakened Mewar unable to come to the aid of Amer, somewhere in CE 1562, Bharmal shifted loyalties from Mewar to Akbar.

Pratap wanted to see how different Man Singh was from his father, Bhagwan Das. He came out of the hills of Gogunda and a meeting was arranged in Udaipur on the banks of Udai Sagar Lake. Pratap sent his son Amar Singh to eat lunch with Man Singh. Pratap also sent his message through his trusted General, Dodiya Bhim Singh that his stomach was upset and hence he couldn't eat with Man Singh.

Man Singh understood the message and is said to have replied to Bhim Singh, *"I know a perfect remedy for an upset stomach, but if that is what Pratap chooses, so be it. I have tried to help Mewar all along, but from now on you must be careful because the goodwill is over."*

This epic conversation between Man Singh and Bhim Singh has been documented in Mewar annals and is part of folklore.

Bhim Singh ended the conversation by saying, *"If I do not hit the elephant you ride with my spear, I will not call myself Bhim Singh. Don't come alone to the war. Do bring your foofa (uncle, meaning Akbar) with you[107]."*

The conversation between Mewar and the Turks ended on this bitter note.

Pratap got the utensils, that Man Singh and his Generals used for food, thrown into the Udai Sagar Lake and got the place where Man Singh and his troops had sat, cleaned with *Gangajal* (holy water of River Ganga).

According to the folklore, Man Singh returned via Udaipur where Pratap met him again and laid down three impossible conditions for maintaining peace with the Turks. They have been described as three च-the equivalent of Hindi alphabet '*cha*':

107. *Veer Vinod*, vol. 2, p. 147.

i. Mewar would not do *chakri* (service) of the Turks.
ii. Mewar would not pay *chauth* (tax) to the Turks.
iii. Mewar would not give any *chhokri* (daughter) to the Turks.

Raja Man Singh of Jaipur : A friend of Hindus

Obviously, Pratap made such an offer to Man Singh that was unacceptable to him and his Turk master.

The parting note between Pratap and Man Singh is said to be this: *"If you will confront me militarily, I will meet you at Malpura (an area under Amer House but was annexed off and on by Mewar). If your uncle (Akbar) wants to fight with me, let him choose the place."*

The third delegation of peace was led by Bhagwan Das of Amer, Man Singh's father. Bhagwan Das was the traitor who had helped Akbar during the siege of Chittor in 1568; hence, Pratap had nothing but hatred for the man. Yet, Pratap welcomed him to Gogunda, treated him with due respect but repeated the same three conditions. It must be mentioned here that Pratap did not dine with Bhagwan Das as well. In September 1573, Bhagwan Das too returned empty-handed.

Bhagwan Das : The traitor of Chittor

In October 1573, Akbar made a final attempt at keeping peace with Pratap and sent Todar Mal, one of his wisest counsels, to talk to him. Pratap cordially received Todar Mal in Gogunda. Pratap is supposed to have offered a war elephant to Todar Mal, which he politely declined. Todar Mal too failed to convince Pratap and thus ended the peace overtures by Akbar to Pratap. War between the two was inevitable now.

Raja Todar Mal - Hindu facilitator of Akbar and traitor of Chittor

All these years, while Pratap gave a semblance of engaging in peace talks, in his heart of hearts he was in no mood to compromise. He was only stalling to assess the strengths and weaknesses of his enemy while his *samants* were preparing for a long-drawn conflict with the Turks.

Let us now dwell on the reasons for Akbar's peace overtures to Pratap, which seemed like a contest between the mighty Mughal power and a lone Hindu state:

1. The repeated peace overtures demonstrate amply that the 'might of the Mughal state' is a figment of imagination of Leftist historians repeated borne out of a servile mindset. Akbar was desperate to purchase the loyalties of Mewar as his entrenchment at Agra was still a distant dream and it would ease a lot of pressure on his troops and treasury, had Mewar compromised. Akbar's clutches on parts of the country were not firm yet, and with a slightest opposition from united Hindus, his plans could fall apart. Akbar himself was an unstable man and from time to time, his hatred for Hindus would surface and alarm Hindu kings around him.

Abul Fazl writes that once in Surat, Akbar was heavily drunk and lost his temper at Man Singh. He tried to throttle Man Singh, another Muslim General, named Syed Muzaffar disentangled them[108].

Akbar knew perfectly that his rule was a castle of cards that could be blown away by even one Hindu king opposing him

108. Mathur, p. 80.

openly. It was Akbar's misfortune that that king turned out to be the great Pratap Singh of Mewar.

A unique combination of intelligence, organisation, sacrifice, patience and commitment to *dharma*, Pratap proved Akbar's suspicions correct. Due to a lone King Pratap, Akbar could not Islamise the natives of this glorious land.

2. Another reason for this fiction of the 'mighty' Mughal is the total dependence of Indian historians on Persian and Turkish history-writers, like Abul Fazal and Al Badayuni, who not only lacked objectivity in their writings but at times recorded many lies which are an impossibility, even on a cursory investigation. For example, Abul Fazal writes that Pratap expressed regret at not accepting the suzerainty of Akbar and sent Amar Singh to the Mughal court as an emissary. If this were true, there would have been no more wars between Pratap and Akbar. Hence, it can be said that the 'mighty' Mughal Empire was actually a work in progress and the scales were evenly balanced between the Turks and Mewar. Akbar's peace proposals were a cunning manoeuvre to purchase peace with Mewar and gradually devour it.

Mistakes by Tod and Shyamaldas in recording incidents around Pratap are understandable because of the time gap. Abul Fazl was a contemporary of Pratap and Akbar. Fazl writng such white lies shamelessly, exposes the fidelity of these Islamic propagandists to their rulers, with truth becoming a casualty.

3. During the siege of Chittor, Akbar got a taste of the bravery and the extreme sacrifice of the warriors and the people of Mewar. Nearly 8,000 armed men of Mewar had slain about 30,000 soldiers of the Turkish army and the eventual capture of Chittor happened only due to the numerical superiority of Turks. Akbar, the cunning man that he was, saw the fortitude and uncompromising valour of a people who had run out of resources, and yet whose womenfolk undertook *jauhar* while the menfolk surged forth for *saka*. Entering the hills of Mewar to fight Pratap would have meant the defeat and annihilation of the Turkish army.

Akbar knew that if another *saka-jauhar* were to take place in Mewar, his rule will crumble. In 1568, Mewar was stunned into inaction because it was led by a weak and indecisive Udai Singh.

If a slaughter of that scale were to happen again, the entire Hindu community would unite under the leadership of Pratap. Rajputs would forget their differences and destroy him.

It is for this reason the Mughal peace overtures were extended.

4. Akbar was faced with constant rebellion against his rule in Afghanistan, Punjab, Bengal, Bihar and Gujarat and this diverted his focus from Mewar. Akbar had to first defeat Raja Chandra Sen of Marwar who was fighting him in central Rajasthan, before he could focus his attention on Mewar. Bahram Khan, the real reason for Akbar's success in the Second Battle of Panipat had fallen out with him and rebelled, because Akbar had grabbed Bahram Khan's wife as his keep. While among the Hindus, the wife of the teacher is considered as mother. Akbar came from a thought process where violating the wife of your teacher and protector was an acceptable phenomenon.

Bahram Khan was a Shia Muslim and the Sunni Imams of Akbar's court hated him.

Akbar was now heavily dependent on Hindu Generals for his survival. Winning Mewar with the help of his Rajput Generals would ease a lot of pressure on him, hence the overtures.

5. Akbar wanted to psyche Pratap into defeat by increasing his hardships for him. By 1572, when Udai Singh died, Akbar had made treaties with all the neighbouring kingdoms of Mewar or subjugated them, and all that remained with Pratap was an area of 300 miles, which was hilly and barren. Akbar had presumed that Pratap would not be able to endure such hardships and would yield.

Akbar was using the age-old tactic of his religion where purchasing loyalties of kafir leadership was an established doctrine. For the spread of faith, bribing your enemy and their leaders had religious sanction. Akbar was exploring that possibility.

Of course, little did he know of Pratap's mettle and his deep commitment to his family honour and Hindu *dharma*. It was Akbar's misfortune that Pratap was not available for sale.

6. With Jagmal and Sagar, the two brothers estranged from Pratap, Akbar also wanted to engineer a revolt in Pratap's family. But Pratap's love and total trust in his *samants* and the rest of the family endeared them to each other to such an extent that all of

Mewar rallied around Pratap to fight Akbar, whatever hardships it would entail.

The Bhils were the backbone of Maharana Pratap's resistance. They were spies, food providers, protectors and messengers for Pratap. The age-old loyalty of Bhils to Mewar only got strengthened in Pratap's time. The entire population of Mewar rallied around Pratap's 'scorched earth policy' and the nefarious designs of the Turk fell flat.

7. Most importantly, Akbar knew that his artillery would be of little or no use in a war against Mewar in the Aravallis. The *tulghuma* and *araba* war tactics, used by his grandfather Babur to damage Pratap's grandfather Sanga at the plains of Khanwa, could not be employed in the hilly terrain of Mewar; hence his only chance of bringing Mewar in his subjugation was through peace overtures with Pratap.

A defeat for Akbar would be a nightmare he could ill afford, since many Hindu kings would rebel against him.

The *samants* of Mewar were eager to take revenge for Chittor, so Pratap kept playing with Akbar's peace proposals while preparing for a long-drawn war campaign against the Turk invader.

8. Akbar was more than desperate to avoid a frontal military invasion of Mewar because he knew that from the fortifications of Aravallis, there was no way for him to defeat, kill or capture Pratap. A military defeat of Akbar would mean a loss of authority and increase the chances of rebellion in the Hindu troops of Akbar. That was a nightmare he wanted to avoid at all costs. But Pratap and his war council were determined and prepared to confront the murderer of Chittor and therefore, merely played with his emissaries while amassing weapons and men.

Preparing for the Battle

Now let us discuss the preparations made by Pratap to take on the combined armies of the Amer Rajputs and Turks of Delhi. These preparations were crucial in this saga of a king who loved his land and people such that he calculated every move with such clinical care and precision that success always stood by him.

Pratap was a leader who was in perfect synchrony with his warlords, army and citizens.

A man whom never had fate favoured, neither time had granted remissions, nor life showered with benevolence, Pratap nevertheless rose to attain heights unimaginable in his predicament. With extreme love for his land and his people and with sharp intellect to plan out and implement a campaign against a formidable foe, Pratap eventually overpowered him.

Pratap was a Mahayogi who never yielded to emotional outbursts, paternal neglect or insults or sibling rivalry. Maintaining a Spartan lifestyle in the face of reverses of fortune, Pratap focused on the singular goal of achieving Mewar's freedom.

A *saadhak* (seeker) who knew the truth and worth of Hindu *dharma* and Sanatana values and protected them with everything at his disposal.

He put every resource he could lay hands on at stake and emerged victorious in the end.

From 1568, with the siege and destruction of Chittor, to 1576, the year of the Battle of Haldighati, both Akbar and Pratap were busy in their own pursuits. Akbar was quelling rebellions in Afghanistan and Bengal, while Pratap was striking alliances with surrounding kingdoms and preparing an army to take on the joint forces of the Mughals and Jaipur's Rajputs. That he would have to fight his fellow Rajputs in the years ahead, weighed heavy on Pratap's heart but he chose war nonetheless, because a much larger principle of his freedom and *dharma* were at stake.

Below is the account of the preparation Pratap made in view of the impending clash. We will decipher as we go through these preparations that Pratap was preparing for a restrained campaign to take on the Turk imperialist and tire him out by guerrilla warfare with the singular aim of recovering every inch of Mewar:

1. When Udai Singh, Pratap's father, retreated from Chittor to Udaipur in CE 1568, he was received by Rawat Harpal, the chief of Ponarwa. Harpal took the royal family into the dense forests of Ponarwa into the fort by the same name. Later, Pratap's women and children would be living in the hilly areas of Chuppan in Kamalnath—an area with ample supplies of water and fruits. Agriculture was practiced on the slopes and thus Pratap was relieved of the anxiety of the well-being and safety of his family.

The Caves of Mayra

2. The most crucial decision taken by Rana Pratap and his counsels was to spot the intricate network of caves at Mayra, Jowarwala and Machinpur where he instructed his men to keep the treasures of Mewar, as well as arms and supplies for the army. We must remember the great pursuits of the valiant ancestry of Pratap, especially Hammir, Kumbha and Sanga who amassed great wealth for the kingdom of Mewar. The foresight of these Maharanas would help Pratap tide over the most difficult period faced by the Mewar dynasty. We must also marvel at the wisdom and logistics management of the kings of Mewar and their chieftains who transported all the wealth out of Chittor when Akbar's attack was imminent. How those huge containers of gold and other jewels were taken out, transported and concealed from the public eye and enemies of Mewar is anybody's guess. How that entire movement was kept secret and how the unflinching loyalty of allies and caretakers preserved this treasure, is a case study in logistics, intelligence and honesty.

3. At many places in the Aravallis, several mountain ranges were only twenty feet long and six feet wide with an abundance of water. The plateaus amid the ranges were extremely fertile, yielding crops perennially. Such areas were marked, and tiny paths constructed to interconnect areas that were to be used by the Mewar army to retreat to and rest. The approach to these areas was such that even 20 to 30 armed men could easily thwart a thousand men trying to come in. These sites were memorised by each war General of Mewar and the accesses and exits were constructed to serve as retreat points.

4. Pratap fortified the network of forts built by his great, great grandfather Kumbha to function as retreat and refresh points for future guerrilla warfare. Gogunda was a special focus for Pratap because of its proximity to the Haldighati pass. He posted his chief of cavalry, Joshi Puna at Haldighati to lead a contingent of Bhils to defend the Haldighati pass by becoming familiar with the terrain.

5. Pratap shifted entire populations from the occupied areas of Mewar to Kelwara, Kumbhalgarh and other fertile areas. The plains of Mewar were left scorched so that the incoming Mughal forces would starve; also, the local population of Mewar could be protected against plunder and rape by the Turks. Wells were poisoned so that invaders would die of thirst. Crops were burnt and everything of utility destroyed.

6. Pratap made adequate arrangements for the training of his people in the hilly retreats. The task of the military training of young and new recruits was given to Ram Shah Tanwar of Gwalior. Akbar had annexed his kingdom of Gwalior and Tanwar had approached Rana Udai Singh for help in winning Gwalior back. Ever since Ram Tanwar was appointed as the General and military strategist for Mewar, he was paid 800 rupees a day to support himself and his family. He also received a few troops in lieu of his services to the Mewar dynasty. Ram Shah Tanwar along with his sons Shalivahan, Pratap and Bhawani Singh had been instrumental in firmly ensconcing Mewar's army in the jungles of Aravallis after the loss of Chittor[109].

7. A solid spy network was erected around the Bhil population of Mewar as they were very intimately connected to Pratap and had his complete trust. Bhils were forest dwellers and masters at camouflaging themselves and could survive in the wild for weeks without food or water, sustaining themselves of from the jungle. Pratap's spy network would prove critical in planning the battle of Haldighati and Dewair, by gathering adequate intelligence regarding the numbers and tactical moves of Mughals. Pratap was always two steps ahead of the invading Turks because of his 'eyes' and 'ears' in the Aravallis.

8. Alliance was stuck with the king of Sirohi, Man Singh.

109. Bhatt, p. 227.

Pratap reached out to his father-in-law Narain Das of Idar and got his support too. The Maharana was aware of his deficiencies with regard to artillery and therefore hired Hakim Khan Suri and his 800 Afghan soldiers to use cannon warfare effectively. Hakim Khan was a relative of Sher Shah Suri, who had briefly ruled Delhi and then died prematurely in an accidental cannon explosion. The Afghan Suris and Turkic Mughals were bloodthirsty rivals of each other. Firepower remained a weak spot of Mewar until Pratap's son Amar Singh became the king and undertook the construction of cannons for Mewar. Pratap also paid Taj Khan of Jalore to join forces with him and hire Muslim mercenaries for his army.

Thus Pratap lead from the front, sacrificing comfort, living in the jungles, vowing never to sleep on a bed or eat in metal dishes until the war was won. His committment and constant criss-crossing the state to galvanize his troops inspired the people of Mewar to rise against the Turkic invaders at the most vulnerable time for Mewar and adjoining kingdoms. That the powerless but vengeful Afghans chose to fight for Pratap is indication enough that Pratap was the only pivot around whom resistance to the Mughals could be offered.

Brahmins, Vaishyas, Shudras, Kshatriyas, Charans and Bhils—all communities rose to fight alongside Pratap's army. Pratap generated unprecedented support, both in scale and committment, as we will find out with the eight-year campaign that Pratap began at Haldighati in CE 1576 and ended at Dewair in CE 1583. It ended with a crushing defeat of the Mughals and Pratap recovering every inch of Mewar, except Chittor.

Appointment of Man Singh

Akbar came to Ajmer in March 1576 and set up his camp. Despite the reservations of his Muslim nobles, Akbar nominated Man Singh as the leader of the expedition against Pratap. The Mughal contingent also had Asif Khan, Syed Ahmed, Hashim Barha, Jagannath Kachchawa, Syed Raju, Bahlol Khan, Mehtar Khan, Madho Singh, Rao Loonkaran, Mujahid Beg, etc.

Al-Badayuni, the writer of *Muntakhab-ul-Tawarikh*, also accompanied the Mughals and the Muslim side of history was recorded by him as a witness of the Battle of Haldighati.

Man Singh, whom Akbar referred to as *beta* (son), was chosen to lead the Turk army for the following reasons:

Man Singh was a fierce and courageous warrior and a shrewd General with a lot of experience in warfare.

- It was a strategic masterstroke by Akbar to create permanent enmity between two powerful Rajput houses of Amer and Mewar. Not only between Pratap and Man Singh, but with both Rajput armies fighting each other, there would be multiple layers of enmity between the two kingdoms which would be irreparable.
- Akbar knew that the Rajputs of Jaipur would not be at their best in the offensive if a Muslim was to lead them. He thus optimised his chances by pitching Rajputs led by a Rajput. But Akbar also sent Asif Khan and his best warriors along with the Syeds to fight under Man Singh. If his Rajputs were to put a weak offence, Akbar reinforced it with his Muslim troops.
- Akbar was also aware of the psyche of the kings of Mewar and their armies, who were the protectors of Hinduism. Hence, he knew that the assault of Mewar armies on the fellow Hindus of Jaipur would be half-hearted at best. He thus used this dilemma of Mewar's Hindus to weaken Pratap's position.
- Akbar being a shrewd manipulator had educated himself on the hierarchy among Rajput kingdoms and was aware that till Maharana Sanga's time, Jaipur used to pay taxes to Mewar and was subservient to it. He knew that the house of Jaipur would certainly be nursing some grudges against Mewar and hence, the undercurrent could be capitalised on to expand his own imperialistic designs.

On 20th April 1576, Man Singh marched towards Mandalgarh in Mewar with a contingent of approximately 10,000 troops. He stayed at Mandalgarh for two months while ensuring food supply and other logistics from Ajmer. From Mandalgarh, Man Singh proceeded to Khamnor, which is a kilometre from the Haldighati pass. Hearing of Man Singh's arrival at Mandalgarh, Pratap wanted to confront him there itself but was advised against it by his *samants* for two reasons:

- It would be impossible to defeat a larger army of Man Singh in the plains; it was better to lure them into the hills.
- Man Singh was a representative now. This war was no scuffle between two perennial armies. The outcome of this battle would decide the fate of Mewar and thus Hindus. Hence, extreme caution had to be exercised, as losing was not an option.

Pratap consented and decided to wait. With Man Singh's movement to Khamnor, it was certain that Haldighati was where the two forces would clash. So he moved his forces from Kumbhalgarh to Gogunda, about 10 kms south-west of Haldighati. Pratap's war council met at Raja Ram Shah Tanwar's residence in Gogunda and was attended by Tanwars of Gwalior, represented by Ram Shah and his three sons. A teenage grandson of Ram Shah, Dharmagat, was also present. The *samants* and allies of Mewar who attended the war council were Rao Sangram Singh, Jhala Bida, Jhala Man, Bhim Singh Dodia, Durga Singh Parmar, Hari Das Chouhan, Natha Chouhan, Pragya Das Bhakrot, Alam Rathore, Net Singh Sarangdevot, Krishna Das Choondawat, Hakim Khan Sur and Bhama Shah, along with his brother Tara Shah. From the house of Mewar itself and the family, the following were present: Man Singh Songara (Pratap's maternal uncle), Kumpa Rathore (son of Jaimal Rathore) and Kalyan Singh Choondawat (son of the legendary Patta Choondawat).

Pratap's eldest son and heir to Mewar, Kunwar Amar Singh, was deliberately kept away from all proceedings of the war. This demonstrates the foresight of Pratap and his *samants* to avoid any harm to the young prince so that the war against the Turks would continue even if Pratap was martyred in the battle.

The seniors of the council were of the opinion that Mewar's army shouldn't leave the hills and wait for the Mughal army to come inside. Ram Shah Tanwar, Net Singh, Krishna Das and other seniors said that except for the few Rajputs of Jaipur, the Mughals were not experienced in warfare in the hilly areas and would be easily taken care of by the Mewar army.

But the young scions of the council favoured a meeting in the plains. Ultimately, it was decided that the Mewar army would attack from three directions and descend out of the Haldighati pass to fight in the plains of Khamnor near the banks of the Banas river. This decision was in contradiction to Mewar council's earlier strategy of fighting the invading army from the safety of Aravallis[110].

Analysing Pratap's persona, it can be conjectured that Pratap yielded to the younger members because of a strategic plan in his mind. The plan was that the enemy must be shown the fierce face of the Mewar army. If they were to defeat the Mughal army, then fellow-Hindu kingdoms would gravitate towards Mewar.

If, on the other hand, the Mewar warriors were to lose because of being outnumbered, at least a message would be sent to Akbar and other Hindu kingdoms that Mewar would not surrender to the Turks at any cost.

Pratap also wanted to measure the resolve of Man Singh and his Rajput army to kill fellow-Rajputs in alliance with a *vidharmi* (an adherent of another religion). Pratap hoped that the lower rung of Rajputs in the Jaipur army would at least introspect on witnessing the killing of fellow-Hindus of Mewar. At Gogunda, before departing, it was decided that if the Mughal army were to overwhelm the Mewar army, then the latter would retreat to the hills. This decision of Pratap's and his council to attack from the hills and stay close enough to them for retreat also meant that the Mughals would be unable to use their superior firepower against Mewar.

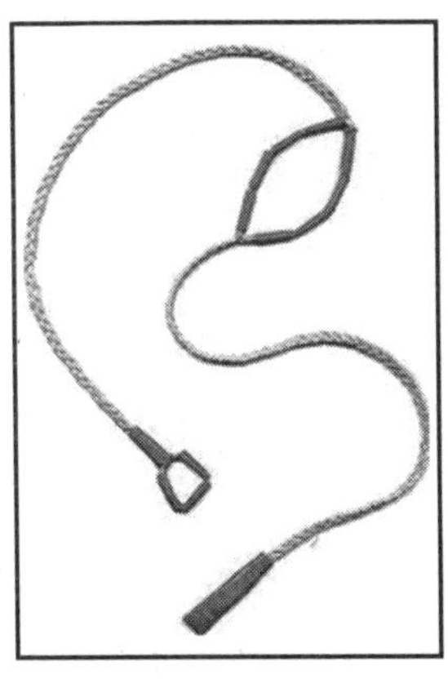

Gofan

In any case, Pratap would be protected from all sides and it was agreed that if the main Generals gave a call to Pratap to retire, he would heed it and not sacrifice himself needlessly.

The Bhils were to climb up on trees

110. Mathur, p. 103.

and hit the Mughals with a barrage of stones by using *gofan*—a stone pelter made of jute and rope. These stones hurled from the pelter would hit like a bullet and cause extensive damage.

The annals of Mewar and Col. Tod mention 20,000 as the strength of the Mewar army and 80,000 as that of Man Singh. Muslim historian, Al Badayuni puts the number of troops at 3,000 for Pratap and 5,000 for Man Singh. If we analyse the numbers objectively, the tilt would be on the side of number of troops at least in five digits.

First, it has been well documented and a settled fact that Akbar attacked Chittor in 1568 with a force of 80,000 which was resisted by 8,000 from Mewar from inside the fort. If 8,000 troops were a fraction of Mewar army, surely 20,000 troops could have easily been present at Haldighati.

Second, the strategic significance of the Battle of Haldighati implied that both sides came with adequate numbers; hence the figure of 20,000 troops of Mewar seems closer to the truth.

Third, Mewar folklore narrates the expanse of war from the neck of Haldighati to the fields of Khamnor, where Mughal troops were chased as far as Banas river, 5 km from the battlefield. This indicates a larger army most likely in five digits.

Furthermore, the contradictions in Al Badayuni's writings give away a lot. On one hand, he says, praising Man Singh, that he became the sword of Islam that day, and then he puts the numbers of Mewar troops at 3,000, which would make Haldighati nothing more than a skirmish instead of a battle that changed the course of history.

All in all, to belittle Pratap, it would be a sound ploy to show Haldighati as a minor battle and hence the Islamic literature downplayed the size and scale of Haldighati. Whatever be the numbers, one thing is sure that Pratap was up against an army two to three times his own army; hence, his tactic of fighting close to the hills would prove crucial to his victory.

Pratap marched and camped with his army at Losing, a village 10 miles south-west of Khamnor. Man Singh camped at Motela, near Khamnor. Thus, the two camps were set up approximately six miles from each other.

An interesting incident deserves narration here. The Bhil spies informed Pratap that accompanied by fewer than 100 horsemen, Man Singh had strayed into the jungles near Losing while chasing game. A few advisors asked Pratap to seize the chance and kill Man Singh. Only Jhala Bida opposed the move saying that Hindus could not afford a perpetual enmity between Jaipur and Mewar for a relatively small gain. Pratap consented and let Man Singh go back unharmed.

This action would prove crucial to the coming generations when Jaipur *samants* eventually aligned with Mewar to defeat Aurangzeb during the tenure of Raj Singh, Pratap's great-great-grandson. Had Pratap killed Man Singh that day by deceit, the enmity between Jaipur and Mewar would have become irreconcilable.

The Battle

Before describing the war in detail, a particular terminology of Mewar's warfare must be understood. The Mewar army usually attacked in two waves. The first one was called, *harawal dastaa* or advance guard and the follow-up group was called, *chandawal dastaa,* meaning the rear attack formation.

The Battle of Haldighati is best understood and explained by the relative movements of these two formations with respect to both the armies. On 18th June 1576, Maharana Pratap Singh descended from the Haldighati pass to an open space just at the northern end of the pass—an area referred to today as Badshahi Bagh.

Man Singh had posted eighty very experienced Syed Barha soldiers at the point of exit for Pratap and his army.

Maharana Pratap had divided his army into two flanks and a central core. The left-wing of Mewar's *harawal dastaa* was led by Jhala Man, Jait Singh, Jhala Bida and Man Singh Songara; the right-wing was led by Ram Shah Tanwar and his sons and the lone grandson along with Bhama Shah and his brother Tarachand. The central *harawal dastaa* comprised Bhim Singh Dodiya, Rawat Krishna Das, Rawat Sanga, Ram Singh and Hakim Khan Sur; the central *chandawal dastaa* was made up of the king of Bhils Poonja

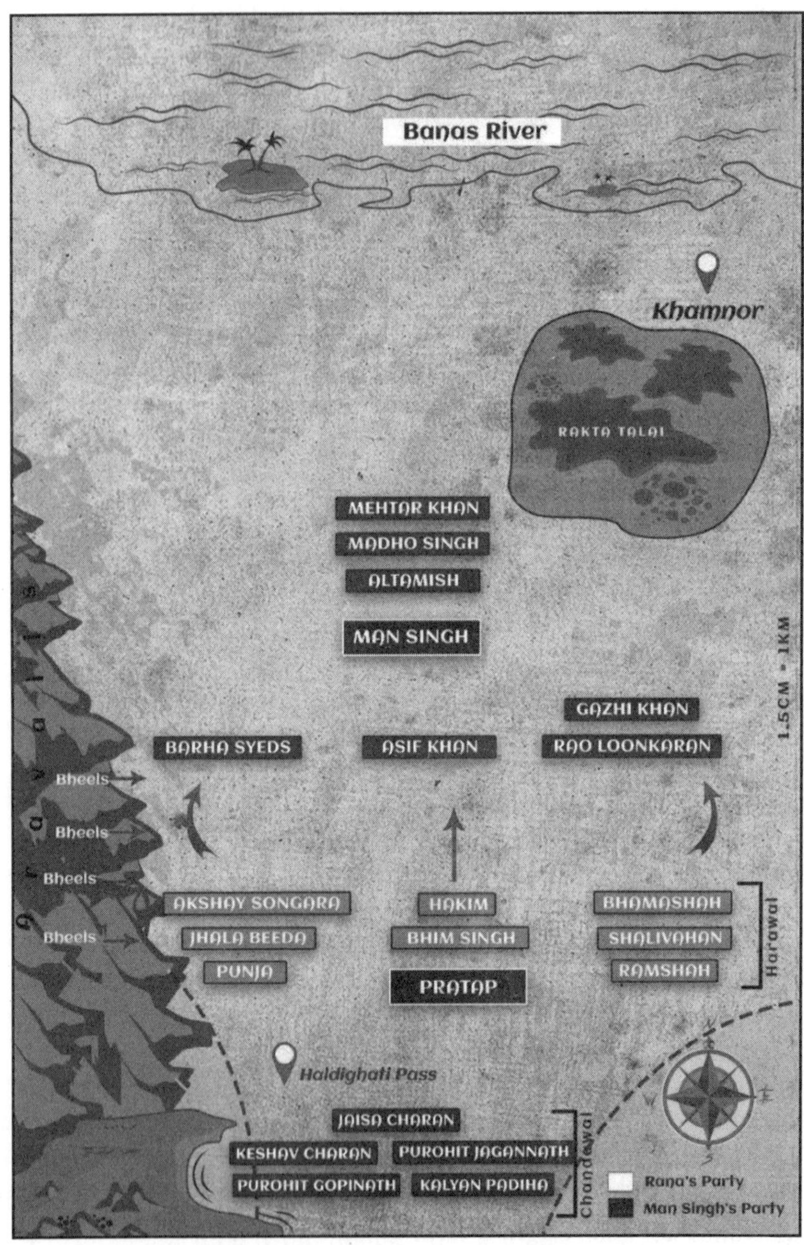
Banas River
Khamnor
RAKTA TALAI
MEHTAR KHAN
MADHO SINGH
ALTAMISH
MAN SINGH
1.5CM - 1KM
GAZHI KHAN
BARHA SYEDS
ASIF KHAN
RAO LOONKARAN
Bheels
Bheels
Bheels
Bheels
AKSHAY SONGARA
JHALA BEEDA
PUNJA
HAKIM
BHIM SINGH
PRATAP
BHAMASHAH
SHALIVAHAN
RAMSHAH
Harawal
Haldighati Pass
JAISA CHARAN
KESHAV CHARAN
PUROHIT JAGANNATH
PUROHIT GOPINATH
KALYAN PADIHA
Rana's Party
Man Singh's Party

Rana, Purohit Gopinath, Purohit Jagannath, Kalyan Padihar, Jaimal Bhachaawat and the Charans Jaisa and Keshav.

The Maharana was kept at the centre of this formation. The Mughal army was placed in an almost equivalent manner. The right-wing of the Mughal army was led by battle-hardened Syed Barhas, who were known for his courage and experience. The left-wing was led by Ghazi Khan and Rao Loonkaran along with Jagannath Kachchawa and Asif Khan.

Man Singh was placed at the centre but was adequately shielded by the *harawal* of Mughals. The most important thing that changed the course of this battle was the two batches of reserve forces of the Mughals. The frontal reserve force referred to as *altamash* was led by Madho Singh and was to reinforce any flank that was seen to be weakening. The rear reserve force of Mughals was led by a cunning General, Mehtar Khan. Thus, these two formations clashed on the noon of 18th June 1576, on the fields of Khamnor, for a battle that was to decide the fate of Hindu survival in the region.

Pratap is said to have scanned the war arena, giving a long, hard and angry look at the Mughal army. He was flanked only by Hakim Khan and Bhama Shah as he looked piercingly at the Mughals. Abul Fazl writes: *"Keeka Rana looked at our brave soldiers menacingly. The day was so hot that our brains were melting in our skulls."*

And with conch shells reverberating the battlefield, Hindu warriors led by Pratap commenced the attack. Mughals too sounded the war bugle.

Al Badayuni writes in his memoirs: *"The two armies were friends of war and enemies of life. They turned life cheap and honour costly."*

The central Harawal of Mewar led by Hakim Khan Sur led the first attack on the Harawals of the Mughals, who were decimated. Pratap followed Hakim Khan and attacked Kazi Khan in the centre, who was stationed at the exit of Haldighati pass with his eighty soldiers.

Killing them, Pratap attacked Syed Hashim Barha and the advance Mughal guard (harawal) under Jagannath Kachchawa and Asif Khan. Pratap's assault stupefied these Generals and they huddled together and their forces rolled into a rugged and bushy plain. Asif Khan retreated to the safety of the centre of the Mughal army, close to Man Singh. Jagannath Kachchawa, a very courageous and seasoned warrior, was about to fall from his horse when the advance reserve force led by Madho Singh came to his rescue.

Pratap pushed even this reserve force on the defensive and but for Syed Barha's soldiers, all Mughal central forces began disintegrating. Meanwhile, the right-wing of Mewar's army attacked the left-wing of the Mughals and defeated it completely. The Rajputs of Sambhar, under Loonkaran, fled like a flock of sheep and took shelter under the right-wing of Mughal forces, the Barha Syeds. Jhala Bida from the left-wing of Mewar army attacked the Syeds and resoundingly defeated them. To the credit of these Barha Syeds, they stood ground despite the slaughter and did not flee.

Badayuni writes, *"Had the Syeds withdrawn from their posts, a great disaster would have befallen the imperial army."*

Here an incident that denotes the mindset of Islamic invaders must be narrated. This incident has been narrated by Al Badayuni himself in his memoirs. This is an incident that should educate Hindus as to the real designs of Islamic invasion of India and the stupidity of Hindus in believing that by striking an alliance with Islamist extremists, they can be safe and prosperous.

When both armies had intertwined in such a fierce manner at the centre, left and right flanks, it became difficult for the Mughals to differentiate between the Rajputs of Amer and Mewar since both were wearing saffron coloured scarves.

Al Badayuni turned to Asif Khan, the main General besides Man Singh and asked, *"I see saffron-wielding Rajputs on both sides how to distinguish between friends and foes?"*

Asaf Khan replied, *"Continue showering arrows indiscriminately. Either way, only kafirs will die and Islam will win[111]."*

If only Hindus of yesteryears and even today would grasp the true implications of these words of Asif Khan.

111. Ojha, Bhatt, both quote Al Badayuni.

If only Hindus were to understand that we were dealing with invaders with no moral compass at all, except a mad desire to Islamise their enemies.

If only Hindus were to understand the message of this confession by Badayuni that to them, friendship, honour and loyalty meant nothing before the expansion of Islam.

If only Hindus would even today understand that such an obsession with spreading Islam on this globe overrode any designs of progress, goodwill or peace with these marauders.

If only Hindus were to see this singular obsession of Islamists of spreading Islam instead of viewing them as mere imperialists.

If only Hindus had truly understood the real nature and motive of Islamic invaders, the resistance to them would have been firmer and more organised.

If only Hindus had responded to the Islamic onslaught with a similar dedication to save Hinduism and had firmly stood their ground, the history of this region would have been entirely different.

Returning to the battle, with the defeat and plunder of both flanks, the Mewar army converged to the centre of the battlefield. Ram Shah Tanwar and his sons now attacked Man Singh himself. Man Singh fought bravely against Ram Shah and the combat was of such ferocity that even the fighting soldiers were distracted and began watching the duel in awe.

Mullah Sheeri, another Islamic historian, although openly favouring only Islamic warriors, was forced to write about the valour of Man Singh, saying, *"The Hindu wields the sword of Islam*[112]*."*

Pratap shot an arrow to penetrate the buttock of an escaping Sheikh Mansur, who was the leader of the Sheikhzadas of Fatehpur Sikri and the son of Salim Chishti. Mansur limped for the rest of his life. Kazi Khan, a war General, received a big slash in his right hand which forced him to retreat, shouting, *"Flight from overwhelming odds is one of the traditions of the Prophet."* Kazi was referring to the teachings of the prophet of Islam[113].

---

112. Mathur, p. 110.
113. Bhatt, p. 232.

The Mewar army had conclusively pushed the Mughal army in all the three flanks and the latter literally ran with their lives in a northward direction for approximately 5 kilometres, running even beyond the Banas river. Here is where the critical turn to the Battle of Haldighati took place. With a quick exchange of glances between the main Generals, the Mewar army chased the Mughal army northwards and came to an open space, just west of the village of Khamnor.

Mehtar Khan, a General commanding the rear reserve forces came up with a plan to revive the broken morale of Mughal troops and instructed his drummers and trumpeters to falsely announce the arrival of Akbar with more troops. Islamic invaders were known to concoct such lies and propaganda to their advantage. This has also been documented by Maulvi Abdul Qadir in his memoirs of the battle.

Hearing this noise and proclamation, the escaping Mughal army was reinvigorated and gathered again to fight, while Mewar forces were anxious and filled with doubt that if more Mughal troops had arrived, how were they to face them?

The trick worked to the advantage of the Mughals and hand-to-hand combat commenced in the field near Khamnor. The slaughter that occurred at Khamnor was a decisive one. Thousands of warriors and soldiers fell near the local water pond, fighting each other. The pond was filled with so much blood that the locals named the pond *Rakt Talai*, or a 'pool of blood,' a name that has been retained even today.

The two armies were engaged in hand-to-hand combat and Mewar's warriors started falling, outnumbered 3:1 by Mughals. The fight at *Rakt Talai* lasted approximately three hours.

As death danced around them, the Hindus of Mewar joined her, matching step to step, beat to beat and note to note. All boundaries were forgotten in the combat and only slaughter filled the heads of the Mewar army.

Ram Shah Tanwar, along with his three sons and a teenager grandson, Dharmagat, were the first ones to sacrifice their lives in service of Mewar. Jagannath Kachchawa killed Ramdas Rathore, the son of Jaimal Rathore in a one-to-one combat. Jhala Bida and the Charans Keshav and Jaisa too fell.

At this point, Bhim Singh Dodia, who had personally had a verbal duel with Man Singh when Man Singh had come to Mewar with a peace proposal, called out to Man Singh, and shouted, "I, Bhim Singh have come, save yourself." He launched his spear at Man Singh which hit his *hauda*[114] (canopy seat atop an elephant), but Man Singh was unhurt.

A dozen Mughal soldiers descended upon the mighty Bhim Singh and overpowered him with multiple injuries. Pratap immediately followed Bhim Singh and the epic scene of Pratap's horse, the beautiful white Chetak putting his forelegs on the body of the elephant that Man Singh was mounting ensued, and Pratap dispatched his spear with full might.

Pratap roared while hurling his spear, *"Pratap Singh aaya, jahan tak ho sake tujhse, veerta dikha."* (Pratap Singh comes. Show as much valour as you can)[115].

114. The metallic tub-shaped seat on the back of war elephants (Hindi word).
115. *Veer Vinod*, vol. 2, p. 152.

Man Singh ducked and hid inside the *hauda,* fearing Pratap's assault. The elephant's tusks were fitted with straight swords, called *khaanda* and a lunge by the elephant cut through one of the hind legs of Chetak and the brave mount was crippled.

At this time, a brief description of the battle of the elephants of both sides must be mentioned. Pratap's elephant Loona fought with Gajmuktha of the Mughals and both animals crushed many of the enemy soldiers. Loona's *mahout* was then hit by a bullet and Loona turned back to remove himself from the battle. Then the best elephant of Pratap, Ramprasad was brought in, and he wrought havoc on the Mughals, when they brought an elephant named 'Ran Madar' to fight Ramprasad.

Ramprasad was about to overpower Ran Madar when his *mahout* too was killed by an arrow. Ramprasad was a very special and intelligent animal, whose popularity had reached even Akbar's ears.

Ramprasad kept crushing the Mughals even without a *mahout.* The superintendent of the Mughal elephant army, Hussain Khan, seized the opportunity, mounted Ramprasad and drove it into the possession of the Mughal army. This amazing animal was later taken to Akbar as a war bounty by Asif Khan and Akbar was overjoyed to win this elephant. He renamed him Peerprasad. According to legend, Ramprasad gave up food and water in Mughal captivity and eventually died within days.

Maharana Pratap had no reserve forces to back him and hearing of the arrival of Akbar himself with fresh forces, he called for a retreat to the hills as had been decided by the war council. Pratap had himself endured eight wounds by this time. It was 3 o'clock in the afternoon, the Mewar forces had tired out and Pratap signalled his Generals to retreat to the mountains. Mewar's sons had been fighting in the unforgiving heat of Aravallis for four hours now.

The Bhils were the first ones to retreat under Rana Poonja. The Mughals decided to pursue Pratap and kill him as he turned his limping Chetak towards the hills. At least two dozen archers started shooting arrows at the Sisodia lion and an equal number attacked him physically.

Hakim Khan Sur and Jhala Man then decided to make the ultimate sacrifice for their master. Hakim Khan came between the arrows of Mughal archers and Pratap. Jhala Man took the royal *chhatri* or the royal emblem which only the king of Mewar could don and put it on his horse. Jhala Man also took the twin swords of Pratap in exchange for his own and started shouting, *"Come and get me, you Turks, I am Pratap, your destroyer."* It helped matters a lot that Jhala Man much resembled Pratap in height, build and complexion.

The Samadhi of the Tanwars of Gwalior *Samadhi of Jhala Man*

Rakt Talai

Both Hakim Khan and Jhala Man perished in this combat with the Mughals, but both these great warriors laid down their lives with immense satisfaction in their hearts that their king had been saved and the struggle for freedom would go on. Man Singh ignored the escape of Rana Pratap Singh and kept fighting, but Asif Khan sent two Mughal Generals after Pratap to finish him off.

Chetak breathes his last

A remarkably interesting turn of events took place at this juncture, which deserves mention for multiple reasons. Shakti Singh, Pratap's estranged brother, gave hot chase to the two pursuing Mughal Generals. As the Mughals gained on Pratap, Shakti Singh also caught up and shouted, *'Are O neele ghode ra aswar'* in the Marwari language meaning, 'Listen! O rider of the blue horse.'

Pratap looked back and witnessed Shakti Singh killing both his Mughal pursuers. The latter approached Pratap with tears in his eyes. This episode happened at the village of Bilocha, about 5 kilometres from Haldighati. Both brothers hugged each other, and Shakti Singh offered his horse to Pratap to continue his escape. At Bilocha, the wounded Chetak fell and breathed his last in Pratap's arms. Both brothers cremated the animal; a *samadhi* of Chetak today stands at Bilocha. Pratap continued his journey southwards and retreated to the safety of Kolyari village.

There are different accounts of the number of troops killed at Haldighati. While Persian and Mughal historians put the number of the dead at 500, 180 Muslims and 320 Hindus, the annals of Mewar and Col. Tod estimated the numbers at 16,000. Whatever be the number, it is an established fact that Pratap managed to inflict a mortality rate of 2:1 in favour of Mewar since at least 50 per cent of dead Hindus were fighting for Mughals.

Samadhi of Chetak at Bilocha

On the other hand, in terms of Generals lost, Mewar lost heavily, as no General of significance was lost by Mughals, but Mewar lost Ram Shah Tanwar and his entire clan, Jhala Man, Bhim Singh, Jhala Bida, Hakim Khan, Man Singh Songara, Ram Das Mertia and warriors of very high calibre. Those of Mewar who escaped were Rawat Kishan Das, Gopal Das Mertia, Bhama Shah and Tarachand.

As for the outcome of Haldighati, there have been proponents of both sides being victorious but here we try to present facts to establish Haldighati as a victory for Mewar:

1. The Mughal army was so thoroughly decimated and defeated by an army one-fourth its size that it could not chase Pratap or his army even for 100 metres into the hills.
2. Akbar had clearly instructed Man Singh to kill or capture Pratap to conclusively finish this expedition, but Man Singh failed to do either and hence Akbar was denied his objective.

3. The stature of Asif Khan and Man Singh upon returning to Delhi was much reduced and both were reduced at the *dyodhi* (doorstep) of Akbar as a punishment for the failure of conclusively defeating Pratap or capturing him.
4. The Mughals could not capture any General of Mewar or lay hands on any treasure or weapons of consequence except Ramprasad, the magnificent war elephant.
5. In November, 1576, Akbar himself led an expedition to attack Mewar and came up to Gogunda. If Pratap had lost Haldighati, what was Akbar doing in Mewar within six months of that victory invading the same geographical area with a much larger force?
6. Three *tamra patras* (copper letters) issued by Bhama Shah on behalf of Pratap have been found with their owners in Sathana, Peepli and Mohi villages. These are all dated around August and September of 1576, the year of Haldighati. If Pratap had lost Haldighati, how was he issuing *jagirs* to his men? Land revenue records are one of the most reliable pieces of historical evidence.
7. The most important thing is the state of the Mughal army in the days following Haldighati and which most Indian historians have failed to record and/or describe for unknown reasons.

Next day, Man Singh moved to Gogunda in pursuit of Pratap and this was exactly what Pratap and his counsels had planned post-Haldighati. Pratap let Man Singh walk into the hills of Gogunda after killing twenty odd defendants. It was believed that those who died defending the forts would attain *moksha* and only the weak and old had been left to perform this favour.

Pratap's army then blocked all routes out of Gogunda and Man Singh was trapped in the jungles without food and water as Gogunda had been emptied of its residents and resources beforehand.

Man Singh remained trapped at Gogunda for months and several hundreds of his soldiers died of hunger and disease. It has been recorded in various annals that the Mughal army survived by eating mangoes from the jungle and horse meat, killing their own war horses. Ultimately, Man Singh and Asif Khan were asked to return and were demoted by Akbar. The Mughal emperor, in fact, did not even receive them personally[116].

Now, we look at Maharana Pratap's strategy and his achievements from the Battle of Haldighati.

1. Pratap was able to send a clear, unambiguous message to Akbar and his Generals of his resolve to defend his freedom and territory. It was crucial not only for the enemy but for the *samants* and people of Mewar to know that this was a king who was not ready to bend to Akbar, whatever the cost.
2. The Maharana was able to assess the strength and resolve of the Mughals as well. This was his first war with the Mughal army in frontal combat and being an astute learner, Pratap learnt the war tactics of Mughals.
3. Before Haldighati, Ram Shah Tanwar of Gwalior had been of the firm opinion that the Mewar army should not come out of the hills but instead lure Mughals into Aravallis and decimate them. The younger generation wanted to fight in the plains and Haldighati ensured for Mewar that in the coming years, the only way to fight would be in the form of guerrilla warfare—a system of warfare that suited the topography, courage and genius of Mewar's people. Instead of fighting pitched battles, Pratap decided to bleed the Mughals with a hundred cuts.
4. Haldighati established Maharana Pratap Singh of Mewar as the unquestioned leader of Hindus.
5. Both Pratap and Akbar now realised that the Mughals had no answer to the mountain warfare of the Sisodias and their army. It was through the safety of Aravallis that the future consolidation of Mewar was to happen.

Implicit in the preparation that Rana Pratap had made was his resolve of a long campaign against the Mughals. We also see no sign of dejection in Pratap or his scattered army. His name and

116. Mathur, p. 117.

fame travelled far and wide across Rajasthan and all kings, even those subservient to Akbar, started talking about Pratap's rise as a challenge to the Turks.

After Sanga, Pratap was the only king of consequence who rose to fight the joint forces of the Mughals and Jaipur's Rajputs.

It was Pratap's unbending resolve that forced defections in the Rajput armies of Rajasthan when the small chieftains gravitated to him.

Pratap became the epicentre of resistance and a lot of poetry recorded in Rajasthan and even in Akbar's courts eulogised Pratap. Most Hindu kings now began supporting him without the knowledge of Akbar. After Haldighati, the rulers of Banswara, Dungarpur, Sirohi, Jalore and Idar entered into friendly alliances with Mewar.

The ground was laid for a sustained campaign to root out the Mughals from Mewar and recapture every inch of the land. Thus, Pratap was able to achieve and establish his objectives at Haldighati, though it came at a heavy cost in lives to Mewar. The Maharana moved on to the next stage of resistance to Mughals without any delay.

We can safely proclaim Haldighati as a victory for Maharana Pratap in both the short and long term.

Thermopylae is a pass in coastal Greece where the Greeks had fought a massive Persian invasion in 480 BC. James Tod compares Haldighati with the Battle of Thermopylae. Just like the resistance at Thermopylae made a hero of the Spartan king Leonidas, Haldighati catapulted Pratap to the platform of *Hindwa sooraj*, making him a living legend.

Just like the Greeks were hopelessly outnumbered by Persians at Thermopylae, the Mewar warriors too were outnumbered by the Turks. But the comparison ends there.

While Thermopylae resulted in the defeat of the Greeks, Haldighati was won by Pratap and the grounds were laid for a final battle at Dewair, where Pratap would uproot all Mughal ingress into Mewar, regaining every inch of territory, except Chittor and live a free ruler, till his *moksha* in CE 1597.

□

14

Battle of Dewair: The Marathon of Mewar

Seven years of preparation for a showdown with the Mughals reached its culmination when Maharana Pratap Singh walked towards thana *thaana* of Dewair with approximately 15,000 troops to kick off a campaign to vacate eighty-four *thaanas* of the Mughals littering Mewar, to regain every inch of his land in the shortest time possible.

Bhama Shah and Tarachand in Malwa

Immediately after Haldighati, Pratap despatched Bhama Shah and Tarachand to neighbouring Malwa as his vassals.

On the eastern side of Mewar, Malwa was a vital conduit on the trade route from Delhi and Agra to Gujarat sea ports.

Bhama Shah was instructed by Pratap to loot Mughal caravans freely and amass as much wealth as he could.

Akbar was using the sea-route to send huge amounts of gold and wealth of Hindustan to Turkey and Arabia.

For Akbar and other Islamic invaders, Hindustan was a part of the Islamic Caliphate and hence, areas under Islamic occupation were tributaries of the global Islamic empire.

M.A. Khan in his book, *Jihad: A Legacy of Forced Conversions, Imperialism and Slavery* writes:

"Money and resources, extracted from the sweat and toil of non-Muslim subjects of India, used to be siphoned to the treasuries of the Islamic Caliphate in Damascus, Baghdad, Cairo or Tashkent, to the Islamic holy cities of Mecca and Medina and to the pockets of

Muslim holy men throughout the Islamic world. At the same time though, the infidels of India were being reduced to awful misery."

This should expose the hollow claims of Leftists that the Mughal rule over Bharat was just and benevolent or an era of economic progress.

Mughals destroyed the Hindu economy to fund the Islamic lands, far away.

Shortly after killing Ibrahim Lodhi at the first Battle of Panipat in CE 1526, Babur took the keys to the imperial treasury at Agra. He writes in his autobiography, *Baburnama*:

"Suitable money, gifts were bestowed from the treasury to the whole army. To every tribe there was—Afghans, Hazara, Arab, Baluch, etc. according to his position.

"Every trader, and student, indeed every man who had come with the army, took ample portion and share of bounteous gifts and largesse.

"And indeed, to the whole various train of relations and younger children went masses of red and white (gold and silver), of planishing jewels and slaves."

In contrast to the Hindu kings who taxed the farmers a mere 16 per cent of their total production, Mughal tax rate was 30-50 per cent plus some additional cesses.

Bernier writes about the tax system of Aurangzeb: "It is a tyranny often so excessive as to deprive the peasant and the artisan of the necessities of life, and leave them to die of misery and exhaustion."

Thus, while the Mughal elite and their courtiers splurged the money in mindless indulgence, the land of the Hindus was being impoverished by a gang of thieves and murderers.

Akbar also funded the Haj pilgrimage by state money.

During the Mughal era, on an average, 15,000 pilgrims visited Mecca to perform Haj, every year. This religious sponsorship began after Akbar conquered Gujarat in CE 1573 and Mughals got access to the port of Surat.

In 1576, a Mughal Haj caravan left Agra with its party of sponsored pilgrims and a massive donation of 600,000 rupees. In

1577, a caravan left with double this amount of money[117].

Mewar troops under the fierce leadership of Bhama Shah and Tarachand attacked these caravans and robbed them. There was no way Akbar could have defended these caravans from the attacks of Mewar since the time and place of attack was always chosen by the Mewar troops and they would escape with the looted wealth before the Mughals could even respond.

This unique way of generating wealth to fund his army shows the great acumen of Pratap in attacking the weak spot of Mughals.

In a period of approximately five years, Bhama Shah and Tarachand amassed 2.5 million in local currency and 20,000 gold coins and presented themselves to Pratap with that money.

Bhama Shah brings the money to Pratap

Can the Hindu *samaj* ever be free of the debt of these two great sons of Mewar?

What was the mettle of these two brothers!

117. https://indiafacts.org/islamic-loot-how-the-mughals-drained-wealth-out-of-india/

Master strategists, fierce warriors, unflinching loyalty and honesty and such dedication to Pratap! Without doubt it was the great fortune of Pratap to have such trusted friends as lieutenants in this war. Without Bhamashah and Tarachand, Pratap would have been reduced to merely being a brave rebel.

After Haldighati, Akbar sent one of his ablest Generals Shahbaz Khan, to capture Pratap.

Shahbaz chose to attack Kumbhalgarh and for one year Pratap fought him. In CE 1578, Pratap had to escape from Kumbhalgarh and take refuge in the hills of Abu.

It was around CE 1580-81 that Bhama Shah came to Pratap with the money.

According to *Veer Vinod*, Bhama Shah came with enough funds to pay the salaries of an army of 25,000 infantry and 5,000 cavalry for a period of 12 years. Besides arranging for funds, Pratap also kept fighting the Mughals at various places to keep crucial passes and *thanas* under his control. Two significant battles that need mention are being narrated below.

Battle of Mohi

Humiliated by his loss in the battle of Haldighati, Akbar was furious. He himself invaded Mewar in November 1576, and snatched Gogunda from Pratap.

He loitered around for a few days in Mewar in search of Pratap, but after a few unsuccessful attempts, he went back to Agra. Before leaving, Akbar seized some important posts of Mewar from Pratap.

In the month of May 1577, the moment Akbar set his course for Agra, Pratap started invading and seizing those important posts back-to-back.

Akbar had named Udaipur as Muhammadabad and started his own coins there. Pratap fought and won Udaipur back and revived Udaipur's name from Muhammadabad to Udaipur and also melted all the Mughal coins.

After getting Udaipur and Gogunda back from the Mughals, Pratap wanted to win the significant post of Mohi.

Situated in Rajsamand district, Mohi was a vital post held by the brave Bhati Rajputs.

A Mughal commander Mujahid Beg, forced peasants and farmers to work and arrange ration for his forces. Pratap knew that if this continued, Mughals will be entrenched comfortably. If Mughal army was successful in feeding itself from Mewar, they would end up winning every inch of Mewar in no time.

Pratap sent a message to the Bhati Rajputs in September 1577 and asked them to be ready for the attack.

Allied forces of Mewar and Bhatis destroyed all the farms and corn fields. Mujahid Beg had 3000 horsemen and pawns too. Mujahid's force and allied Hindu forces fought a fierce battle wherein Mujahid died with hundreds of his soldiers.

Mohi was now in the grip of Pratap and the rest of Mughal posts were again forced to depend on Ajmer for their reinforcements and food, etc.

Abul Fazal writes in *Akbarnama*: *"Rana started destroying fields in his attack on Mohi. At this time, Prince Man Singh Kachhwaha of Amer moved his forces to the hilly areas of Mewar. Mujahid Beg got to know of this and he rushed with his forces towards the fields but sans his artillery and weapons. He fought bravely and died like a valiant soldier."*

Once again it is observable how Man Singh overlooked Pratap's attack and helped Hindu resistance by his silence.

Battle of Banswara

On learning that the Rawals of Banswara and Dungarpur accepted suzerainty of Akbar, Pratap sent Rawat Bhan Sarangdev to subdue them in October, CE 1578.

Since both these states bordered Mewar, it was necessary for Pratap to bring them under control. A fierce battle was fought on the banks of Som River, where the combined armies of both the states were defeated by Rawat Bhan. Rawat Bhan was severely wounded in the battle but emerged victorious. An uncle of Rawat Bhan, Ran Singh was immortalised in this battle by his valour and sacrifice of his life for Mewar.

On the death of Dungarpur Rawal Askaran, his son,

Shastramal was installed by Pratap. Shastramal was already supporting Pratap. Ugra Sen was put in charge of Banswara. Both the rulers were ardent supporters of Pratap and thus the south-west borders of Mewar were secured[118].

Fighting skirmishes and battles all around Mewar, Pratap was amassing weapons and personnel for a frontal assault on Mughlas. He wanted to strike with maximum force instead of fighting in patches. Pratap planned to sweep Mewar in entirety within the shortest time and slay as many Mughal forces as he possibly could, thus striking fear into the Mughal thanedaars and giving them no time to regroup or offer resistance to Mewar's army. Flush with money and resources provided by his own wealth hidden in the Maayra mines and huge funds provided by Bhama Shah and Tarachand, Pratap amassed a huge army and was assisted by the kingdoms of Sirohi, Idar, Dungarpur and Banswara. A large contingent of the Solankis and Chauhans from the surrounding areas and Shaktawats under Pratap's brother Shakti Singh were organised to fight from Mewar's side.

Amar Singh, Pratap's eldest son, had grown up to be a fine young man and an excellent warrior with his sword and spear alike. Amar Singh led one flank of the Mewar army and was the main strategist as well. Bhama Shah and Tarachand were given charge of one flank and the Bhils were, as usual, placed on surrounding trees. Since very patchy details of this war are available to us, the estimates for Pratap's army vary from as high as 25,000 men on foot and 5,000 on the cavalry to as little as a total army of 5,000. But given the money Pratap had in 1582, and the support of most of the nobles of Mewar along with supporting kingdoms, it can be said without doubt that this army exceeded 10,000 on the side of Mewar and this was a fight for Pratap to win as he had brought all his finest warriors to this war.

On the Mughal side, Serima Khan Sultan who oversaw Dewair *thaana* had 2,000 men under his command and at least one elephant on his side along with a few dozen cavalry. Serima was a spiritually-inclined person and was a distant relative of Akbar himself, probably an uncle. Serima believed in Hindu customs and

118. Mathur, p. 143.

rituals and was tolerant towards Hindus in his area of influence.

An incident that stresses Serima's tilt to Hinduism is that when he was injured by Amar Singh's spear, he asked for *Gangajal* on his deathbed. This account has been narrated by various authors[119]. Rana Pratap himself served *Gangajal* to the dying Mughal.

Serima had prior intelligence about Pratap's impending attack and he summoned more troops from fourteen neighbouring Mughal *thanas*. Shyamdas writes in his *Veer Vinod* that the usual number of troops in each Mughal *thana* was approximately 1,000[120].

Thus, it can be safely assumed that at least 15,000 Mughal troops were involved in the Battle of Dewair

If we compare the sheer number of troops, the choice of Dewair as the point of contact by Pratap and the involvement of almost all major warriors of Mewar in the Battle of Dewair provides ample evidence for us to conclude, that this was the decisive battle between a cornered Pratap and a well-entrenched Mughal besiegement of Mewar. The Maharana chose the time and place where he would be equipped not only with the element of surprise but the advantage of terrain. Pratap had nothing but a ruthless slaughter in his mind when he was planning the campaign of Dewair.

The lull of seven years after Haldighati was to be shattered by an all-out offensive by Pratap. Only the closest *samants* and trusted Generals of Pratap knew what was being planned

The writer chooses to call this a campaign of Dewair for the simple reason that within days of the victory at Dewair, thirty-six *thaanas* of Mewar were conquered by splitting the army into two parts, one led by Pratap and the other led by his son Amar Singh.

After winning Dewair, Amar Singh led half of his troops eastwards to Amet and slew everyone who stood for the Mughals. Pratap meanwhile turned westwards and regained Kumbhalgarh and Udaipur.

Now, let us attempt to draw a picture of the actual Battle of Dewair based on various accounts available.

119. *Amarkavyam*, p. 262.

120. Veer Vinod, Vol.2,p. 158.

The Strategy of Mewar

The war council met somewhere 10 kilometres around the south-east of the valley of Dewair. Those who attended besides Pratap, were Amar Singh, Bhama Shah, Tarachand Shah, Shakti Singh, Bhil king Rana Punja, Rawat Krishna Das, Gopal Das Mertiya and a whole clan of Shakti Singh's sons, the Shaktawats.

It was unequivocally decided that the Mewar army would not venture into the plains north of Dewair and instead engage the Mughals towards the south of the Dewair opening in the hills. The mistake of fighting in the open, like at Haldighati, was not to be repeated at any cost. A few hundred soldiers were to mingle with the local population and get close to the *thana* without getting noticed.

Pratap, Bhama Shah and all Generals were to stay in the base of the valley in the centre and the Bhils would attack from the trees atop the mountains with arrows and stones using *gofan.* Amar Singh was to encircle the village and wait at the northern end of the valley to cut off any attempt by Mughals to escape to the plains.

The Battle

Armed with a well-equipped army, adequately paid and trained in mountain warfare, with trusted Generals and aides like Amar Singh, Shakti Singh, Bhama Shah, Tara Shah, Rawat Kishan Das and various nobles of Mewar leading their contingents and courageous Bhils ready to climb trees and attack the Mughals from heights, Maharana Pratap Singh set out on the final military mission of his life in which he had resolved to destroy every *thana* and a local unit of Mughals occupying Mewar. Pratap was free of the moral baggage of fighting and killing his own Rajput brothers, unlike at Haldighati.

Akbar had placed only his trusted Muslim lieutenants guarding the *thanas* of Mewar because he didn't trust the Rajputs of Jaipur or Jodhpur to man the outposts of another Rajput kingdom of Mewar. He knew that the Hindu comradery could find its feet anytime, if the Mewar Rajputs were to be guarded by fellow-Rajputs from other regions. This was of tremendous advantage to

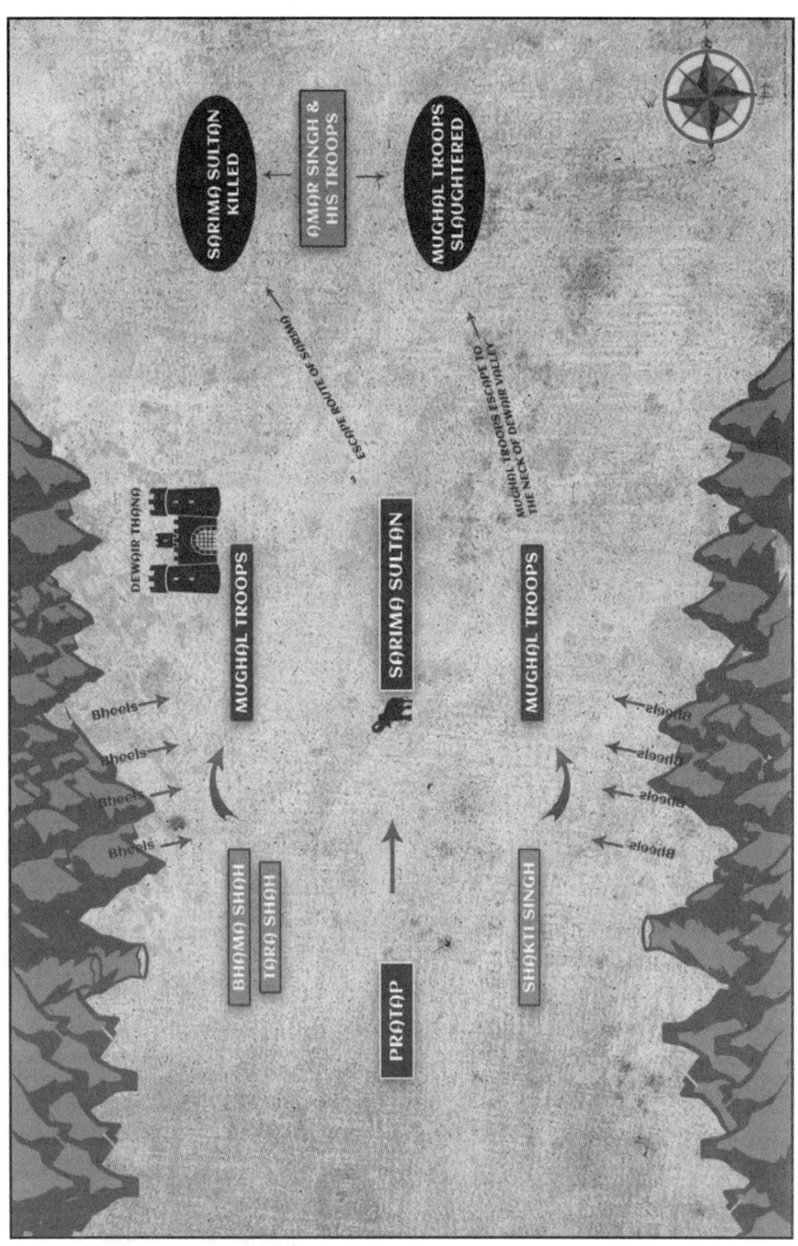
SARIMA SULTAN KILLED
AMAR SINGH & HIS TROOPS
MUGHAL TROOPS SLAUGHTERED
ESCAPE ROUTE OF SARIMA
MUGHAL TROOPS ESCAPE TO THE NECK OF DEWAIR VALLEY
DEWAIR THANA
MUGHAL TROOPS
SARIMA SULTAN
MUGHAL TROOPS
Bheels
Bheels
Bheels
Bheels
Bheels
Bheels
Bheels
Bheels
BHAMA SHAH
TARA SHAH
PRATAP
SHAKTI SINGH

a hardcore Sanatani like Pratap, as his sword would not hesitate in slaughtering well-defined enemies of Hinduism and his beloved state of Mewar which had been fighting the marauders of the Arabian desert for 800 years.

The shrieks of women and children committing *jauhar* on 25th February 1568, at Chittor, fuelled Pratap's agonised soul on that day when he set out to avenge the murder of his people at the hands of Mughals. The fallen friends, like Jaimal and Patta and Tanwars of Gwalior, Jhalas of Sadri, Bhim Singh of Dodia, would come alive on that day to prod Pratap to seek revenge on their behalf from Turk invaders squatting on the pious land of Mewar. The *Poorvajas* of Mewar dynasty would shower blessings upon Pratap on that glorious day as Pratap rose from the ashes of the plunder of Mewar to fulfil his promise to his glorious ancestors to evacuate Mewar of *vidharmis*.

Friends and relatives, subjects and servants, well-wishers and teachers would have raised chants of '*Har Har Mahadev*' to reverberate the skies of Mewar and convulse the very beings of Pratap's army to attempt a final assault on Turks occupying his motherland. All fear, concern and anxiety for his own survival or his families' lives being carried on were dissolved at the altar of the singular pursuit of a victory at Dewair by Pratap.

He went 'all in' to this dice that fate had thrown with only slaughter engaging his mind. The hooves of the horses, the ranklings of the spears, the clutter of the swords, the rubbing of the shoulders of man and animal with each other, the glances of fortitude at each other, the cold resolve of the king of Mewar and his people joined on Vijayadashami, 16th of September 1583 to take shape as a mammoth Hindu beast ready to devour the *mlechcha* who had been tormenting them for 800 years.

At daybreak, Pratap's army attacked the Mughal army from three sides and started slaughtering the enemy mercilessly. Below are a few incidents from the war which need to be described in detail to understand what actually transpired on that glorious day at Dewair.

The main General from the Mughal side was Serima Khan Sultan who was leading the Mughal defence, sitting atop his

war elephant. Pratap confronted Serima and fierce spear fighting ensued, but using the advantage of height, Serima ducked all attempts made at him by Pratap. Then a Padihar[121] Solanki Rajput got between the forelegs of the elephant and chopped them both with his dagger. The animal stooped low and at this moment, Pratap broke open the skull of the elephant. As the animal collapsed,

Pratap opens the skull of the elephant at Dewair

121. A subcaste of Rajputs.

Serima jumped off it and his assistants got him a horse to ride on.

Serima continued fighting and led his men on horseback. But soon, Serima and his men realised that they stood no chance of survival against the stones and arrows that were shot from treetops and decided to retreat northwards into open space. Serima led the retreat only to be met by Amar Singh and his men waiting for them at the neck of the Dewair valley.

The sons of Mewar started slaughtering the Mughals who were sandwiched between Pratap's assault from the rear and Amar Singh's from top. Death surrounded the Mughals from all sides. Amar Singh then took a long spear, hurled it at Serima with such force that the spear perforated the body of Serima, the hind part of the horse and rested six inches deep into the earth below. This act of Amar Singh proves the legend around his muscular strength as someone who was about 7 feet tall and supposed to be blessed with great military skill as well as the temperament to use his strength and skills. We can only imagine the morale of the Turks on seeing this state of their commander, perforated by a spear along with the horse rendered immobile in the midst of war by a single stroke of Amar Singh.

Amar Singh pierces Serima and his ride with his spear

Serima was still alive and he looked around for help, but his troops had all scattered and only Mewar soldiers were around him. Serima asked the soldiers as to who was the warrior that had put the spear through him. He said, *"I want to see him."*

Amar Singh looked at Pratap and Pratap nodded to him to come ahead. In the meanwhile, Mewar's soldiers disarmed Serima to avert a treacherous act upon their prince.

It is noted in various records of this incident that no soldier could extricate the spear out of the horse and the body of Serima when Amar Singh came forward and with one hand disengaged the spear from the earth and the bodies of the man and his ride.

Serima is believed to have uttered these words, *"I am seeing a divine man resplendent with rays of light from the skies to earth. I am indeed fortunate to have been killed by the weapon of this devpurusha."*

Then, Serima is believed to have asked for *Gangajal*, which Pratap himself served to him. Serima is said to have breathed his last thereafter and his body kept respectfully by the Mewar soldiers as instructed by Pratap. The battle in Dewair ended after this incident with the Mughal army being completely routed. Every single Mughal soldier who was left fighting or attempting escape was chased and put to the sword without mercy. There were to be no prisoners at Dewair. By mid-noon, Dewair was taken by Pratap, and the saffron flag was planted over its *thana*.

Serima asks for Ganga Jal while dying

Dewair was won by sheer ferocity and by Pratap's strategy of overwhelming the Mughal forces in one day. Thus began the campaign to conclusively eradicate the Mughals from Mewar.

Bahlol Khan, an Uzbek Mughal commander, who was much feared by his enemies and was known for his brutality and fighting skill, was posted at the other end of the Dewair valley that led to the fort of Kumbhalgarh. Without wasting time, Pratap gathered some soldiers and attacked the relatively small outpost.

Maharana Pratap had an undimmed memory of the friends and relatives lost at the hands of the Uzbek at Haldighati and had personal scores to settle. It was in this encounter with Bahlol Khan at Dewair that history was written in metal and blood at the altar of retribution, by the 43 year old Maharana.

Pratap attacked Bahlol Khan with such vengeance that before the Uzbek could even comprehend what was happening, the Rajput's sword had sliced the Uzbek from the head to his midriff. Pratap's mighty blade did not halt there. The sheer power of his blade coming down was such that even Bahlol's horse was sliced open from the middle.

Hundreds of soldiers fighting on the side watched this spectacular sight in utter amazement and awe. It was as though all fury of Hindu retribution against *jihadi* sins was visited by Pratap in that single blow.

The silent surrender of Maharani Padmini to the flames of *jauhar*, the deceitful murder of Rana Ratan Singh, the treachery against Pratap's grandfather Rana Sanga at Khanwa, the slaughter of Hindus at the third *saka* of Chittor, the decades of suffering, of roaming in the Aravallis, the pain of losing friends and family at Haldighati, all converged at that singular point of conflict between Hindus and Muslims of the region.

Pratap did not merely slay a Mughal General on that day but sent a message to the whole world that this was the terrible form Hindu fury would assume when it manifested out of the deep desire for freedom. Such Hindu fury is also entirely capable of unthinkable vengeance. Nowhere in the recorded history of humankind has such a battlefield feat been recorded.

Rana Pratap did not merely avenge Haldighati that day but cleaved open the entire edifice of deceit and cowardice that Akbar had so laboriously built to subjugate the Hindus.

From that day in 1583 to the day of his *moksha* in January 1597, no warrior of any significance ever engaged Pratap in a one-to-one combat. No wonder that after this day, Akbar kept pleading with his Generals to invade Mewar, but none ventured to do so. Such was the intensity of the assault on the Mughals that day that 32 *thanas* all around Mewar were vacated overnight.

Putting Hindu vassals in charge of Dewair, the army was divided into two parts on the very same day that Dewair was captured. Amar Singh took half of the army to the east and fugitives of Dewair were chased up to Amet and put to the Rajput sword. The garrison at Amet was cut to pieces by Amar Singh. Pratap turned westwards and reached Kumbhalgarh. The Mughal troops deserted the posts there and Pratap entered Kumbhalgarh after slaughtering a few hundred who chose to resist.

Shahbaz Khan, the Mughal General, had taken Kumbhalgarh from Pratap in 1578. Pratap regained it in merely five years. These five years were the only ones when Kumbhalgarh had been out of the hands of Hindus. Pratap must go down in history as one of the bravest and most determined warrior kings to have lost and regained such a critical fort from the so-called 'mighty Mughal Empire.'

A powerful Mughal General, Abdulla, was then confronted by Pratap and killed by his army. The *thana* of Hammirsar, near Kumbhalgarh was similarly overrun. After this, Pratap marched to the southern Ovro village and retook the Javra mines of silver and tin. This takeover was critical to empower Mewar economically. All thirty-two *thanas* encircling Mewar were attacked and troops put to death mercilessly.

To use the words of the Mewar annals: *"Pratap made a desert of Mewar; he made an offering to the sword of whatever dwelt in its plains."*

This was an appalling but indispensable sacrifice by Pratap for his motherland. In one short campaign, Pratap and Amar Singh had recovered all of Mewar, except Chittor. Encircling Mewar from either side, Pratap and Amar Singh entered Udaipur to find it vacated by the Mughals. Such was the impact of Pratap's campaign that a city as critical as Udaipur was deserted by the Mughals without a single skirmish and was regained effortlessly.

The battle of Dewair and the subsequent campaign to regain Mewar, established Maharana Pratap Singh of Mewar as the unquestioned Hindu leader of the region against Akbar's occupation.

A lot of details and records of this victory of Pratap have been overlooked or erased by Mughals by destroying temples and burning the books that kept the records, but the folklore and a buoyant Pratap kept the memory of this great battle alive in the consciousness of Mewar.

Records by Ranchod Bhatt, *Veer Vinod*, James Tod, and many contemporary historians of universities of Rajasthan establish the veracity of events at Dewair. But as laymen, for us, the biggest evidence of the successful campaign of Dewair lies in the fact that from CE 1583-1597, Pratap ruled Mewar uninterruptedly and the so-called mighty Akbar and his imperial army never dared to attack Mewar again, till Pratap roamed the jungles and fields of Mewar.

The shameless historians of this unfortunate nation have tried to not only erase but also belittle Pratap's glorious resistance to Akbar. They said that Pratap ruled freely because Akbar was busy in other campaigns around India.

The truth is that all the plans of Akbar to subjugate Hindus completely, were burnt in the pious fire of the rage and valour of Pratap and Kunwar Amar Singh.

To trivialise Pratap's victory, the pseudo liberals invented a lie as petty as themselves.

If Akbar was really busy elsewhere, then for fifteen years from CE 1568-1583 why did he destroy Chittor? Why did he send four peace proposals? Why did he organise ten fully armed invasions of Mewar? Why did he spend millions of rupees and get thousands of his soldiers killed?

The truth is that to the slaves of Islamic expansionism and their Hindu stooges, it was an issue of unbearable pain that a lone Pratap didn't allow Mughals to breach Mewar. Because of one Pratap, Akbar's dream to Islamise the Hindu land remained just that—a dream.

It is this pain that torments the self-proclaimed intelligentsia of this besieged nation. To ease this pain, their crooked mind churns up new lies regularly to belittle Pratap's achievements.

And yet, these liars could not erase the truth of Pratap. With the advent of internet, the truth of Pratap will be spoken from every Hindu home. It is the responsibility of every Hindu to take Pratap's story to the world—a story that this world will listen with amazement and utmost gratitude.

After kicking out the last Mughal from Mewar, Pratap began amassing wealth and an army with the support of fellow-Hindu kingdoms to have a decisive battle for Chittor and then Delhi before fate intervened. Pratap was injured in a hunting incident which eventually took him away from the glorious land of Mewar. But, before the dissolution of his mortal body, Pratap redeemed the honour and prosperity of Mewar and passed on a kingdom to Amar Singh that had full coffers and a vibrant economy along with a strong military.

Dewair was fought at a time when the Hindu resistance had been totally subdued by Akbar and his Hindu commanders. Dewair should be written in golden words in Hindu history because it was from Dewair that Pratap regained lost territory and infused new blood into the diminishing morale of Mewar, Rajasthan, and the northern plains.

The victory of Dewair and the scale of the destruction of the Mughal forces by Pratap sent the most unambiguous and penetrating message to invaders eyeing the land, that Hindus would not yield their *dharma* through force or deceit. Dewair was indeed the decisive day in Mewar history that invigorated the Hindus to keep fighting against forces of slavery and darkness till the last Hindu lives on this globe.

As Dr. L.P. Mathur, eminent historian writes in his book, *"The conquest of Dewair proved to be the turning point in the Mughal-Mewar conflict*[122]*."*

The Battle of Marathon was fought in 490 BC between invading Persian army and Greeks in which Persians were crushingly defeated. Drawing comparisons between the Greco-

122. Mathur, p. 146.

Persian conflict with the Mughal-Mewar conflict, James Tod writes:

"It is worthy of attention of those who influence the destinies of states in more favoured climes, to estimate the intensity of feeling which could arm this prince (Pratap) to oppose the resources of a small principality against the then most powerful empire of the world whose armies were more numerous and far more efficient, than ever led by the Persians against the liberties of Greece.

"Undaunted heroism, inflexible fortitude, that which "keeps honour bright", perseverance, with fidelity no nation can boast, were the materials opposed to a soaring ambition, commanding talents, unlimited means and the fervour of religious zeal; all, however, insufficient to contend with one unconquerable mind.

"There is not a pass in the alpine Aravallis that is not sanctioned by some deed of Pratap—some brilliant victory or, oftener, more glorious defeat.

"Haldighati is the Thermopylae of Mewar; the fields of Dewair her Marathon."

Pratap was the *mahapurusha* who single-handedly kept the flame of Hindu resistance burning at a time when there was no hope, not even a fair chance of revival of the fortunes of Mewar. If we are Hindus today, it is due to Pratap alone. Let Dewair be the *teertha* (pilgrimage) every Hindu visits once in his lifetime to shed a tear of gratitude to one of the bravest sons of Mewar, who staked everything to defend Hindu honour and *dharma*.

Let Dewair be the symbol of the indomitable Hindu spirit that has fought Islamic invasions for 1400 years and let us promise as Hindus of today with confidence that, if need be, we will fight subjugation for another 1,400 years as well.

That alone would be a fitting tribute to Pratap.

That alone would be our gratitude to the sacred valley of Dewair.

□

15

Maharana Amar Singh: A Worthy Son

(CE 1597-1620)

This is the story of one of the bravest and physically strongest kings of Mewar, whom fate had bestowed the duty to carry forward the legacy of the greatest son of Hindu *dharma*, Maharana Pratap Singh of Mewar. This was not an easy feat by any standard, more so because Amar Singh was an extremely sensitive and honourable man and had no dearth of valour and will to take on the Turkish Islamic invaders.

The circumstances of Pratap's death have been described variously by historians but a story that deserves mention is that after being injured in a hunting accident, Pratap was mortally injured but clung on to life even in pain. The nobles approached Pratap and asked him the reason for his agony. Pratap quoted an incident to his lifelong friends and comrades:

'Once while residing in the mountains of Aravalis, we were camping at a secluded spot when it started raining. We were encamped along with 'Amra' (Amar) and his family and a few aides in makeshift huts. Amar was in his hut with his wife when I heard his wife say to him, *"Will our days of suffering ever end or not?"*

Amar replied, *"What can be done? Who can question the will of Dajirajsa? (Father in Mewar royalty)".*

Quoting this incident, Pratap said to his *samants* that he knew that Amar Singh was not of steely resolve like him and sooner or later, he would surrender to the Turks.

"For his own comforts, he would destroy the honour of our family."

Hearing this, Amar Singh rushed to his dying father's side and swore on his honour that he would never surrender to the Mughals. The *samants* and nobles of Mewar too raised their swords and swore to stand with Amar Singh till death. A reassured Pratap blessed his son and the other warriors of Mewar and slept peacefully that night.

Painful as it might be to describe the process of the dissolution of the physical body of Maharana Pratap, when even Yogeshwar Krishna is bound to the laws of nature, what is the worth of mortals like us... let us use the imagination of our poets and our ancestors to draw a caricature around the *moksha* of Pratap.

Rana Raso, the chronicle of Pratap describes the next day's events thus:

'Maharana Pratap got up from his bed and took a bath in *Gangajal.* He looked lovingly at his family and friends. He was reassured of the bravery and the dutifulness of his son Amar Singh and grandson Karan

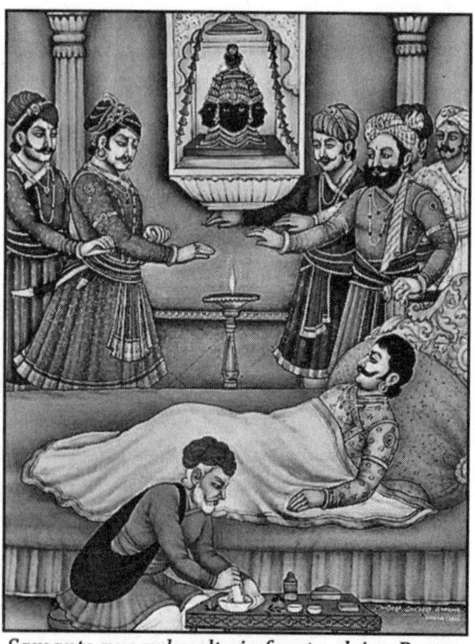

Samants swear loyalty in front a dying Pratap

Singh. Sitting down in *padmasana*, Maharana Pratap focused his consciousness on Shri Vishnu residing at the three lines of his forehead. He had the *'darshan'* of blue-skinned Shri Krishna himself which put Rana in ecstasy. Maharana Pratap sucked in his *praan vayu* (air of life). Breaking all *pranic* bonds of attachments with this mortal world, the *aatma* of that *mahayogi* ascended to *moksha* at the feet of Shri Hari.'

Tod writes thus on the *moksha* of Pratap:

"Thus closed the life of a Rajput whose memory is even now idolised not only by every Sisodia, but by every Hindu and will continue to be so, till renewed oppression shall extinguish the remaining sparks of patriotic feeling. May that day never arrive!

"Yet, if such be her destiny, may it, at least, not be hastened by the arms of Britain[123]*."*

Pratap attains Moksha. After the Saka-Jauhar of 1568, Pratap vowed to sleep only on floor. He lived up to his vow, even in death

At the age of fifty-seven years, on 19th January of CE 1597, the greatest Hindu king of all times, Maharana Pratap Singh, having

123. Tod, Vol.1, p. 278.

achieved the unthinkable feat of freeing his beloved nation and *dharma* from the clutches of one of the most powerful kingdoms of its time, left his mortal body and crossed over to the world of *devas* from where he had descended to save a besieged Hindu *dharma*.

The father-figure of Mewar's courageous people performed his duty of making a defeated people bounce back from the brink of submission and made them stand on their feet and move on to the next world.

A real hero, a protector of women and men, who bore the brunt of barbaric Islamic assault on his chest and repulsed it so effectively that even 500 years after his *moksha*, Hindus are inspired by his deeds and memory.

A chivalrous warrior like Shri Rama, who never used his might, skills and weaponry for petty personal gains, but used them only for the establishment of *dharma* and fighting for freedom and honour of his people, rode into the glory reserved only for the greatest amongst greats, like Bhishma, Pandavas, Porus, Bappa Rawal, Kumbha and Sanga.

The lineage of Bappa Rawal was brimming with pride and joy that glorious day when one of his sons who brought back Hindu *dharma* from certain annihilation, fulfilled his *kartavya karma*, and merged his mortal body into Mewar's *punyabhoomi* forever.

It was this heavy mantle that was passed on to Amar Singh, aged thirty-eight years, that glorious day and as we will witness in his life and deeds, Amar Singh indeed lived up to the highest standards set by his father. After Pratap's *moksha*, Akbar renewed his attacks on Mewar, though, for three years, Amar Singh continued the policies of Pratap to build Mewar economically and militarily.

Amar Singh continued attacking Mughal caravans in Malpura, Gujarat, Malwa, Idar and Abu to amass wealth. A very important shift that he initiated militarily was to import trained military men from Godwar and Multan in Punjab to train Mewar in cannon warfare and optimise the use of firepower.

This game-changing decision of Amar Singh would prove crucial in his twenty-three year conflict with the Mughals and the eventual defeat of Aurangzeb at the hands of Amar Singh's great grandson, Maharana Raj Singh. Amar Singh was the first king of Mewar to import high-grade weapons from other states and start the production of advanced cannons and firepower in Mewar. For the first time, Mewar was no longer thinking of defending but was actively attacking Mughal forces. Amar Singh continued the 'scorched earth' policy exercised by Pratap and built new centres and cities in the hills of Mewar.

Mewar's arch enemy, Akbar, had almost forgotten Mewar for two decades as he ran around quelling rebellions in Gujarat, Afghanistan, Balochistan, Punjab and other parts of north-west. Akbar lost some of his valuable advisors like Bhagwan Das, Todar Mal, Abul Fazl and others to time and death. On 15th September 1599, Akbar appointed Salim as subedar of Ajmer and tasked him with capturing Amar Singh and annexing Mewar. Akbar also asked Man Singh to shift from Bengal to Ajmer to assist Salim. Man Singh did not like Salim, as Man Singh wanted his sister's son from Jehangir, Khusro, to become the Mughal king after Akbar.

Fortunately for Mewar, Salim was a drug addict and a womaniser with little interest in wars and slaughter. Salim kept roaming here and there wasting time around Gwalior. This suited Man Singh who stationed himself at Ajmer, keeping an eye on Salim's indulgences with relief in his heart. Abul Fazl writes of Salim as, *"the ignorant son of the empire*[124]*"*.

Akbar was furious with Salim and instructed him to fight Amar Singh with seriousness. Amar Singh in the meantime attacked Oontala, Mohi, Koshithal, Bagar, Mandal, Madariya, *thanas* and won them.

An amazing story about the capture of Oontala fort deserves a mention to show how extreme the idea of honour was to Rajputs and the extent they could go, to protect it. As discussed in the chapter on Haldighati in this book, the front formation that is meant for attacking the enemy is known as *harawal* and the rear group for the attack is referred to as *chandawal*.

The norm was that Choondawats were to be in the *harawal* and Shaktawats in the *chandawal*. Shaktawats were descendants

124. Bhatt. p. 352.

of Shakti Singh, the brave brother of Pratap who saved him at Haldighati. It so happened that Choondawats and Shaktawats got into an argument on why only the Choondawats should get the honour of being in the *harawal*. Amar Singh intervened and said that whosoever set foot on Oontala fort first was to get the honour of leading the *harawal*.

Ballu Shaktawat and Rawat Jait Singh Choondawat attacked the fort simultaneously. Ballu Shaktawat prodded the *mahout* of his elephant to break open the gates from where the Mughals were firing bullets and shooting arrows constantly. The *mahout* expressed his inability saying that the elephant was without tusks and huge spikes prevented the animal from attacking it directly. Ballu stood in front of the spikes and asked the *mahout*, "Move the elephant on my body or I will kill you." The *mahout* complied. Ballu's crushed corpse provided the cushion to the animal to break open the gates. On the other side, Rawat Jait Singh started climbing the wall and was shot by a Mughal. The wounded noble asked his men to behead him and throw his head inside the fort. Thus, both Shaktawats and Choondawats entered the fort simultaneously.

Amar Singh showered accolades on his warriors and the Choondawats retained the honour of heading the *harawal*.

What could a murdering, womanising Akbar or his son Salim even comprehend of the sense of valour and honour of such great Rajputs who competed with each other in sacrificing their lives to capture the fort with such extreme acts of martyrdom!

Thirty *thanas* were recovered by Amar Singh in a short span of time and Akbar's attempt at annexing Mewar was an abject failure. Though it must be said that Mewar won at the huge cost of losing some great war Generals, like Ballu Shaktawat, Rawat Jait Singh Shaktawat, Tej Singh Khangarot, Achal Das Choondawat, Jaimal Sangawat, etc. At last, frustrated with Salim's indifference, Akbar put forward Salim's son, Khusro, whom Akbar started liking more than his own son due to his fighting capacity and loyalty to the throne.

Another move that Akbar made was to appoint Sagar, an

The Masjid on the walls of Kashi Vishwanath Shiva Temple

The Sacred birth place of Sri Krishna shares wall with a Masjid

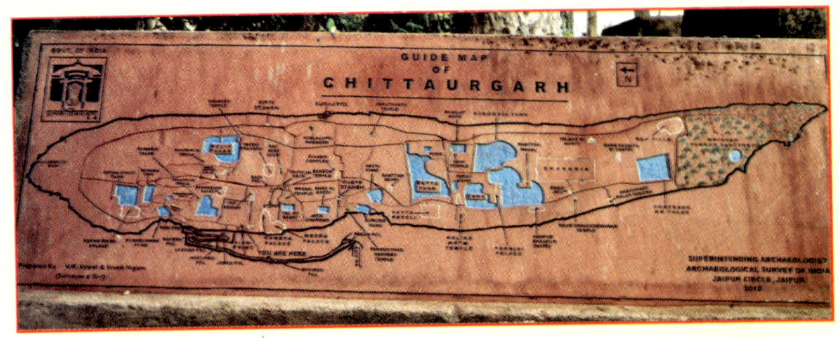

The guide map of Chittorgarh

Kunwarpada—the place where Pratap spent his childhood

Pratap melts the boundary between prince and his subjects

The third Saka-Jauhar; Chittor scarred forever

Every Hindu idol was destroyed by Akbar's Muslim army

Islamic dome over Hindu Temple constructed by the ASI

Jaimal Rathore's Haveli that witnessed the first fire of Jauhar in 1568

Bheem Taal where maximum Jauhar pyres were lit

The spot of Pratap's coronation at Gogoonda

Banbeer's wall to separate the royalty from the citizens of Chittor

One of the places where Rajput queens committed Jauhar

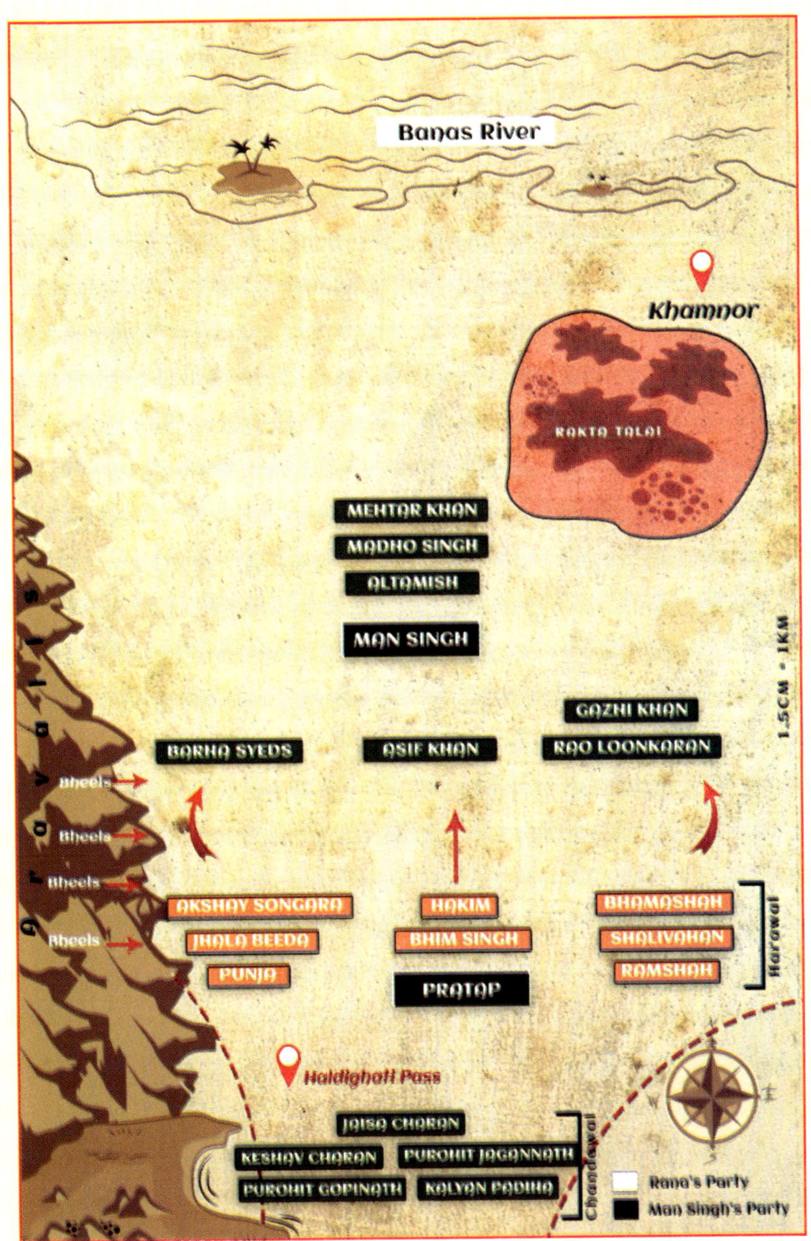

Battle of Haldi Ghati

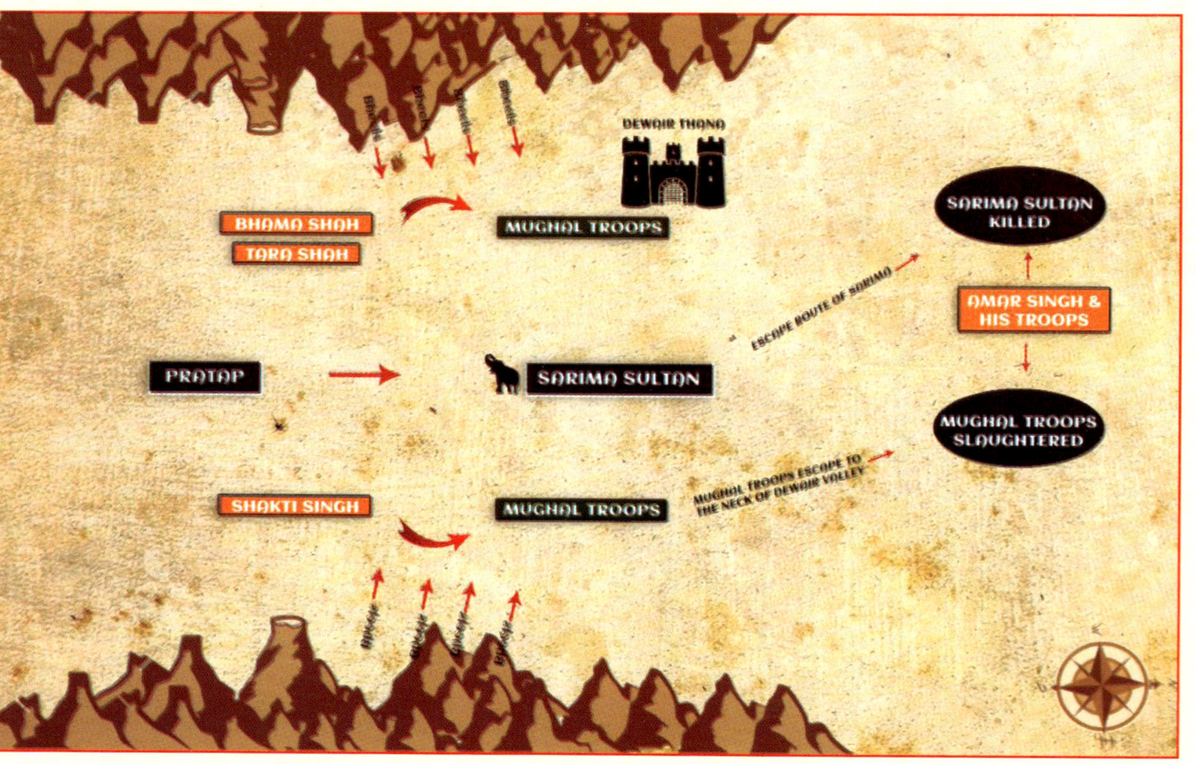

Battle of Dewair

Pratap cuts Behlol and his steed into two

Shakti Singh rescues Pratap

The withering ancient trail of Haldi Ghati which connects to Badshahi Bagh

Samadhi of Maharana Pratap at Chawand

The Samadhi of Amar Singh

The beautiful Rajsamand

Veer Durga Das Rathore with child Ajit Singh in the Aravallis

Samadhi of Raj Singh near Nathdwara; deserted by an ungrateful Hindu Samaj

Si Vis Pacem, Para Bellum—if you want peace, prepare for war. Mewar lived this Latin adage

Meera Bai Temple at Chittor—spirituality and war can coexist

Writer with Hindu refugee child Dileep Bhil

Writer with Jai Ahuja at a rally in Jaipur in support of Citizenship Amendment Act. (CAA)

Who were the fools to tell you that brute force can not defeat an idea? Nothing is simpler. And once an idea is dead, it is nothing but a corpse. —Simone Weil

A society that can't protect it's women, deserves to die

One Man's realisation is enough to save the world

estranged brother of Pratap, as the vassal of Chittor and promised to make him Maharana of Mewar if he helped capture or kill Amar Singh. Sagar came to Chittor and sat on the throne of his glorious ancestors but could never gain the love and respect of the people of Mewar. For seven years, Sagar's hollow rule was endured by Mewar. Tod sums up Sagar's predicament beautifully:

Sagar, though flinty as a rock to a brother and nephew, would not support the silent admonition of the altars of the heroes, who had fallen in her defence. The triumphant column raised for victory over a combination of kings was a perpetual memento of his infamy; nor could he pass over one finger's breadth of her ample surface, without treading on some fragment which reminded him of their great deeds and his own unworthiness.

Sagar left Chittor out of shame and sometime later, went to the court of Jehangir, where he drew his dagger and slew himself in the presence of the Mughal. An end befitting a traitor. Thus, Akbar's trick to split the Rajputs ended.

In Delhi, as Khusro was amassing a huge army to invade Mewar, fate intervened and on 15th October 1605, Akbar died of poisoning.

The *Akbarnama* records:

"Wherever Allah's mercy remains, it remains,
That which cannot be done, gets done,
That which can be done, does not get done."

Akbar was never destined to see the annexation of Mewar. Even seven years after his *moksha*, Pratap snatched victory from the hands of the Mughal. The story of Akbar's death is as treacherous as his life.

Tod quotes the annals of Bundi state which were recorded by the kings of Bundi themselves[125].

Man Singh, Akbar's trusted aide whom he referred to as *beta* or son, wanted Khusro, Jehangir's talented son to become the next emperor after Akbar. Akbar, on the other hand, had made up his mind about Jehangir. Anticipating a civil war in the Mughal army, Akbar decided to poison Man Singh's food and eliminate him, since Man Singh was too powerful to be openly assaulted.

125. Tod, vol. 1, p. 279.

A lot of authors and historians like Manucci, Beveries and Vincent Smith have quoted numerous examples of Akbar's treacherous poisoning of clothes and food to eliminate the enemies he couldn't defeat in war.

He would usually sweet-talk such people to the dining table and carry out his design with the help of his tailors and cooks. By a twist of fate, it so happened that the food meant for Man Singh was served to Akbar and he consumed it. He developed bloody dysentery from the effect of the poison and after three days of consuming it, on 15th October 1605, the vilest Muslim ruler of Delhi got entangled in the web of his own creation and died an inglorious death befitting his deceitful life.

The record-keepers write that on his last day he couldn't recite the customary *kalma* to his gods and sank into everlasting darkness where *yamdoots* (messengers of Yama) would drag him to justice for the slaughter of 40,000 innocent Hindus at Chittor.

After Akbar's death, Jehangir (Salim) became the king of Delhi, but his own son Khusro rebelled against him in 1607. Jehangir defeated Khusro in the Battle of Bhairowal in Punjab and blinded him before imprisoning him. Jehangir then deputed Mohabbat Khan, an apostate (Mohabbat, son of Sagar, was a Sisodia by birth, but converted to Islam) to subjugate Amar Singh. An interesting story is woven around the abject defeat of Mohabbat Khan.

Jahangir (1605-1627 CE)

With a force of around 12,000 horsemen, 500 infantries, seventeen cannons, sixty war elephants along with 20 lakh rupees,

Mohabbat Khan entered Mewar and started destroying Rajput *thanas* and penetrated Oontala.

Here, Rawat Megh Singh and Govindasot Choondawat devised a plan to overwhelm the Turks with a mere force of 500 men of Mewar. A dozen Mewar warriors dressed as shepherds took a huge herd of cows and buffaloes close to Mohabbat's army. The Mewar warriors tied watermelons filled with fireworks to the horns of the cattle and let them loose on the Turk camp. Nearby 500 Mewar men then attacked with their arrows and spears, utilising the commotion to slaughter the Turks. Mohabbat's army started fleeing northwards to Ajmer thinking that a huge army had attacked them. A few kilometres ahead, Amar Singh was waiting with a full army of Mewar and the entire Turk force was slaughtered. All its weaponry and valuables were looted by Mewar men and all *thanas* were freed of the Turks.

Then Jehangir deputed the brother of Abdul Raheem Khankhana to attack Mewar. Amar Singh met the Turk army at the pass of Dewair in CE 1608 and after a prolonged combat, the Turk army was decimated. The honours of this battle are chiefly attributed to the brave Kana, an uncle of Amar Singh, whose children were called Kanawats after him.

A brief truce followed the second battle of Dewair. In the pass of Ranpur, the Mughal army, under its new leader Abdulla, was exterminated. But all these victories came at a heavy cost to Mewar as well. Dooda Sangawat, Narayan Das, Soorajmall, Aaskaran, all Sisodias of first rank were lost. Pooran Mal Shaktawat, Haridas Rathore, Bhopat Jhala, Kahirdas Kachchawa, Kesudas Chauhan, Mokund and Jaimalote Rathore laid their lives for these victories.

Alarmed at these defeats, Jehangir appointed his other son, Parvez, to take on Amar Singh with fresh reinforcements and adequate firepower to overwhelm the Rana. Jehangir raised the imperial standard at Ajmer and sent Parvez to attack Mewar with the following instructions, *"If Rana or his elder son Karan should repair to him, to receive them with becoming attention and to offer no molestation to the country."*

Amar Singh took Parvez head-on and met the Mughals at the spot oft moistened with blood—the pass of Khamnor. The

Mughals were defeated and pursued with great havoc to Ajmer. Even the Mughal historians admit that it was a glorious day for Mewar.

The Mughal historians describe Parvez entangled in the passes, rebellions in his camp, his supplies cut off and his precipitous flight and pursuit by Mewar horsemen leading to loss of a vast number of men.

Jehangir then appointed Parvez's son, who had been tutored in warfare by Mohabbat Khan, to lead expeditions to Mewar. Even this army was beaten badly by Amar Singh, but the Mughals kept coming to Mewar like a *raktabeej*[126]. *The more the Mewar sons slayed the Mughals, more sprang up.* The hydra appeared indestructible.

For every victory, while Mewar lost its best sons, the numbers of the enemy kept multiplying. Seventeen pitched battles were fought by the illustrious Amar Singh after the *moksha* of Pratap and each ended in victory of Mewar. But, the loss of Mewar's veterans withered the laurels of victory and Mewar did not have sufficient repose to husband her resources or rear her young to replace the fallen.

On his part, Jehangir too lost many valuable Generals and this he mentions in his memoirs. He writes grievingly about one Fareed Khan Barlas that he was the last of the Barlas clan. Jehangir also mentions loss of Sikandar Moin Karawal to wars with Mewar. Karawal's corpse was transferred to Jehangir and he personally oversaw the burial of his old time-keeper. More significantly, Rajput Generals like Madho Singh and Jagannath Kachchawa too were dead, and Jehangir was desperate for a truce with Mewar.

In CE 1613, Jehangir despatched Khurram (Shahjahan), his ablest son and gave him a huge army to attack Mewar. Khurram was a cunning general. He divided his vast army into smaller units and started capturing Mewar *thanas* one by one, pushing Amar Singh into the Aravallis. Then he used the very tactics used by the Mewar army to cut supplies of food and water to the besieged Mewar battalions engaged in guerrilla warfare.

---

126. A demon in Hindu *Puranas* who could not be killed because every drop of his blood falling on ground would regenerate a demon like him.

The entire northern Mewar was thus brought under Mughal control and Amar Singh was pushed to the southern Aravallis. All major cities of Mewar, including Kumbhalgarh and Udaipur were lost and Amar Singh had to stay in the jungles of Aravallis permanently.

The account that follows is a mix of the immense sacrifice of Amar Singh and his son Karan Singh along with the nobles and the people of Mewar, and extreme suffering that Mewar endured in fighting Islamic invaders along with the remarkable foresight shown by Amar Singh and his family and the illustrious nobles of Mewar.

Bhama Shah, who was instrumental both as a war General and financier of Pratap's army, continued to serve Amar Singh until his death in CE 1600. He filled the coffers of the Mewar house, working ceaselessly till his death. The night before his death, he gave away the entire account statement of Mewar and maps of the hidden wealth around caves and forts of Mewar, to his wife and son. For a very long time, even after his death, Bhama Shah ensured the funding of Mewar's war campaigns. Amar Singh appointed Jeeva Shah, Bhama Shah's son, as the cash-keeper of Mewar and he served him all his life.

With Khurram choking all trades of Mewar, in a few months, the nobles of Mewar sensing the disquiet amongst masses of Mewar, approached Amar Singh and made the following request: *"We do not have the numbers or resources to fight the Mughals now. Without a treaty, Mewar cannot be retained."*

Maharana Amar Singh had promised his father that he would never surrender, but he couldn't ignore the near rebellion in his army against the hardships. He asked his chieftains to wait as he wrote a *doha* to Abdul Raheem Khankhana, a General with Mughals and a friend and well-wisher of Pratap's family. The Rana wrote:

गौड़ कछावा राठवड़, गोखां जोख करंत।
कहजो खांनांखान नै, वनचर हुआ फिरंत।।

(The Gauds, Kachchawas and Rathore Rajputs are savouring the cool winds of compromise.

We, the Sisodias, are condemned to the jungles like animals, O Khankhana.)

Raheem got this message while he was fighting in Deccan. His reply:

धर रहसी रहसी धरम, खप जाशी खुरसाण।
अमर विशंभर ऊपरा, राखौ निहचो राण।।

(This earth will stay, so will stay *dharma*, the Mughals will perish.

Abdul Raheem Khankhana : The Muslim who found truth in Hinduism

Trust the immortal divine lurking in the skies and have patience, O Rana!)

The saga of the Mewar-Mughal rivalry apart, can we pause and absorb the spiritual quantum of these giants. An enemy General speaking such soothing words to the king of the opposite side!

After this conversation with Khankhana, Amar Singh continued to fight the Mughals for one more year[127].

The Mewar nobles now decided to bypass Amar Singh and approach Karan Singh, the wise and able son of Amar Singh. The nobles pleaded:

"Nothing to eat and cover our body remains.

We do not even have enough weapons.

There are households that have lost four generations of men.

If some children fall into Muslim hands, they are used as sex slaves.

More than dying, we are fearful for our women and children facing this fate.

Forty-seven years have passed since we have endured all kinds of sufferings, but no end seems in sight.

Mewar sons fought Mughals for decades surviving on figs from

127. *Veer Vinod*, vol. 2, p. 234-35.

jungles of Aravallis, but now, even the trees have gone barren."

Karan Singh listened patiently and thanked the nobles for their service and loyalty. He explained to them that Dajirajsa (Amar Singh) was bound by a promise to a dying Pratap and that as long as he was alive, he would not settle for peace with the Mughals.

Jhala Haridas and Shubhkaran Panwar, two wise nobles, then retorted that if all the nobles of Mewar refused to fight, what could the lone Maharana do? Both nobles advised Karan to let them approach Khurram to discuss the terms of the treaty and if they were honourable, there was no harm buying time for Mewar to replenish its resources and regroup lost forces.

In the Mewar hierarchy, the prince is lower in rank than the Umraos and Rawats. The Mughals would think the prince was yielding, but in Mewar that would amount to the surrender of merely one noble.

This was the value that the royal house of Mewar attached to the chieftains fighting for them. Even the royal heir was considered inferior to the loyal *samants* of Mewar. Such was the respect for merit and fidelity and voice of the majority in Mewar. Can our current politicians and power-brokers even fathom this and learn from these great traditions?

Both nobles also assured Karan that they would go to Jehangir and get his written assurance on the terms of the treaty and if the terms were not honourable, they promised to fight till death.

Karan, without the permission of Amar Singh, sent both the Mewar nobles to Ajmer to meet Jehangir. As stated earlier, Jehangir had lost many of his close relatives and Generals in the war with Mewar. By CE 1614, Man Singh and Jagannath Kachchawa, the main facilitators of the Mughal army, were dead too. Jehangir was tired of fighting with Mewar and was hard-pressed for resources due to rebellions in various parts of the land.

In the summer of CE 1615, eighteen years after the *moksha* of Maharana Pratap and after fighting seventeen major battles and winning all of them, Mewar entered into a treaty with Jehangir, when the two nobles were received with celebration by the Mughals. Jehangir wrote a letter to Maharana Amar Singh, sending him his deepest regards. A costly shawl from Dhaka and the emblem of his palm in saffron colour, which was an assurance by the Mughal that he would honour every word of the treaty, was also sent to Amar Singh.

Jehangir wrote to his son Khurram to seal the treaty on whatever terms the Rana was to decide and to bring Prince Karan to Delhi. All this happened without the knowledge of Amar Singh, who was residing in Gogunda, when the news of this treaty reached him. Karan explained everything to his father and advised him to accept the honourable treaty.

Amar Singh's face turned dark with sadness and the Rana went completely silent and shocked.

After some time, Amar Singh spoke these words, *"What can I alone do if all of you have made up your minds? I didn't wish to break my promise to Dajirajsa (Pratap), but God has made me see this day with my own eyes."*

Amar Singh retreated into solitude and gradually ceded all matters of state to Karan Singh. As we will see, this treaty, though the need of the hour and done on very honourable terms for Mewar, was the cause of Amar Singh's untimely demise as he could not stomach the fact that it was during his reign that Mewar was to accept Mughal suzerainty. He would have to bear the humiliation of bending to Muslim invaders, a tragic event that his ancestors averted for 900 years.

The main points of the treaty between Mewar and Mughals were:

- Maharana will meet Khurram at a place of Rana's choosing.
- Maharana's son Karan will be sent to Mughal court as a representative of Mewar.
- The place of Mewar prince in Mughal court will be above the other Mughal princes on the right side of Jehangir.
- Maharana of Mewar is excused from appearing in Mughal court.
- Chittor fort will be returned to Maharana, but neither can it be repaired nor fortified.
- Maharana Amar Singh will give 1,000 Mewar horsemen to Mughal army[128].

128. Bhatt, p. 402.

Thus, from 8th century onwards to the 17th century, for 900 years after fighting Islamic invaders, a truce was agreed upon by Mewar and the Mughals. Some historians term this treaty as a capitulation of Mewar, but that is an unfair and skewed view of things at that time. In their hearts, Mewar's people never surrendered and agreed upon this peace treaty only to replenish their resources and regroup their scattered forces.

What were the norms at that time that were completely overlooked by the Mughals in a haste to seal this treaty?

Firstly, the Maharana was excused from appearing in the Mughal court and bowing to the Mughals personally. This was crucial because the message of Mewar's Rana kneeling to the Mughal would have had a devastating effect on the morale of not only Mewar, but of entire Bharatavarsha.

Secondly, Amar Singh clearly refused marital bonds with the Mughals. It was, again, a major blow to the prestige of Mughals who always connected the subjugation of Rajput kingdoms with matrimonial bonds.

Prince Karan and chieftains of Mewar adopted a strategic retreat for the benefit of his courageous people who had stood with him and his forefathers for a thousand years. The other option to this honourable treaty was plunder and annexation with all doors closed to any chance of a bounce back by Mewar. Mewar had seen several bounce-backs in the tumultuous history of her conflict with the Islamists and this treaty was one such low which was needed for Mewar to rise again.

As we shall see in the chapter on Raj Singh, the interim of peace between Mewar and the Mughals gave Mewar the requisite time to replenish its economy and people to take on the vilest and most hideous enemy of Hindus—Aurangzeb.

History should judge Amar Singh kindly for this treaty which had been forced upon Mewar due to the prevalent geo-political situation at the time, but the core principles of Rajput honour and Hindu freedom were not compromised and Mewar bounced back within five decades of this honourable treaty.

Two major advantages of this treaty for Mewar that deserve special mention are the regaining of Chittor, fifty years after it was captured by Akbar and Amar Singh's insistence that Mughal artisans be given to Mewar to establish workshops to build advanced cannons and allow effective use of firepower.

Chittor was of huge symbolic value to Mewar and the entire population of Mewar rose to celebrate the regaining. The training of Mewar's warriors in Mughal firepower would prove crucial in the future wars between Mewar and Aurangzeb. Thus, we witness an amazing turn of events where even a besiegement of Mewar is turned into an honourable compromise by the wise and brave Mewar nobles and Amar Singh.

Besides the Mewar annals and the Hindu writers presenting their side of this turn of events, let us take some references from *Tuzak Jehangiri*, the autobiography of Jehangir where he talks so respectfully and fondly of Amar Singh and Karan Singh, respectively. On 18th February 1615, the Mewar prince, Karan Singh, accompanied by Prince Khurram reached Ajmer and Jehangir personally received the Mewar prince.

According to the records of the British imperial agent in Mughal court, Thomas Roe, representing the British monarch, James I:

"Jehangir rose from his throne and kissed the forehead of Karan Singh and made him sit on the right side of his throne, above all the other courtiers present."

Jehangir writes himself in his memoirs:

"Karan, owing to the rude life he has led in his native hills, was extremely shy, and unused to the pageantry and experiences of a court. In order to reconcile and give him confidence, I daily gave him some testimonies of my regards and protection for him and his family.

"On the second day, I gave him a jewelled dagger.

"On third, a choice steed of Iraq in the rich caparisons.

"On the same day, I took him with me to the queen's court, when the queen, Noorjehan, made him splendid khelats, caparisoned elephant and horse, jewels, etc.

"The same day, I gave him a rich necklace of pearls, another day an elephant and it was my wish to give him rarities and choicest things of every kind.

"I gave him three royal hawks and three gentle falcons trained to the hand, a coat of mail, chain and plate armour.

"On the last day of the month, carpets, state cushions, perfumes, vessels of gold and a pair of bullocks from Gujarat."

If we look at the treatment that Karan Singh received from the Mughal king, we can understand the real value of honour and valour. The kings who served the Mughals were never treated in the respectful and even doting manner in which Karan was treated by Jehangir.

Thomas Roe, the British agent writes on the respect Jehangir gave to Karan:

"The right issue of Porus is here a king in the midst of Mughal dominion, never subdued till last year; and, to tell the truth, he is rather bought than conquered.

"Won to own a superior by gifts and not by arms. The pillar erected by Alexander is yet standing at Delhi, the ancient seat of Rama, the successor of Porus."

Thomas Roe acknowledges that the Hindu line of kings from Shri Rama to Porus to the modern-day Mewar king continues uninterrupted[129].

Alas! It is only the Hindus who are blissfully unaware or ignorant of the fact that Hindus alone are the heirs of the oldest human civilisation and that we thrive today because of some extreme valour and intelligence demonstrated by our great ancestors at an extremely adverse time. Karan Singh returned to Mewar and then his son Jagat Singh visited Jehangir at Delhi and was treated with the same love and respect as his father.

Karan's return to Mewar was immediately translated into the economic and social progress of Mewar. The population descended from the mountains to the plains and massive economic activity was initiated with farming and trading resuming at their fullest.

Mewar was geographically expanded with the addition of many new districts, like Kheirar, Phoolia, Badnor, Mandalgarh, Jheerum, Neemuch, and Bhainsror, with Mewar's supremacy established over Deola and Dungarpur. The regaining and repairing of Chittor were of tremendous psychological advantage

129. Tod, vol. 1, p. 288-89.

to the great people of Mewar, who worked overtime to restore its lost glory. Fate had intervened in a strange manner in the story of the Maharanas, as Amar Singh entered into a ceasefire with Mughals—a ceasefire that lasted for five decades during which time Mewar experienced some well-deserved rest and tranquillity. This will be detailed in the chapter on Karan Singh and Jagat Singh.

Little did the Mewar Maharanas and its people know that one final battle against the Islamic invaders was still written in the fate of these magnificent people.

The divine had given Mewar an interim period to rest and regroup to finally take on the evilest of the enemies of Hinduism—Aurangzeb, under the great Raj Singh, who was the brave son of Jagat Singh.

This unsung story of Mewar's final assault on Mughal occupation was the biggest tremor that shook the very foundation of Aurangzeb's occupation of Delhi and eventually led to the end of the Mughal dynasty forever.

Amar Singh's treaty with the Mughals and the interim of the tranquil rules of Karan and Jagat Singh were the coiling of the Hindu resistance to Mughals to be uncoiled during the rule of Raj Singh, who would finally defeat Aurangzeb in Mewar and build a strong Rajput confederation in the process which would ultimately lead to the downfall of Mughals after Aurangzeb's death in CE 1707.

Let us return to Mewar at the time of the treaty to witness what Amar Singh, the great son of Maharana Pratap, endured while Karan and Jagat were being wooed by the Mughals. Amar Singh sent through Karan and Jagat, innumerable precious gifts for Jehangir and exercised his dues to honour the treaty.

But, to a lofty mind like his, no consideration by the Mughals was enough. Amar Singh could not free himself of the burden of his promise to Pratap in the true tradition of *raghukul*, which has been immortalised by Goswami Tulsidas as:

रघुकुल रीति सदा चलि आई।
प्राण जाये पर वचन न जाई।।

(In the line of King Raghu, this tradition is unbroken. Life may be lost, but never a promise.)

Although Mewar lost nothing in the bargain with the Mughals, and only gained more territory and affluence for her deprived population, the binder of a promise was too much to bear for Amar Singh. Though Mewar regained the highly prized and valued Chittor, Amar Singh was constantly immersed in the singular obsession of having gone back on his promise to a father he loved so deeply.

Even transiently, Amar Singh could just not endure the blot of becoming a *jagirdar* of Mughal rule and his *soul* withered into the sad corridors of solitude.

To the noble Amar Singh who took the resolution to abdicate the throne he could no longer hold:

"Rather than be less, cared not be at all."

Assembling his nobles and chiefs, and announcing his decision, Amar Singh put the *teeka* on Karan's forehead; observing that the honour of Mewar was now in Karan's hands, he left the capital and secluded himself in Nau Chauki on the banks of Pichola Lake.

Amar Singh was physically the most powerful prince of Mewar as demonstrated in the Battle of Dewair. He was fully worthy of Pratap and his clan. He displayed all mental, physical, emotional and spiritual qualities of a Hindu king at the most challenging time that Mewar faced historically.

He was reserved personally, but an aggressive military strategist and executioner, a compassionate king and tolerant of other streams of thought and lifestyles. Of the sixty years of his life, Amar Singh kept fighting for forty years in pitched battles against Mughals in and around Mewar. Of the twenty-three years that Amar Singh ruled Mewar, eighteen were spent in fighting Akbar and Jehangir and he won every single battle convincingly. The last five years of his rule brought tranquillity and economic progress to a war-ravaged Mewar.

Being an extremely sensitive man, the failure to keep his word to Pratap weighed heavily on Amar Singh and his *aatma* withered away due to that burden. On 30th October CE 1620, Amar Singh, the worthy but unsung son of Pratap, attained his *moksha* on the banks of Pichola and his ashes were merged with those of his illustrious ancestors.

Being the son and heir of Pratap, Amar Singh carried the heaviest mantle of Mewar with the perfect balance and grace that were expected of him. His honourable treaty with the Mughals helped Mewar extend its limits and replenish its resources which proved to be of immense value to his great grandson Raj Singh. Maharana Raj Singh went on to defeat Aurangzeb and laid the foundations for the eventual fall of the Mughals in CE 1707.

Karan Singh (CE 1620-1628) and Jagat Singh (CE 1628-1652)
Three Decades of Tranquillity

In CE 1620, Karan Singh was officially proclaimed the Rana of Mewar. Karan Singh was a brave yet soft-hearted and benevolent king, who focused his eight-year rule on bringing prosperity to a war-ravaged Mewar. He expanded Mewar into large areas of Malwa and Gujarat, without fighting wars, through diplomacy and coercion.

Maharana Karan Singh (1620-1628 CE)

As we have read in the chapter on Amar Singh, Karan went to the courts of Jehangir at Agra and Ajmer and had an excellent rapport with Khurram, the son of Jehangir who later ascended the throne at Delhi, as Shahjahan. During Karan's reign, Khurram revolted against his father Jehangir and the Mughal Empire was split vertically in this war of dominance.

Karan gave shelter to Khurram in Udaipur for years but managed to avoid the enmity of Jehangir, who loved Karan like a son. The Muslim annals completely ignore the reference to Shahjahan being Mewar's guest probably because they find it demeaning to admit that a future Mughal ruler had to seek shelter in a Hindu kingdom. But there are enough pieces of evidence to substantiate this reality.

The reference to Shahjahan finds a place in very reliable Hindu historical sources, like *Rajprashasti* by Ranchod Bhatt Tailang, the Telugu history-keeper of the Mewar royal house. Shahjahan is also mentioned in the Bikaner and Boondi annals. James Tod mentions it as well. The red Mughal turban of Shahjahan remains with the Mewar royal house even today. In those times, when two kings proclaimed friendship, they would exchange their turbans. Thus, we can be reasonably sure that Karan Singh indeed gave shelter of Shahjahan for years in Mewar. This shows the extent of influence Mewar exercised over the affairs in Agra and Delhi.

Jehangir simply overlooked Karan's decision of protecting Khurram. Karan, on his part, as the Rana of Mewar, never visited Agra again but sent his son Jagat Singh as a representative to Mewar. Jehangir was thus placated and could devote his time to fighting other wars all over India.

After the death of Jehangir in 1627, Karan sided with Khurram in the war of succession at Delhi. This was a step, which by providence would prove of immense value to the future king of Mewar, Jagat Singh. Khurram killed all his brothers with the help of his father-in-law, Asaf Khan.

A brief account of the fate of the other children of Jehangir is written below to underscore the brutality and blind ambitions of Mughal princes, who had scant regard for the parental will, or a rule of succession. Only the more wicked and merciless would prevail in this bloodbath of sibling rivalry. The Islamic rulers were not only brutal upon Hindus but equally barbaric with each other where brute power was the only worthy goal, whatever be the cost. Contrast this with the Hindu kingdoms like Mewar. Pratap faced similar circumstances during his ascent to the throne of Mewar, but he never ever hurt his blood relatives.

The eldest son of Jehangir, Parvez, was supported by many Mughal chiefs and the royal houses of Jodhpur and Jaipur.

A brother of Karan Singh, Bhim Singh grew very close to

Shahjahan and aligned all his forces with him in this war of succession. Bhim was a great warrior. A major battle took place in Jaunpur in today's Uttar Pradesh, in which he lost his life fighting for Shahjahan. This sacrifice was to weigh heavily on Shahjahan all his life, as he was very considerate, not only to Karan, but also his son Jagat Singh and his grandson Raj Singh.

Shah Jahan Friend of Mewar (1628-1658 CE)

Parvez was an alcoholic and died of cirrhosis at the age of thirty-eight in CE 1626. Khusro Mirza, the eldest son of Jehangir, was Akbar's favourite and Akbar wanted to bypass/circumvent/sidestep Jehangir and make Khusro the next ruler kingdom. Khusro fought Jehangir after Akbar's death in 1605 but was defeated and blinded by Jehangir at Lahore in CE 1607. He was murdered in CE 1622 by Asif Khan on the orders of Shahjahan.

Shahryar, Jehangir's youngest son, was defeated in a battle by Khurram and killed in CE 1628. After eliminating all his brothers, Khurram assumed the title of Shahjahan and ascended Delhi's throne in CE 1628. Karan Singh's help to Shahjahan during his war of succession was amply recognised and reciprocated by Shahjahan.

In fact, Karan sent a few of his leading nobles to Surat where Khurram was living in exile and informed Khurram of Jehangir's demise and immediately invited Khurram to Udaipur. It was in 'Badal Mahal' at Udaipur that Khurram was named 'Shahjahan' by nobles and princes from around Mewar[130].

Shahjahan, on reaching Agra, restored five alienated districts of Mewar, presented Karan with a red ruby of inestimable value and allowed the fortification of Chittor as Karan desired. Authority to set up a larger number of ordinance workshops was granted to Mewar.

There is another interesting incident from Karan's life that is being narrated to highlight how destiny intervened to preserve

130. Tod, vol. 1, p. 295.

the line of these amazing Maharanas and one more instance of the close affinity of the Charans with Mewar's royal house.

In CE 1625, Karan ordered the execution of a Naruka Rajput of Jaipur for reasons unknown. The younger brother of the slain Naruka Rajput swore revenge and came to Mewar on a very strong family horse. Khemraj Charan was a young man serving with an arms-keeper in Udaipur at the time. Naruka Rajput called upon Khemraj and asked him to sharpen his sword for a disproportionate amount of money. Khemraj grew suspicious and followed the former. The next morning, Jagat Singh, Karan's son and heir to Mewar was returning from a hunting expedition. Karan was watching his son's arrival from the royal house.

Maharana Jagat Singh (1628-1652 CE)

Near Krishna Pol (Krishna Gate), Naruka attacked an unprepared Jagat Singh, shouting, *"I claim enmity with you for my brother's murder,"* and charged towards Jagat Singh. Karan shouted in despair, *"My house has sunk!"* But Khemraj had already positioned himself between Naruka and Jagat and in one slice cut the head and arm of the charging Naruka Rajput.

Thus, by foresight and loyalty of a vigilant citizen, the heir to Mewar was saved. Khemraj was taken as the fourth son by Karan and employed as Jagat's personal bodyguard[131].

Karan Singh had a short rule of eight years and died of an unknown disease at the young age of forty-five in the year CE 1628. Karan's son, Jagat Singh then became the Rana of Mewar and for twenty-four years, ruled Mewar without much interference or opposition from the Mughals. Jagat Singh's reign passed in uninterrupted tranquillity. The interim was used by him to cultivate peaceful arts, especially architecture.

Udaipur owes much of its present beauty to this Maharana,

131. *Veer Vinod*, vol. 2, p. 316-17.

after all the disasters and suffering endured by the people of Mewar. Jagat built the city to become a wonder and Udaipur is one of the most famous tourist spots in the country even today besides being renowned throughout the world as 'Venice of the East'.

Jagat Singh visited many Hindu centres of pilgrimages. A huge army would accompany him on these pilgrimages.

On innumerable occasions, Jagat was resisted by local Muslim lords but did not relent and quelled them. His expeditions to Dwarka and Haridwar were marked by freeing Hindu traders from taxes and harassment by Muslim warlords. Once, he even had a frontal confrontation with the *subedar* of Malwa, who was forced into retreat but then wrote a very vengeful letter against Jagat to Shahjahan. Shahjahan ignored all such complaints against Jagat.

Jagat Singh built the famous Jagannath temple in Udaipur and also fortified Chittor. Jagat also strengthened Mewar's forces in Dungarpur, Banswara and Sirohi as Shahjahan looked away.

At the young age of forty-five, Jagat Singh too ascended to *swarga* (heaven) to be with his glorious forefathers, leaving a hugely prosperous kingdom of Mewar for his son. His son Raj Singh, became the king of Mewar in CE 1652. The great Raj Singh would need every penny of these funds and every ounce of those resources to take on the deadliest enemy of Hindus: Aurangzeb.

□

16

Maharana Raj Singh: Saving of Srinathji and Defeat of Aurangzeb (CE 1652-1680)

With Maharana Raj Singh, we come to the end of the thousand-year saga of the Mewar Maharanas who had resolutely stood against the Islamic invaders for a thousand glorious and uninterrupted years. A saga that is so surreal, that without the meticulously preserved annals of Mewar and brilliant documentations of this saga by James Tod and Shyamaldas, would have remained unbelievable folklore only. We must also express gratitude to writers like Ranchod Bhatt Tailang, Gaurishankar Heerchand Ojha, Dr. Chandrashekhar Sharma, Rajendra Shankar Bhatt, Dr. L.P. Mathur, Prof. K.S. Gupta, Dr. Manish Shrimali and many more who kept reinforcing the research and documentation around the lives of these great Maharanas.

From Bappa Rawal in the 8th century, to Raj Singh towards the end of the 17th century, this royal house of Mewar kept producing kings who ceaselessly owed their allegiance to Hindu *dharma* and paid every price conceivable to the human mind to live up to that allegiance.

Mewar forged alliances with friendly and like-minded kings to defend Hinduism and honour of the kingdom, but at times, she was deserted by all and stood alone in her fight against the barbarians from West Asia.

The epicentre of Mewar, Chittorgarh, was lost and regained by Mewar's kings at least twice during these thousand years of conflict. Each stone and brick of Chittor is a mute witness to the glory of these amazing Maharanas who kept the flag of freedom and *dharma* flying high through the sheer grit and determination of their conscience. There couldn't have been a better king than Raj Singh to have written the concluding chapter of this thousand-year saga.

Raj Singh inherited a prosperous and rejuvenated Mewar from Jagat Singh and was crowned the Maharana of Mewar on 22nd October CE 1652. For the next twenty-eight years till his death, Raj Singh changed the course of Hindu history in the subcontinent irreversibly and thus, his life became a saga of legends that are part of everyday folklore of Rajasthan.

We can look at the life of Raj Singh under three broad events:

- The great famine of Mewar and digging and construction of Rajsamand Lake
- Expansion of Mewar and war with Aurangzeb
- Manufacturing a pan-Hindu alliance

1. The Great Famine of Mewar

A mere seven years after Raj Singh's ascension to the throne of Mewar, a devastating famine hit the kingdom. There were no rains for three consecutive years. The Rana went to different temples to pay homage to the gods to relieve the suffering of his people. Charbhuja (the four-armed), Jagannath Mandir, among others, were visited by him to implore the grace of the divine, but the skies remained quiet.

The condition of people is described in detail by the poet Maan, in his work *Raj Vilas,* which has been translated into English by James Tod and draws a horrifying sketch of Mewar's sufferings.

Tod writes:

"For want of water, the world was in despair and people went

mad with hunger. Things unknown as good were eaten.

"The husband abandoned the wife, the wife the husband; parents sold their children; time increasd the evil; it's spread far and wide;

"Even the insects died; they had nothing to feed on.

"The wind was from the west, a pestilential vapour.

"The constellations were always visible at night, nor was there a cloud in the sky by day, and thunder and lightning were unknown.

"Such portents filled mankind with dread.

"Rivers, lakes and fountains were dried up.

"Men of wealth meted out the portions of food.

"The ministers of religion forgot their duties.

"There was no longer distinction of caste and the Shudra and Brahmin were indistinguishable.

"Strength, wisdom, caste, tribe; all were abandoned, and food alone was the object.

The char varna (four varnas) threw away every symbol of separation; all was lost in hunger.

"Fruits, flowers, every vegetable thing, even trees were stripped of their bark, to appease the cravings of hunger; nay, man ate man!

"Cities were depopulated. The seed of families was lost, the fishes were extinct, and the hope of all extinguished[132]."

Such is the simple yet terrific record of this pestilence from which Raj Singh extricated Mewar with his vision of constructing a massive artificial lake 50 kms north of Udaipur.

In CE 1661, Maharana Raj Singh visited the famous Roop Narayan temple and chanced upon the dry Gomti river and enquired if a lake or an embankment could be dug to collect the waters of the river. The *samants* and the royal priest informed the king that his great-grandfather Amar Singh had attempted to construct a pond on this river, but because of the might of the river, the task could not be completed.

If a huge lake were constructed, then this would be a worthy endeavour. Raj Singh, meditating on the extreme distress of his people, was determined to raise a monument by which the wretched might be supported, monsoon water be harvested and

132. Tod, vol. 1, p. 310.

his own name perpetuated. It was named Raj Samudra (Royal Sea).

The digging of the Raj Samudra began on 12th January CE 1662. The foundation for the embankments began to be laid on 8th May CE 1665. It took sixteen years to complete the construction of the Raj Samudra, now known as the Raj Samand. Hundreds of thousands of ordinary people were given work and Raj Singh opened the state coffers to his people through this magnificent construction.

The Raj Samand was fed by three rivers, namely, the Gomti, Tali and Kelwa. The dam forms an irregular segment of a circle embracing an extent of nearly three miles, encircling the waters on every side, except the space between the north-western and north-eastern points. This barrier, which confined a sheet of water of great depth, is about 12 miles in circumference, entirely of white marble, with the flight of steps of the same material, throughout this extent, from the summit to the water's edge—the whole buttressed by an enormous rampart of earth.

The Raj Samand is an architectural masterpiece with the town and fortress situated on the southern side and upon the embankment stands the temple of Kankroli, dedicated to Shri Krishna.

According to Tod, £1150,000 sterling contributed by the Rana, his chiefs and opulent subjects, was expended on this work. Shyamaldas records that 1,05,47,584 rupees were spent on its construction.

Such is the simple yet terrifying record of this pestilence, when Aurangzeb provoked religious warfare with all its attendant atrocities, which despite Raj Singh's benevolent works, was to devastate this fair and just region still further. This assault met with just retribution, as Aurangzeb was cast into ignominy, causing grave prejudice among the Rajputs and laying the ground for the end of the Mughals.

Maharana Raj Singh, having taken care of the worst suffering and economic disaster of Mewar, prepared for a final assault on the Islamic zealotry of Aurangzeb to weed out Muslim imperialism permanently.

The beautiful Rajsamand

2. Expansion of Mewar and Wars with Aurangzeb

As we have seen in the chapters on Amar Singh, Karan Singh and Jagat Singh, after the Mewar-Mughal treaty of CE 1616, Mewar witnessed uninterrupted tranquillity and prosperity for half a century, which helped her to replenish its resources and manpower to fight one final war with the Mughals, which eventually hastened the downfall of Mughal rule in Delhi.

Shahjahan had grown old at the time of Raj Singh's ascendance to the throne of Mewar. A bloody war of succession broke out between his sons Dara Shikoh, Shuja-ud-Daula, Muhiuddin Aurangzeb and Murad Baksh.

The Mughals had no tradition of primogeniture, i.e. the systematic bequeathing of rule upon a ruler's death, to his eldest son. Instead, it was customary for sons to overthrow their father and for brothers to war to death amongst themselves.

The final outcome of the succession war rested heavily on whose side Mewar would tilt. All the four sons of Shahjahan wrote letters to Raj Singh seeking help from him. Raj Singh was personally inclined towards Dara Shikoh who was an extremely liberal individual in matters of religion and had even gotten the *Upanishads* translated into Persian. Besides, Dara was also recognised as a scholar.

Dara Shikoh, The liberal Mughal we never got

Aurangzeb eventually outmanoeuvred and killed everyone who opposed his ambitions. His father, his brothers and even his sons who opposed him became victims in his mad lust for power, which eventually destroyed the Mughal rule itself.

Dara was defeated by Aurangzeb in the Battle of Samugarh (near Agra) and was finally put to death in CE 1659. Murad was abducted at Mathura and executed in Gwalior at the behest of Aurangzeb in CE 1661. Shuja had been the Governor of Bengal but grew ambitious and was eventually overcome by

Aurangzeb's forces. He escaped eastwards to Burma and was killed there by the locals.

The policies of Jehangir and Shahjahan of aligning with the powerful Mewar dynasty, in order to cement a strong foothold in the north-west, were abandoned by Aurangzeb, to his peril. It is noteworthy that Shahjahan and Jehangir had Rajput Hindu mothers and thus, belonged to the bloodline that made them relatively tolerant and wise to rule a nation as complex as Bharat, which was 95 per cent Hindu.

Aurangzeb's unmixed Tatar blood brought no Rajput sympathies to his aid. On the contrary, every noble family of Rajasthan stood with Shahjahan and Dara in the Mughal war of succession. Aurangzeb's bigotry and evangelistic lust outweighed any policy making and he began an unrelenting and self-destructive persecution of Hindus in general and Rajputs in particular.

Renewal of resistance to the Mughals after the treaty of CE 1616 between Mewar and the Mughals can be credited to Raj Singh. His legacy as a protector of Hindu *dharma* and as an able, just and fearless ruler should forever be etched in Indian history. He was a deeply ambitious Hindu monarch who not only wanted to regain every inch of Mewar, but also expand its horizons to the entire north and west India and eventually defeat the Mughals in Delhi.

Raj Singh began his work many years before Aurangzeb grabbed power in Delhi. He used *teekadaur*, the name given to hunting expeditions by Mewar kings, to slowly nibble away at the neighbouring kingdoms. He annexed Malpura in one such hunting expedition and thus expanded Mewar to the frontiers of Ajmer, challenging the Mughals directly.

Shahjahan, who was the Mughal king then, chose to look the other way amidst these adventures by Raj Singh and is quoted as saying, *"Oh, it is only a folly of my nephew."* Shahjahan thought of Karan Singh, Raj Singh's grandfather, as his adopted brother.

Raj Singh continued his moves to irritate Shahjahan by repairing the Chittor fort on a war footing (which was disallowed according to their treaty), destroying *masjids* in and around

Mewar and publicly beheading Muslims who would indulge in cow slaughter. Shahjahan then decided to move to Ajmer with a force of 30,000 horsemen with an intention to confront Raj Singh in CE 1654.

The Mughal emperor deputed a Brahmin, Chandrabhan, to reach out to Raj Singh and get him to tone down his ambitions. Before Chandrabhan could reach Mewar, Raj Singh himself sent his emissaries, Madhusudan Bhatt and Raj Singh Jhala to the Mughal General, Sadulla Khan, who had captured Chittor and was laying it waste. Given below is the conversation that took place between Sadulla Khan and Mewar's emissaries:

Sadulla: *"How come Udaipur Rajputs behave so autonomously? Have you guys forgotten that Shahjahan is the emperor?"*

Mewar's emissaries: *"Udaipur Rajputs have earned their right to be in Delhi and Udaipur simultaneously. This is a tradition being followed since Rawat Megh Singh and Shakti Singh went with Jehangir and Akbar, respectively."*

Sadulla: *"Does this mean that you Rajputs have started considering Delhi a second-grade power?"*

Mewar's emissaries: *"No, but neither is Mewar a second-grade power. Mewar's Rajputs will settle in Delhi or Udaipur, depending on their own will."*

Sadulla: *"Really? If Udaipur wants to pick a fight with Delhi, you are most welcome. How many horses does Raj Singh have?"*

Mewar's emissaries: *"26,000."*

Sadulla: *"Shahjahan has one lakh. How can you fight us?"*

Mewar's emissaries: *"26,000 are sufficient for a fight[133]."*

That was the kind of army Raj Singh commanded besides the infantry and elephant force in the early days of his confrontation with Mughals. By the time Aurangzeb invaded Mewar, Maharana's army had multiplied to take on frontally with Aurangzeb.

After this failed attempt, Raj Singh approached Dara Shikoh and sent his trusted nobles along with his son Sultan Singh to the court of Shahjahan. Shahjahan treated the boy Sultan Singh with love and respect and a temporary truce materialised between Mewar and Mughals once again. Raj Singh understood

---

133. *Veer Vinod*, vol. 2, p. 412.

that a disunited Hindu leadership and an ill-conceived strategy to fight the Mughals would stymie the plan he had in his mind, and therefore decided to fortify Mewar further. He now reached out to the other princely states of Rajasthan, mainly Jodhpur, Bikaner, and Jaipur to forge a Hindu alliance. He even sent emissaries to the intrepid Maratha leadership.

As mentioned earlier, by CE 1659, Aurangzeb had eliminated all his three brothers.

The magnanimous Dara, the impetuous Murad and the hyperactive Shuja, all met the same tragic end. Aurangzeb imprisoned his father Shahjahan and thus began the final chapter of conflict between Mewar and the Mughals under the two most committed and ablest leaders on either side. It is shameful and tragic for Hindus of this land that the amazing saga of Hindu victory over Mughals has been completely erased from our history.

This story gains immense significance for the simple fact that for the initial twenty years of his vengeful reign, Aurangzeb was challenged and defeated by Raj Singh. If Aurangzeb had not been challenged and defeated by Raj Singh, we can only imagine the slaughter and plunder that the Hindus of the subcontinent would have faced.

This is a saga of humongous significance, as it forced Aurangzeb to completely abandon his desire of conquest of Rajasthan and shift forever to Deccan and the far east (Assam).

This is a saga that demonstrates the abilities of Rajput kingdoms to forget their differences and forge alliances against a common enemy when Hindu *dharma* was under siege.

It is a saga that brings us to the closure of the immortal conflicts of Mewar with Islamic imperialism.

Who better than the great Raj Singh of Mewar could be the protagonist of the culmination of this thousand-year old saga of civilisational conflict with a great Hindu *dharma* on one side and a barbaric death cult of the invaders on the other?

Three events, all of equal significance, need to be narrated and understood clearly to grasp the scope and build-up of the Mewar-Mughal conflict under Raj Singh.

After Aurangzeb, the Mughal rule over Delhi crumbled for

the singular reason that Mughal-Rajput alliance was completely shattered by Raj Singh. Mughals and Rajputs were now enemies. From this point of view, Raj Singh was the most important pivot of Rajput unity after Sanga.

The Charumati Episode

Kishangarh was a small estate near Mewar at the time and was ruled by Roop Singh, who had an extremely beautiful daughter, Charumati. When the fame of her beauty reached Aurangzeb, he ordered Man Singh, Charumati's brother, to give her in marriage to him (Aurangzeb). The men of Kishangarh's royal house had to consent to this order fearing a war with the Mughals. But when Charumati heard of this, she outrightly declared to her brother and father, her refusal to be married to a Musalman. Charumati was a deeply devotional Hindu and had total faith in Shri Krishna. She told her family that she would prefer death than marry a *mlechchha*.

But receiving no assurance of help from her family, Charumati wrote a letter to Raj Singh and sent it to the Maharana through her family's trusted head priest. The letter is preserved in Mewar's annals even today. Charumati, in her letter stated, thus, "Is a swan to be a mate of the stork; a Rajpootni, pure in blood, to be the wife of a monkey-faced barbarian?" She concluded her letter with a resolve of ending her life if she were not saved from the dishonour of being forced to become a Mughal's sex slave.

Raj Singh made up his mind to respond to the call of the Rajput princess, gathered an army of his trusted nobles and sent a letter to Ratan Singh Choondawat, the keeper of Saloombar house, under the auspices of Mewar. Ratan Singh was an extremely courageous warrior and commanded a few thousand troops under him. Raj Singh instructed him to immediately leave for Ajmer and intercept Aurangzeb's army which had been dispatched in large numbers to attack Kishangarh and prevent Raj Singh from marrying Charumati on the date of the wedding.

Aurangzeb did not trust his Rajput Generals to fight the Mewar army. A large Mughal force was therefore dispatched under a relatively insignificant Muslim General to attack Kishangarh.

Ratan Singh Choondawat had been married only for a few days, when Maharana Raj Singh's letter reached him. He immediately responded to Rana's call and prepared to leave with his few thousand troops for Ajmer to intercept the Mughal army. But Ratan Singh was enamoured by his beautiful wife who belonged to the Hada clan of Bundi. The wise and brave Hadi Rani (the name for Ratan Singh's wife in folklore) convinced Ratan Singh to look ahead to the task of defeating the Mughals while she would eagerly await his return.

The story goes like this:

Ratan Singh just couldn't get the image and memory of his beautiful queen out of his mind and kept sending emissaries to her even from the battlefield. To the two initial emissaries, the Hadi Rani gave a ring and a fragrant handkerchief as mementos to be given to her husband. When the third emissary appeared, the Hadi Rani understood that her husband would be constantly distracted from his responsibility. Something drastic needed to be done to remind Ratan Singh of his duty towards Mewar at such a critical juncture when Raj Singh's survival depended on Ratan Singh's success. Hadi Rani did the unimaginable. She decorated a plate and gave a red cloth to the emissary to cover it and then beheaded herself and had her head placed on that plate to be delivered to Ratan Singh. Such were the sacrifices that our amazing ancestors made to keep fighting *jihadi* predators.

Can we imagine the message such an action would have sent to the whole state of Mewar? Can we imagine the impact of the visceral image of the queen's head being carried by an emissary to her husband at war? Can we even comprehend what it would have done to Ratan Singh to see his beloved wife's head in a *thaali.*

Ratan Singh's life collapsed in the instant when he lifted the red cloth from the *thaali*. It is through such numerous acts of extreme sacrifice of our women over the millennia, that Hindus managed to thwart and defeat the most violent barbarians ever to have walked on the globe.

Ratan Singh, now free of all worldly baggage, turned to the war with full ferocity and led his men to attack an enemy four times the size of his army and decimated it. Ratan Singh and most of his troops sacrificed their lives in this battle but gave enough time for Raj Singh to marry Charumati and return to the safety of Mewar.

.*The ultimate sacrifice of the Hadi Rani*

Raj Singh, who left for Kishangarh with a chosen few by his side, cut down the Mughal imperial guards and went off with Charumati back to Udaipur. The surreal turn of events around Raj Singh's marriage with Charumati provided a huge boost to the morale of Rajputs in Rajasthan and the Rana used it as a pretext to throw away the scabbard. This was done in order to initiate a war with the Mughals in which he was determined to vanquish those who menaced his country and his faith.

Raj Singh weds Charumati

Charumati's audacious rescue by a Rajput king crushing the evil designs of a Musalman to marry a pure Rajpootni was also an omen of success to his war-like and deeply religious vassalage. Ratan Singh Choondawat and the immortal sacrifice of Hadi

Rani facilitated the grounds for the resurgence of Rajput pride in Rajasthan.

Raj Singh demonstrated to the Hindus of Rajasthan that the bullying might of the Mughals was largely a bluff premised on two key factors, namely, the internal divisions of Rajputs and the incentivising of mercenaries with the wealth and women of Hindus.

If Rajputs could forget petty differences and align with each other, the Mughal kingdom was easily surmountable. If Hindus would protect their women and properties ferociously, this vicious cycle of Islamic encroachment could be broken.

As if to endorse Raj Singh's challenge to Aurangzeb's authority, the latter did not pursue Raj Singh into Mewar and brooked this insult by marrying Charumati's sister to his son Muazzam, to assuage his bruised ego.

Srinathji comes to Mewar

Aurangzeb, in his religious zeal, issued two *firmans* (orders) that brought him to a head-on confrontation with Raj Singh of Mewar. The Mughal ruler sent an order to the *gosains* (priests)[134] of Mathura saying if they claimed divinity, they had to show him some miracle, else he would destroy the Krishna temples of Mathura and Vrindavan[135]. On 10th October of CE 1669, the priests of Srinathji temple of Mathura, Damodarji, Bal Krishna, Vallabhji and Ganga Bai took the *moorti* (icon) of Bhagwan Krishna and left for Rajasthan to seek shelter for the precious divine idol of Shri Krishna.

No other Rajput kingdom could muster the courage to pick enmity with Aurangzeb. On some pretext or the other, they politely asked the priests to seek shelter elsewhere. Finally, after traversing the entirety of Rajasthan, through Jaipur, Kota, Jodhpur, Boondi, etc., the priests approached Maharana Raj Singh of Mewar to seek shelter and protection from Aurangzeb to build a temple of Srinathji in Mewar.

Following was the reply of the great Raj Singh to the priests,

134. Brahmin priests of Krishna temple.

135. *Veer Vinod*, vol. 2, p. 452.

"Only when one lakh Rajputs of mine have been beheaded, can Aurangzeb touch the moorti of Srinathji[136]."

Raj Singh gave state protection to the idol and the priests and asked them to choose a place of their liking to build a temple for Srinathji. The priests chose Sihaad village near River Banas about 50 kms north of Udaipur. On 20th February 1672, Saturday, Srinathji's idol was reinstalled at the village, which remains till date as one of the most significant and sacred pilgrimage centres for Hindus and Vaishnavites in particular, the Nathdwara.

Srinath Ji

Giving state protection to the priests of Vrindavan was the second major bone of contention in the relationship between Aurangzeb and Mewar, but Raj Singh chose to stand for honour and love of his *dharma* than to forsake it at the altar of fear and greed, both traits quite distant from the great Sisodia clan of Rajputs.

Aurangzeb wrote a letter to Raj Singh forbidding him from giving protection to the priests and Srinathji's idol. The Maharana completely ignored Aurangzeb's rantings and dispatched a large army to the village of Sihaad to prepare for a battle, should Aurangzeb attack the temple. The nobles of Devgadh, Saloombar and its neighbouring areas geared up for battle to protect the icon of the Hindu deity.

Raj Singh sent an emissary to the Rathore clan of Jodhpur to assist him in fighting Aurangzeb.

136. *Veer Vinod*, vol. 2, p. 453.

Raj Singh's Alliance with Durgadas Rathore and Shelter to Infant Ajit Singh of Jodhpur

As though destiny had started to tilt towards Hindu fortunes, during the tenure of Aurangzeb, all the three major kingdoms of Rajasthan were ruled by three incredibly talented, brave and staunch Hindu rulers. Raj Singh in Mewar, Jaswant Singh in Jodhpur and Mirza Raja Jai Singh of Amer (Jaipur) were the formidable trio that prevented Aurangzeb from pursuing his plans for the full-blown Islamisation of the region. Jai Singh and Jaswant Singh were devout Hindus but were committed to fighting for the Mughal ruler because of their ancestral loyalty. However, both were displeased internally and adequately demonstrated it to Aurangzeb from time to time.

Aurangzeb's continuous conflict with Hindu kings all over north-western region and with the Afghans in Afghanistan resulted in mass-scale migration of Hindus from Mughal-controlled regions to Hindu-controlled areas. Cities were vacated by Hindus and small villages sprung up all along the rural countryside. A major economic slowdown began gathering pace and Mughal coffers started depleting.

Aurangzeb then planned to implement the *jaziya* or religious tax on the Hindus of his kingdom. *Jaziya* is an Islamic practice of taxing non-Muslims under Muslim rule simply for adhering to their faith.

Aurangzeb knew that as long as the Rajput kingdoms of Jaipur, Jodhpur and Mewar stood tall, his plan of implementing *jaziya* would invite rebellion from Rajputs, and the possible effacement of the Mughals from Delhi. He now planned the murder of Mirza Raja Jai Singh and Maharaja Jaswant Singh.

He ordered Jai Singh to go to the Deccan to quell a local rebellion and sent Jaswant Singh to fight in Afghanistan. On 28th August 1667, under the orders of Aurangzeb, Jai Singh was poisoned and thus eliminated[137]. Besides his opposition to *jaziya*, Aurangzeb held Jai Singh responsible for secretly helping his deadly enemy, Chhatrapati Shivaji Maharaj of the Marathas, by planning his escape from the clutches of Aurangzeb.

137. James Tod's *Annals & Antiquities of Rajasthan*, vol. 1, p. 302.

The writer could lay hands on two written accounts that prove that Jai Singh was indeed murdered on orders of Aurangzeb.

The first one is very poignant. Shri Shankar Singh Ashiya writes in his book *Charan Digdarshan* that clearly describes that angered at Shivaji's escape, Aurangzeb ordered his minister, Nizam-ul-Mulk to get Jai Singh assassinated.

Nizam prepared one Jagannath Ratnu for this job. Jagannath was a very powerful warrior, called *Yakka* in those times. A warrior who had killed 100 soldiers in war was referred as *Yakka*.

Jagannath took Jai Singh to the jungles on the pretext of hunting. Jagannath drew his sword on the Jaipur king and challenged him to a duel. Jai Singh was incapable of fighting him, yet he also drew his sword. Jagannath then kept his sword at the feet of Jai Singh and showed him the *farmaan* by Nizam ordering Jai Singh's execution.

Jagannath said, *"A warrior born in Charan family can never slay a Rajput. A Charan can never be accused of treachery."*

Jagannath continued; *"Though dharma cannot be bartered for the sake of survival, but I have fed myself with Aurangzeb's money. To free myself from that burden, I had to draw the sword on you. I am free of that burden now. From here on, I am tied to dharma. This sword is for your defence now. You should go to Amer now and I will tell Nizam that you escaped."*

Jai Singh hugged Jagannath and said, *"You are like a father to me. If you go back to Delhi, you will be killed. No one will believe that Jai Singh could escape a Yakka. You too come to Amer with me."*

Jai Singh took Jagannath to Amer and granted him Bhojpura, Jhodunda, Sunara, Nangal and eight other villages in Chaksu area of Jaipur. Jagannath Ratnu settled down in Nangal, where Jai Singh used to go to meet him. Jagannath's progeny still lives in these villages and some of them happen to be related to the writer[138].

This event underlines the huge paradoxes that our ancestors endured and overcame with such amazing clarity and saved themselves and our *dharma*.

The second mention happens in Jaipur annals where

138. Ashiya, p. 357.

Maharaja Jaswant Singh of Jodhpur (1638-1678 CE)

Aurangzeb is supposed to have instructed the female cook of Jai Singh to poison him. Shyamaldas and Tod argue that Jai Singh was murdered by Aurangzeb because Jai Singh helped Chhatrapati Shivaji Raja to escape from his clutches[139].

Recently, Shri Mahendra Khadgawat from Bikaner has unearthed a vital clue from the records of Bikaner annals about the role of Mirza Raja jai singh and his son Ram Singh in arranging the escape of Shivaji Maharaj.

In the same year of 1667 CE, Aurangzeb presented Jaswant Singh's brave son, Prithviraj Singh, with a poisoned khilat, an Arabic robe, which caused the latter's death. Jaswant Singh was shattered at the murder of his son because he had no male heir left to rule Jodhpur. Jaswant Singh still kept fighting for Aurangzeb. On 28th December 1678, Jaswant Singh too was poisoned and put out of the way by Aurangzeb.

Jaswant Singh's queen was pregnant at the time of his death but was forced by Aurangzeb to move to Delhi and was confined with his queens. Aurangzeb also annexed the kingdom of Jodhpur under the pretext of the absence of a rightful heir at the time of Jaswant Singh's death. Jaswant's widowed queen delivered a son who was named Ajit Singh. Aurangzeb planned to raise that Rajput prince as a Muslim[140].

Veer Durgadas Rathore (1638-1718 CE)

139. *Veer Vinod*, vol. 2, p. 1293-94, 1986.
140. Bhimsen Burhanpuri, quoted by R.S. Bhatt on p. 143.

And then arose a warrior from the deserts of Thar, who changed the entire course of the history of Marwar by raising the banner of revolt against Aurangzeb. He was a warrior of such calibre that history had to attach the prefix of 'Veer' to his birth name—Durga Das Rathore. *Veer* is the Sanskrit word for brave. Durga Das was a simple soldier in Jaswant Singh's army but rose to the level of a much respected and feared noble of Marwar. Before Jaswant Singh's poisoning, Durga Das promised to protect the unborn child of Jaswant Singh and one day coronate him as the Maharaja of Jodhpur.

How Durga Das lived up to his promise and eventually crowned Ajit Singh as the king of Jodhpur is an unbelievable saga of chivalry, loyalty, intelligence and selflessness which needs another book to be narrated in its full detail and glory.

Suffice to say, that Durga Das decided to extricate the infant Ajit Singh from the clutches of Aurangzeb and a brief account of that needs to be mentioned here because this one event of the rescue of the infant Ajit Singh catapulted Durga Das to the status of a true leader and protector of Jodhpur's dynasty.

This act would also prove to be crucial as Ajit Singh grew up to finally weed out Mughal rule from Marwar and Jodhpur totally. This escape has been documented in detail in Marwar's annals and needs to be quoted not only for historical accuracy, but also for the sheer poetry of the valour of each noble of Marwar, who laid down his life protecting its legal and rightful heir.

Faulad Khan, with a contingent of 20,000 troops surrounded the Jodhpur *haveli* in Delhi with the orders of 'Arrest or Kill 'for the two queens and the infant Ajit Singh.

The Rathores and their soldiers were furious on hearing the demand of Faulad Khan.

When these brave men saw that Aurangzeb desired nothing short of the surrender of all that was dear to a Rajput, their first instinct was the preservation of their prince; the next was to safeguard their own honour and that of their late king Jaswant Singh.

The means by which they achieved their objectives were terrific.

The womenfolk of the Rathore contingent who were stationed with the queen and infant prince were placed in an apartment filled with gunpowder and torched. All was over in an instant, instead of the long agony of *jauhar*.

With what heart could the great Rathores and Charans and other warriors of Marwar have blown their families to pieces, is beyond the writer's capacity to describe.

Once free of the bonds of family and love, Marwar's Hindu warriors had nothing to look forward to except a niche in the immortal temple of valour when the motto was, *"Youth who died, to be by poets sung."*

Hidden in a basket of sweetmeats, Ajit was taken out of the Mughal palace and a contingent of about 500 Hindus of Marwar under the able leadership of Durga Das Rathore made oblations to their deities, took a double portion of opium and mounted their steeds to achieve the impossible.

The first one to attack was Raghunath Bhati with his 100 soldiers. Durga Das and 400 soldiers left for Marwar from the other gate.

Raghunath slaughtered thousands of Mughals and laid his life with seventy of his soldiers.

Durga Das had gained nine miles by then.

Nearby 10,000 Mughal troops were put in pursuit of the Marwar contingent.

The second challenge to Mughals was thrown by Ranchod Das Jodha and his 60 men. After slaughtering thousands, Jodha and his men too laid their lives.

Finally, Durga Das along with the rest of Rajputs decided to take on the Mughals.

Chandrabhan Jodha of Panchla was accompanied by his two wives in this escape. He beheaded both of them and surrendered the body to the holy waters of Yamuna River and joined Durga Das.

Can we ever fathom the resolve of those young queens who sat down in front of their husband to be beheaded?

What samskaras would prompt such an act of self dissolution for the sake of protecting their little prince?

Such disregard for one's life for the sake of duty towards the land.

Without any noise, free of all doubt, no loud arguments, just simple surrender to the task at hand...

The Rajput girls freed thier husband of all conflict and responsibility in that act of wilful surrender to destiny.

No wonder that with such women ready to die for their duty , Islam could not subjugate us for 1400 years.

The Hindu warriors were electrified in their assault on the Mughals. Each Hindu took down thirty to forty Mughals before falling. They kept fighting till the evening.

All that was left of Marwar contingent was a badly wounded Durga Das and six equally battered men, but the Mughals were completely decimated. The names of the other six warriors who made it alive are as follows:

1. Roop Singh Rathore, 2. Mohkam Singh Rathore, 3. Bhojraj Rathore, 4. Doodi Rathore, 5. Maha singh Rathore and, 6. Panchayan Das Pancholi.

The queens and the infant were well beyond the reach of the *Mlechchas.*

The sons of Marwar had achieved the impossible[141].

The Marwar annals describe this war with poetic connotations and is being shared with the reader because the writer is numb with this mind-blowing sacrifice of Rathores and incapable of bringing out the intensity of what happened on that glorious day for Hindus.

The lust for this sacrifice was so intense that it often defeats the very purpose of revenge!

The Rathore warriors and their friends wished to die gloriously rather than to inflict death.

Thus spoke Ranchor and Govind, the son of Jodha, and Chandrabhaan, the Darawut and the son of Raghunath, with the fearless Bharmal, the Ooda, Soojawat and Raghunath, 'Let us swim,' they exclaimed, 'in the ocean of battle. Let us uproot these *asuras* (demons) and be carried by the *apsaras* (heavenly damsels) to the mansions of the Sun.'

As thus each spoke, Soojah the bard took the word: 'For a day like this,' he said, 'you enjoy your fiefs to give in your Lord's

141. R.S. Bhatt, p. 147-48.

cause, your bodies to the sword and in one mass to gain *swarga* (heaven). As for me who enjoyed his friendship and gifts, this day I will make his salt resplendent. My father's fame, I will uphold, and lead the death in this day's fight, that future bards may hymn my praise.'

Durga Das, the son of Asoh, spoke thus: 'The teeth of *yavanas* (foreigners) are whetted, but by the lightning emitted from our swords, Delhi shall witness our deeds and the flames of our wrath shall consume the troops of the Shah.'

As Aurangzeb's troops approached, lances in hand, with faces resembling Yama (the deity of death), the Rathores and the rest of Hindus of Marwar rushed upon the foe. Wave followed wave in the field of blood.

Shiva's *tandav* (dance of death) was unfolding on the streets of Shahjahanabad, Delhi.

Shankar completed his chaplet in the streets of Delhi.

Ratna contended with nine thousand foes.

Dilloh, Darawut made a gift of his life to *devas*.

Chandrabhan was conveyed by the *apsaras* to Chandrapur.

The Bhati was cut piecemeal and lay on the field besides the son of Sultan.

The faithful Udawat appeared like crimson lotus.

Sandoo, the Charan bard with a sword in both hands, was in front of the battle and gained the mansion of moon.[142]

Every tribe and every clan performed its duty in this day's pilgrimage to the stream of the sword, in which Durga Das ground the foe and saved his honour.

Five hundred Hindu warriors of Marwar slew more than ten thousand soldiers of Aurangzeb on this one day of August CE 1679 and ensured the survival of their valuable prince and the queens of Jaswant Singh. Only six horsemen along with Durga Das made it out alive and reached the house of Thakur Mokham Singh Balunda, who took the infant Ajit and the mother in his care.

Ajit Singh was taken to Maharana Raj Singh of Mewar by Durga Das. Raj Singh immediately granted protection to the infant heir of Marwar. Raj Singh allotted twelve villages around Kelwa as

142. Tod, vol. 2, p. 35.

a *jagir* to the infant and said to Durga Das, *"Aurangzeb cannot dare to attack a united force of Sisodias and Rathores. Stay without fear in Mewar."*

Durgadas on horseback

Thus, a bond was cemented between the Sisodias of Mewar and the Rathores of Marwar and it would prove instrumental in the final uprooting of Mughal rule from Rajasthan.

Durga Das took shelter in the Aravallis of Sirohi and Abu and kept inflicting heavy casualties on the Aurangzeb army. There is an incident that deserves particular mention here.

Aurangzeb commanded that pictures to be drawn of two of his most mortal foes, Shivaji Maharaj and Durga Das. Shivaji was drawn on a couch and Durga Das on horseback. Aurangzeb at first glance exclaimed, *"I may entrap that fellow (Shivaji), but this dog is born to be my bane."*

Aurangzeb even offered a bribe of forty thousand gold dinars to Durga Das if he were to surrender Ajit to the Mughals. Durga Das laughed it off contemptuously. He kept the banner of resistance to Aurangzeb flying and outlived Aurangzeb to reinstate Ajit Singh as the Maharaja of Jodhpur[143].

After Aurangzeb's death in CE 1707, Durga Das drove out the Mughal army from Marwar and crowned young Ajit Singh as its new Maharaja. For reasons beyond the scope of this book to be discussed, Durga Das fell out with Ajit Singh in his old age. Thus, the lionheart Durga Das, after fulfilling the promise he made to Jaswant Singh, rode silently into oblivion.

Durga Das left Marwar to die a lonely man with a few loyal chieftains around him on the banks of Kshipra river, in the holy city of Ujjain on 22nd November CE 1718. The writer intends to write a full book on this son of Marwar, as his next project.

143. Tod, vol. 2, p. 50.

Returning to Raj Singh, as narrated earlier, after the rescue of Ajit Singh from Aurangzeb's clutches, Durga Das kept the child-prince of Marwar in the custody of Raj Singh for a few months. This too became a bone of contention between the Mughals and Mewar.

Opposition to Jaziya—the Game-changer in the Hindu-Muslim Conflict

The last act that evaporated all possibility of peace between Aurangzeb and Raj Singh was the implementation of the *jaziya* tax on non-Muslims of his kingdom.

Sri Guru Gobind Singh ji

Jaziya, though, became a blessing in disguise for the Hindus as the mask of a tolerant Islam was fully thrown off by Aurangzeb. He was now using muscular force to convert Hindus to Islam, causing a massive rebellion not only in the troops serving the Mughal army under Hindu kings, but also among the general Hindu populace.

Jaziya also ensured that Rajput kingdoms of Jodhpur, Jaipur and Mewar would begin to forget their differences and align with each other. Raj Singh was the pivot under whom the Rajput unity was crystallised. He also wrote letters to Chhatrapati Shivaji Maharaj and the tenth Sikh guru Sri Guru Gobind Singh ji, thus laying the foundations of pan-Hindu resistance to Islamic rule over the country.

The cunning Aurangzeb knew that as long as Maharaja Jaswant Singh of Jodhpur and Mirza Raja Jai Singh of Amer were alive, any move to implement *jaziya* would mean immediate and unmanageable revolt by both these devout kings and would also push them both into the willing and waiting arms of Raj Singh of Mewar.

As has been narrated, Aurangzeb poisoned both these great Hindu kings of Jodhpur and Jaipur and then imposed the *jaziya* order on India in CE 1679. Promulgation of *jaziya* immediately evoked a response from Raj Singh.

Following are random passages from the letter Raj Singh wrote to Aurangzeb, almost challenging him to attack Mewar if his love for taxing Hindus needed quenching:

"I have been informed that enormous sums have been dissipated in the persecution of the designs formed against me, your well-wisher; and that you have ordered a tribute to be levied to satisfy the exigencies of your exhausted treasury.

"While your great ancestors pursued generous principles, wheresoever they directed their steps, conquest and prosperity went before them and they reduced many countries and fortresses to their obedience. During Your Majesty's reign, many have been alienated from the empire and further loss of territory must necessarily follow since devastation and rapine now universally prevail without restraint. Your subjects are trampled underfoot and every province of your empire is impoverished.

"When indigence has reached the habitation of the sovereign and his princes, what can be the condition of the nobles?

"As to the soldiery, they are in murmurs; the merchants complaining, the Mohammedans discontented, the Hindu destitute, and multitudes of people are beating their heads throughout the day in rage and desperation.

"At this juncture, it is told that you, jealous of the poor Hindu devotees, will exact a tribute from Brahmins, Samorahs, jogis, bairagees and sanyasis.

"If Your Majesty places any faith in your own books, by a distinct called divine, you will then be instructed that God is the God of all mankind, not the God of Mohammedans alone.

"In fine, the tribute you demand from Hindus is repugnant to justify; it is equally foreign from the good policy as it will impoverish the country. Moreover, it is an infringement of the laws of Hindustan.

"But if the zeal for your own religion hath induced you to determine upon this measure, the demand ought, by requisites of equity, to have been made first upon Ram Singh (then king of Jaipur), who is an esteemed principal among the Hindus.

"Then let your well-wisher (referring to himself) be called upon, with whom you will have less difficulty to encounter; but to

torment ants and flies is unworthy of a heroic and generous mind.

"It is wonderful that the ministers of your government should have neglected to instruct Your Majesty in the rules of rectitude and honour[144]."

Around the same time, Chhatrapati Shivaji Maharaj too wrote a letter to Aurangzeb challenging him to extract *jaziya* from Raj Singh of Mewar. The grounds for the final conflict between Mewar and Mughals were thus laid, which would conclude a great resistance to the Islamic invasion of India before the mantle of fighting the Mughals shifted to the great Marathas. A chapter that establishes the greatness of Mewar for defeating the mighty Aurangzeb and forced him to the plains of Deccan and eastern areas of India.

In a strange way, Hindus should be grateful to Aurangzeb for exposing the true designs of Islamists in the subcontinent.

Aurangzeb's impatience of converting Hindus to Islam was a slap on the face of Hindu kings deluding of coexistence with Islam. Thus, with the mask of liberal islam shattered, Hindus saw the barbarity and bloodshed that Islamic rule was thrusting upon them. All over Bharatvarsha, Hindus rose in revolt.

Raj Singh was the last great king of Mewar who militarily matched and defeated the Mughals conclusively.

Raj Singh's progeny did continue the struggle but with the rise of Maratha power, the Hindu flag of resistance went into the hands of Shivaji Maharaj and the Peshwas. The crucial role of Raj Singh in weakening and pushing Mughal forces out of Rajasthan and thus laying grounds for the pan-Hindu resistance cannot be overstated.

Aurangzeb Humiliated and Driven out of Mewar

The account of the war between Raj Singh and Aurangzeb which was an enduring conflict lasting two years between CE 1679-80 and ended with Aurangzeb's army decimated, humiliated and driven out of Rajasthan completely, merits narration here.

The preparation Aurangzeb made for the conquest of Mewar resembled those of the conquest of a potent kingdom than for the

144. Tod, vol. 1, p. 303.

subjugation of a local *zamindar* (the title by which the Mughals referred the local Hindu princes), a vassal of the so-called mighty Mughal empire on whose colossal spread, Mewar was but a speck. He called his son Akbar from Bengal, Azim from Kabul and also Muazzam (the Mughal's heir) from Deccan. With this formidable array, Aurangzeb entered Mewar.

Raj Singh responded adequately to Aurangzeb's assault. He first sent emissaries to all big and small Rajput kings to appeal to their Hindu pride and amassed a massive army. Raj Singh's life and deeds inspired every Hindu youth of Rajasthan to enlist in massive numbers with a fierce determination to destroy a *vidharmi* (adherent of an alien creed) who was out to destroy Hindu *dharma*.

The Bhils, Palindas and Palipats (lords of the passes) embarked with thousands of bows and hearts devoted to the cause of a *Hindupat* (chief of the Hindus).

The red banner of Mewar was raised high and mighty against the most powerful and vicious sovereign anywhere in the world at the time by the Sisodias and Rathores—Maharana Raj Singh of Mewar. The first royal edict of the Maharana was to follow the centuries-old tactic of the 'scorched earth policy' of his great ancestors. The peasantry, the mercantile class, the shepherds, blacksmiths, entire villages vacated the plains and moved to the hills where, once again, the Bhils fed them and served them.

Magnificent Jagdish temple

This caused extreme hardships for the Mughal army, as food supply had to be ensured from Ajmer which was regularly attacked and looted by Mewar's Hindus. Raj Singh divided his forces into three armies. He dispatched his eldest son Jay Singh to the crest of Aravallis, ready to attack the invaders from either side of the mountains. The younger son, Bhim Singh, was dispatched to the western side of Mewar, around Abu, to keep channels of communication open with Marwar and Gujarat. Maharana Raj Singh kept the main body of the Mewar army with himself on the left flank of Aravallis, ready to cut off any possibility of retreat by the Mughals.

Aurangzeb entered Debari, on the outskirts of Udaipur and instead of entering the valley where Jay Singh was waiting for him, sent his General, Tyber Khan and his son Akbar to Udaipur with 50,000 troops. The Mughal emperor must have been tipped off about the placement of Raj Singh's troops by an insider and this one move of Aurangzeb to stop at Debari and not commit his entire army into the valley leading to Udaipur, saved his army from a complete slaughter.

Aurangzeb's son Akbar advanced into Udaipur from the northern passes, unresisted. Palaces, gardens, lakes and isles met his eye, but no living thing; all was silent. Akbar set up camp at Udaipur and instructed Taj Khan and Ruhilla Khan to start demolishing temples and destroying sculptures. More than 200 temples in and around Udaipur were razed to the ground. Numerous skirmishes took place around these temples, where twenty to fifty Mewar Hindus killed three times their numbers before being overwhelmed by the invading Mughals. The battle around the famous Jagannath temple was very fierce.

The gatekeeper of the royal Udaipur house was a warrior named Naru Barhath. As Raj Singh was vacating the palace and leaving for the hills, someone mocked Naru, saying, *"You have taken gifts for decades as the gatekeeper; won't you stay back and fight for the temple?"*

Naru sent his family with the Rana to the hills and stayed back at the gates of Jagannath temple with chosen warriors.

When Taj Khan and Rohilla Khan came to the Jagannath

temple, Naru and his twenty men gave battle to an entire army of Mughals and killed close to 500 troops before being overpowered. Thus, the people of Mewar kept giving a foretaste of the things to come, to the Mughals. Aurangzeb moved to Udai Sagar from Debari to re-join Akbar. At Udai Sagar, Aurangzeb destroyed three beautiful temples of Shiva and Vishnu.

Raj Singh moved in with his troops and placed them in such a way that neither Aurangzeb could proceed further, nor could Akbar retreat from Udaipur. Raj Singh was a master war strategist and used his immaculate knowledge of Mewar's topography to his advantage. Mewar's Maharana pushed Akbar to commit a blunder, and after weeks of waiting, Aurangzeb's son made the suicidal move. He chose the mountains and passes of Gogunda as his exit, and this was the worst choice he could make. Prince Jay Singh, along with his troops and the Bhil army waited precisely for this move.

To quote James Tod:

"The allodial vassals of the mountains, along with Bhil auxiliaries, outstripped Akbar's retreat and blocked up farther egress in one of the long-extended valleys termed as Naal, closed by natural ramparts or col, on which they formed post of trees, and manning the crests from each side, hurled destruction on the foe; while the prince, in like manner, blocked up the entrance and barred retrogression too. Death menaced them in every form."

The trapped Mughal army was starved and was headed towards annihilation when Prince Jay Singh showed mercy to them, admitting overtures from Akbar, confided in protestations to renounce the origin of the war and gave them guides to conduct them out of the trap to the defile of Jilwarra onwards to the eastern side, till they reached the safety of the walls of Chittor. While Akbar was trapped in the Aravallis, another Mughal General, Delhire Khan, approached from the west through Desuri pass from Marwar to rescue Prince Akbar.

Mewar's army allowed Delhire to approach unopposed and when they were fully inside along an intricate gorge, Vikram Solanki and Gopinath Rathore, both gallant nobles of Mewar, attacked the Mughals and after a desperate conflict, destroyed the Mughal contingent completely.

A huge amount of money and weaponry fell into the hands of the Mewar army. Their plan had worked out to perfection. With the Mughal army dissipated, trapped and partly destroyed, it was the right time for Raj Singh to attack Aurangzeb himself somewhere around the mountains between Udaipur and Chittor.

Tod quotes the British historian Robert Orme, who is credited to have many historical details of that period:

"The Mughal army advanced among the defiles with incredible labour, and with so little intelligence, that the division which moved with Aurangzeb himself was unexpectedly stopped by insuperable defences and precipices in front; whilst the Rajputs on one night closed the straits in his rear, by felling the overhanging trees and from their stations above, prevented all endeavours of the Mughal troops, either within or without, from reversing the obstacles."

"Udeperri, the Circassian wife of Aurangzeb, accompanied him in the arduous war, and with her reticence and escort was enclosed another part of the mountains; her conductors, dreading to expose her person to danger or public view, surrendered. She was carried to the Rana, who received her with homage and every attention.

Meanwhile, the emperor himself might have perished by famine, of which the Rana let him see the risqué, by confinement of two days; when he ordered his troops to withdraw from their stations and suffer the way to be cleared[145]."

Orme's account is also endorsed by R.S. Bhatt in his book[146].

As soon as Aurangzeb was out of danger, the Rana sent back his wife, accompanied by a chosen escort. The Rana only requested in return that Aurangzeb should refrain from destroying the sacred animals of their religion, but Aurangzeb, who believed in no virtue but self-interest, imputed the generosity and forbearance of the Rana to the fear of future vengeance and continued the war.

Soon after, he was again well-nigh enclosed in the mountains. The second experience of difficulties well beyond his age and constitution and the arrival of his sons, Azim, and Akbar, determined him not to expose himself any longer in the field, but to leave the conduct of operations to his sons. Thus, the great clan

145. Tod, vol. 1, p. 305.
146. Tod, vol. 1, p. 196.

of Rajputs of Mewar, ably assisted by the general population of Mewar and an alliance with gallant Rathores of Jodhpur under Veer Durga Das, nobly contested the palm of glory.

Aurangzeb simply could not withstand the fury of the Sisodia-Rathore forces. Though equipped with superior firepower manned by European gunners, the Mughal army was no match for the just cause and avenging steel of the Rajputs. Aurangzeb was humiliated, ignominiously defeated and compelled to a disgraceful retreat with an immense loss of men and equipment.

Raj Singh captured the imperial standard of Mughals, horses, elephants and immense state equipment. The humiliation of Aurangzeb and his sons by Raj Singh and his sons and his nobles did not end here, but continued for two more years. Of the multiple battles fought, a few deserve special mention and are being described briefly.

Aurangzeb retracted to the safety of Chittor and joined his sons Akbar and Muazzam there. In spite of the reverses and hardships endured by Aurangzeb and his army, he continued one act of barbarity very religiously and that was, destroying of Hindu temples. Even while retreating and nursing his wounds and contemplating how to respond to an ascending Rajput power, Aurangzeb is recorded to have destroyed seventy-six Hindu and Jain temples in and around Chittorgarh.

Meanwhile, a noble of Mewar, Sanwal Das Rathore (direct line of Jaimal Rathore) was wreaking havoc on the supply lines of Mughals from Ajmer to Chittor. This caused alarm to Aurangzeb with regard to his personal safety. Leaving the perilous warfare of Mewar to his sons, Aurangzeb retreated to the relative safety of Ajmer.

Foiled in his vengeance, personally disgraced, twice granted a pardon by the great Maharana himself, his women captured and returned, his armies depleted, his invincibility crushed, his religious zeal blunted, Aurangzeb, the Tatar, was pushed out of the sacred lands of Mewar by the pious and glorious blood of Bappa Rawal and Maharana Pratap Singh flowing in the veins of one of the greatest Maharanas of Mewar, Raj Singh.

A Maharana whose name finds no mention in the history curriculum of this unfortunate nation of ours. A Maharana who did not rest on the affluence and calm created by his father and grandfather but chose to respond to the Islamic zealotry of Aurangzeb in kind and with equal force.

Upon his return to Ajmer, Aurangzeb dispatched Rohilla Khan with 12,000 troops to capture or kill Sanwal Das. The Marwar troops came to the rescue of Sanwal Das and the joint army defeated the Mughals at Poor Mandal, pushing them back to Ajmer. While Rana and his elder son Jay Singh succeeded in destroying Aurangzeb in the east, the younger son Bhim Singh continued with his own pursuits in the west and made a powerful diversion against the Mughals by invading Gujarat and seizing it. Bhim also annexed the crucial state of Idar and mercilessly slew the Mughal vassal Hassan and his troops.

Bhim went on to Badnagar and Pattan and plundered them. Siddhpur, Mhourassa and other towns of western Gujarat shared the same fate. Bhim was advancing to Surat when Raj Singh recalled him out of benevolence to the local *nawab* and sultan, who sought mercy from Mewar's Maharana.

Bhim was a staunch Hindu prince and inflicted retribution for the Muslim plunder of temples with an equally furious demolition of mosques all over southern Rajasthan and northern Gujarat. Shyamaldas says in the *Veer Vinod*:

"The Maharana sent his son Bhim Singh with 4,000 horsemen to Badnagar in Gujarat, where he demolished 300 mosques and extracted 40,000 rupees as penalty from the city dwellers and returned triumphant."

One episode of the vengeance of Hindus under the Maharana needs special mention after which we shall come to the three major battles fought by Maharana and his two sons, which led to the conclusive victory of Mewar and ended with Aurangzeb extending a hand of friendship to Raj Singh. A treaty ensued. This treaty not only ensured total safety and prosperity of Mewar, but it also secured the freedom of Marwar from the clutches of the Mughals.

For two years, the intense Mewar-Mughal conflict for

superiority went on with Raj Singh and his two sons and a dozen-odd noblemen of Mewar fighting for Hindu supremacy over the murderous Aurangzeb, who had bared all his *jihadi* fangs.

One such noble man was a Jain civil minister of Mewar, Dayal Shah, who had shown great military acumen and loyalty to the Rana and earned his trust. Dayal Shah headed a flying force that would indulge in 'shoot and scoot' tactics to harass the Mughals. Raj Singh sent a large contingent with Dayal Shah eastwards to Malwa, and the latter ravaged the region up to Narbada and Betwa rivers.

Tod describes Mewar's retribution by Bhim Singh and Dayal Shah against Islamic onslaught thus:

"Contrary to the Rajput character, whose maxim is parcere subjectis, Mewar's military leaders were compelled by the utter faithlessness of Aurangzeb to retaliate against his excesses."

Dayal Shah ravaged Sarangpur, Dewas, Sarong, Mandoo, Ujjain, and Chanderi. Every Mughal supporter in these areas was put to the sword. To continue using the words of annals:

"Husbands abandoned their wives and children, and whatever could not be carried was given to the flames. The Qazis were bound and shaved, and the Qurans thrown into wells[147]."

For once, the Mewar army avenged themselves in the imitation of the Islamic tyrant, even on the religion of their enemies. Dayal Shah is said to have razed hundreds of mosques to the ground. He was unrelenting in his vengeful slaughter and turned Malwa into a desert. Once again, Malwa was ravaged to fill the coffers of Mewar, just as had happened at the time of Pratap when Bhama Shah did the same to Malwa, albeit on a smaller scale. Flush with the looted riches and weaponry from Malwa, Dayal Shah met the forces of Prince Jai Singh at the foothills of Chittor and fought a battle with Aurangzeb's son Azim near Chittor.

Jai Singh camped at Chittor with 13,000 horsemen and 26,000 soldiers when Dayal Shah joined him. The night before the decisive battle for Chittor, Mukhim and Ganga Shaktawat, Ratan Choondawat of Saloombar, Chandrasen Jhala of Sadri and Sabal

---

147. p. 307.

Singh Chauhan of Baidla made powerful, motivating speeches to the Mewar army, as recorded in the Mewar annals.

Some day, in July 1680, the Mewar army sneaked around the fort at night and under the cover of rains, wiped out the Mughal force. The Mewar army returned to Prince Jai Singh with looted elephants, horses, *nagadas* (war drums), tents, weaponry, etc., which the prince distributed among the nobles and the men. Chittor was finally regained by the Rajputs after years of bloodbath and sacrifices, never to be lost again.

Azim fled from Chittor with his life and was hotly pursued by the Mewar army till he reached the safety of the fort of Ranthambore and sealed himself inside. Maharana Raj Singh, in the meantime, was stationed on the western frontiers of Mewar, touching Marwar. Raj Singh fulfilled his promise of protecting the infant Ajit Singh, the Rathore heir of Marwar by taking on the Mughals at Ganora, the chief town of Godwar. The Rathores under Durga Das fought jointly with Mewar against Aurangzeb. The Mughal army was totally decimated and kicked out of Mewar and Marwar after this battle.

Somewhere in north-central Mewar, Prince Bheem gathered his Sisodias and was joined by Rathores to fight a battle with Prince Akbar and his General Tyber Khan, whom they completely defeated. This victory is mainly attributed to the moves of a Rajput chief, who first looted 500 camels from the Mughals and then hurled flaming torches on them, unleashing mayhem on the Mughal camp. The pandemonium that ensued gave the right opportunity to Mewar soldiers to attack and comprehensively defeat the Mughals. Thus, the Mughal-Mewar conflict premised on multiple reasons of hatred between the two powers reached culmination with the expulsion of Aurangzeb and his sons from Mewar permanently.

Aurangzeb was so overwhelmed by the ferocity of Mewar's valour that he never set his eyes or foot on the pious land of Mewar again, till his death in CE 1707.

Raj Singh and his nobles, along with the Rathores of Mewar dented the myth of Mughal superiority permanently and depleted the army and resources of the Mughals to such an extent that it

The dilapidated Samadhi of Maharana Raj Singh at Oda village, 20 kms from Nathdwara

took the Mughals years to replenish them. By then, they had to shift their focus to the Deccan and eastwards, towards Assam.

Aurangzeb, in his religious zeal, provoked a fight that spun out of his control and ended the Rajput-Mughal alliance of 150 years, which had been the main reason for the continuance of Mughal rule in Delhi.

With the twin states of Marwar and Mewar alienated and the Rajputs of Jaipur under Ram Singh remaining indifferent, Aurangzeb had no alliance left with the Hindus to placate the Hindu masses. Hindus all over the country rose in revolt against the temple destruction and *jaziya* imposition by this intolerant Mughal zealot.

Aurangzeb's madness and bigoted zeal to Islamise India led to an unparalleled consolidation of Hindu forces in India when Raj Singh wrote letters to Sri Guru Gobind Singh Maharaj in Punjab, Chhatrapati Shivaji Maharaj in Maharashtra and fellow nobles and Rajput kings of Rajasthan to form a Hindu confederation to eliminate the Mughal scourge permanently.

Proposed Hindu alliance by Raj Singh

All this would have shaped the trajectory of the thousand-year-old Hindu-Muslim conflict in this region very differently, but for one more act of treachery by Hindus who were close to Rana Raj Singh.

On 3rd November 1680, after the Mughals had been convincingly kicked out of Rajasthan and when Raj Singh was planning to terminate the very seed of Islamic rule in India, he sat down to have lunch with a Charan friend, Aaskaran, whom he used to refer to as his 'brother'. Both friends consumed rice porridge, *khichdi*, and minutes after that, both died due to their food being poisoned.

At fifty-one years of age, the great Maharana's life came to an abrupt and tragic end by the unchivalrous connivance between one of his insiders and his enemies.

Looking at Aurangzeb's record of poisoning the Rajput kings of Jodhpur and Jaipur and the conduct of his great-grandfather Akbar, eliminating his enemies in a similar deceitful manner, it can safely be assumed that Aurangzeb might have been behind the poisoning of Maharana Raj Singh, although we may never be able to prove this conclusively. Thus, the sun set on the greatest dynasty of kings to have ruled anywhere at any time in recorded human history.

Raj Singh remained true to the glorious legacy of his ancestors.

Like Bappa Rawal, he forged a Hindu alliance to take on the murderous assault of the Islamic invaders on India.

Like Kumbha, he was a man of exquisite tastes and nurtured art and architecture in Mewar, the most notable being the construction of the Raj Samand, when a great famine struck the people of Mewar.

Like Sanga, he never let an iota of weakness and crippling thought, intervene in his instincts to take on the Islamic zeal of Aurangzeb on the flimsiest of grounds. His fortitude in rescuing Charumati, giving protection to Srinathji, and granting state protection to the infant Ajit Singh demonstrate his traits of fearlessness, like his great ancestor Rana Sanga.

Like Pratap, Raj Singh demonstrated the steely resolve and meticulous military panning to fulfil the aim of never being subjugated by Islamic onslaught at the time.

Though Raj Singh never faced an economic crisis of the scale that Pratap did, the range and degree of armed opposition faced by him was also several degrees more severe than Pratap. Yet Raj Singh stood like a rock around whom the bereaved Hindus of the region could rally or seek refuge. He was the chief reason for the eclipse of Mughal rule in Delhi after Aurangzeb's death. He was a king who gave up the comforts of palatial retreats of Udaipur and moved to the jungles of the Aravallis to endure the torments of weather and terrain to lead Hindu resistance against Aurangzeb. He was a devout Hindu who picked up the sword to protect the *devas* (celestials) when no other Hindu king would dare to. A compassionate ruler, who opened the coffers of the state to his subjects to endure the great famine, that struck Mewar and an honourable man who rose to Charumati's defence when she beckoned help from him.

Raj Singh was a family man who chose to protect the infant Ajit Singh from the most powerful and evil army at that time. Raj Singh was a visionary king who saw the reality of the Islamic onslaught and was not lulled into complacency, either by sloth or avarice and instead, forged an alliance with all the Hindu kings of the time to fight this evil.

There couldn't have been a greater Maharana to write about, than Maharana Raj Singh of Mewar, as we end the saga of the uninterrupted line of the Sisodia kings of Mewar—a surreal saga of resistance to the most intolerant and treacherous horde of invaders motivated only by religious bigotry, unrestrained plunder and merciless slaughter.

The Sisodia Rajputs of Mewar matched the Islamic invasion of our great Vedic land, soldier to soldier, steel to steel, fire to fire, animal to animal, guts to guts and blood to blood.

They kept the Hindu saffron flag flying for an awe-inspiring thousand years from the ages of Bappa Rawal to Maharana Raj Singh.

The *Annals of Indian History* are not just about the Mughal kings and their puny sultanates or the colonising greed of the British Empire. In fact, India's magnificent history is about how the oldest, surviving, and continuous civilisation, stood solid in face of thousands of years of barbaric atrocities that annihilated all other civilisations except the Hindu civilisation.

India cannot be free till every child hears this story of the survival of Bharat and *dharma.* This is a story that deserves to be told, again and again.

A story of a multitude of generations that fought the most barbaric cruelty with heroic sacrifice.

A story that survives in the dusty library of books of unsung authors who recorded against the grain, the truth of this survival.

A story of sung ballads that are a part of folklore, which have travelled through generations passed on from father to son and mother to daughter, an unbroken unchained melody that sings the glory of their ancestors.

A story that many have tried to erase and ignore in our history books and civic life by 'historians' who seem to have written with a singular purpose of filling Hindus with an inferiority complex.

A story that has waited in the wings for its time, to take centre stage and a story that we can forget only to our abject peril.

A story that opens our eyes and hearts to the unbelievable resolve and grit of the great Maharanas of Mewar who endured heat and cold, fire and death, insults and forsaking, loss and desertions, pettiness, and treachery, and yet stood firm in one resolve—freedom from the bigoted zeal and barbaric atrocities of Islamic invaders.

A story that stares us in the eye and asks us to follow the footsteps of these giants to the path of glory and freedom and fills our hearts with unmanageable pride and voluminous gratitude to these *avatars,* who could only have descended from the heavens so we may celebrate forever the traditions and their legends.

This is a story that should adorn our *pooja grihas*[148] (places of worship), like the *Ramayana* and the *Mahabharata,* for us to imbibe, act upon and recreate in our lives.

It is time to recognise that the once all-pervasive and universal faith of Sanatan Dharma survived in just one corner of the world, in Bharat, only because the great Maharanas and Hindus of Mewar

148. Places of worship.

and other great Rajputs of Bharat nourished it with their blood for a thousand years and more.

It is time to drag out of the dungeons, our amazing valour and heroic past and place it again on the pedestal it deserves, so that future generations can look back with pride at the honour of the *dharmic* culture and at the Maharanas who never surrendered in face of such vicious atrocities.

It is time to take back our dignity from the hands of fake historians and show our everlasting indebtedness to James Tod and Shyamaldas and other writers of *shilalekhs* (rock edicts) because of whom this story is not buried forever in the passes of Mewar.

History will never forgive us if we do not revive, record and narrate the truth for our future generations—the truth of a story that isn't a story but the painstaking sacrifice and endless endeavour to never bow down to barbarians and never cow down in face of unimaginable suffering for one single reason—preservation of Sanatana Dharma.

It is with a profound sense of fulfilment, honour and gratitude that I come to the end of the story of the resistance of Maharanas of Mewar to the Islamic invaders of India.

What better way to close this story of Hindu resistance than with the saga of the honourable, compassionate and mighty Raj Singh of Mewar.

I am well aware of my incapacity to do justice to the great saga of these *devapurushas*, but if this book is able to give even the slightest of glimpse into the unimaginable sacrifices and struggles of these celestial beings, then I would consider this book to be worthy of being kept at the feet of these great ancestors of Hindu *dharma*.

□

Part-III

"It was the disfigured version of India's history which gave a good conscience to the British imperialist while he pulverised Hindu society, plundered Hindu wealth and poured undisguised contempt on the Hindu culture. It was this version of history that emasculated Hindu society and emboldened the residues of Islamic imperialism to stage street riots and then walk away with precious parts of the Hindu homeland, thus consolidating an aggression that had not succeeded even though mounted repeatedly for more than a thousand years."

—Sita Ram Goel

17

The Lies of Thousand Years of Hindu Slavery

Although there is no historical data to validate this claim, but how often do we get to hear this phrase, 'Thousand years of Hindu slavery under Islamic rulers!'

This colonised and fabricated narrative is repeated AD nauseum in media, academia and research papers and has for the longest time been the only acceptable version of the history of Bharat. Even Hindu opinion makers parroted it and we have all internalised this lie as a civilisational truth of the Hindu-Muslim conflict in this subcontinent.

In its journey of thousands of years, Hinduism gave birth to numerous ideologies. These were tested on the parameters of time and intelligence and were either adopted or discarded accordingly.

To settle a difference of opinion, Hindus used to indulge in debates, called *shaastraartha*. Whosoever presented his point logically and with evidence, was victorious and society followed that ideal.

Islam came as a brute force which was not interested in any debate. It demanded total surrender.

A land which had been blessed by Buddha, Mahaveer, Adi Shankara, Madhaw, Vashishtha, Kautilya, Nagarjuna, Gorakh and hundreds of such ancient traditions, refused to surrender.

Thus, a nation reverberating with the message of selfless *karma* by Shri Krishna rose to struggle against Islam.

The Christian civilisation too suffered at the hands of Islamic expansionism with the long crusades, the Battle of Tour, Spanish occupation, and subsequent freedom, but the Hindu resistance to Islamic invaders can be said to be exemplary because of the geographical proximity of Arabic and Central Asian region to the Indus Valley and the Indo-Gangetic Plains and the nature of the Hindu people of this region.

Hindu society has been beautifully diverse from the beginning. A section of Hindus was busy in spiritual pursuits through Vedanta, Jainism, Buddhism,Tantra, etc. with some engaged in trade and commerce, some indulged in art and architecture, a lot were invested in day-to-day labour of life and it was left only to the Kshatriyas, mainly the Rajputs, to lead the fight against the invaders.

Hence, with a fraction of the population engaging in combat and that too with a very ethical code of conduct during the wars, the Hindu resistance to Islam makes an awe-inspiring study of the lust of human spirit to cling to the religion of the forefathers and the uncompromising quest to be free.

In those centuries of conflict, communication was so tenuous that it would take weeks for a letter asking for help to reach from one king to another. To organise and mobilise large armies against murdering thugs was a huge challenge.

This was when the true nature and intent of Islamic invaders had not even dawned upon the kings and people of northern and north-western Bharat; while the plundering armies of mercenaries from the west were ceaselessly invading Bharat with a singular aim of converting us to their faith.

While a large segment of the population of Hindus was engaged in trade and commerce, and intellectual and spiritual pursuits.

While India was the richest economy in the world for past 1000 years.

While ills like sex slavery, human slavery, *dhimma* and its enforcement by Islamic rulers, the slaughter of non-combatant population at the hands of a merciless army, absolutely amoral and lacking rules of engagements of armies, unpredictable barbaric behaviour against civilisational values, purchasing loyalties of dissatisfied Hindus and a ruthless will to annihilate anything un-islamic by any means possible, left the Hindus of this region bewildered and confused as to how to deal with this tyranny;

While the Hindu society was busy discovering the laws of physics and mathematics and creating poetry of the calibre of Jayadev's *Geet Govind* and Tulsi's *Ramcharitmanas.*

While Hindus were erecting architectural marvels like *Vijaya Stambha* (victory tower), Ranakpur temples, Konark sun temple, etc., we were attacked by a people from a barren desert who had no concept of beauty and civility, whose singular obsession was to spread the word of a person whom they thought to be a divine messenger.

A people who had nothing to lose in their barbaric pursuits since there was nothing of value or splendour in their native lands.

A people who were obsessed with money and women of those whom they couldn't subjugate.

A people who justified rape, murder and plunder of everything that did not conform to their theology.

A people who were merciless killers and looters of wealth since they did not know the art of wealth creation.

A people who baffled our ancestors with their desire to die and kill for their religion without any consideration for morality and civility.

Such was the uneven conflict that our glorious and extremely intelligent ancestors endured, survived and eventually overcame in fourteen centuries.

When the world analyses this amazing feat of Hindus dispassionately, it will truly realise the value of this extreme sacrifice that Hindus have made not only for themselves but for the entire globe. The global community should be grateful and remember the Hindu kings and their fighters who stood as a bulwark between Islamic expansionism and salvaged the Far East and China in the process.

Author Ian Austin writes in his book that the world must be grateful to Hindus of the subcontinent for saving it from Islamisation of the globe.

And then we have the self-proclaimed intelligentsia of modern India inventing and peddling a lie that Islam ruled over Hindus for one thousand years and that this rule was a benevolent visitation by some very advanced people who had come to civilise the primitive natives of this glorious land. The ill-conceived notion of a 'Ganga Jamuna *tehzeeb*' was an invention to humanise rape and massacre that cannot possibly be humanised, leave alone justified.

The central thrust of this book is to bust the lie perpetrated and established in the day-to-day discourse of this besieged nation, that Islamists ruled us for a thousand years.

Let us examine this theory of the 'thousand-year slavery of Hindus' critically and try to uncover the truth objectively.

Following are the reasons that Islamic invasions of this land are not one-sided conquests that ended up enslaving Hindus of India:

Chronology and Durations of Islamic Rule

If we look at hard historical data recorded by both the Hindu as well as the Persian and Turk historians since 7th century CE when the first Islamic attack happened on Raja Dahir of Sindh by Mohammad bin Qasim, we realise that the passage of years of Islamic rule in Delhi is one big lie.

Qasim returned to Arabia after killing Dahir and the second wave of Arabs then attacked Rajasthan. The Arabs were opposed by the combined forces of Bappa Rawal, Nagabhatta of Gurjara Pratihara dynasty and Pulakesiraja of Gujarat. The Arabs were comprehensively defeated by the Hindu forces and chased back to Iran by Bappa. The Arab annals of that time quote the fury of Hindu warriors thus: *"Not a place of refuge was to be found from the wrath of Rajputs."*

From the 7th century onwards, repeated Islamic invasions were repelled by the Mewar dynasty in alliance with other Hindu kingdoms. Khumaan I, II & III, Shakti Kumar, Rawal Jaitra Singh and Samar Singh of Mewar stand out as names that did not let the Arabs get past Sindh.

Mahmud of Ghazni, an Afghan of Turk origin, attacked Bharat

in the beginning of the 11th century and was resisted by Jayapala, Anangapala and Trilochanpala of the Shahiya dynasty. Mahmud managed to plunder the Somnath temple and destroy the sacred *lingam*, but he witnessed the fury of 50,000 Hindu warriors who died defending Somnath.

Mahmud beat a hasty retreat and fearing attack by Chalukya Bhimdeva, returned via Multan and Mansurah. Gardizi, a Muslim historian writes, *'The Badshah of the Hindus stood in his way, disputing his path. Mahmud decided, therefore, to leave the right track back to Ghazni, from fear, lest this great victory of his turn into a defeat*[149]*."*

The Jats of Sindh still molested the retreating army of Ghazni causing heavy losses of men and riches.

The first major defeat of Hindus at the hands of Muslim invaders happened around CE 1192 when Shahabuddin Muhammad Ghori defeated Prithviraj Chauhan in the second battle of Tarain where Prithivraj was killed.

Muhammad Ghori appointed Qutub-ud-Din Aibak as his ambassador and thus began the war against Islam by various Hindu kings that would last for the next 500 years, until the advent of East India Company. Thus, even on the scale of years, the Islamic penetration on our nation lasted a total of 600 years. Of these 600 years, the first 300 are attributed to a euphemism called 'Delhi Sultanate' as if it was a great, powerful Sultan ruling Delhi, whereas in reality, these were mercenaries and robbers whose rule extended from Yamuna to today's Mehrauli at the most.

All of these so-called Sultans were running around north-west Bharat plundering our cities, destroying our temples and killing innocent Hindus randomly.

Dr. R.C. Majumdar writes about Feroz Tughlaq, one of such robbers around Delhi, "Feroz proved to be the most bigoted Islamist who preceded Ibrahim Lodhi and Aurangzeb. Feroz was the first such Islamic mercenary who started taking *jaziya* from Brahmins of Bharat. "

But all through their pillaging they were being resisted by Hindu kings.

149. Mishra, p. 66.

Now, let us examine the duration of the much-acclaimed Mughal Empire. Firstly, the Mughal rule is said to begin with the victory of Babur at the famous Battle of Khanwa in CE 1527, where lakhs of soldiers from both sides were killed. As detailed in the chapter on Sanga, we can reasonably infer that Khanwa was not a defeat of Maharana Sanga but a victory or at best a stalemate. Sanga managed to inflict enough damage on the Mughals that they dared not follow him. Sanga stayed in that area for another year and continued fighting Babur before being poisoned by him in CE 1528. Babur himself died three years after Khanwa.

Secondly, Babur's son Humayun had to keep fighting his brothers, Bahadur Shah of Gujarat and Sher Shah to retain even Delhi under him till his death in CE 1556. In a longish interregnum from CE 1540-45, Humayun was defeated and chased away to Iran by Sher Shah Suri, an able but ruthless Afghan. The real Mughal rule began only with Akbar in 1556 and continued through Jehangir and Shahjahan and culminated with Aurangzeb's death in CE 1707. So, even if we grant the capture of Delhi as an empire to the Mughals, it lasted only about 150 years.

Hindus must ponder as to where this figure of 'thousand years' come from.

By what logic, constant attacks by Islamic invaders constitute a victory for them?

Why do we lap up the white lie of a thousand years of slavery which is beyond comprehension even on a mere time scale!

Civil War among Islamic Rulers and Hindu Resistance

If we look at the successive reigns of Islamic invaders trying to retain their foothold in Delhi, it appears like an incessant civil war with occasional plundering of Hindu temples and educational institutions. For example, in the first 300 years after Mohammad Ghori killed Prithviraj Chauhan in CE 1192, five dynasties, twenty-four so-called emperors and one 'empress' lasted in Delhi through assassinations, rebellion and dethronement.

The bloodbath that happened in the post-Muhammed Caliphate in Arabia was replicated in India by the Muslim invaders. Besides this infighting, the Hindu kings of India kept fighting Islamic invaders without a break. One wonders what kind of 'Sultanate' was established by these plunderers when the average rule of a Delhi king comes out to be ten to twelve years[150]!

There is a saying in Punjabi that mocks the time of a robber from the Sayyad dynasty named Shah Alam. 'सल्तनत ए शाह आलम, आज दिल्ली ता पालम' meaning what is the extent of the Sultanate of Shah Alam? It is from Delhi to Palam. Palam being a village few kilometres from Delhi.

Where are the universities, palaces or pieces of architecture? What art was patronised by these power-crazy plunderers? What was the geographical extent of this so-called Delhi Sultanate when all five so-called dynasties were running around the vast nation of ours to fight one kingdom or another? Was Delhi even a centre of power at the time of this so-called Delhi Sultanate? It was only in CE 1639, that Shahjahan decided to shift capital from Agra to Delhi that Delhi becomes a power centre.

These 'Sultans' of the Delhi Sultanate were conclusively defeated by Mewar's Maharanas and the Vijayanagar Empire. Three of these 'Sultans' were imprisoned in Chittor in the most humiliating manner. Rana Hammir Singh kept Mohammad bin Tughlaq captive in Chittor for six months and set him free only after levying huge penalties on him. Rana Lakha captured Firoz bin Tughlaq at Chittor and also Maharana Mokal captured a ruler of Delhi.

Rana Kumbha fought fifty-six battles in his life against the Islamic rulers of Malwa, Gujarat and Nagaur and didn't lose a single one. Kumbha also captured the Sultan of Malwa, Mahmud Khilji and held him captive for months in Chittor.

Sanga fought more than 100 battles, winning every single one. Sanga too kept the Malwa Sultan as his prisoner and defeated Delhi's king, Ibrahim Lodhi twice at Bakrole and Khatauli. Sanga also captured a son of Lodhi and released him after taking adequate compensation for the war.

Sanga's arms reached up to Afghanistan in the west and beyond Malwa in the east.

Pratap defeated Akbar's imperial army conclusively at

150. Tod, vol. 1, p. 231.

Dewair in 1583, slaughtering thousands of Mughals in three days. Jehangir's army was defeated seventeen times by Pratap's son Rana Amar Singh before concluding an honourable treaty with the Mughals whereby Mewar retained its freedom and even Chittor was freed from the clutches of Mughals.

When was the last time slaves signed honourable treaties with their captors? Shahjahan had to run around the country quelling rebellions. Aurangzeb was conclusively defeated by Rana Raj Singh of Mewar in CE 1680, and later by the Ahoms of Assam. He met his nemesis at the hands of the Marathas in the Deccan and died, a defeated and broken man.

So, who was enslaving whom in medieval India? Contrast this with the spread of Islam in Arabia and the Middle East. Persia lost its original civilization and religion, with its entire Zoroastrian population killed or converted; Mesopotamia became 100% Islamic and Egypt's ancient civilisation was destroyed; all in a matter of decades. Hindu civilisation stands today even after 1,400 years of incessant attacks.

No Uprooting of Indic People from Bharat

Another especially important phenomenon is that people flee the city or country of their inhabitation when they are attacked by barbaric invaders, as happened with the Zoroastrians, who had to flee Persia.

A few hundred of these landed in India, off the coast of Gujarat or take the case of the Jews escaping Europe in the last century.

Is there a single incidence of Hindus fleeing Bharatvarsha to escape the Islamic invaders? None at all.

The first exodus and slaughter of Hindus in modern times happened in 1971, from Bangladesh. But because Hindus had a modern, well-equipped army, this exodus was responded to adequately. East Pakistan was broken from West Pakistan and Bangladesh was born with 92000 Pakistani soldiers taken captive by India. Migrating populations are most vulnerable to slaughter and hunger. While this murder of Hindus and Sikhs happened in the so called modern times, we have no such record of mass scale migrations of Hindus in medieval Bharat. Hindu kings and armies have consistently resisted Islamic gangsters in this manner for 1,400 years.

Even today, we see persecuted people from Syria, the Yazidis and Kurds in Iraq fleeing to safer nations.

As we are writing this, Hindus, Sikhs and Christians in Pakistan and Bangladesh are fleeing their homes to escape persecution because they have no choice left.

Either they would be killed or converted, so they choose to flee to the safety of more civilised societies.

Three underage Hindu/Sikh/Christian girls are picked up every single day from their homes in Pakistan while the world looks away[151].

If this is happening in the 21st century in full view of the global community, we can imagine what Hindus must have endured for centuries.

An exodus occurs when the people and their leaders capitulate. If people rise and fight back, there is no exodus. A fight gives hope to people to endure the sufferings and stay on.

In the Kashmir valley, in 1990, Muslims were shouting from their mosques that Hindus living there should either convert, flee or die. Kashmir exodus of 1990 happened when Hindus in the valley lost all hopes of being protected. Unlike our forefathers, who were muscular Hindus and fought all such threats, we Hindus looked away as our brothers and sisters were kicked out of their ancestral homes by a mafia masquerading as religion. The shame of the Kashmiri exodus of Hindus is on us and our pathetic leadership, which capitulated.

Even today, these unfortunate Hindus are struggling to get this heinous act of 1990 declared as a genocide, but nothing has been achieved.

Our glorious ancestors were not weak kneed, hence all threats of Islamists were responded to, in kind. Medieval amoral conduct in the 21st century should be dealt with in a similar fashion and our present leadership should learn from history.

Hindu kings raised the banner against Islam and kept fighting

151. https://economictimes.indiatimes.com/news/international/world-news/pakistan-institutionalised-discrimination-against-minority-groups-eu-parliament-report/articleshow/69329724.cms?from=mdr.

it and the Hindus stood behind their kings to fight Islam than to flee to other nations. The firm entrenchment of Hindus in this subcontinent is an undeniable indicator of their resolve to take on Islamic invasions and exposes the lie of the claim of a 'thousand years of Hindu slavery.'

Art and Architecture in the Hindu Kingdoms

If Hindus were slaves for a thousand years, who erected the magnificent forts of Mewar, the architectural marvels of Chittor, the observatories in Rajasthan, the beautiful *havelis* (mansions) and palaces adorning Rajasthan, the sun temple at Konark, the grandest temples at Mahabalipuram, Khajuraho and Ranakpur?

Maharana Kumbha of Mewar alone built thirty two forts in the 15th century besides the architectural wonder, Vijay Stambha, in the fort of Chittor. He did this while he fought fifty-six pitched battles with Islamic armies of Malwa, Gujarat and Nagaur.

How did the Hindus write brilliant commentaries on the *Gita*, *Upanishads*, like the ones written by Madhavacharya, Vallabhacharya and Ramanujacharya?

How did Mira Bai compose such sublime poetry and the entire chain of the saints of the Bhakti movement propagate and serve Hinduism if we were slaves? How could Hindus preach their religion if Islamists had completely subjugated them? Can slaves even dream of writing works of art and constructing architecture marvels? Which slaves erected empires like the Vijayanagara Empire spreading and spanning through the entire southern India for 300 years? Which slaves keep worshipping idols, singing Vedic hymns, running dance and drama schools under regal patronages and performing *mangal artis* (ceremonial worship) to their gods in mammoth temples when still under Islamic rule for one thousand years?

Hindustan has always stuck like a thorn in the heart of Islamists because Hindu resistance against Islamic expansionism continued unabated for centuries and they could not convert the Hindu masses of this subcontinent.

The thriving Hindu culture, traditions and festivals are ample evidence that the monotheistic Islamic invaders were forced to endure all the polytheistic rituals much to their distaste and discomfort and were helpless to stop them, unlike what they had done to the Pagan civilisations of West Asia.

It is the callousness of the mediocre intelligentsia of this unfortunate nation that instead of applauding the Hindus for a the staunch defence of their culture, literature and traditions the fabricated lie of Ganga Jamuni tehjeeb is perpetrated and attributed to the tolerance of Islamic invaders.

The double-mouthed historians of this nation call Hindus slaves of Islamists and at the same time the Islamic invaders are desperately shown to be tolerant.

No one asked the history writers of this nation that if indeed Hindus were enslaved by Muslims, how can Muslims be considered tolerant?

The truth is that Hindus continued with their investigation into their spiritual, scientific and cultural pursuits in spite of the Muslim invasions.

If Hindus were morbid slaves of Muslims, Bharat too would have been cursed to be in the 'Dark Ages' like Europe.

Hindus weren't taken as Slaves by Islamic Invaders

The slavery of a fellow-human being is a disease brought to Bharat by Islamic invaders.

All through 8,000 years of Vedic civilisation, with all its ups and downs, human slavery was an inconceivable idea in Sanatan Dharma.

Opposing slavery was one of the reasons for Hindu kings and populations resisting Islamists so vehemently.

Almost all annals of Rajput states are filled with conversations amongst kings and their advisors about the fate that would fall upon the population, if Islamic plunderers were not resisted.

Tod describes this trait of Rajputs to fanatically defend the honour of their womenfolk in beautiful words:

"If devotion to the fair sex be admitted as the criterion for civilisation, the Rajpoot must rank high.

"His susceptibility is extreme and fires at the slightest offence to female delicacy, which he never forgives[152].

The unique practice of *saka-jauhar* is an extreme example of

152. Tod, vol. 1, p. 223.

Hindus of India choosing a painful death over slavery.

Islamic invaders were known to keep Hindu women as sex slaves as a means to humiliate the local population because the barbarians found sanction for such a practice in their religious books. Hence, Rajasthan witnessed at least a dozen *saka jauhars* in Chittor, Ranthambore, Jalore, etc. where Hindu women immolated themselves to avoid sex slavery.

Many a times a question is raised as to why die such a painful death? The women could have consumed poison or stabbed each other to death. The answer is in the horrible practice of necrophilia practiced by Islamic invaders. The Islamic invaders were known to humiliate even the corpses of Hindu women, hence *jauhar* was done. Burning oneself in *jauhar* also sent a message to the rest of the Hindu population to keep fighting the invaders. Can we even imagine the level of intelligence and determination of an entire state's regal line and also its general population to devise such a tool to counter Islamic slavery?

With the rising flames of the *jauhar*, the message to *jihadis* at the time as well as to fellow-Hindus was loud and clear.

Violence and torture can never subdue us.

Never will we forsake the religion of our ancestors.

Never will we surrender our freedom at the altar of slavery.

James Tod describes the first *jauhar* of Rani Padmini of Chittor in these words:

"Rana Ratan Singh called his chiefs around him and said, 'Now I devote myself to Chittor.'

"But another awful sacrifice was to precede the act of Rana going to fight Allauddin Khilji.

"In a horrifying rite, the jauhar, where the women are immolated to preserve them from pollution or captivity. The funeral pyre was lit within the 'great subterranean retreat,' in chambers impervious to the light of the day. The defenders of Chittor beheld in procession, the queens, their own wives and daughters, to the number of several thousand. The fair Padmini closed the throng, which was augmented by whatever of female beauty or youth could be tainted by Tatar lust. They were conveyed to the cavern and the opening closed upon them, leaving them to find security

from dishonor in the devouring element of fire."

Nowhere on this globe, at any time in human history, does one find such resolve in an entire population to fight for their freedom as we do in the extremely courageous act of *jauhar*.

Even in defeat, Hindus sent a message to their plunderers that they might have defeated and killed them, but Hindus could never be subjugated. A message for the entire world to see that the death of honour is far superior to a few years of a wretched life as a slave.

Never was a more audacious and bold statement written against the vile practice of slavery, than in the unparalleled act of Saka Jauhar, the self immolation by women and a warrior's death in the battlefield for men. An act of supreme defiance in the face of insurmountable odds.

People who surrender their freedom do not commit acts of *jauhar*, that too on such a massive scale and so consistently.

The mass migration of Hindus from cities to multiple small habitations across Bharat was a consequence of the determination of Hindus to refuse slavery of Islamists.

According to an estimate, Kashmir alone has witnessed seven such mass migrations in the past one thousand years.

This migration happened at huge economic cost to this prosperous nation of ours, as centres of trade and commerce were abandoned by the mercantile class and artisans, just to escape persecution at the hands of barbarians, singularly obsessed with conversions and sex slavery.

Yes, there are recorded instances of Arab and Turk invaders, like Mohammad Qasim, Taimur Lung and Nadir Shah taking thousands of Hindus as slaves back to their native nations.

This has been a standard practice of Islamic plunderers, but it was resisted fiercely by the Hindu kings.

These instances happened when a Hindu opponent was temporarily defeated and these barbarians would capture some locals and take them as slaves.

The Sikh warriors during the 17th and 18th centuries would ceaselessly attack Muslim forts where Hindu women were kept prisoners to be transported to Middle East for sex slavery. The message to the Islamic barbarians was loud and clear. Hindus will not yield to slavery and would pay every conceivable price to avoid that. including martyrdom to defend and protect their women.

Hindu-Muslim Ruler Alliance

In every human society, there are losers; not everyone can be a winner. And for an external enemy to invade and tap on the grudges of the loser and find an ally in him is one of the easiest things in the world.

Islamic invaders exploited these human follies to gain a foothold in India, but does it mean they enslaved Hindus or tricked them by fuelling infighting among Hindus? That is a question we need to ponder upon.

Not a single Muslim invader ruled even an inch of India without striking alliances with the local Hindu kings.

Islamic invasion of the Indian subcontinent was not a story of outright military conquest by Islam, but a saga of Hindu opposition to the invaders and resolve to save *dharma* at all costs. Hence, Muslims were forced to change their tactics and purchase peace with Hindu kings, however temporary and artificial that peace turned out to be. But it does underline the truth that Hindus could never be defeated by the Islamic invaders unless aided by Hindu kings in resources, strategy or information.

Would Haldighati have witnessed such a bloodbath of Rajputs if Jaipur had allied with Mewar?

Could Akbar even dream of becoming an emperor of India without the help of mighty Man Singh and Jagannath Kachchawa? It was Man Singh who had won Kabul for Akbar, not any Muslim General.

The wars of succession between the sons of Akbar, Jehangir and Shahjahan were all fought by direct or indirect support of Hindu kings to one Mughal or the other.

This meant a great control of Hindus on the destiny and conduct of the Mughal who was ruling Delhi.

What can be a bigger proof of defiance of Mughals than this?

It was the Hindu kings who crushed revolts by Muslims

against Islamic rulers.

Akbar's reign would have crumbled if Hindu warriors like Man Singh, Jagannath Kachchawa, Bhagwandas and Madho Singh of Jaipur hadn't fought Akbar's wars for him against fellow-Muslims. Jaswant Singh of Jodhpur was instrumental in quelling the rebellion of Pathans in Afghanistan for Aurangzeb.

Before Akbar, few Hindu kings supported the Islamic invaders and hence we see that the whole edifice of Islamic rule over India was too fragile and shaky to pose a real threat to Hindu survival in the subcontinent.

It was Akbar who changed this and aligned with Hindu kings to augment his power and created a quasi-Islamic rule in the heart of the country. Akbar's next two successors, Jehangir and Shahjahan continued this policy of humouring Hindu princes and used them to quell rebellions all over the land.

Aurangzeb abandoned this policy and attacked Hindu lives and values openly by destroying Hindu temples and imposing the *jaziya* tax on Hindus. Jaipur's Mirza Raja Jai Singh and Jodhpur's Jaswant Singh were murdered by Aurangzeb, who pushed the Rathores of Marwar straight into the arms of Raj Singh of Mewar. The direct consequence of the Sisodia-Rathore alliance was the conclusive defeat and ouster of Aurangzeb from Rajasthan permanently in CE 1680. Aurangzeb spent the rest of his life fighting the Hindus in the Deccan and Assam. With Aurangzeb's death in CE 1707, Mughal rule crumbled like a pack of cards, reinforcing this doctrine that Muslim rule in this nation was only possible as long as they were in alliance with Hindu kingdoms.

We may question the intelligence and loyalty of such Hindu kings who facilitated Islamists instead of their own brothers, but it does show us the truth of the Islamic invaders who were mere 'managers' of power in medieval India instead of great conquerors that they are falsely portrayed as.

Reference to Islamists in Contemporary Literature

If we look at the last 1,400 years of conflict, there was not a period when Hindu kings stopped constructing forts and palaces and/or Hindu writers stopped composing all kinds of literature.

A lot of this literature, especially the short *dohas* (couplets) and *sorthas* (verse in meter) written in Rajasthan and Mughal courts were scathing attacks on the anti-Hindu policies of Muslim rulers. These writings were crucial in infusing education and opposition to the plunder of the Hindu ethos by the Islamic invaders.

Prithviraj Raso, *Khumaan Raso* and *Rana Raso* were written by local Hindu bards of Rajasthan, describing various wars and the glory of Hindu kings against the Islamic invaders.

Medieval vernacular literature is studded with words, like '*mlechchha*, Turk, Tatar, *hatyaro* and *asur* for Islamic invaders.

Dursa Aadha, a poet in Akbar's court is supposed to have written *Vrihad Chiyattari,* a collection of seventy-six *dohas* in praise of Maharana Pratap, where he has used words like a 'jackal', 'dark cloud' and 'greedy murderer' for Akbar while referring to Pratap as a 'lion', 'sunlight' and 'valorous Kshatriya'. Which slaves could write such derogatory language for their captors and not only stay alive but flourish?

The literature of that time kept invigorating the masses to stand against the dark forces of this repression and stay united behind the Hindu kings who were fighting it.

The might and penetration of the written and spoken words were used by the Hindu poets and masses to the hilt. Fire of resistance against Islamic invaders was kept burning by a fiercely honest and creative articulation of the threat to Hindu *dharma* if Islamic imperialists were not resisted.

One doha is being shared to demonstrate the evolution of literature in response to Islamic invasions.

धर जातां धरम पलटतां, त्रियाँ पड़न्ता ताव।

तीन दिवस ऐ मरण रा, कुण रंका कुण राव।।

meaning, if someone takes your land, converts your faith or hurts your women, you should die resisting these, it doesn't matter if you are a king or a Pauper.

It is obvious that the poet is referring to the Islamic design of converting Hindus or attacks on the Hindu women by Islamic armies.

Hindu theological creativity also continued unabated during these centuries and thousands of *ashrams* (hermitages) and *mathas* (monasteries) spread all over the nation were indulging in the uninterrupted pursuit of Hindu religious practices. The *Ramcharitmanas, Geet Govind,* dozens of *teekas* and commentaries on the *Vedas, Upanishads* and the *Bhagwad Gita* were written in this very phase of India's history.

It is when the Hindu writers, especially Charans and Brahmins, were forced to stop penning the truth of the barbarity of Islamic invasions that the lies of Hindu slavery were invented.

On their part, Charans too, expecially in the post independence era, stood idle while the Leftists erased the glorious Hindu resistance and are partly responisble for the lies of Hindu slavery finding roots.

The power of spoken and written word was effortlessly taken over by the Islamists masqerading as Bollywood writers and Shayars charming the middle class Hindus with their lies laced in chaste language.

The literary and acedmic capitulation of the Hindu poets and bards is a major reason for the lies of slavery being trumpeted unresisted.

Aurangzeb's Repentance on His Life and Deeds

History must never imprison us.

History must liberate us from our prejudices and blindness and thus help us continue on our trajectory of evolution.

The entire saga of Mewar Maharanas, the noble and gallant *samants* and the amazing people of Mewar stands on the singular edifice of opposition to Islamic invasions of this Vedic land. An incessant, brutal assault by gangsters, motivated by the blind pursuit of a theological doctrine of monotheism, on a people who had already discovered monotheism thousands of years ago and monotheism too was only one of the ways to explore one's divinity.

A people who gave principles of mathematics, the *Upanishads,* the *Gita* and *yoga* to the world. Such evolved people were brutalised by robbers who used the cover of religion to cause immeasurable suffering not only to Hindus, but to the entire globe.

In the *Annals and Antiquities of Rajasthan,* Col. James Tod quotes a letter written by Aurangzeb to his religious teacher, Mulla

Saley in CE 1684, in which Aurangzeb is livid with his teacher for making him a religious bigot, instead of a liberal man. Tod narrates that Francois Bernier witnessed this letter being written and preserved it with him. Another letter is by a dying Aurangzeb to his grandson and son.

× × ×

The purpose of sharing the contents of these letters is to discover the truth of Aurangzeb's life.

The content of these letters is explosive because it destroys the claims of violence and strife as tools to impose an unjust and immoral way of life on others. Aurangzeb is the benchmark of success of Islamists and if he dies a sorry and dejected man, it should be known to the Mullahs and their followers.

The content of these letters is sublime because they gives hope to mankind, that if a hate-monger like Aurangzeb can repent his indoctrination, maybe the liberals in Islamic world too can realise the darkness of indoctrination. If all his life, living like a model Muslim, leads to such a pathetic death in his own words, shouldn't the Muslim world reflect that mayhem, hatred and murder that *jihadis* are causing in the world, is all meaningless.

Aurangzeb is idolised by a vast number of Muslims as their *gazi*: a victorious Muslim fighter against non-Muslims.

In the first letter, Aurangzeb clearly states to his religious teacher that because of his religious teachings, Aurangzeb missed out on the beautiful things in life. He even goes on to blame Saley for the indoctrination that caused him to be so stone-hearted that he ended up killing his own brothers.

Aurangzeb writes:

"You told my father Shahjahan that you would teach me philosophy. This is true, I remember very well, that you have entertained me for many years with airy questions of things that afford no satisfaction at all to the mind, and are of no use in humane society, empty notions and mere fancies, that have only this in them, that they are very hard to understand and very easy to forget, which are only capable to tire and spoil a good understanding and to breed an opinion that is insupportable.

"I still remember that after you, but amused me, all I retained

of your philosophy was the multitudes of barbaric and dark words, proper to bewilder, perplex and tire out the best wits, and only invented the better to cover the vanity and ignorance of men like yourself, that would make us believe that they know all, and that under those obscure and ambiguous are hid great mysteries which they alone are capable to understand."

He continues then lamenting his missing out on the more liberal and happier worldview because of his teachings. It is almost as though Aurangzeb is talking about the wisdom of *Gita* and *Upanishads* to which he was surely introduced by his brother Dara Shikoh sometime in his childhood.

"If you had seasoned me with that philosophy which formeth the mind to ratiocination (perhaps rationality) and insensibly accustomed it to be satisfied with nothing but solid reason, if you had given me those excellent precepts and doctrines which raise the soul above the assaults of fortune and reduce her to an unshakeable and always equal temper, and permit her not be lifted up by prosperity, nor debased by adversity.

"If you had taken care to give the knowledge of what we are, and what are the first principles of things, and had assisted me in forming in my mind a fit idea of the greatness of the universe and of the admirable order and motion of the parts thereof; if, I say, you had instilled into me this kind of philosophy I should think myself incomparably more obliged to you than Alexander was to his Aristotle[153]*."*

This letter is adequate proof that Aurangzeb realised the hollowness of his faith.

When he saw the courage and fortitude of the Maharanas and the people of Mewar to fight and die for Hinduism, he was forced to introspect that there was a higher principle that Hindus were ready to fight and die for. The lives and deeds of Maharana Raj Singh, Chhatrapati Shivaji Maharaj, Sri Guru Gobind Singh Maharaj, Veer Durga Das, etc. must have shown him the mirror that it wasn't only Islam that evoked the passion for religion, Hinduism did the same too.

But while Hinduism evoked the passion only in times of

153. Tod, vol. 1, p. 299.

crises and as a matter of choice, Aurangzeb's passion was an uncontrollable, mindless and continuous torment of his being.

Auragzeb goes further to blame Mullah Saley's teachings for his violent temperament:

"Should not you, instead of your flattery, have taught me somewhat of that point so important to a king, which is, what the reciprocal duties are of a sovereign to his subjects and those of subjects to their sovereign; and ought not you to have considered, that one day I should be obliged with the sword to dispute my life and the crown with my brothers?

"Is not that the destiny almost of all the sons of Hindustan?

"Go, and retire to the village whence you come, and let nobody know who you are or what is become of you."

Tod also quotes a letter by Aurangzeb to his grandson Shah Azim Shah from his deathbed:

"Health to thee! My heart is near thee. Old age has arrived; weakness subdues me and strength has forsaken all my members. I came a stranger in this world, and a stranger I depart.

"I know nothing of myself, what I am, and for what I am destined.

"I have not been the guardian and protector of the empire.

"My valuable time has been passed vainly.

"I brought nothing into this world and, except the infirmities of man, carry nothing out.

"I have a dread for my salvation, and with what torment I will be punished. Though I have strong reliance on the mercies and bounties of God, yet, regarding my actions, fear will not quit me.

"Farewell! Farewell! Farewell!"

Aurangzeb murdered Hindus and Muslims of this nation thinking it to be his religious duty. We have dealt in detail with how he murdered Rajput kings, slaughtered villagers and destroyed Hindu temples in blind pursuance of his faith.

Most modern-day Muslims and their religious teachers are proud of what Aurangzeb did to Hindus and Hindu temples. The *madrasas* in this nation teach the plunder caused by Aurangzeb as an example to emulate.

Consequently, Islamisation of this nation has been an ongoing project from Aurangzeb's demise to the 21st century.

As *halal* economy, love *jihad*, victimhood narratives, Sufism, population inversion, RULLS violence[154], Hindu genocides, Bollywood brainwashing and underworld blackmail go on unabated, what are the options for Hindus?

Morality and righteousness are not inborn in man. These are traits that the family, teachers and society teach us. A world devoid of morality and justice simply cannot survive.

If religious zealots read these letters of Aurangzeb and ponder, mankind can progress at an unimaginable speed. The needless investing in defence budgets and securities around the globe can be diverted to pharmaceutical, oceanographic, space, cancer, medicine and climatic research and we can all progress to a safer, saner and happier humanity.

Hindu kings and Hindu philosophy shook even a fossilised mind like Aurangzeb into contemplating the futility of his actions. No slave culture can force a tyrant to submerge in such self-doubt. Slavery only evokes contempt in the heart of the enslaver.

That our glorious ancestors fought Aurangzeb and that within his court and around him millions of Hindus kept practicing their Hindu faith and didn't convert, is itself a glaring example of Hindu resistance.

Aurangzeb continued hating and killing Hindus in spite of these realisations, but these letters show the split consciousness with which he continued his dance of death.

Hindus continued to torment him with their resistance and forced him to regret his life and deeds. No slave ever achieved such a feat.

How are we 100 Crores Today?

A cursory look at Islamic expansion in the Middle East reveals that once Islam gains a foothold in a society, it soon starts going for the power centres either by subjugation or alliance. So, in a matter of decades, all of West Asia became Islamised with not even a remnant of the past cultures left behind.

Pagan temples in the Middle East were razed to the ground.

154. Random, unceasing, low-level, scattered violence.

Every beautiful sculpture was crushed to dust, every symbol of life itself was annihilated in a blind quest to establish dull, sad and angry monotheistic societies which considered dance, music and sculptures as *kufr* or heresy.

Yet, it was Hindus alone who kept on thriving through this incessant military onslaught on our people, economy and culture.

Yes, we lost entire Hindu/Buddhist/Sikh lands to this onslaught and kept shrinking, but fourteen centuries is a very, very long time to fight a bigoted mass of people whose singular pursuit was to grab the women and property of affluent Hindus under the cover of their expansionist ideology. That Hinduism survived this invasion by motivated psychotics against overwhelming odds, speaks volumes of the might, resolve and intelligence of the Hindus.

The writer has had the great fortune of serving Hindu and Sikh refugees from Pakistan migrating into India in the 21st century.

One thing that stands out is the steely resolve of these

Writer with Bhag Chand Bhil on way to Kumbh Mela

Hindus and Sikhs to forsake everything dear to them—their land, properties, businesses, memories, even relatives, for the sake of their *dharma*.

If we want to understand what *dharma* means to most Hindus, we must meet these wonderful Hindus and Sikhs, who migrating from Pakistan and Bangladesh to India just so they can remain Hindus. I quote a conversation I had with a Hindu refugee, Bhag Chand Bhil, few years ago:

Bhag Chand's son was kidnapped by *jihadis* in the district of Rahim Yar Khan in Pakistani Punjab, where Bhag Chand had a thriving business as a wholesale cloth merchant.

Bhag Chand spent his entire life's savings and recovered his son from the jaws of *jihadis* in the north-western area of KPK region of Pakistan. The *jihadis* had converted the young boy to Islam and were keeping him prisoner in a *madrasa*.

Within months of this incident, Bhag Chand and his entire family migrated to Bharat. I have personally witnessed Bhag Chand's struggles to keep his family afloat through a life of poverty and insecurity. Our NGO, Nimittekam, supported him all through these years and today he is the main coordinator of Pakistani-Hindu refugees in Jaipur.

One day, while talking to him, I asked Bhag Chand, "Why didn't you read the *kalma* (Islamic ritual to convert) and become a Muslim, Bhag Chand? Why choose a life of such hardships and uncertainty when all that was needed of you was to convert your faith and you could have retained your business and family?

Bhag Chand looked at me puzzled, contemplated for a second, and smilingly replied, *"बाप-दादों का धरम ऐसे कैसे छोड़ दें साहब?"* (How can we forsake the *dharma* of our ancestors, sahib?)

I melted when I heard this reply of Bhag Chand. Such utter simplicity and matter of fact understanding of life is a gift not many of us are aware of.

I got my answer that day to this question that had intrigued me for decades as to what was that element that kept us Hindus alive through this civilisational battle with Islam. And the answer is the robust understanding of life and its forces by ordinary Hindus.

Never did our ancestors allow pseudo morality to confuse us in this war of thousand years with Islamic invaders. In fact, we chose the morality of the *Gita* as explained by Shri Krishna, where it was a higher duty to kill anyone who violated our women and gods.

Ahimsa was an immoral argument when confronted by a barbarian because *ahimsa* in front a murderer is only a cover up for our cowardice.

Our ancestors knew that the sublime principles pf Hindu *dharma* were worth living for, worth fighting for and if it comes to that, worth dying for.

Bhag Chand Bhil is a living embodiment of that understanding of Hindu *dharma*. He let go of all his worldly possessions for the sake of a promise—a promise that his glorious ancestors had passed on to him through the millennia.

This is an amazing loyalty and unfathomable understanding of Sanatan Dharma that has withstood the most violent onslaught on the values and freedom of this great land and continues to do so even today.

Why and how of this lie

Against this background, we try to find the answer as to why did the Leftists and Islamic historians of this nation concoct this lie of a thousand-year of Hindu slavery.

These prostitutes of mind aligned with the Islamic expansionist for money and power and sold us without our knowledge.

What Islamic invaders could not achieve through force, they tried to achieve through deceit.

What they couldn't get through the cruelty of their sword, they tried to get by the might of the pen.

How else to subvert proud people like Hindus than to turn the entire truth of their glorious resistance to Islamic invaders right on its head!

Islamists have always known the power of controlling the mind and narrative, even if it is through fear or lies and in Bharat, they found allies in the Leftist academicians manning almost every educational institution of this nation.

The Congress party actively colluded with the Leftists in this distortion of history. Rakesh Batabyal in his book,' JNU: The Making of a University' writes that Subhadra Joshi, a Congress MP took the lead in writing a 'secular' history of India in the NCERT books.[155]

History is just history.

What kind of perverted minds would advocate writing secular or communal history!

Leftists provided Islamists with access, justification and resources to invent and propagate the lies of Hindu slavery.

A look at the speech of Babur on the eve of the Battle of Khanwa in CE 1527 is a glaring example of how religious zeal can fill even a mentally defeated army to rise and fight.

Only this time, the reverse was to be applied to the Hindu population. The lie was circulated so that Hindus are filled with a sense of inferiority complex and get convinced that the docile, cowardly, inward-looking Hindu was no match to the aggressive, cruel and extroverted Islamic warriors.

Islamic expansionism is a work in ceaseless progress and the best simile that can explain this phenomenon is that of hydra (a creature that lives in water).

Just as a hydra has multiple heads or arms where it uses one to hypnotise its prey and catch it with the other arms as it stands mesmerised by the dance, Islamists too put on various kinds of faces when confronted by Hindu resistance.

In the past seven decades especially, instead of a scholarly, honest analysis of the Hindu-Muslim conflict in India, the lie of a thousand years of slavery was invented and circulated. So, the obvious question would be that if indeed Hindus were slaves of Islamists, then how come the entire land was not converted? How come 100 crore Hindus still populate this area of the globe?

That the lie of a 'thousand years of slavery' was forcibly inserted into Hindu consciousness without being questioned, also speaks volumes of the mediocrity and mendacity of Hindu academicians and the political and spiritual leadership of Hindus.

155. Batabyal , p 58

Perhaps, Hindus got tired of fighting Islamic imperialism or were outdone by the religious zeal of Islamic invaders; still, the fact of a compromised Hindu leadership cannot be overlooked.

Hitler's propaganda minister, Joseph Goebbels once said, "You tell a lie a hundred times, it becomes the truth."

Both Islamic zealots and Hindu thought, or shall we say thoughtless, leadership have worked in cahoots to prove Goebbels right.

The end game of Islamists is to take over the resources and land of an unconquered area and convert all the natives to their faith. That singular obsessive pursuit has not changed its course in the last 1,400 years.

Of course, like a hydra, it keeps changing the means to achieve that end.

So, sometimes it is the sweet-talking, singing and dancing *Sufi* that is sent to charm (fool) Hindus. At other times, it is spreading lies by controlling the history-writer and record keeper as we see in the extreme biases of Muslim historians, like Abul Fazal and Al Badayuni, who openly used words like 'soldiers of Islam' for Muslims while referring to Hindus as 'stone-hearted infidels'.

Sometimes, it is the play of victimhood, when the civil war within Mughals and other dynasties would make one of them seek refuge and alliance with Hindu kings. Sometimes, it is the ploy of tolerance, as used by Akbar to buy the loyalties of Jaipur's Rajputs and strategists, like Todar Mal.

At other times, it is outright barbarism like Aurangzeb passing diktats for *jaziya* and plunder of Hindu temples.

But every single time, the end game is the same: Islamisation of the land through conversions.

Our intelligent and brave ancestors understood this truth even in those tough times when there was no effective means of communication and chose to fight it.

Even Muslim thinkers and writers have acknowledged the glorious Hindu resistance to Islamic invaders and spoken the truth, which our Leftist pseudo liberal historians have tried to erase.

'That audacious armada of the religion of Hijaz
Whose insignia reached every corner of the world
Which learnt no obstruction from any fear
Which felt no hesitation in Persian Gulf or faltered in the Red Sea
Which valiantly crossed all the seven oceans
Oh, drowned was that armada (of Islam), when it reached the mouth of Ganga!'

—Mawlana Khwaja Altaf Husain Hali

James Tod describes the resistance of Rajasthan to Islamic imperialism in beautiful words:

"What nation could have maintained the semblance of civilisation, the spirit, or the customs of their forefathers, during so many centuries of overwhelming depression, but one of such singular character as the Rajpoot?

"Rajasthan exhibits the sole example in the history of mankind, of a people withstanding every outrage barbarity can inflict, or human nature sustain, from a foe whose religion commands annihilation and bent to the earth, yet rising buoyant from the pressure and making calamity a whetstone to courage."

Tod then goes on to compare how his own people, the British, kept yielding to oppressors through the ages and writes:

"How did the Britons at once sink under the Romans, to the Saxons they alike succumbed; then, again, to the Danes; and this heterogeneous breed then succumbed to the Normans.

"Contrast this with Rajputs of Mewar; not an iota of their religion or customs have they lost.

"Mewar alone, the sacred bulwark of religion, never compromised her honour for her safety and still survives her ancient limits; and since the brave Samar Singh gave up his life fighting alongside Prithviraj, the blood of the princes of Mewar has flowed in copious streams for the maintenance of their honour, religion and independence."

This is a British writer penning his thoughts on the people his own nation was trying to rule.

After careful inspection and piecing together of historical facts, we can reasonably arrive at the deduction that the whole business of Hindu *ghulami* is a mind game played by the *jihadi* cabal facilitated by the conniving Leftists of our nation to keep us deluded by a false narrative of inferiority and defeatism.

In the *Mahabharata*, there is a story of King Shalya who was made to steer the chariot of the great warrior Karna in the battle. Shalya was an arrogant king and Karna was the son of an ordinary person. Throughout the war, Shalya kept demoralising Karna against Arjuna. Karna was dejected by Shalya's rants and eventually, this ended with Karna being slain by Arjuna in the war.

The Leftists have been the Shalya for Hindus since the past seven decades.

Now it is up to us to deny or believe the lies of a thousand-year slavery being parroted by the Shalyas in our midst.

But if we continue to believe this lie, we must accept that by doing that, we turn our backs to our own glorious past.

Believing this lie means disowning the sufferings and struggles of the amazing Maharanas and people of Mewar.

Believing this lie means we are ready to tread on the charred remains of the glorious women and children of Rajasthan who committed *jauhar*, to a spurious future.

Believing this lie means that our hollowed spines cannot even bear simple truths which define us.

Believing this lie means that '*satyameva jayate*' is a mere slogan and not a principle worth living and dying for.

Believing this lie means to stab the memory of Pratap, who stood absolutely alone to preserve *dharma* but did not yield.

Believing this lie amounts to a chuckle shamelessly on the limbs and bodies littered around Khanwa, Haldighati, Dewair, Panipat and hundreds of such places, which only insensitive dolts can do on witnessing an overwhelming sight.

Believing this lie means to mock and ridicule the extreme sacrifices of the unsung people of Bharatvarsha as they silently supported their kings, enduring whatever suffering came along.

Believing this lie means looking over the unlived lives and uncared corpses of our courageous ancestors with indifference, reserved only for the worst kind of traitors.

Believing this lie means to actively collaborate with the

prostitutes of mind in erasing our sublime past.

But if we can comprehend the truth and stand up to unshackle ourselves of this mental albatross of slavery around our necks, we would perhaps have taken the first steps to the claim of being heirs of the legacy of giants like Pratap, Sanga and Bappa.

Only then we can safely say that the lie of thousand-year slavery of Hindus is just that—a lie.

And lies have consequences.

Horrible consequences. Consequences that are borne by the whole society. If we want to evolve as humanity and travel towards a brighter, safer, happier future, all civilisational lies have to be defeated objectively and comprehensively.

Lies can be destroyed by speaking the truth. Lies can be defeated by scholarly research and honest articulation of the truth. That is what the Hindu *samaj* (society) needs to do in the 21st century—speak and broadcast truth from their rooftops, because truth is non-negotiable. Truth liberates. Only when we seek and speak the truth shall the true *shakti* (power) of our great nation be unleashed and Hinduism can find its rightful place in the global order.

With technology, internet and the gift of the algorithm, we see today a knowledge economy where information is democratized. The age of the "presstitutes" and the age of the "Distorians" is reaching its end. Agenda driven narratives peddled by the Lefto-Islamist or the indologists cannot hide behind fancy creatives that portray hindus as weak and subvert our proud and courageous resistance against invaders and colonizers.

While the rest of the world succumbed to the onslaught of the Red (communism) White (Christianity) and Green (Islam) forces, India stands as that sole beacon of hope, that vestige of a civilisation that pervaded the entire globe at one point.

The hope of revival of civilisational ethos and its triumph over ideological forces is a beautiful hope that can solve and resolve issues as complex as environmental damage, reduction of crime, evolution of humanistic values and collective growth of spiritual energies that can bring about egalitarian principles to the world again.

Sold out media that have been classified as presstitutes or the sold out narrative builders in academia, who write fake history and are called distorians have to be replaced by truthsayers and intellectual giants with no hidden agenda.

Hindu Dharma and Indian civilisation are the audacious hope that truth will shine through the darkness of chauvinistic narratives. Satyamev Jayate. Let truth alone triumph.

The slavery of fellow-human beings is an evil that cannot be endured at any cost.

Slavery is worse than murder because it kills the *atma* (soul) of the individual.

Slavery must be fought, whatever be the cost.

Our glorious ancestors fought slavery and succeeded.

Hindus were not enslaved even for a microsecond. And as long as even one Hindu remembers the truth of Pratap, Hindus will never be enslaved.

Har Har Mahadev!

□

18

Silence of the Lions

While we are in awe of the amazing stories of valour and fortitude of the Maharanas of Mewar in fighting the onslaught of Islamic imperialism on our soil, we must also assess as to what happened to this glorious dynasty in particular and the martial spirit of Rajputs and other martial communities in general, especially after CE 1700.

With the death of Aurangzeb in CE 1707, as the Mughals went into oblivion, so did the Mewar Sisodia dynasty very mysteriously.

We will try to assess the causes of this overall decay of the Rajputs, Charans, Jats, Sikhs and the associated martial communities in fighting the imperialistic forces.

With the advent of the British, a huge complicating factor had taken birth in the already muddy waters of the geo-politics of the subcontinent. British imperialism is a separate topic with its own dynamics and connotations; we will restrict ourselves to studying and deciphering the changed contours of Islamic imperialism in the Indian subcontinent.

The Rajputs and allied martial communities of Rajasthan and the great people of Mewar, irrespective of their castes, had been fighting Islamic imperialism for a thousand years, hence it is safe to conclude that a civilisational fatigue set in the people of Mewar and Rajasthan.

James Tod put it in beautiful words when describing the conflict between Prithviraj Chauhan and Mohammad Shahabuddin Ghori at the second Battle of Tarain in CE 1192.

"The capture of Delhi and its monarch Prithviraj, the death of his ally of Chittor, with the bravest and the best of his troops speedily ensured the further and final success of the Tatar arms; and when Kannauj (Raja Jaichand) fell, now was left to contend with Shahabuddin, the possession of the regal seat of Chauhans. Scenes of devastation, plunder and massacre commenced which lasted through ages; during which really all that was sacred in religion and or celebrated in art was destroyed by these ruthless and barbarous invaders. The noble Rajput, with the spirit of constancy and enduring courage, seized every opportunity to turn upon his oppressor. By his perseverance and valour, he wore out entire dynasties of foes, alternatively yielding 'to his fate' or restricting the circle of conquest.

Every road in Rajasthan was moistened with torrents of blood of the spoiled and the spoiler.

"But all was to no avail; fresh supplies were ever pouring in, and dynasty succeeded dynasty, heir to the same remorseless feeling which sanctified murder, legalised spoliation and defied destruction.

"In these desperate conflicts, entire tribes of Rajputs were swept away; whose names are the only mementos of their former

existence and celebrity[156]*."*

The key words in Tod's explanation are *"fresh supplies were ever pouring in"*. How long could the citizenry of an affluent, educated and progressive society like Hindus endure the barbarians pouring in from our western borders?

It is quite a natural turn of events in the source of the trajectory of a nation that people get tired of fighting and simply give in to the wishes of the tyrants.

Fortunately for Hindus, this fatigue against Islamic imperialism happened when other powers, like the Marathas in the south and the Sikhs and the Jats in the north along with the Ahoms in the east, picked up the baton from the tired Rajputs and Kshatriyas of Rajasthan and hence, the fight against Islamic imperialism continued.

The power struggle with the Hindus of this nation changed its dimensions to the advantage of the rise of Marathas as the bearers of the Hindu flag against Islam. Thought it was a great blessing for our Vedic motherland, but the Kshatriyas of Rajasthan were relegated to the background of this new force of Hindu resistance.

There is little to complain about this spontaneous shift of the Hindu resistance from Mewar to the Marathas as events ran their natural course.

What is shameful and highly objectionable is the systematic degradation of Rajputs and other martial communities their struggle with Islamists in the next 200 years by Leftists, British imperialists, *jihadis* and a section of Hindus themselves.

This entire cabal got together to create lies around the glorious Rajput resistance, especially in the last seventy years of post-British India, where it has become an industry to belittle Hindu martial castes and traditions.

The direct consequence of this onslaught on Hindu martial races was the introversion of our warriors, especially the Rajputs. When people are constantly attacked for their lineage and the deeds of their ancestors, they respond either by belligerence or introversion. The Rajputs responded by both. A section of Rajputs took to rowdy behaviour on streets and in family lives, while the

156. Tod, vol. 1, p. 214.

majority succumbed to this propaganda and receded from public life. The gross indifference in the psyche of Rajput population to Hindu plight has been a direct consequence of this Leftist-*jihadi* onslaught on the glorious past of Rajputs.

Broadly, Rajputs became a schizophrenic society, confused between their actual, innate, martial leanings as protectors of women and Hindu *dharma* on one side, versus the Leftist-*jihadi* depiction of Rajputs as losers, and exploiters of the rest of the Hindu *samaj* (society).

This introversion and inaction of the martial communities suited the Leftist-*jihadi* agenda as Islamic imperialism would continue unabated in the subcontinent now, with the Hindu muscle paralysed or atrophied into inaction.

The poison of *ahimsa* as an absolute principle, injected into Hindu consciousness by Mr. Mohandas Gandhi and his followers proved to be the last nail in the coffin of Hindu martial resistance to Islamic imperialism. *Ahimsa* is a relative principle definitely worthy of pursuit in civilised societies but has no place when dealing with violent ideologies.

The average Hindu was fed the falsehood of submission as a virtue and resistance as a vice.

The 'meek Hindu,' who was always preoccupied with sterile speculations, was glorified to such an extent that the Kshatriya Hindu simply receded into oblivion. The lie of Islamic victories and the falsehood about continuous defeat of Hindu kings was mainly popularised by British historians alike in the 19th and the 20th century.

Many Hindus, blinded by the veil of *ahimsa*, participated in furthering these lies in the mistaken belief that they were somehow proving the 'superiority' of India's 'spiritual culture' over the materialistic culture of the West.

None of these Westerners and Hindu propagandists realised that the cowardice, sloth and capitulation to violent invasions may have no place in Hindu spirituality. But since this version of Hindu history became a very convenient tool to advancing Islamic imperialism, it continued unresisted. This dilemma has been beautifully explained by the great *maharshi* of the last century,

Sita Ram Goel:

"Indian history became a history of foreign invaders—Arabs, Turks, Uzbeks, Persians, Portuguese, Dutch, French and the British—rather than a history of the greatest civilisation that the world has known, and later on of Hindu heroism which fought and ultimately frustrated all foreign invaders."

Goel goes on to sum up this existential schizophrenia of Hindus thus:

"India itself became a sub-continent seething with a mass of heterogeneous humanity rather than an ancient and invisible Hindu homeland. Indian people became a conglomeration of nationalities, racial groups and religious communities which are finding it difficult to coexist in peace, rather than a national society that is trying to reform itself and reclaim some of its unfortunate sections alienated from it by successive waves of attacks by Islamic, Christian and modern Western imperialism."

Goel goes on further to exactly describe the consequences of such deracination of Hindus through the propagation of such lies:

"It was the disfigured version of India's history which gave a good conscience to the British imperialist while he pulverised Hindu society, plundered Hindu wealth and poured undisguised contempt on the Hindu culture. It was this version of history that emasculated Hindu society and emboldened the residues of Islamic imperialism to stage street riots and then walk away with precious parts of the Hindu homeland, thus consolidating an aggression that had not succeeded even though mounted repeatedly for more than a thousand years."

It is this version of India's history that is being invoked by the fifth columns of Islam, Christianity and Communism, each of which looks forward with the help of foreign finances, and if need be, foreign firearms. And it is this version of India's history which is being promoted by power-hungry politicians who woo the Muslim vote bank while they divide the Hindu society into mutually hostile camps[157].

The surest way of propagating this defeatist version of Hindu history was to demean and demoralise modern-day Rajputs along

157. Goel, p. 2.

with other martial communities.

Let us now decipher and simultaneously counter the myths propagated around the Rajput resistance to Islamic invaders one by one.

1. Rajputs (Hindus) lost all battles

The first attack of Islamists on India was by Mohammed bin Qasim on Raja Dahir in the 8th century CE. After being repulsed twice by Dahir, Qasim aligned with the Buddhists of Sindh and managed to defeat and behead Dahir. A Hindu confederation led by Bappa Rawal defeated subsequent Arab invaders even chasing them up to Iran. Bappa then went to Afghanistan, uprooted the Islamic ruler Salim, and put his nephew in his place.

For 500 years, Arab Islamists continued attacking Hindu kings and only succeeded in defeating Prithviraj Chauhan of Ajmer in CE 1192 at the second Battle of Tarain. All we hear from our history books is the defeat of Prithviraj by Mohammed Shahabuddin Ghori, but there is no mention of the 500 years of interim when each and every attack of Arab invaders and Islamic zealots was repulsed by great kings, like Gurjar Pratihara king Nagabhatta, Lalitaditya Muktipada (CE 720-764) of Kashmir, Khumaan II and III of Mewar, Shakti Kumar, Jaitra Singh, Anandapala, the Shahiya dynasty, the Chandelas, the Chalukyas and numerous such kings who faced and defeated Arab Islamists. Ghori himself was defeated by Mul Raja of Gujarat in CE 1178 and his army destroyed. These names have simply been erased from our history.

Mahmud of Ghazni (971-1030 CE)

Do we even realise how Islamic murderers have been forced to change their ways and goals in the sub-continent due to the glorious Hindu resistance?

The most violent assault on our nation happened at the end of the 10th century when Mahmud of Ghazni attacked Bharat twelve times, before finally plundering Somnath temple in CE 1026. Every single time Mahmud had to retreat back to his home. He did cause massive plunder and destroyed temples, but was always being chased by Hindu armies led by very courageous and committed Hindu kings. The initial years from CE 1005-1015, Mahmud was resisted by the Shahiya dynasty. Anandapala, Trilochanapala and Bheempala kept fighting him in his campaigns.

Then, from CE 1018-1022, Raja Nanda of Khajuraho and Vidyadhar Chandella resisted him and three times he had to return to Ghazni after exchanging gifts' with these kings[158].

A glimpse into what Mahmud of Ghazni faced in his raid on Somnath temple in CE 1026 will tell us a lot about the grit and resolve of Hindu resistance.

To quote from the Muslim annals;

Ferishta writes, *"The Hindus, urged by despair, returned to the defence of the works and made so spirited a resistance that the Mohammedans, unable to retain their footing and wearied with fatigue, fell back on all sides."*

Ibn-ul-Asir's account makes a very sad reading as to how our forefathers fought literally with bare hands against the well-armed Afghan barbarians. *"Band after band of the defenders entered the temple of Somnath, and with their hands clasped round their necks, wept and passionately entreated him. Then again they issued forth to fight until they were slain."*

Khond Mir also testifies to a bitter struggle lasting two days after which, *"those ignorant men ran in crowds to the idol temple, embraced Somnath, and came out again to fight until they were killed. Fifty thousand infidels were killed around the temple."*

It is a documented fact that after destroying Somnath, Ghazni was deliberately led astray by two Hindu soldiers posing as guides and hundreds of Mahmud's soldiers died of thirst and hunger.

On his way back, the Chalukya king, Bheem was waiting with his army to finish Mahmud, but he took a detour and returned from a different path avoiding present day Marwar, where Bheem was waiting[159].

---

158. Mishra, p. 63.
159. Mishra, p. 66.

Finally, on his way back, Mahmud's army was decimated by Jats of Sindh.

Thus, the Hindus fought for every street, every village and every temple with these mindless barbarians. It was the spirited defence of Somnath that saved so many temples of our nation.

It is mindboggling that only the destruction of Somnath is rubbed on our wounds constantly, but no one even talks about the thousands of temples saved.

Of course, if a bunch of sex-starved, religiously-indoctrinated murderers will attack a civilised and humane society relentlessly, they are bound to cause some damage, but this was no walkover as propagated by *jihadi* writers of this nation. For 500 years, Hindus didn't let our soil be polluted by the filth of a totalitarian darkness that engulfed Middle East in few decades.

500 years of Hindu victories simply erased from the collective consciousness of Hindus also speaks volumes of the mediocrity of the post-British Hindu leadership that allowed this to happen.

Then came the lie of the 'Delhi Sultanate'. At least four recorded instances of the Sultans of the Delhi Sultanate have been recorded by independent historians where the Mewar Maharanas captured and imprisoned these so-called Sultans or their children in the Chittor fort.

Mohammed bin Tughlaq, Firoz Shah Tughlaq and Ghiasuddin Tughlaq were captured and imprisoned by Maharana Hammir Singh, Maharana Lakha and Maharana Mokal of Mewar, respectively. Mahmud Khilji of Malwa was defeated and imprisoned by Kumbha.

Maharana Sanga of Mewar fought close to 100 battles in life and won all of these, but what is trumpeted around in our books is only the 100th battle, the Battle of Khanwa against Babur as a fable of the final defeat of Sanga in CE 1527. So many layers of lies have been woven around Khanwa that it has become almost impossible to decipher the truth. We have proved in the chapter on Sanga in this book that Khanwa was a victory for Sanga, according to Mewar annals.

While conveniently shoving the *saka-jauhars* committed by Rajputs and Hindus of Rajasthan under the carpet, the decisive victory of Pratap at Dewair finds absolutely no mention in India's post-Independence history. All we hear of is the hotchpotch around the Battle of Haldighati and the lies spread around it. It is a mark of the success of the Leftist-*jihadi* cabal that Hindu society, because of its intellectual sloth and lack of aggressive scholarliness, has allowed the mutilation of facts around the life and struggles of the greatest Hindu king of medieval India, Maharana Pratap Singh of Mewar.

Pratap's son, the mighty Amar Singh fought seventeen battles against the mightiest force on the globe at that time and won all of them. Yet the lie that 'Rajputs lost all battles' continues to be parroted.

Maharana Raj Singh defeated Aurangzeb and even captured him twice, but this fact doesn't suit *jihadi* narrative and hence, Raj Singh himself has been erased from the collective consciousness of Hindus. Like Mewar, the glorious victories of Jats of Sindh, Lalitaditya, Chandelas, Gurjar Pratiharas, the Vijayanagara Empire, Kakatiyas, Ahoms, Marathas, etc., were also erased and only the victories of the Islamic invaders trumpeted as some sort of unilateral walkover over Hindu kings.

Even a cursory look at the records and annals of each princely state will reveal the truth and demolish this lie of Islamic victory over Hindus.

Rajputs put Their Women to Fire

This is the vilest and the nastiest allegation put against the singular glory of Rajputs.

Jauhar was an act of supreme sacrifice of Hindu women in refusing to accept Islamic debauchery. Honour was not for barter. That message was vehemently conveyed by Rajput princesses leading the march to jump into funeral pyres with their children.

Can we imagine the impact of this one act on Islamic marauders themselves? While Islam spread into the Middle East and northern Africa in a matter of decades, no race, or people, be it Persians, Byzantines, Egyptians, Mesopotamians, could even conceive of *jauhar*. These people simply capitulated. Men were killed or converted, and women and children taken as sex slaves.

It was only the Rajput women who devised the ultimate tool of *jauhar* to prevent Islam's entry into the Indian subcontinent.

Women of all communities of Hindus joined the Rajput ladies in *jauhar*, but it was the resolve of the glorious Rajput foremothers of ours, that led the way.

In one move, the message that Hindu women led by Rajput princesses would burn themselves to ashes instead of becoming their sex slaves was conveyed to the Islamic marauders.

In one move, the singeing skin, shrieking children, rising embers and smoke from the pyres of *jauhar* galvanised the Hindu masses of this nation to never surrender, never yield to subjugation.

Hindu women raised the cost of surrender to unimaginable heights by this supreme sacrifice.

The parting kisses and hugs of their beloved, filled the Hindu men with such fortitude that one Hindu slaughtered four *yavanas* on an average when *saka* was to begin. *Jauhar* ensured Hindu resistance would go on forever because the ultimate cost of honour and safety had already been paid by the Hindu society. There was no looking back from the ashes of their loved and respected ones for Hindu men.

The quantum of a man's attachment to his womenfolk is immeasurable.

It is a deep, *pranic* bond which surpasses all levels of sensitivities.

A man, whose mother, daughter, sister or wife is forced to have sex with an outsider, gets reduced to a corpse. He becomes soulless. Such a man might appear to be alive, but within himself, he dies a thousand deaths.

Our glorious foremothers freed their men from this dishonor by giving themselves to the purity of fire.

Our mothers burnt themselves alive to extinguish all possibilities of their sexual exploitation by barbarians of the Arabian desert.

Hindus fought with a liberated being once they knew the fate of their women.

All fear, doubt and anxiety had evaporated with the ambers of *jauhar*.

As a society, our confidence was never shattered because we knew our women were not carrying the seeds of these animals.

Jauhar was not a momentary thing; it was a *kaaljayi* (timeless) phenomenon that transcended time, as the mere mention of *jauhar* inspires a resolve in Hindus even today after centuries of its happening—a resolve to fight and resist Islamic expansionism.

We can only extrapolate on how *jauhar* was critical for Hindu resistance to Islam in the subcontinent. To give *jauhar* a twist and an angle of Rajput defeat and surrender is definitely a product of an evil mind.

To say that *jauhar* implied the inability of Rajputs and Hindu men to protect their women is to spit on the memory of these amazing people.

To suggest that Hindu women should have surrendered and lived as sex slaves instead of choosing death by self-immolation amounts to putting our families up for sale at the altar of violence and goonism.

Jauhar was not a case of surrender or forsaking of their womenfolk and children by Hindu men of Mewar and Rajasthan.

It was the resolute defiance to a sex-obsessed invader when Hindu women chose honour above life.

Which people on this globe prefer death to barter their freedom to a barbaric invader except for the Hindus?

Which people would devise this unique form of denial to their body and spirit to an invader who was unrelenting in his attacks, except for the Hindus?

Which people would deny the Islamic barbarians the joy of touching even their dead bodies by burning themselves alive, except the Hindus?

To mock this kind of supreme sacrifice of life at the altar of freedom and honour as a meek surrender of Rajputs and to belittle this amazing feat of Hindus as a defeatist step is an *adharmic* understanding of life and deserves to be rejected vehemently.

Jauhar was a terrific expression of love.

Epression of unfathomable love for one's spouse, *Dharma*

and nation. Out of this love, the Hindu women chose to immolate themselves than to sleep with the murderers of their husbands, brothers and sons.

In this labour of love, our great foremothers walked this path to protect their *sateetva,* their freedom and their honour.

Hindus should preserve the memory of these great ancestors with pride and gratitude, so that we too can raise ourselves to these highest ideals of human existence.

Rajputs were Opium Addicts and Drunkards

Nothing can be more demeaning than this allegation on the glorious Rajputs of Rajasthan.

Firstly, let us imagine a Jaimal Mertiya or Patta Choondawat or even any ordinary Rajput fighter preparing to set a funeral pyre of his beloved, his children and his mother. What sends a chill down our spine on mere contemplation, was actually done physically by thousands of Hindus led by Rajputs when *saka-jauhars* were committed.

For a few moments, can we transpose our consciousness to that moment when Rajput men would light the pyres of their families and then witness them being burnt alive in front of their eyes? Even the most stone-hearted man cannot undergo this ordeal without losing his mind. The Rajputs gave *amal* to each other in betel leaves as a mark of the parting gift before opening the gates of their forts and setting out for their last stand against the barbarians.

Opium was used by warriors to numb themselves physically and psychologically when confronted by a foe who would stop at nothing short of total annihilation of their families and *dharma*. Nowhere in written history do we find any example of opium consumption—otherwise a social evil—when warriors would en masse consume morphine without compromising their consciousness and conduct.

The second reason for opium consumption in warriors of Rajasthan was the analgesic effect of morphine. Almost all Hindu warriors suffered major and minor injuries during countless conflicts with *mlechchas* and even during training for combat and horse riding.

The great Maharana Sanga had no less than eighty-four wounds on his body as a consequence of more than 100 battles he fought around Mewar.

Many warriors had amputated fingers and limbs which resulted in 'phantom limb' pains to these warriors. Opium was the only respite for these traumatised soldiers. Opium's use was purely medicinal or celebratory in marriages in Rajasthan and to castigate such an innocuous practice as addiction and to mock the practice is not only insensitive but downright evil in all its designs and implications.

Rajputs Kept Fighting Each Other

That Hindus didn't fight Islamists unitedly is another hideous lie that has been peddled by Hindus and Hindu sympathisers themselves.

On a closer look, this is not only erroneous but also demonstrates a gross lack of scholarliness on behalf of Hindu intelligentsia. The most maligned people on this issue are the Rajputs of Jaipur and the writer has dealt with this issue in detail in another chapter.

Hindu Dharma is presently engaged in an existential, civilisational conflict with the two expansive Abrahamic faiths who leave no opportunity to malign Hinduism and are converting Hindus on an industrial scale.

Let's briefly talk about the sects within the two faiths and the consequences of the incessant war between these sects.

While Muslims have dozens of sects, Christians have hundreds of them. Christians have two major sects namely Catholic and Protestants.

Catholics consider the Pope sitting in Rome as supreme, while Protestants don't.

Millions following both the sects have slain and harassed each other for centuries. Crores of Christians killed each other in the Second world war, from 1939-1945 for one mad man's lust for power and dominance. Similarly, Muslims have various sects who even call each other infidel, but majorly, Shia and Sunni conflict has gulped millions of human lives as recently as the Iran-Iraq war.

More than 5 lac Muslims have been killed in Shia-Sunni conflict in Syria in the last 10 years. In stark contrast, Hindus never killed each other for a variance of belief in thousands of years of their existence. When even two blood brothers find it difficult to coexist, expecting 100 crore Hindus to live without frictions is not only Utopian but counter-productive to the ethos of a nation. Let a thousand ideas bloom, but violence can never be a citizen's right. The power to unleash violence must only and only rest with the state.

Hindus have followed this ideal when our Abrahmaic friends were living in caves. Insipte of all the differences of languages-regions - food habits, ethnicities, etc., crores of Hindus live together as a *"Hindu Rashtra."*

राष्ट्र रक्षक
महाराणा सांगा 13 मार्च, 1527 ई.
को खानवा पहुंचे। राणा की सेना में
राजा हसन खां मेवाती(अलवर),
भारमल(ईडर),वीरमदेव,रतनसिंह
(मेड़ता),मेदिनीराय(चंदेरी),राव गांगा
(मारवाड़),रावल उदयसिंह(डूंगरपुर),
रावत रतनसिंह चूण्डावत(सलूम्बर),
नर्बद हाडा और वीर सिंह(बूंदी),रावत
जोगा(कानोड़),पृथ्वीराज(आमेर),
चन्द्रभान चौहान(मैनपुरी),मानिक चन्द्र
चौहान(राजौर–एटा), झाला अज्जा
और झाला सज्जा(बड़ी सादड़ी),
गोकुलदास परमार(बिजोलिया),
रायमल राठौड़(जोधपुर),रावत बाघसिंह
(देवलिया),कुंवर कल्याणमल(बीकानेर),
शत्रुदेव(गागरोन) मोहम्मद लोदी,राजा
ब्रह्मदेव,राय दिलीप,रामदास सोनगरा आदि
अपनी सेना लेकर राणा सांगा के साथ थे।

An inscription at the Khanwa Memorial

There is dissonance but through debate discussions-elections and constructive criticism, society deals with them and stays functional. A hundred crore Hindus can't be a monolith of ideas and practises.

Still Sanatan Dharma provides humanity with a peaceful and progressive model, hence Hinduism should be saved at any cost. The Leftists and pseudo liberal intellectuals should not preach Hindus on tolerance and coexistence. Hindus have never slaughtered each other over imaginary beliefs and spurious principles. Our glorious forefathers knew very well that we had to be united in order to oppose the Islamic Marauders.

Suffice it to say here that power struggle is a game played in all societies ruthlessly and since the Rajputs were the ruling class in most of the northern and western parts of the subcontinent, there were numerous rivalries amongst the various Rajput houses passed on from generation to generation.

One of the most important battles of medieval India was fought between Maharana Sanga and Babur in Khanwa in CE 1527. All Rajputs of Rajasthan and central India fought together in that bloody battle that lasted a full day. In spite of all dirty tactics used by Babur, Hindus managed to defeat Babur's army because wave after wave, Rajputs kept fighting the reverses and dying valiantly to defeat the Mughal.

Some battles were lost to Islamists because the latter always hit below the belt while Hindus kept fighting with a moral code of warriors.

We get innumerable examples of Hindu kings capturing the Islamic rulers and setting them free after extracting heavy penalties. Muslims never did this with Hindu kings, though.

Raja Dahir, Prithviraj Chauhan, Raja Hemchandra were beheaded by Qasim, Ghori and Akbar, respectively.

While the women and families of Islamic kings were never even touched by Hindu kings, Hindu kings had to send their women and family in safety to faraway places. This was not only bothersome but needed diversion of already depleted numbers of the army for the same.

Hindus did not know how to respond to the unchivalrous tactics of the barbarians and were cheated.

How many times were cows or oxen used by Islamists to blunt an offensive by Hindus since these animals are sacred to Hindus?

Hindus were facing a very uneven conflict with an army of rapists and murderers with absent moral compass and simply did not have that hatred for their enemies needed to destroy them.

But to say that Hindus were never united in their opposition to Islamic imperialists is a white lie created to devalue the glorious resistance of Hindus.

How did we manage to defeat the so-called Delhi Sultanate

rulers consistently for 300 years if we were not united?

Bappa Rawal formed a Hindu confederation against Arab invaders with the Gurjar Pratiharas and Parmars and conclusively pushed the Arabs back to Iran and this Hindu federation kept the Arabs at bay for the next 500 years. If we look at the names of the Rajputs who were fighting for Mewar, we see Rathores, Chauhans, Parmars, Tomars, Kachchawas, Solankis, etc., aligning with Mewar and each other to take on the *mlechchas*.

All these subcastes of Rajputs hailed from different principalities of northern and western India. Though the Sisodias were the rulers of Mewar, all Rajputs like Rathores, Jhalas, Chauhans, Hadas, Kachchawas, Kheenchis, Songaras, Gaurs, Padihars, etc., joined the Sisodias to fight the invaders from the desert. The union of Rajputs was premised on a collective understanding that only a united Hindu response could stall the march of the predators from the west, unlike the soldiers of Islam, who were united only because they had been assured a share in the loot of Hindu wealth and Hindu women.

At Haldighati, the chief of cavalry of Pratap was a Brahmin named Poona Joshi. The great Bhama Shah was an Oswal Jain. Bhils were a separate contingent under their king, Rana Punja.

All *jatis* stood by Pratap in fighting the invader of Mewar.

It was an alliance of *dharmics* against the brotherhood of bandits.

The most glaring example of the *dharmic* alliance was the treaty between the Sisodias of Mewar and the Rathores of Marwar when both major clans came together to defend the Srinathji temple at Sihad in the present-day Nathdwara. Aurangzeb was comprehensively defeated by the alliance in CE 1679-80 and had to run to Ajmer to save himself from the wrath of Rajputs.

To say that Hindus, particularly Rajputs, were never united in their wars is not only erroneous but mischievous in design.

And the design is to demean and belittle the supreme sacrifices of Hindus in stymieing the cruelest war machine mankind has ever known.

Of course, the Rajputs were not monoliths of a particular

clan when they fought the Islamic zealots, but like anywhere else, there were conflicting interests in the succession to a throne or rival claims on territories, but faced by a common enemy, Rajputs in particular, and Hindus in general, put up a united front against Islamists and succeeded in defeating them.

All 36 castes of Hindus like Bhils, Meenas, Gurjars, Raigars, Valmikis, Brahmins, Charans, Jats, Yadavs, and many more like them kept fighting the Islamic imperialists.

Every single war of succession within Islamic rulers happened with a blood bath amongst brothers and parents. But the propaganda is that Hindus fought each other.

To say that Hindus, especially Rajputs were not united in fighting Muslim invaders is not only erroneous, but mischievous too. Leftists-Jehadi historians have spread this canard to humiliate and belittle the sacrifices and struggle of Hindus against the cruellest invaders mankind has ever known.

It is upto the Hindus of this globe to break out of ths deathly spell cast upon us by the Leftists.

The warriors of Bharatvarsha especially Rajputs, were the bravest, most intelligent, and utterly selfless people.

Unmindful of the pleasures and pains of sensual pleasures, fixed in *Titiksha,* (indifference to sensual inputs) these lions kept fighting Islamists ceaselessly.

Our freedom, our opulence, our very existence is a blessing of these *Mahapurushas.*

When You can't Beat Them, Mock Them, Divide Them

It isn't that the Leftists and *jihadis* are totally unaware of the valour and sacrifices of the martial communities of Hindus. In fact, they are more aware and alarmed by the fighters of Hinduism than Hindus themselves. Surely, the pseudo-liberal cabal of our nation saw the resolve of Hindus to fight for their *dharma* till the last bullet and the last man.

Hence, they decided to weaken hindus from within by alienating the martial communities from mainstream Hinduism.

Besides erasing the glorious saga of its muscular resistance to Islam and inventing white lies around the valour of Muslims, they used a very potent weapon to demoralise our martial communities—mockery. Gullible Hindus themselves participated in this exercise demeaning the sacrifices of our fighters. The most obvious community to bear the brunt of this mockery is our Sikh *sahodaras* (brethren), but this trick has been also used on Jats, Gujjars and Rajputs to ridicule them for the very trait that was their crowning glory.

Have we Hindus ever paused for a moment to realise as to what impact would it have on a Sikh child to be the butt of all jokes in his class just for bearing *kesh* (hair), *pagdi* (turban) and *kada* (iron bracelet worn on the wrist)?

We have become so depleted in our intellect bordering cruelty that we Hindus, as a society have participated in this bullying of our own Sikh children!

Do we ever pause and ponder upon the trauma we cause to a child when we mock his identity incessantly?

Jat jokes and Rajput jokes have similarly found a place in the colloquial discourse, and we don't even realise how we are damaging the psyche of our own people.

Mockery is a very evil thing, but more evil is if a child has to face it.

During the time of Aurangzeb and up to the reign of Maharaja Ranjit Singh, Punjab was a playground of bitter rivalry between Muslims on one side and Hindus-Sikhs on the other. Muslims are known to take away women and children of Hindus and Sikhs to be used as sex slaves or barter them for gold. At 12 o'clock midnight, when the enemy camp was in deep sleep, the Sikh groups would make a surprise attack on the campus where the women and children were being kept in chains.

How we ourselves have maligned this glorious tradition of Sikhs by weaving jokes around it and mocking our Sikh saviours as 'the gong has struck 12, they have gone bonkers'.

Can there be a bigger example of our stupidity! A tradition that should have been cherished, is reduced to this level!

Similarly, Rajputs and Jats are mocked for being unsmart in chivalry.

The conduct of the rich and educated Hindus towards our Dalit Sahodaras has been no less demeaning.

When did that unfortunate day dawn that we started calling our own brothers and sisters in faith as 'untouchables'?

We haven't even bothered to enquire about the roots of our Dalit Sahodaras. Two stories are being shared to highlight the greatness of our Dalit ancestors and our stupidity of belittling them.

Khateeks, who are Hindu butchers, are supposed to trace their origins in Brahmins who used to do animal sacrifice in temples. The identification of Brahmins with animal sacrifice and meat eating led to gradual drifting away of these Brahmins from the mainstream Hinduism and thus Khateeks became an entirely new *jaati*. The Khateeks fought the Islamists throughout their existence and continue to do so even today.

Second case is of Valmikis. They are believed to be Kshatriyas who were forced to do menial jobs by Muslim rulers and out of shame, they broke their sacred *janeus*. An act of such supreme sacrifice by our glorious ancestors should have been honoured, but unfortunately, we forgot them.

It must also be noted that it was our Valmiki ancestors who started raising pigs and consume pork in daily life to keep away Muslim invaders. A Muslim fears and hates nothing more than a pig or anything remotely related to a pig. Pig farming was such an innovative and effective means of keeping away Muslim invaders that we can only look back on our ancestors with awe and respect.

But with passage of time, all these sacrifices of our great ancestors were forgotten and our own brothers were pushed down the social ladder, physically and economically.

No community on this earth is as ungrateful as Hindus in actively contributing in instilling a massive inferiority complex in our martial races.

The results are there for all of us to see.

People respond differently to insults.

Most will internalise it and move on. Some will rebel. Others will resort to alcohol, like the Rajputs and our Dalit *sahodaras*. A vast number will go into the victimhood mode. Victimhood is the worst state of mind. A victim always blames others for his plight and justifies every wrongdoing on the basis of some injustice of the past. Victimhood is the root of all evil on this earth .

It is because we Hindus have never introspected about the psychological impact of mockery and arrogance that we are at loss to understand why our martial communities are a pale shadow of what their ancestors were.

Many Sikhs have either given up Sikh traditions or become belligerent, engulfed in a deep hatred for non-Sikh Hindus. Rajputs have completely internalised and are missing from action on the national regional stages, or even as a caste group. Many Rajput boys have become rowdy students in universities and almost the entire community is in disarray. The Gurjars and the Jats who fought the Islamic murderers even without organised leadership have been denied their proper due in this beautiful saga of Hindu resistance. The Dalit Sahodaras have taken to alcohol and victimhood narrative.

It was a Leftist-*jihadi* plot that should never have been yielded to by Hindu intelligentsia and leadership.

It has damaged us immensely, but now the time has come to immediately halt this self-damage of mocking our own defence system of some very amazing and valiant people. Nearby 4-5 crore Rajputs cannot be allowed to simply drift away from the Hindu masses due to Leftist propaganda. A people who gave up everything to protect us from a gang of rapists and predators.

Similarly, crores of Jats, Gurjars, Sikhs our Dalit *sahodaras*, Yadavs, Kurmis, Bhils and dozens of Hindu *jatis* who kept fighting for *dharma* need to be honoured and cherished for the sacrifices of their valorous ancestors. These martial *jaatis* are the carriers of the age old *sanskaras* of our ancestors in their genes.

They are modern bearers of *dharma* and if beckoned, these sons of *dharma* will respond with the same loyalty and ferocity as their glorious ancestors. The least we can do is to show our gratitude to these sung and unsung brave hearts.

Human Immunodeficiency Virus (HIV) is a pathogen that attacks the T cells in the human body. T cells are our main defence against deadly pathogens.

The Leftist-*jihadi* complex is the virus that has infected Hindu society and rendered our martial communities paralysed and ineffective.

The complete introversion and aloofness of Rajputs, Sikhs, Dalit *sahodaras*, Bhils and other martial communities is a glaring example of the success of this HIV virus. Only this time, we will conflate HIV to Hindu Immunodeficiency Virus.

Lies have consequences.

Horrible consequences that are borne majorly by the women, children and the weak of the society.

Hindu society was always based on one eternal principle, 'सत्यमेव जयते, नानृतम्। तदा किं विवादेन्!' Meaning that 'Truth alone triumphs, nothing else. What is there to debate?'

If in this era of communication, we can dispassionately establish the truth of the Rajputs, Sikhs, Jats, Marathas, Kakatiyas, Ahoms and other innumerable greats of our great nation and decimate the lies woven around our glorious resistance to Islam for 1,400 years, we would have rebuilt our path to recovery as the most valuable, oldest, living civilisation on this globe.

This civilisational war with Abrahamic faiths isn't over yet. Islamic imperialism has merely changed its methods but persists in its designs.

In fact, it is more dangerous now, with the Left-liberal forces providing the smoke screen to its real intentions: Islamisation of the subcontinent. This is possibly our last chance to correct our history, re-establish the ancient traditions of Hindu valour and reach out with gratitude and respect to our warrior communities so that they can be galvanised to action to completely uproot the Hindu Immunodeficiency Virus forever from our motherland.

The Hindu society has to introspect and realign its forces in this new kind of conflict which has been thrust upon it. All castes (*jaatis*) have to start talking to each other, instead of talking at each other.

When Islamic invaders ravaged Mewar, it was a united Mewar that fought and defeated these barbarians. That is the singular lesson for all Hindus to learn from this glorious saga. We may have thousand differences with each other, but when an external enemy threatened us, we forgot those differences and close ranks to resist that enemy.

The Brahmins have to give up their victimhood and lead the Hindus from the front like the priest, Bhag Chand Paliwal who killed himself to prevent a fight between Pratap and his brother Shakti Singh.

The Brahmins who are the brain of the Hindu society must prepare themselves for *tapasya* (austere penance) to devise ways and means to fight the *vidharmis* who have infiltrated our glorious nation.

The martial communities have to break the spell of slumber and inaction and rise like a Phoenix from the ashes of time to defend the Hindu *samaj* from the all-round attack it is facing.

The martial communities who are the reservoirs of passion and honour of Hindu society must rekindle that fire of *'Kshatriya dharma'* and like Pratap and Hammir, lead the Hindu society to a new state of fearlessness and sacrifice for *dharma*.

The mercantile class, the Vaishyas have to give up myopia and show large-heartedness like Bhama Shah and Tara Shah to not only open their coffers but actually stand and fight for *dharma*.

The wealth creators of Hindu society must use all their acumen to fill the lifelines of *dharma* with an unending supply of resources for our warriors to fight this civilisational struggle.

The Shudras, the Dalits, who I choose to refer to as *sahodaras*, are the muscle of the Hindu body and all the intellect of Brahmins, passion of Kshatriyas and the wealth of the Vaishyas has to flow to the *sahodaras* to activate the muscular response to the continuous onslaught on our *dharma*. The *sahodaras* like the Bhils of Mewar have to form one last ring of defence around *dharma* like they did for Pratap to fortify Mewar and eventually annihilate the enemies of *dharma*.

Fuelled by the support of all *varnas* and *jatis*, our Dalit *sahodaras* have to come out of their under-confidence and claim the leadership and resurgence of the Hindu society.

Defeat is no longer an option for Hindus.

Defeat this time will not allow us for a tactical retreat.

We have run out of places to retreat to.
A defeat for Hindus this time will mean
total annihilation of Sanatan Dharma.
That simply cannot be allowed to happen.

Hence, a spirituo-politico-economic awakening of Hindus is a matter of life and death, not only for Hindus but for the very survival of this little globe of ours.

The Bourgeois and the Samurai

It would be prudent to end this book by sharing the writings of the greatest *mahayogi* of modern times—Sri Aurobindo.

Mahayogi Sri Aurobindo

He brilliantly underlines the follies of the Hindu upper and middle class and thus helps us decipher the decay set into our social fibre today. Through this understanding only, he prescribes the path to recovery as well.

Comparing the fortunes of Japan and Bharat, which are both ancient civilisations and faced external enemies, he goes on to analyse how Japan became a world power and Bharat remains a wretched, Third World country struggling with poverty, corruption and abject moral decay.

He ponders on a fundamental question: Why has Japan so admirably transformed herself, and why has the attempt at transformation in India been such a failure[160]?

Sri Aurobindo writes: *"The solution of problems of this kind has to be sought not in abstractions, not in machinery, but in men. It is the spirit in man which moulds his fate; it is the spirit of a nation that determines its history.*

"Japan remained faithful to her ancient spirit, the spirit of the Samurai.

"In Bharat, the mass of the nation has remained dormant;

160. https://satyameva.org/the-bourgeois-and-the-samurai/

but in the upper strata, a new type has been evolved to serve the necessities of foreign rule. This type is the bourgeois.

"Who is the bourgeois?

"The bourgeois is the average contented middle-class citizen. He is a man of facile sentiments and skin-deep personality; generally 'enlightened' but not inconveniently illuminated.

"In love with his life, his ease and above all things of his comforts, he prescribes the secure maintenance of these precious possessions as the first indispensable condition of all action in politics and society; whatever tends to disturb or destroy them, he condemns as foolish, harebrained, dangerous, or fanatical and is ready to repress by any means in his power.

"In the conduct of public movements, he has an exaggerated worship for external order, moderation and decorum and hates over-earnestness and over-strenuousness.

"He has ideals and likes to talk of justice, liberty, reform, enlightenment and all similar abstractions. The bourgeois is the man of good sense and enlightenment, the man of moderation, the man of peace and orderliness, the man in every way 'respectable,' who is the mainstay of all well-ordered societies.

"For great adventures, tremendous enterprises, lofty achievements, the storm and stress of mighty and eventful periods in national activity, he is unfit. These things are for the heroes, the martyrs, the criminals, the enthusiasts, the degenerates, geniuses, the men of exaggerated virtue, exaggerated ability, exaggerated ideas. He enjoys the fruit of their work when it is done, but while it is being done, he opposes and hinders more often than helps.

"A little art, a little poetry, a little religion, a little scholarship, a little philosophy, all these are excellent ingredients in life and give an air of decorous refinement to his surroundings. They must not be carried too far or interfere with the great object of life which is to earn money, clothe and feed one's family, educate one's sons to the high pitch of the B.A. degree or the respectable eminence of the M.A., marry one's daughters decently, rank high in service or the professions, stand well in the eye of general opinion and live and die decorously, creditably and respectably."

Doesn't this brilliant description by Sri Aurobindo sum up

the entire schizophrenia of the Hindu society?

Our education and tilting towards Western civilisation makes us bourgeois while something within us keeps telling us that we are fierce and formidable Samurais, the Kshatriyas.

Sri Aurobindo writes further,

"Bourgeois may give stability to a society; it cannot reform or revolutionise it.

"Bourgeois may make the politics of a nation safe, decorous and reputable. It cannot make that nation great or free.

"Bharat was an amalgam of the highest ideals man's nature could achieve and use for the society.

"The Brahmin who devoted himself to poverty and crushed every desire in the wholehearted, selfless pursuit of knowledge and self-discipline;

the Kshatriya who, hurling his life joyously into the shock of chivalrous battle; held life, wife, children, possessions, ease, happiness as mere dust in comparison with honour and the Kshatriya dharma, the preservation of self-respect, the protection of the weak, the noble fulfilment of princely duty;

the Vaishya, who toiling all his life to amass riches, poured them out as soon as amassed in self-forgetting philanthropy, holding himself the mere steward and not the possessor of his wealth;

the Shudra who gave himself up loyally to humble service, faithfully devoting his life to his dharma, however low, in preference to self-advancement and ambition; these were the social ideals of the age.

"The bourgeois came up as a class of their own in independent Bharat and from sheer inanition, from want of light, room and air, the Kshatriya died out of the soil which had first produced him and the bourgeois took his place. But if room was none for the soldier and the statesman, little could be found for the Brahmin, the sage, or the sannyasin.

Independent Bharat had no need for scholars, it wanted clerks."

The bourgeois infected every sphere of Hindu life;

he was speaking lofty lies as slogans to the nation as a politician, teaching lies of secularism and socialism to unsuspecting students as a professor in universities;

spreading falsehood of Ganga-Jamuna *tehzeeb* through Bollywood;

preserving the deathly status quo via the bureaucracy;

inventing and sustaining historical lies like Delhi sultanate and Mughal Empire;

pursuing falsehoods of weekend theme parties and foreign vacations premised on the spurious freedom from the British, while the real task of character building and nation building was completely forgotten.

The bourgeois even infected two sacred institutions of our great *dharma*, the military and the Hindu *ashrams* and *Mathas*.

The Hindu and Sikh military man is devoid of the '*shatru bodh*' (enemy consciousness) even as he valiantly performs his duty because our *dharmacharyas* and *mathadheeshas* have failed to identify, comprehend and articulate the actual enemy of our civilisation—the *jihadi* and the missionary.

So, we continue fighting Pakistan, without realising that we are not fighting a nation state, but an idea. An idea of pan-Islamism, aiming at takeover of the Vedic *bhoomi* of ours, through *ghazwa-e-Hind* (assault on Hindustan).

The Hindu *sadhus* have thus been reduced to moral science teachers instead of carriers of the nectar of Vedantic wisdom.

This spiritual bankruptcy of our *acharyas* and teachers has been the single biggest reason of the existential predicament Hindus find themselves in.

Politics saw mediocre minds like Mohandas Gandhi, JL Nehru and his coterie sitting over a mindless and botched up partition of this glorious nation. A *madrasa*-educated Abul Kalam Azad became the first Education Minister of this nation. No questions asked about the merit or competence of a person without any formal education holding a post as crucial as Education Minister. The history taught in this nation is an edifice of slavery built on stinking lies that only evoke repulsion and anger in the reader.

And this slaughter of our history continued in full worldview as five Muslims became Education Ministers while the bourgeois looked on indifferently.

From Maulana Azad to Humayun Kabir, Mohammad Chagla, Fakhruddin Ali Ahmed and Nurul Hassan controlled the Education Ministry and played havoc with our history.

This book has raised the issue of inactivity and mediocrity of Hindu intellectual leadership in almost every chapter.

Here too, the bourgeois gave his due, for peace, comfort and safety are the very breath of his nostrils. But he gravitates to a peace for whose preservation he is not called on to wear armour and wield the sword; a comfort he has not to purchase by the discomfort of standing sentinel over his liberties. The bourgeois intelligentsia simply allowed this murder of Hindu ethos and rolled over under Islamic propaganda.

We read and thought, but did not live what we read and thought. Our experiences were mere mental imaginations.

So, our existence grew ever more artificial and unreal. The fighter and the thinker in us dwindled as the bourgeois flourished and grew.

The bourgeois delights in convention, because truth is too hard a taskmaster and makes too severe a demand on character, energy and intellect.

Thus, *Bhagwad Gita* which demands extreme action from each of us was relegated to the background and spurious memes flood our social media, spreading lies of peace and coexistence with *adharma*.

Bourgeois craves superficiality because to attain depth requires time and energy, which would have to be unprofitably diverted from his chief business of making his individual way in the world.

Thus, all our interactions have this weird platonic feel about them. Our professional and personal relationships lack the roots needed to nourish a healthy society.

Thus, the deracinated bourgeois created by Western education is the biggest facilitator of *jihadis* and missionaries gnawing at our nation.

To this extent, the fact that Western education could not percolate to a vast mass of Hindus has become a blessing in disguise. For among the rural and semi-urban Hindus, we still find the remnants of the Kshatriya who, given the right leadership, will not hesitate to die and kill for *dharma*, like a true soldier. A people true to itself, a race that hopes to live, will not comfort itself and sap its manhood by the opiate of empty formulas and specious falsehoods; it will rather prefer eternal suffering and disaster.

For in truth, as our old thinkers used to insist, the whole universe stands; truth is the root and condition of life and to believe a lie, to live in a lie, is to deliver oneself to disease and death.

The teaching that peace and security are more important and vital to man than liberty is a lie. Bourgeois lives this lie.

Hence, he scuttles any remnant of resistance that the Kshatriya element of Hinduism puts to the Abrahamic onslaught on our *dharma*.

The doctrine, that social and commercial progress must precede political strength and liberty is another extremely dangerous lie; for a nation is no aggregate of separable functions, but a harmony of functions, of which government and political arrangement is the oldest, most central and most vital and determines the others.

Without a just political system, impartial policing and a functioning judiciary, along with an army of honourable men manning government institutions, all social and economic progress will crumble like a pack of cards.

Bourgeois are simply incapable of being those men of honour.

Fortunately for Hindus, the ancient traditions of some of our great *rishis* and sages have managed to survive this onslaught and great minds keep taking birth on this blessed land of ours to remind us of our real worth and place in this mysterious existence.

Referring to Swami Vivekananda, Sri Aurobindo writes,

"British rule in India has been a record success in history in the hypnosis of a nation. It persuaded us to live in death of the will and its activities, taking a series of hallucinations for real things and creating in ourselves the condition of morbid weakness the hypnotist desired, until the Master of a mightier hypnosis laid His finger on India's eyes and cried 'Awake'.

Then only the spell was broken, the slumbering mind realised itself and the dead soul lived again."

Swami Vivekananda infused confidence and vigour in the collapsing veins of the Hindu society just before the Leftist-Jehadi cabal started its stoat dance. Hindu samaj has to give up on the bourgeois and respond to Swami ji's clarion call.

Swami Vivekananda : The Yogi who revived Hinduism

For good or bad, it is the middle class that now leads in India, and whatever saving impulse comes to the nation, must come from the middle class. But for that to happen the middle class must, by a miracle be transfigured and lifted above itself; the natural breeding ground of the bourgeois, it must become the breeding ground of the Samurai.

It must cease in fact, to be a middle class and turn itself into an aristocracy—an aristocracy not of birth or landed possessions, not of intellect, not of wealth and commercial enterprise, but of character and action.

India must recover her faculty for self-sacrifice, courage and high aspiration.

We are the luckiest people on this globe who are the heirs of the most noble and glorious Kshatriya traditions.

Kshatriyas who looked into the eyes of death and did not blink.

Kshatriyas who suffered loss of life and limb joyously.

Kshatriyas who refused to be lulled into complacency by a sweet-talking Islamist.

Kshatriyas who fearlessly attacked and defended their women, land and gods.

Kshatriyas that are not a *jaati* but a trait to stand for truth and freedom.

Kshatriyas that struck fear in the heart of rapists and murderers attacking our motherland.

Kshatriyas that drank from the cup of loyalty even as they were torn to shreds.

Kshatriyas who were living embodiments of valour and sacrifice.

Kshatriyas who were preservers of fragile beauty and sublime art.

Chatrapati Shivaji Maharaj : The greatest Hindu warrior ever

There is only one way for Hindus to survive, as this crucial civilisational battle enters its most critical and final phase—

It is the death of the bourgeois.

It is the rebirth of the Samurai, the *Kshatriyas*.

The entire Hindu society has to unite and rise as *Kshatriyas* against the demons of antagonistic faiths and the Leftist ideology to break them physically, economically and morally. Time has passed on the baton of Hindu revival to our generation. This golden opportunity is for us to destroy the murderous ideology that had devoured our ancestors for 1,400 years now. It has fallen upon our shoulders to destroy the very seed of this darkness from our glorious nation.

Let us imbibe the words of the greatest Maratha warrior Chhatraptai Shivaji Maharaj when he roared to his samants from his death bed:

"आम्ही जातो, आमचा काल झाला।
तूम्ही सप्तसिंधू यवनांच्या हातून मूक्त करा।
काशीचा श्री विश्वेश्वर सोडवा,
बाराजोतिर्लिंग या यवनांच्या हातून मूक्त करा।
हिंदवी स्वराज्यात आणात। चूकूर होऊ नका।"

Meaning,

"I leave, my time has come.

You have to liberate the seven seas from the yavanas. Liberate the lord of the world, Kashi and the twelve jyotirlingams from the clutches of yavanas.

Establish Hindwi swarajya anyhow.

Let there be no deviation."

Do we Hindus have it in us to carry out the final order of our great General, Chhatrapati Shivaji Maharaj?

This victory of Hinduism must be final.

We have to establish a just, fair and prosperous Hindu *rashtra* so that the demons of *jihad* do not ever rise again.

It is our honour and duty to finish the unfinished work of the Maharanas of Mewar. That would be the true *shraddhanjali* (homage) to the great Maharanas of Mewar who watch us from the *swarga* above.

Never forgive! Never forget!

□

Glossary

The glossary is an alphabetical listing of many of the key terms from the chapters, along with their meanings. The definitions listed in the glossary are the ones that apply to the way the words are used in this book.

Aatma—a Sanskrit word which means soul

Adharma—the Sanskrit antonym of *dharma*. It means that which is not in accord with the *dharma*

Agni—a Sanskrit word meaning fire and connotes the Fire god of Hinduism

Agyaatvaas—an incognito exile

Ahimsa—an ancient Indian principle of non-violence which applies to all living beings. It is a key virtue in the *dhārmic* religions: Hinduism, Buddhism, Jainism, and Sikhism

Akhaadaas—wrestling grounds, a place of wrestling

Amal—morphine

Araba—war tactic used by Babur

Asuras—a demon or devil

Bharatbhoomi—Hindustan, India

Bhakta—a devotee, one devoted to *bhakti-yoga* and one's deity

Brahmahatya—the Sanskrit term for 'the act of killing a Brahmin'

Brahmin—a Hindu of the highest caste traditionally assigned to priesthood.

Chandawal dastaa—the rear platoon

Chhand—the term is derived from the Sanskrit word *chhanda*, which refers to the study of the Vedic meter. However, in North India and Pakistan, *chhand* has come to mean a specific poetic style associated with the modern languages native to the region, such as Punjabi, Hindko, Dogri, Hindustani and Rajasthani

Darshan—witness, a Sanskrit term for 'viewing', also spelled *darshana*, in Indian philosophy and religion, particularly in Hinduism, the beholding of a deity, especially in image form, revered person or sacred object

Devapurushas—divine men

Dharma—in Sanskrit *dhr*-means 'to hold' or 'to support', *dharma* means 'right way of living' and 'path of rightness'

Dharmic—one who follows *dharma*

Dhimma—a non-Muslim in an Islamic state

Doha—a very old 'verse-format' of Indian poetry. It is an independent verse, a couplet, the meaning of which is complete in itself.

Dyodhi—a gatehouse or step in royal parlance

Farman—the Mughal constitutional term Farman refers to an irrevocable royal decree issued by the emperor

Ghulami—slavery, the system by which people are owned by other people as slaves

Harawal dastaa—the forward platoon or advance guard

Ishta Dev—a term used in Hinduism to denote a worshipper's favourite deity

Jagirdar—landlords of *jagirs*

Jagirs—a type of feudal land grant, a piece of land assigned to an individual for the purpose of collection of revenue in lieu of cash/salary was an age-old practice in the Delhi Sultanate period

Jal jauhar—voluntary submerging in water by women to avoid capture, enslavement and rape by invading army

Janeu—the sacred or sacrificial thread worn by the Hindu

Janmashtami—an annual Hindu festival that celebrates the birth of Krishna, the eighth *avatar* of Vishnu

Jauhar—a Hindu practice of mass self-immolation by women to avoid capture, enslavement and rape by invading army, when facing certain defeat during a war

Jaziya—a forced tax paid by non-Muslim population to their Muslim rulers in an Islamic state

Jihad—the doctrine of violent struggle in Islam

Jihadi—Islamic religious fighter

Kaaljayi—timeless, ageless

Kalma—the fundamental proclamation of Islamic scripture

Karma—the term refers to both the executed 'deed, work, action, act' and the 'object', 'intent'

Karmayoga—The principle of detachment from the fruits of one's labour. The corner stone of Bhagwad Geeta.

Kartavya karma—designated action

Khelats—male gowns worn in the medieval Mughal times

Khyatis—records by the local history keepers in Rajasthan

Kshaatra dharma—the duty or function of a Kshatriya

Kshatriyas—one of the four *varnas* (social orders) of Hindu society, associated with warriorhood. The Sanskrit term *kṣatriyaḥ* is used in the context of Vedic society wherein members were organised into four classes: Brahmin, Kshatriya, Vaishya and Shudra

Mahant—a religious superior, in particular the chief priest of a temple or the head of a monastery

Mahapurusha—great men

Mangal artis—morning congregational prayers in Hindu temples

Melas—fete, fair

Mlechchas—a Sanskrit term used by the Vedic people meaning 'ill-willed people' The word is a portmanteau of two Sanskrit words: '*Mal*' (negative/bad) and '*ichcha*' (intentions/desires) meaning one with bad intentions. Much as the ancient Greeks used *barbaros* to indicate the uncouth and incomprehensible speech of foreigners and then extended to their unfamiliar behaviour

Moksha—freedom from cycle of life and birth

Moorti—a general term for an image, statue or idol of a deity or mortal in Hindu culture. In Hindu temples, it is a symbolic icon. A *moorti* is itself not a God in Hinduism, but it is a shape, embodiment, or manifestation of a deity

Muni—an inspired holy person; an ascetic, hermit, or sage

Nagaadas—a huge drum which is played as a bass instrument in war-time

Navroza—nine days of debauchery by the Mughal emperor, Akbar

Niyama—recommended activities and habits for healthy living, spiritual enlightenment and liberated state of existence

Panchmakkars—also known as the five *m*, is the *tantric* term for the five transgressive substances used in a *tantric* practice. These are *madya* (alcohol), *māṃsa* (meat), *matsya* (fish), *mudrā* (gesture) and *maithuna* (sexual intercourse). Here in the context of this book, the author has used the term for Mulla, missionaries, Macaulayputras (offspring of Thomas Macaulay, the English administrator who introduced British colonial education in India), Marxists and the media

Pattals—a kind of plate which is used for eating in many rural areas in the country. It is made up of sal or banyan tree leaves and it is simply joined with small wooden

Poorvaja—someone born before; a word used to refer to ancestors.

Praana—the Sanskrit word for 'life force'; in yoga, Oriental medicine and martial arts, the term refers to a cosmic energy believed to come from the sun and connecting the elements of the universe.

Ragas—(in Indian classical music) each of the six basic musical modes which express different moods in certain characteristic progression, with more emphasis placed on some notes than others

Raghukul—the dynasty of Raghu/Rama

Raginis—(in Indian classical music) a derivative melody related to a *raga*

Raj Kavi—state poet laureate

Rajmata—the mother of the king

Rajpootni—a Rajput lady

Rajyabhishek—a coronation, the ceremony at which a king or queen is crowned

Raktabeej—ancient mythological demon. Every drop of his blood would give birth to another demon like him; used as a metaphor

Saadhak—related to the Sanskrit word *sādhu*, which is derived from the verb root *sādh*–'to accomplish'. As long as one has yet to reach the goal, they are *sādhaka* or *sādhak* or *saadhak*, while one who has reached the goal is called a *siddha*

Samant—a baron is a man who is a member of the nobility

Sadhu—derived from the verb root *sādh* or 'to accomplish'; a religious ascetic, mendicant or any holy person in Hinduism and Jainism who has renounced worldly life. They are sometimes alternatively referred to as yogi, *sannyasi* or *bairagi*

Saka jauhar—act of final war by men while women give themselves up to fire

Sahodaras—born from the same mother/womb

Samaj—society

Sampradaaya—a *sampradāya* (Sanskrit: संप्रदाय) can be translated as 'tradition', 'spiritual lineage', 'sect' or 'religious system'. It relates to a succession of masters and disciples to serve as a spiritual channel and provide a delicate network of relationships that lends stability to a religious identity

Sanatana—a Sanskrit word referring to eternal; having no beginning or end

Sanatan Dharma—a term that refers to the eternal truth of Hinduism. The roots of this phrase can be traced back to ancient Sanskrit literature as a kind of cosmic order. Sanatan denotes 'that which is without beginning or end' or 'everlasting'. *Dharma*, no direct translation into English, but comes from *dhri*, meaning 'to hold together or sustain'. *Dharma* is often interpreted as meaning 'natural law'. As such, the whole term, Sanatan Dharma can translate as 'the natural and eternal way to live'.

Sanatani—follower of Sanatan Dharma

Sanchit karma—the totality of all *karma* accumulated in an individual's past lives, including all good and bad actions. *Sanchit* is a Sanskrit word meaning 'piled up' or 'collected', while *karma* is from the root *kri*, meaning 'to act', so *sanchit karma* means 'actions that have accumulated'.

Sankalp—an intention formed by the heart and mind; a solemn vow, determination, or will or a one-pointed resolve to focus both psychologically and philosophically on a specific goal

Sati—the practice of wife burning herself on funeral pyre of husband

Sattva—pious energy

Sattvic ahamkara—ego or pride borne out of good deeds

Satyameva Jayate—Truth alone triumphs

Shaiva—follower of Shiva, the God of dissolution

Shaiva Tantra—a mystical form of practice by followers of Shiva

Sorthas—a popular meter (couplet) in medieval Hindi poetry

Shraddhanjali—tribute

Swarga—heaven, specifically the heaven presided over by the king of gods Indra, where virtuous souls reside before reincarnation

Taharrush—a practice in Islamic societies where a crowd of men sets upon, violently molests and rapes a woman

Tantric—follower of *tantra*

Tapa—a variety of austere spiritual practices

Tatva—element

Teeka—a coloured spot or mark, worn by Hindus, generally of sandalwood paste or vermilion on the forehead

Teekadaud—ancient practice in kingdom of Mewar to chase game for kilometres and then claim the land as their own by the kings of Mewar

Teerth—pilgrimage centre

Thaali—Utensil to eat food in

Thaanas—police stations

Thaanedaars—in charge of police station

Tilak—a coloured spot or mark worn by Hindus generally made of sandalwood paste or vermilion on the forehead

Titiksha—The capacity to be free of sensual inputs.

Tulughma—a war tactic by Mughals

Upanishads—ancient Hindu religious texts

Vaanprastha—The third quarter of Hindu social life when a couple starts disengaging from family and society

Vedic Bhoomi—a name for India

Veena—Musical instrument

Veergati—martyrdom

Vidharmi—one belonging to another religion

Vijaydashmi—auspicious day in the Hindu calendar. Historically, the day Shri Rama slew Ravana, the king of demons

Yamadoots—agents of death

Yogi—one who practises yoga

Zamindar—landlord

□

References and Bibliography

- *Veer Vinod* by Kaviraj Shyamaldas Dadhwadiya
- *Mewar ke Maharana aur Shahanshah Akbar* by Rajendra Shankar Bhatt
- *Udaipur Rajya ka Itihas* by Gaurishankar Heerchand Ojha
- *The Delhi Sultanate* by R.C. Majumdar
- *The Baburnama, Babur,* Translated by Wheelee M Thackstone
- *Annals and Antiquities of Rajasthan* by Colonel James Tod
- *Veer Shiromani Maharana Pratap* by Gaurishankar Heerchand Ojha
- *Heroic Hindu resistance to Muslim Invaders* by Sitaram Goel
- *Maharana Pratap aur Solahveen Shatabdi ka Mewar* by Sajjan Singh Ranawat & Prof. K.S. Gupta
- *Amarkavyam* by Ranchod Bhatt Tailang
- *Rajprashasti* by Ranchod Bhatt Tailang
- *War Strategy of Maharana Pratap* by Prof. L.P. Mathur
- *Indian resistance to Muslim invaders upto 1206 AD* by Dr. Ram Gopal Mishra
- *Maharana Raj Singh aur Aurangzeb* by Rajendra Shankar Bhatt
- *Vansh Bhaskar* by Surl Mal Misran
- *Six Golden Pages in the Histroy of Bharat* : V.D. Savarkar, Translated by Vaishali Borker
- *Maharana Pratap* by Bhawan Singh Rana
- Storia da Mogur, History of the Moghul Dynasty in India: From its Foundation by Timurlane in the Year 1399 to the Accession of Aurangzeb in the Year 1657
- *About Akbar* by Niccolao Mannucci
- *The Navroz Incident* by Suranya Sengupta
- *Bikaner Museum*
- *Jaipur Museum*
- *Saffron Swords* by Manushi Sinha
- *Eminent historians* by Arun Shourie
- *Islamic Jehad: A Legacy of Forced Conversion, Imperialism and Slavery* by M.A. Khan
- *Saltanat kaal mein Hindu pratirodh* by Ashok Kumar Singh
- *Muntakhab-ut-Tawarikh* by Abd al-Qadir Badayuni
- *Akbarnama* by Abu'l-Fazl ibn Mubarak